PEDAGOGY and the CATHOLIC EDUCATOR

Nurturing Hearts, Transforming Possibilities

by
Jim & Therese D'Orsa

BBI - THE AUSTRALIAN INSTITUTE OF
THEOLOGICAL EDUCATION
MISSION AND EDUCATION SERIES

Published in Australia by
Vaughan Publishing
32 Glenvale Crescent
Mulgrave, VIC 3170

vaughanpublishing.com.au
A joint imprint of BBI – The Australian Institute
of Theological Education and Garratt Publishing

Copyright © 2020 Jim and Therese D'Orsa
All rights reserved. Except as provided by the Australian copyright law, no part of this book may be reproduced in any way without permission in writing from the publisher.

Text Design by Mike Kuszla, J&M Typesetting
Cover image iStock
Images
Excerpt from *Transforming Worldviews* by Paul G Hiebert, copyright 2008. Used by permission of Baker Academic, a division of Baker Publishing Group. (Fig 6.1 Hiebert Worldview) p 82.

Printed by Tingleman

ISBN 9780648524625

Nihil Obstat:	Reverend Gerard Diamond MA (Oxon), LSS, D.Theol
	Diocesan Censor
Imprimatur:	Very Reverend Joseph Caddy AM Lic.Soc.Sci VG
	Vicar General
	Archdiocese of Melbourne
Date:	1 August 2020

The Nihil Obstat and Imprimatur are official declarations that a book or pamphlet is free of doctrinal or moral error. No implication is contained therein that those who have granted the Nihil Obstat and Imprimatur agree with the contents, opinions or statements expressed. They do not necessarily signify that the work is approved as a basic text for catechetical instruction.

A catalogue record for this book is available from the National Library of Australia

The authors and publisher gratefully acknowledge the permission granted to reproduce the copyright material in this book. Every effort has been made to trace copyright holders and to obtain their permission for the use of copyright material.

The publisher apologises for any errors or omissions in the above list and would be grateful if notified of any corrections that should be incorporated in future reprints or editions of this book.

There are some expeditions that should only be undertaken by the most experienced explorers. Therese and Jim D'Orsa's deep educational experience is on display as they travel through pedagogical territory that is vast and diverse. They stay close to their compass bearings grounding Catholic pedagogy in the spirituality of John Baptist De La Salle and Ignatius of Loyola, as they survey scholarship as diverse as Longerganian epistemology and philosophical hermeneutics and as they engage with developmental theory and the more recent empirical research of John Hattie. Their compass bearings are true and they provide sure and accessible guidance for any Catholic educator who wishes to reflect a little more deeply on sources that will illuminate and enlargen their educational vision and practice.

Dr Paul Sharkey, Director of Catholic Leadership and Governance, Catholic Education Archdiocese of Melbourne

The need to develop an imagination and worldview that is open to faith and to engaging with the world we inhabit is an urgent matter for Catholic educators today. How we do this depends on our pedagogy. This book shares a rich vision and understanding for what it means to talk about a Catholic pedagogy. Rooted in both the historical faith tradition and the changing contemporary contexts of church and society, the book offers original insight and valuable scholarship for Catholic educators in the Australian context but internationally as well. Rooted in a variety of discourses, pedagogy is considered through wide-ranging dialogue with education theory and practice alongside the theological legacy of the faith tradition and the heritage of spiritual giants. Questions and actions are posed for the reader, seen as teachers in Catholic schools, but such prompts invite all involved in Catholic education to deeply consider the pedagogy they bring to their work. The book presents pedagogy as that which goes beyond the technical or instrumental to seek a missional imagination and a relational and ethical practice. This is an exciting and inspiring vision for a Catholic pedagogy, one that can indeed nurture hearts and transform possibilities.

Dr Ros Stuart-Buttle, Senior Lecturer in Theology & Education, Director of the Centre for Christian Education, School of Humanities, Liverpool Hope University

Pedagogy and the Catholic Educator: Nurturing Hearts, Transforming Possibilities, by Therese and Jim D'Orsa builds on their earlier work, *Catholic Curriculum*. It applies the same approach and method as in their earlier text, namely to explore the field in question, in this case pedagogy, firstly by expounding on seminal work in the wider world of education and then focussing on ramifications and practice in the Catholic school context. In doing the latter, it draws on some of the deeper and most distinctive educational paradigms in Catholic history, including the ground-breaking works of Loyola and De La Salle. It is a most comprehensive, almost encyclopaedic, work that will no doubt take its place in the long list of contributions to Catholic education by the authors.

**Emeritus Professor Terry Lovat,
Faculty of Education and Arts, University of Newcastle Australia**

Once again, Jim and Therese D'Orsa take us below the surface of a crucial issue confronting Catholic Education in today's Australian context. Drawing on a range of perspectives from the human sciences and education theory, the authors underline the urgent need for a new awareness on the part of Catholic teachers. They argue for an authentically Catholic pedagogy that is both critical and transformative, informed by Jesus' vision of God's kingdom, and fully engaged with the multiple worldviews of Australia today.

**Rev Dr Kevin Lenehan, Master of Catholic Theological College,
Senior lecturer in theology, Archdiocese of Melbourne**

In this comprehensive examination of the complex relationship between teaching and learning in the religious education domain, Therese and Jim D'Orsa have once again helped Catholic educators in understanding and gauging the effectiveness of their work, not just through the vital lens of student learning outcomes, but also through a conceptualisation of their work as an intricate component of the mission to make real the Kingdom of God for their students. This is a must-read book for leaders and teachers in Catholic education.

**Mr Dominic Ryan,
Manager Catholic Identity and Religious Education,
Diocese of Sale**

Pedagogy and the Catholic Educator: Nurturing Hearts, Transforming Possibilities is an exciting contribution to the exploration of questions that exist about learning and teaching. Therese and Jim D'Orsa's deep knowledge and expertise is evident throughout the book as they engage with theory, theology, scripture, scholarship and research in the development of an authentically Catholic pedagogy, that helps students to develop an imagination and worldview that is both contextualised and open to faith so as to ensure human flourishing. Crucially, the authors remind us that a Catholic pedagogy of possibility results in actions, not just the transmission or consumption of content. The text offers many possibilities for individuals, schools and systems to re-contextualise their own current practices.

Dr Sandra Harvey, Assistant Director System Improvement, Catholic Education, Diocese of Ballarat

As with all their works, Therese and Jim D'Orsa's latest offering in the Mission and Education space provides Catholic educators with an excellent balance of theory, history and practicality. The study allows teachers to understand the theological foundations on which they build, invites them to consider their teaching as part of a continuing community of practitioners in the hermeneutical tradition and encourages them to make pedagogical choices for their specific context.

Ms Audrey Brown Director of Catholic Education, Diocese of Ballarat

For all who seek to awaken a pedagogical consciousness within a comprehensive examination of relevant disciplines and philosophies: look no further. This resource is extraordinary. It is foundational to undergraduate studies; refreshing and important for continuous learning; and, a rich source of inquiry for researchers. Underpinning a spectrum of relevance: *Pedagogy and the Catholic Educator: Nurturing Hearts, Transforming Possibilities* is eminently readable; outstanding in clarity and presentation of relevant, accessible and connected chapters. The work from start to finish engages and seeks engagement, develops understanding, reaches the heart and invites authenticity. The text is bountiful in insights: a scholarly, reflective, practical, and much-valued contribution to pedagogy for mission in Christian faith-based educational settings.

Dr Bill Sultmann, Associate Professor, Deputy Dean La Salle Academy, Office of the Vice-President, Australian Catholic University

BBI – THE AUSTRALIAN INSTITUTE OF THEOLOGICAL EDUCATION MISSION AND EDUCATION SERIES

The Mission and Education Project seeks to bring together, in the one conversation, the light that human experience, culture, and faith each throw on particular topics now central to Catholic education.

It also seeks to honour the significant efforts that Catholic educators make on behalf of young people to address contemporary mission agendas within the total process of education. It provides a forum designed to stimulate further conversation about the 'why', the 'what' and the 'how' of Catholic education as a work of the Gospel in our complex society and culture.

The Mission and Education publishing project is currently divided into two series. The Exploratory Studies are designed to serve leaders in Catholic education. They explore aspects of contemporary Catholic education in the light of the Church's official teaching on mission, and the experience of those who attempt to embrace this missional challenge in their personal and professional lives. The Educator's Guides are introductory texts prepared specifically for teachers in Catholic schools and for those for whom such a text might be helpful, for example parents, board members and others who serve Catholic education.

The mission-based resources now at the disposal of those who seek to explore Catholic education theologically are rich and deep. Because the faith held by the Catholic community is a living faith, Catholic Church teaching on mission has developed, and continues to develop, in the light of contemporary societal and cultural changes. Similarly, Scripture continues to yield its treasures. Only now, for example, is the Bible being widely recognised as a witness to God's purpose or mission in the created universe, and as an account of human response to the unfolding of that mission.

We live in a period of rapid cultural change driven by global dynamics. This has its impact on how we understand what knowledge is, how it is acquired, and how schools are best led and organised so as to maximise student learning, and facilitate the social and economic benefits that are assumed to flow from sound educational policies. Very often the emphasis in such policies shifts from 'the learning student' to the more abstract 'student learning'. This sits uneasily with the concept of a Catholic education.

A consequence of rapid societal change is that, in our time, new areas of mission present themselves with real urgency. It is now clearly necessary to include within the mission agenda both the processes of knowledge construction and of meaning-making, as well as the modes of Christian participation in the new public space created by both globalisation and the communications media. These new areas of mission take their place alongside those fields already familiar to the faith community.

It is the hope of the Mission and Education Editorial Board that Catholic educators, both in Australia and beyond, will view the series as an invitation to contribute their own creativity to this vital conversation.

Therese D'Orsa, Professor of Mission and Culture
BBI – TAITE (The Australian Institute of Theological Education)

FINANCIAL SUPPORT

Since the inception of the program, the Mission and Education series has received financial support from a number of Catholic Education authorities. Their assistance with research and publication costs is gratefully acknowledged:

- *Queensland – the Catholic Education Offices of Brisbane, Cairns, Rockhampton, Toowoomba and Townsville.*
- *New South Wales – the Catholic Education Offices of Armidale, Bathurst, Broken Bay, Maitland-Newcastle, Parramatta, Sydney and Wagga Wagga.*
- *Australian Capital Territory – the Catholic Education Office of Canberra-Goulburn.*
- *Victoria – the Catholic Education Offices of Ballarat, Melbourne, Sale and Sandhurst.*
- *South Australia – Catholic Education South Australia (Archdiocese of Adelaide and Diocese of Port Pirie).*
- *Tasmania – the Catholic Education Office of Hobart.*
- *Northern Territory – the Catholic Education Office of Darwin.*
- *Religious Congregations – the Good Samaritan Sisters, Marist Schools Australia, Edmund Rice Education Australia, De La Salle Brothers.*

ALSO IN THIS SERIES

Explorers, Guides and Meaning-makers: Mission Theology for Catholic Educators
Catholic Curriculum: A Mission to the Heart of Young People
Leading for Mission: Integrating Life, Culture and Faith in Catholic Education
New Ways of Living the Gospel: Spiritual Traditions in Catholic Education
Now with Enthusiasm: Charism, God's Mission, and Catholic Schools Today
Stirring the Soul of Catholic Education: Formation for Mission
Educator's Guide to *Catholic Identity*
Educator's Guide to *Catholic Curriculum: Learning for 'Fullness of Life'*
Educator's Guide to *Mission in Practice: Discipleship in Action in Catholic Schools*

This volume is dedicated to those teachers who, in the spirit of Jesus the teacher, guide young people, in good times and bad, to grow in their capacity to co-create a better world for themselves, and for their communities.

*The authors would like to acknowledge the assistance of
Br Ben Boonen cfc in preparing the diagrams
and appreciation to Fr Kevin Lenehan, Terry Lovat,
Paul Sharkey and Jim Quillinan for helpful advice on the text.*

CONTENTS

Foreword	1

ORIENTATIONS

Chapter 1.	Opening up a Conversation	9
Chapter 2.	Mission and the Catholic Imagination	25

PART A
CONFIDENCE BUILT ON FIRM FOUNDATIONS

Introduction		43
Chapter 3.	A Heritage of Giants	45
Chapter 4.	Spiritual Leadership and the Theological Legacy of Ignatius of Loyola	53
Chapter 5.	Spirituality of Teaching: Enduring Insights of John Baptist De La Salle	65

PART B
KEY TOOLS FOR ANALYSING THE PEDAGOGICAL LANDSCAPE

Introduction		77
Chapter 6.	Worldviews and Their Role in Meaning-making	81
Chapter 7.	Culture and the Pedagogical Relationship	89
Chapter 8.	The Worldview of Faith	103
Chapter 9.	The Changing Relationship between Faith and Culture: From Christendom to Vatican II	113
Chapter 10.	The Changing Relationship between Faith and Culture: From Vatican II to the Present	123

PART C
CONTEMPORARY PERSPECTIVES ON PEDAGOGY

Introduction — 139

Chapter 11. Pedagogy as Ethical Endeavour: Robert Starratt and Max Van Manen — 143

Chapter 12. Values Pedagogy: Evaluating Approaches — 157

Chapter 13. The Empirical Research Tradition: The Quantitative Approach of John Hattie — 177

Chapter 14. 'Deep Learning': Quantitative Studies — 201

Chapter 15. The Qualitative Research Tradition: Michael Fullan — 195

PART D
LEARNING AND PEDAGOGY: ESSENTIAL VOICES

Introduction — 211

Chapter 16. Insight into Knowing: Contribution of Bernard Lonergan, Part 1 — 213

Chapter 17. Insight into Knowing: Contribution of Bernard Lonergan, Part 2 — 229

Chapter 18. Introducing the Hermeneutical Tradition — 237

Chapter 19. Understanding from a Hermeneutical Perspective — 251

Chapter 20. Traditions and Culture from a Hermeneutical Perspective — 261

Chapter 21. Hermeneutics and the Educator: Locating Critical Pedagogy — 273

Chapter 22. Contextualising Critical Pedagogy — 285

Chapter 23. Human Development, Cognition, and Pedagogy — 295

Chapter 24. Dialogue and Pedagogy: the Mission Connection — 311

PART E
PEDAGOGIES FOR THE KINGDOM

Introduction — 329

Chapter 25. Transforming Possibilities: Pedagogies for the Kingdom — 331

Select Bibliography — 349

Index — 358

FOREWORD

The Mission and Education series of exploratory studies aims to open up conversation about various elements of the educational process. This conversation explores how each contributes to the mission of Jesus within the context of the ministry of education in schools. Over the years, various authors have contributed to this conversation focusing on such areas as curriculum, formation, leadership, and charism.

A few years ago (2012), we authored a study in the Mission and Education series entitled *Catholic Curriculum: a Mission to the Heart of Young People*. This study was well received, and at that time and since, people have asked us whether we might turn our attention to pedagogy and Catholic schooling. We indicated that we hoped we might do so, but have always been unsure as to when this might be possible. Thus *Pedagogy and the Catholic Educator* has been some years in the making, having been delayed by other writing and teaching priorities. Finally, the latest offering in the Mission and Education invitations to conversation has been completed.

Every day teachers make decisions about how they intend 'to make a difference' for the students they teach, and so realise the hopes they had in becoming teachers. Most of these decisions are not made consciously, but 'on the run'. They are often dictated by the culture of the society, or the culture of the school or school system, in which teachers are employed.

How teachers make pedagogical decisions is also shaped by how they construe their role as teachers. It is our contention that cultural changes now underway mean that the role of the teacher is being reformulated and this has an important impact on what is considered to be 'good teaching', and how teachers in Catholic schools design learning and make pedagogical choices. Teachers are called upon to play a number of roles in the classroom and this complicates the process of making pedagogical choices. Added to this, the advent of the Coronavirus has tended to emphasise the indispensable role that teachers play in the lives of children and young people.

This book aims to bring to consciousness the considerations that inform pedagogical choices, or perhaps should inform them, in order that they become more open to critique. It also invites teachers to become more aware of the changes that are taking place in church and society, as various approaches and movements gain ground and then wane in importance. This may often be for no reason other than a shift in political orientation. While the educational and cultural changes underway affect all schools, they have a particular relevance for Catholic schools where teaching practices are grounded in long-standing traditions. It is these traditions which are the carriers of, not only important values, but shared understandings of what those values demand in terms of life and action.

There are a number of issues to be explored in working towards an understanding of what a 'Catholic pedagogy' might look like. A principal challenge lies in the term 'pedagogy' and what it actually encompasses. Literature and research in the English-speaking world has an orientation in Australia that is different from that to be accessed in Europe. In Australia we tend to interpret 'pedagogy' in quite pragmatic terms – 'what works well in the classroom' – whereas in Europe it is interpreted in more philosophical and phenomenological terms – 'how we make sense of the experience of teaching in a classroom'. A central issue, we believe, is to find an approach which is faithful to the best insights of both our faith and our culture.

When teachers face their new classes each year, they bring with them a number of assumptions about how students learn, how they develop, and what learning is all about. These assumptions are sourced in their culture, their pre-service training (now many years in the past in some cases), their own experience of schooling, and their experience of working with students. Their conception of their role as teacher and what constitutes 'good teaching' is predicated on these assumptions, but the assumptions themselves, because they are beyond awareness, are not open to critique or challenge. The result is that much teaching happens on the basis of what is termed 'common sense', without clear theoretical underpinnings that explain why certain approaches are better than others.

As we proceeded with this study, we were very surprised to find that the pragmatic approach to pedagogy, in either its quantitative or qualitative form, is not underpinned by an explicit theory of learning or of what constitutes knowledge. Nor does 'brain science' provide such a theory.

Irrespective of how we construe 'pedagogy', it is directed to helping students learn. 'Learning' is often regarded as being a self-evident good. However, if teachers are not sure what 'learning' is, then they have a problem. The same applies to knowledge. Too often educators operate from an implied understanding of these terms, and this needs to be brought to consciousness and critiqued. In developing a theory of learning we ask ourselves: Do we look to psychology, neuroscience, theology, or philosophy? How do 'mind' and 'brain' come together in such a theory?

Some teachers see learning in instrumental terms – as actions performed to reach a goal. They seek to help students learn to 'make a difference' of some kind, which raises the question: What is the goal of our pedagogy? Is it better scores in testing regimes? Intuitively, most teachers would baulk at such a limited answer, and if pushed would indicate, however inchoately, that their goal relates to the human flourishing of the student. How then does the teacher understand what is involved in human flourishing? Here two factors become important – culture and one's faith tradition. Both contain understandings of 'human flourishing' based on different worldviews. How do teachers understand these worldviews, and which of them ultimately underpins the teacher's own personal worldview? This is a key issue, as it is a person's worldview which shapes their pedagogy. These are just some of the issues explored in the chapters that follow.

STRUCTURE OF THE STUDY

Orientations

This Foreword is followed by Chapters 1 and 2 which orient the study. Chapter 1 aims to provide an overarching framework, and poses conversation-starters to act as key questions that are pursued within the text. Chapter 2 focuses on the issue of mission and how changes in the way this is understood are beginning to impact on our understanding of the worldview of faith, which is one of the major resources open to teachers and young people in making sense of their lives.

Part A: Confidence Built on Firm Foundations

This section sets pedagogy in Catholic schools in its historical context by examining the foundational contribution of pioneering Catholic educators in developing the notion of 'pedagogy', and giving this a home within the Catholic tradition.

Part B: Key tools in Analysing the Pedagogical Landscape

The meaning of important human endeavours such as pedagogy is open to interpretation, and consequently it depends on the perspective that people bring to this endeavour. In trying to understand what 'pedagogy' might mean, it is necessary to develop conceptual categories appropriate to the task. This is the aim of Part B where key concepts such as 'culture', 'worldview', 'mission' 'faith' and 'values' are addressed, drawing on insights from cultural anthropology, mission anthropology, missiology, theology and phenomenology.

Part C: Contemporary Perspectives on Pedagogy

As an area of study, pedagogy is relatively new. Like many other human sciences, it has had to develop its own methods and ways of validating what it knows. This has resulted in two broad approaches:

- *the phenomenological approach where the focus is on harnessing insights that flow from the lived experiences of teachers in the classroom as these are subjectively understood*
- *the pragmatic approach that is concerned with insights that derive from observing teachers in action and reflecting on the significance of what is happening in light of the theoretical model guiding the research. This approach has two strands: insights drawn from quantitative research studies and insights drawn from qualitative studies.*

In this section we explore the contributions that Van Manen, Starratt, Hattie and Fullan have made to an understanding of pedagogy and related concepts. The section includes discussion of 'deep learning', the 'new pedagogy', and values pedagogy, including the ECSI critique of 'values education'.

Part D: Learning and Pedagogy: Essential Voices

One of the surprises encountered in this study is that contemporary approaches to pedagogy seem to lack a coherent or well-developed theory of learning. This seems to be a consequence of the fact that pedagogy sits in the middle space between 'mind' and 'brain', neither of which are, in our view, well connected at this point in time.

In Part D we consider the contribution philosophy can make to a theory of learning, the implications this has for assessing the assumptions that teachers hold about what constitutes learning, and, by extension, 'good' pedagogy and its place in the development of the student. Such an assessment has implications for how teachers define the pedagogical relationship, and for their role. The philosophical tradition includes discussion of critical pedagogy.

Part E: Pedagogies for the Kingdom

The final section brings together themes that have surfaced in previous sections. It proposes that pedagogy is an inherently ethical endeavour that centres on the 'good' that a teacher seeks to achieve within her or his pedagogical relationship with students, and how this 'good' is conceptualised and pursued when insights from faith and culture are 'befriended' and brought into 'dialogue'. We argue that the result is a 'transformation of possibilities' that allows teachers to understand pedagogy, their relationship with students, and their role as teachers in the classroom in new ways, ways that 'nurture hearts'. Such a transformation of possibility for the teacher is also transformative for students: they in turn are empowered to develop the type of imagination that is necessary to be Catholic and make a positive contribution to the world as co-creators of the Kingdom of God.

Since the worldviews of faith and culture change over time, and can be interpreted by teachers in a number of authentic ways, a pedagogy that is 'Catholic' can take a number of forms. The question educators face today is: What form best suits the situation of this student, and this group of students, growing up in a postsecular culture?

ORIENTATIONS

Catholic pedagogy is a shared understanding that provides teachers with guidelines in their decision-making as to how best to advance the learning and development of their students.

This shared understanding is nourished by a community of educators striving to be faithful to the mission of Jesus in their time and place.

Enriched by the wisdom of both faith and culture, Catholic pedagogy advances the mission of the Catholic school community, and seeks the 'good' of each child.

Catholic pedagogy assumes sound analysis of the student's situation, and adequate understanding of what constitutes learning, including the conditions under which this occurs.

Catholic pedagogy engenders responsiveness to God's invitation to be co-creators of a more just and loving society and a flourishing natural world.

Catholic pedagogy is a profoundly ethical endeavour.

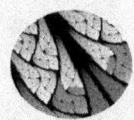

1
OPENING UP A CONVERSATION

As an evangelizer, Christ first of all proclaims a kingdom, the kingdom of God; and this is so important that, by comparison, everything else becomes "the rest," which is "given in addition."[16] 'Only the kingdom therefore is absolute and it makes everything else relative.'
(Pope Paul VI, *Evangelii Nuntiandi*, # 8).[1]

In this book, the starting assumption is that a person can deal with issues or challenges only if she or he can articulate them clearly, so early in our work we identify some of these and present them in question form. Given our continuing role as teachers over many years, we occasionally take the liberty of using the pronoun 'we' when posing questions for the consideration of educators. The questions below are among those which must be explored by teachers and educating communities in choosing, and where necessary creating, pedagogies which help young people to grow as co-creators of what Jesus, attuned to his people's hopes and expectations, termed the Kingdom of God. His was a vision of radical newness leading people beyond their religious and political expectations, and into a qualitatively new and different place. The pedagogies that Catholic educators choose can do no less.

For those of us who stand in the Judeo-Christian tradition, each person is made in the image and likeness of God (Gen 1:27). In order to appreciate this, we need to consider how God revealed Godself to our ancestors in the faith, as the One who is at work in creation, and in history. Thus, for the faithful within this tradition, within creation and history, to be human is to share in God's creative processes in the world, and act to move creation forward positively as the circumstances of human life unfold. For a person of faith within the Judeo-Christian tradition, to be the image and likeness of God is to assume, within the limits of our humanness, God's vision for creation, and God's saving and reconciling work within history.

---

1 Pope Paul VI. *Evangelii Nuntiandi*, 1974, # 8. http://www.vatican.va/content/paulvi/en/apost_exhortations/documents/hf_p- vi_exh_19751208_evangelii-nuntiandi.html

In the fullness of time Jesus, the 'perfect image of the invisible God' (Col 1:15) showed us very clearly what this looks like in practice. By entering human history in a particular time, place, and culture, he demonstrated the central importance of time, place and culture in personal and communal involvement in God's creating and redeeming action in our world.

As teacher par excellence, Jesus utilised many methods. He taught by example, and also by means of direct instruction in which he used words, images, and imaginative stories that people understood. He also taught by involvement with people followed by reflection on the experience, and by his choice of relationships, especially those that were personally demanding. He clarified that creation and human life are heading towards a 'new creation'[2] and he called this, as both goal and process, 'the Kingdom of God', a kingdom that is both partially present and yet to come in its fullness only in God's time.

> *The Kingdom is a gracious gift from God, who comes with unconditional love to seek out humankind and to offer ultimate salvation to all ... It is a gift from God which people can only receive in gratitude and awe. God is coming toward us as unconditional love, seeking communion and intimacy. Since it is a gift of love, the only concrete description can be in terms of symbols and images.*[3]

Jesus modelled what must be the kind of values and actions which can move the present situation towards the 'not yet' direction of God's Kingdom. Most tellingly of all, he demonstrated in his own life and death that a creative, redeeming, and faithful life is very costly in personal terms. Leaving no room for an 'arm's length' or purely 'academic' view of the Kingdom of God, Pope John Paul II, in a famous passage, speaks of Jesus as the incarnation of the Kingdom of God:

> *The Kingdom of God is not a concept, a doctrine, or a program subject to free interpretation, but it is before all else a person with the face and name of Jesus of Nazareth, the image of the invisible God.*[4]

In the introduction to his seminal work on the Kingdom of God, John Fuellenbach raises the question that, in substance, many scholars and other Christians also confront. The question is: Can *we* see the focal issues

---

2 In his own teaching Paul, who was attuned to the cultures in which he was working, used the phrase the 'kingdom of God' quite sparingly in comparison to the writers of the synoptic gospels. He also used the phrase 'new creation' with much the same meaning, e.g. Rom 8:14–17; Gal 4:1–7.
3 John Fuellenbach, *The Kingdom of God: The Message of Jesus Today*. Maryknoll N.Y: Orbis, 1995, 97.
4 Pope John Paul II *Redemptoris Missio* 1990, # 18.

addressed by Jesus' teaching, or are our interpretations and teachings so encrusted with traditions and secondary concerns that we can hardly see the real issues addressed by his preaching?[5] In fact, today's Christians have privileged access to a vast body of scholarship devoted to understanding Jesus in his historical-cultural setting, work which throws light on this important question. Such scholarship, when pursued within a community of faith, enables the faithful to fuse their own horizons with that of Jesus as he, in his time and place, opened up God's vision and mission to his followers through his involvement in the Kingdom of God.[6] As a result, we can appreciate that Jesus' teaching on the Kingdom dealt with the immediate issues of one's relationship with God, and the authentication of that by the quality of relationship with others, the more marginalised being singled out as of central importance in the determination of authenticity.

Considerations of the Kingdom of God and our part in making it present in today's world frame the pedagogical choices confronting Christian educators. They help us shape the goals of Christian education and the pedagogical choices that will facilitate the achievement of those goals.

- *How confident and competent are we as educators in articulating the goals of Catholic education in terms of Jesus' project of the Kingdom of God?*

1. CONFRONTING QUESTIONS

1.1 The world of the student

The process by which students learn and develop unfolds in a particular cultural context, and the way teachers understand and relate to that context shapes many of the decisions they make about how to teach and how to present materials to students.

Every day the readers of this book make decisions about how 'to make a difference' to the lives of their students in the context of a Catholic school, at a time when Western societies are caught up in an era of unprecedented instability and rapid cultural change.

The speed and extent of change leaves many people today wondering not only if the 'goalposts have moved', but whether they may have been stolen! Leaders of institutions that people once thought they could rely on, such

---

[5] Fuellenbach, 1.
[6] The legacy of 'giants' like the distinguished US scholar Raymond Brown, (1928–1998), who worked in a pioneering way with the historical-critical method, stands out and has opened the way for a host of other scholars. In recent times, the hugely popular work by the Spaniard Jose Pagola, *Jesus: an Historical Approximation*. Revised Edition. Convivium Press, 2014, demonstrates the appreciation scholars and educated 'laity' alike have for work which they regard as authentically opening up Jesus' life and teaching within his social and historical context, thus allowing them and their communities to bring their own lives and issues into 'conversation' with Jesus' teaching and example.

as the churches and major financial institutions, have been exposed as less than honourable, leaving many wondering what is going on. US Protestant theologian, pastor and Church leader, Alan Roxburgh, is accurate when he talks about 'the great unravelling'[7] occurring in the West as traditions that once held society together, and which were taken for granted, lose their power as anchors.

Today both teachers and their students learn in a challenging context, but with an important difference in terms of experience. Teachers have more experience to compare current events than do students. They can more easily reflect on what is happening, whereas their students are 'native' to this new environment. For them it constitutes 'normal', and this makes them vulnerable.

- *How do teachers understand this situation and how do they seek to 'bridge the cultural gap' that separates them from their students?*
- *How does the vulnerability of students shape pedagogical thinking?*

Teachers also formulate their moral purpose by implicitly or explicitly assessing students' needs in a changing context in which technology now plays an increasing role. In recent decades teachers have found themselves playing 'catch-up' because they are not 'native' to the technological world as inhabited by their students.

- *What role does technology play in shaping teaching practice and the relationship between teacher and student in the process of learning?*
- *How is technology shaping decisions about pedagogical practice?*

As part of the cultural shift underway, there has been a profound change in how traditions are viewed and how they can be handed on. Parents find their children are resistant to accepting traditions that they themselves take for granted. This is certainly the case in matters of religion, and is increasingly the case in how students form their view of the world.

- *How do teachers understand and work with students in an era of change that is quite unprecedented, and in which 'business as normal' does not work, because what is taken as 'normal' is being rapidly redefined?*

---

[7] In spoken and written texts Roxburgh uses a phrase made famous by Paul Krugman (US economist, Nobel prize winner and popular columnist for the New York Times) in his 2003 bestselling work *The Great Unravelling: From Boom to Bust in Three Scandalous Years*. Roxburgh's own ministry focuses on the refounding of Christian communities in our time, made necessary by discontinuity and radical newness. See for example Alan Roxburgh, *Joining God, Remaking Church, and Changing the World: The new shape of the church in our time*. New York: Morehouse Publishing, 2015. Part 1.1.

1.2 The world of the teacher

A great dignity of the teaching profession flows from the fact that, in a very complex cultural and religious situation, *teachers consciously choose to make a difference through working with students.* They do so believing that their work has benefit for the students themselves and through them for society and culture. Many do so knowing that the financial rewards associated with teaching will rarely, if ever, be commensurate with the challenges to be faced in making teaching one's career. More so than is generally the case, the profession of teaching forces teachers to develop an orientation towards the future that is unique in its sensibility. *Teachers see the future through the eyes and through the hopes of their students.* This is a privileged position, and one that gives them pause to stop and think when planning the processes of learning:

- *What is 'the difference' that teachers seek to make, and how does this impinge on their day-to-day decisions in teaching students native to the new and unfamiliar world educators share with them?*

Not only are teaching decisions shaped by context, they are also shaped by the assumptions the teacher holds about how students learn in general, and how a particular group learns. Teachers are invited to probe:

- *What are my assumptions about learning and how it occurs, and how do these help or hinder me in making pedagogical decisions?*

The world of the teacher is unique. Schooling is the source of a bewildering volume of research, much of which focuses on 'what works in the classroom'. In many disciplines, researchers conduct meta-studies pulling together insights drawn from numerous previous research studies on a particular topic. In education, researchers in New Zealand now conduct mega-studies developing insights based on meta-study data! John Hattie's *Visible Learning* is an example of this approach,[8] as is Timperley et al's, *Teacher Professional Development and Learning.*[9]

Yet the results of these mega-studies seem to have little influence on teacher decision-making. John Hattie suggests that we have created a profession based on the principle: 'Just leave me alone as I have the evidence that what I do enhances learning and achievement'. He goes on to ask rhetorically:

---

8 John Hattie, *Visible Learning: A synthesis of over 800 meta-analyses relating to achievement.* London: Routledge, 2009.
9 H. Timperley, A. Wilson, H. Barrar, & I. Fung, *Teacher Professional Learning and Development: Best Evidence Iteration.* Auckland: New Zealand Ministry of Education, 2007.

> How can there be so many published articles, so many reports providing direction, so many professional development sessions advocating this or that method, so many parents and politicians inventing new and better answers, while classrooms are hardly different from 200 years ago? Why does this bounty of research have such little impact?[10]

For the students, learning and personal development are complex activities influenced by many variables. These variables are operating in-school and out-of-school so as to render most attempts to isolate *cause and effect* in learning futile. A question for the teacher to ponder is:

- *What attitude do I have towards the empirical tradition in education and how does it shape my teaching practice?*

A teacher's moral purpose is determined in large part by their assumptions about how students learn and make sense of life. For the most part, these assumptions are *culturally acquired* and so rarely explored. This situation becomes dangerous in a change of era when cultural understandings undergo major shifts. We currently live at the confluence of three cultural traditions: modernity, postmodernity and postsecularism. People today cherry-pick from each of these and so have a fragmented grasp of their culture (in much the same way as they have a fragmented grasp of their faith). This impacts on how they construe learning and knowledge.

- *What are my assumptions about how students learn and about what constitutes knowledge?*

Every teacher has a working hermeneutical theory that is largely unexamined, and a working epistemology, similarly unexamined, that shape her or his understanding of how students learn. In later chapters we will open up these issues.

Teaching decisions have to be made with respect to the learning and development needs of particular students by teachers with a 'feel' for what is happening *relationally* in the classroom. Having this type of sensibility enables teachers to create a social ambience in which students feel safe and in which learning and human flourishing become possible.

- *How do teachers develop this 'feel'?*
- *Do we construe teaching as an art in which judgment is the key, or can teaching be regarded as a science where fixed norms apply, or some combination of both?*

---

[10] Hattie, 3.

How a teacher constructs the *social ambience* in his or her classroom shapes whether collaborative learning can occur, and how this may be co-opted in the service of learning.

- *How does shaping the relational environment figure in your classroom practice?*
- *How does collaborative learning figure in this practice?*

A classroom is more than a context in which things learnt in the past are passed on. The class itself can become *a source of new knowledge*. This will be *local knowledge* and will include knowledge about *how this group works together*. It also includes knowledge of what the experience of teaching this class is like for me, the teacher.

- *How does the teacher value and deal with local knowledge?*

Every class has the possibility of becoming a learning community in which new things are tried, some of which succeed and some of which do not, but by reflecting on the experience, the group including the teacher, learns.

- *What attitude might a teacher take to such a possibility? Does she or he encourage this form of learning?*
- *How does collaborative learning sit with the teacher's moral purpose in regard to students and the decisions that flow from it?*

In making decisions about how students learn and develop, teachers consciously and subconsciously operate from an understanding of 'what it means to be human', what therefore is considered to be 'natural', and what constitutes 'human flourishing'. For most teachers, 'making a difference' is interpreted as widening their students' perspective about possibilities in regard to 'human flourishing'. However, in a pluralist, postmodern and postsecular society there is increasing disagreement about what is 'natural' and, ready or not, teachers find themselves, caught up into these debates. They have to develop *a functional anthropology* that values both the present and the past.

- *How do teachers do this?*
- *How does this functional anthropology shape the assumptions teachers hold about what constitutes good teaching?*
- *What notion of human flourishing does this functional anthropology embrace?*

Each teacher has a *worldview* shaped by what they have learned up to the present. Such historical experiences are usually interpreted within a *narrative conception* of what it means to be human, what is considered 'natural' and 'correct'. The problem is that, for the most part, this worldview and its associated narrative operate out-of-awareness and are taken for granted; only rarely are they brought to consciousness. They work away in the background shaping the teacher's conception of what is 'right' and 'proper' in learning, in classroom behaviour, in extra-curricular activities, in the use of technology, in individualised instruction, and in how they interpret their role as teacher. How teachers interpret their role as teacher is most important.

- *What do teachers know about their own worldview?*
- *How do they explore it?*
- *How does it shape the way they understand their role as teacher?*
- *How can they assume responsibility, and be supported, in the formation of a personal worldview aligned with that of Jesus?*

1.3 The world of the school

School life provides an important social context for human flourishing. There is often a tendency among teachers to interpret schooling as a preparation for life in the future, almost as if the present were not important. Students do not see the matter this way. For many, the present is all that there is, so they often interpret their needs in a more immediate way than do their teachers. This can create problems for both groups, particularly when it comes to understanding a student's motivation to learn and his or her willingness to engage in learning.

- *How do teachers construe the life situation of their students?*
- *What expectations do they hold about students' motivations?*
- *In what ways do these expectations shape the way teachers structure learning?*

In a learning community[11], as the phrase has more recently come to be understood, the notions of 'teacher' and 'learner' now have a degree of

---

11 Peter Senge popularised the concept of a *'learning organisation'* in his 1990 book (subsequently revised 2006), *The Fifth Discipline,* and in a number of follow-up publications. People utilising his ideas in education (schools and school systems), or in other settings such as parishes, generally use the phrase 'learning community'. In the view of the writers of this book, Senge's emphasis on communities engaging, *as communities,* in transformative learning, as opposed to individuals pursuing their own learning without much reference to the learning of the whole community, has much to recommend it in terms of the pedagogical goal of making a positive difference in the lives of students.

fluidity not found in more traditional school structures. This impacts on the design of learning as it creates options that did not previously exist.

- *How does the teacher make use of these options in designing learning?*

1.4 The world of the Church

Catholic schools exist within an educational tradition that precedes the institution of education as a public service in the 18th and 19th centuries. This tradition has evolved over time. The form in which we know it today dates from the 16th century as the Renaissance impacted on human consciousness, and teaching congregations were founded to provide a basic education for young people from the rising middle classes (boys first, and later girls), and in due course from the lower classes. A multitude of religious congregations would be founded across Europe in subsequent centuries as the Agricultural and Industrial Revolutions created vast social upheaval and people flooded from the countryside into the towns in search of a livelihood. The members of these groups saw education as a way to assist vulnerable children who otherwise could be readily exploited in factories. As the Catholic educational tradition unfolded, 'the faith' was handed on in the process of creating life chances for students.

- *What trajectory does the Catholic education tradition provide for Catholic schooling today?*

Schools now play only an intermediate role in creating life chances for students. In addition to a change in this traditional role, in Catholic schools today 'the faith' cannot be passed on in the way it once was, and this has a bearing on the purpose, place and process of Religious Education in the school curriculum. The function of Catholic schools within the Church and within society is being reformulated.

- *What roles are teachers playing in the reformulations that are underway?*
- *How does this impact on the way they teach in Religious Education? In other learning areas?*

The Catholic school tradition has a narrative that has shaped the culture of Catholic schools. This narrative is broadly coherent, but varies in the telling from country to country, and in its emphasis. In Australia today the narrative owes much to the religious congregations who were indispensable in establishing Catholic school systems in the late 19th and early 20th centuries. Prior to this, lay people and diocesan priests established the first 'schools for Catholics', so creating a foundation on which the religious would later build. The early lay teachers were generally people who had a limited grasp of their faith in terms of 'book knowledge', but their authority as religious leaders and educators was strongly supported by the Catholic community in which they worked, and so they effectively shared their precious faith heritage.

Many Catholic educators today also share something of the early teachers' situation in regard to their religious knowledge base. Although they have the advantage of opportunities to deal with any deficit in knowledge, they operate without the support provided by the strong Catholic culture that their forebears enjoyed. They and their leaders have to work out how to address the challenges this presents. The strength of the local school community, parish, and educational system is obviously a crucial factor. In our experience, many teachers in Catholic schools are largely ignorant of the educational narrative in which their schools stand, and are unaware of how far back in time it extends. The narrative of Catholic schooling affirms a number of *important values* that stand behind the culture of Australian Catholic schools. However, like all cultural values, these are largely taken for granted and work out of sight, at least as long as they remain unchallenged. In the present era of profound societal change, however, the values and traditions that have made Catholic schools 'Catholic' are being challenged. Hence, it is important that teachers begin to learn what these are, and how they affect what is happening in their particular schools. This involves greater familiarity with the narrative of Catholic schooling so that the *pedagogical significance* of its core values is understood.

- *What are the values that characterise your school's participation in the Catholic school narrative?*
- *How do these play out in the goals the school seeks to achieve?*
- *How do they play out in teaching practice?*

Schools associated with religious congregations undertake this project under the rubric of *charism*. It is easy for a teacher to assume that, if their school is not associated with a religious congregation, then it has no charism. However, every Catholic school has its own charism as each school community provides its *own graced witness to the Gospel*. The challenge is to discover what this charism is, to celebrate it, and determine how the values central to it shape school life and influence pedagogical choices.

Many schools now interpret their charism in terms of important values drawn from Catholic social teaching. One of these values is expressed as 'exercising a preferential option for the poor and marginalised'. This emphasis in school life brings Catholic schools into the ambit of what is known as 'critical pedagogy' pioneered by Paulo Freire and the liberation theologians in Latin America, and developed in the US by educators such as Henry Giroux, Joe Kincheloe, and in the US Catholic sector by Thomas Oldenski. These people ask:

- *Who is being left behind or marginalised by the way in which teaching and learning function in schools today, and how are we going to address this issue?*

It is not possible for a Catholic school community to achieve its mission to make present God's Kingdom without thinking through the implications of such questions as:

- *How are marginalised students taught in this school?*
- *How are they taught in my classroom?*
- *In what ways do our school structures, including teaching methods, marginalise students or compound their situation?*

Critical pedagogy highlights the moral dimension of the Catholic school tradition.

In 1977 the Vatican's Congregation for Catholic Education[12] published *The Catholic School*. Since then, this body has consistently attempted to chart, promote, and clarify thinking about what is important in Catholic schooling. Given that Catholic schools operate in widely different political and cultural situations, this is not an easy task. As a consequence, the *normative documentation* on Catholic schooling tends to be fairly general, and dioceses are encouraged to interpret it while taking local contexts into account. This task usually falls to Catholic Education Offices and leaders of religious congregations.

The major emphasis in the normative documents has been on the goals of Catholic schooling, rather than on pedagogy. Consequently, these documents do not feature a consistent focus on pedagogy either conceptually or practically. However, across time they have continued to highlight important aspects of pedagogy. These range from an exhortation to embrace 'pedagogical excellence' in the Second Vatican Council document on Christian education[13] through reference to the responsibilities of teachers

---

12 A division of the administrative apparatus of the Holy See responsible for education in schools, universities and seminaries.
13 The document on Catholic education from the Second Vatican Council (*Gravissimum Educationis*) concludes by urging educators to 'excel in pedagogy', an exhortation repeated towards the end of *The Catholic School* (1977), the document which provided the post-Council comprehensive treatment foreshadowed in *Gravissimum Educationis*.

of 'pedagogical science' in the 1980s[14], to the pedagogy of 'intercultural learning' today[15].

As the foregoing makes clear, there are a multitude of questions to consider in attempting to make links between 'Catholic', on the one hand, and 'pedagogy' on the other. We hope this book will help do this by opening up conversation about what these links are, and how they can be made in the context of a particular school.

Catholic bishops in many parts of Australia have recognised that traditional approaches to Religious Education have become ineffective in educating students native to the emerging cultural environment. Consequently, the purpose and function of Religious Education is being re-conceptualised and translated in terms of classroom practice.

In the emerging thinking, as well as its religious purpose as traditionally understood, Religious Education has both a social and a cultural purpose. The analysis of the situation provided by Belgian theologian and educator Lieven Boeve has been influential, as has the work of his colleagues at Katholieke Universiteit Leuven (KUL) in establishing the *Enhancing Catholic School Identity* (ECSI) project in which many Australian dioceses are participating. Boeve suggests that, in the face of the current pluralism in belief and the devaluing of traditions that once held society together, the purpose and practice of Religious Education needs to be reformulated. Furthermore, he suggests that the Catholic tradition itself needs to be 're-contextualised' if it is going to be meaningful to students and help them live in a pluralised, multi-faith, and de-traditionalised world.

'Re-contextualisation' involves developing a contextualised critical consciousness so that students are able to evaluate the many options open to them, including belief or unbelief, in making important life choices. Boeve's position shares much in common with the advocates of critical pedagogy. His suggestions for reformulating and re-contextualising Catholic education, when taken up, have an important bearing on how teachers construe their moral purpose and the 'difference' they seek to make through their teaching. The development also impacts on how Religious Education, as a specific area of study, is approached. The development also has much to offer other areas of study in terms of teaching methodology, given that our culture as a whole faces the same problem in regard to context.

---

14 Congregation for Catholic Education, *The Religious Dimension of Education in a Catholic School* 1988, 62.
15 Congregation for Catholic Education, *Educating to Intercultural Dialogue in Catholic Schools: Living in Harmony for a Civilization of Love* (2013). All normative documents on Catholic education are downloadable from the Vatican website.

- *What does 're-contextualisation' mean for teachers and how does it shape their pedagogy?*

An important argument of this book is that the role of the teacher in a Catholic school is being transformed. This is driven by changes in the context in which these schools now operate, and this impacts the meaning that 'mission', as a religious goal pursued through Catholic education, has for many. Some of the changes underway reflect changes in the wider culture; others reflect changes in the way members of the Catholic Church now see the world, understand their place in it, and understand their relationship to traditional sources of authority in the Church. Whereas once social conditions were such that teachers understood their role as *knowledge experts and creators of life chances*, today they act more as *designers of learning, models of learning*, and *mediators of meaning* for the young people in their care. All three roles have a particular orientation in the context of a Catholic school and its mission to the young, and to society and culture.

In school education there has been a shift in pedagogical emphasis from *what the teacher does* to *how well the student learns*. The role of the teacher seems to be moving closer to that of the *accompaniment* that characterised the role of the original pedagogues.[16]

2. WHAT IS PEDAGOGY?

While we have used the term many times already, one of the biggest challenges in researching this book has been giving a precise meaning to the term 'pedagogy'. Understandings of pedagogy seem to lie along a spectrum of meanings. At one end of this spectrum the meaning is narrowly *technical*. In this understanding, pedagogy is *what the teacher does in the classroom to promote effective and measurable student learning*. At the other end of the spectrum the understanding of pedagogy is framed in *ethical terms. Pedagogy is a particular form of relationship between an adult and a vulnerable child or young person in which the former accepts responsibility for the care, growth and development of that vulnerable child or young person*. The narrow definition of pedagogy is specific to teaching. The broader definition covers parenting, as well as

---

16 In ancient Greece pedagogues were slaves who accompanied the children (boys only) of the wealthy to school, carrying their books. It was a menial role that developed over time. In Roman times pedagogues were well-educated slaves who stood *in loco parentis* and were responsible for ensuring that their charges (boys or girls) actually learned from their teachers. They became the supervisors of learning. This is the role of modern social pedagogues in Europe who accompany troubled young people and help them negotiate the social challenges associated with growing up in a pluralist society. The notion of 'accompaniment' is also prominent in Pope Francis' approach to young people.

teaching, counselling and other services devoted to the proper development of the child.

As an ethical activity, pedagogy focuses on *what is 'good' for the child* (Van Manen 2016).[17] Teachers will have their own understandings of what 'good' means in the context of Catholic education. There are normative Catholic understandings that grow out of the experience of Catholic education worldwide that provide helpful resources in expanding understanding, and these play their part in pre-service education for teachers and in the formative programs which system leaders provide.[18]

By exploring 'the good' teachers seek to achieve and the way in which this plays out, *Pedagogy and the Catholic Educator: Nurturing Hearts, Transforming Possibilities* seeks to address the questions raised above and the changing role of the teacher in:

- *how they teach*
- *how they interact with students in helping them learn and develop*
- *how they define their role.*

The book uses a multi-disciplinary approach in exploring these issues.

3. CATHOLIC PEDAGOGY

For those who understand pedagogy as narrowly defined, 'Catholic' may seem an unusual adjective to juxtapose with it. The juxtaposition will seem more appropriate for those who interpret pedagogy in a broader way.

In this book we interpret 'Catholic' as embracing *a constellation of values* that are used to justify the 'good' that pedagogy seeks to achieve. The primary Catholic values are those contained in Jesus' message about the Kingdom of God as exemplified in the way Jesus lived his life and engaged in his mission. We call these *Kingdom values*. They apply to human life, to societal arrangements, and to the earth itself.

Jesus' Kingdom values do not exist in some absolute, ahistorical, acultural form. They have to be contextualised. As cultures and times change, they must be *re-contextualised* if they are to remain meaningful and maintain their role in playing a part in ushering in changes that can inaugurate a better future. When this process of re-contextualisation is not carried out effectively, a warping occurs in the fabric of Christian life. We are witnessing

---

17 A key theme in *Pedagogical Tact*. Routledge: London, 2016. See for example 'The Nature of Pedagogy' (chapter 3), 33–48.
18 Readers are encouraged to familiarise themselves with the normative tradition of Catholic education as contained in the magisterial documents which have been issued by the Congregation for Catholic Education since the Second Vatican Council (1962–5). These are listed and downloadable from the Vatican website.

the consequence of this at the present time, and it is a malady that Pope Francis, along with recent popes, is seeking to address. The Kingdom value of 'mission' is, therefore, complex, since the specific demands of God's mission as we learn these from the life, teaching, death and resurrection of Jesus, also change in response to changing historical and societal circumstances.

The word 'mission' is widely used today. In general usage, 'mission' means 'purpose'. In Christian life, the term also refers to the 'purpose' or 'raison d'etre' of the community which is *to continue the salvific ministry of Jesus, the teacher, healer, and reconciler, in the here and now.* Christian churches including the Catholic Church have been through much serious reflection on mission in recent decades. The normative teaching on mission is now rich and extensive. It will be discussed further as we proceed. The mission or goal that Jesus saw as the focus of all his endeavours was to make present and very concrete God's own vision and ongoing work in creation. Jesus called this project 'the Kingdom of God'. For him the Kingdom of God was very clear and concrete, even if fundamentally different from the political triumph his followers were expecting vis-à-vis the Roman occupation. As we have noted, Jesus made the Kingdom of God very real through his down-to-earth teaching, including his arresting parables, his personal choices of relationships, his usage of time and energy, and his prayerful communication with the one he called 'Father'.

As the demands of mission shift, so too does our conception of 'Catholic identity' and our understanding of our role as Christians – 'what it is that expresses who we are', 'what is right for us'. A consequence is that the 'good' that a Catholic pedagogy seeks to achieve has to be re-conceptualised. For example, mission and pedagogy in a postmodern, postsecular society have different emphases and pursue different directions from those appropriately taken in modernity.

A constant temptation for Church leaders has been to take a particular contextualisation of Jesus' Kingdom values as being definitive of Christian life for all cultures and all times. However, *Christian life can have no such definitive form in human history*, for it is always *in process*. This understanding is integral to Jesus' teaching about the Kingdom of God *which was cast in process terms* and included an orientation to the future, God's future. We will open up this important element of pedagogical vision in our final section.

The privilege and challenge of re-contextualising mission is to honour the God who, in Jesus, both entered human history in a particular time and place, and continues through the Holy Spirit to quicken and empower us through the particularities of histories and cultures. Thus there is, or should be, always a fluidity and newness in the concept 'Catholic'.

Jesus' Kingdom values, discernible from how he engaged in his teaching, healing, and reconciling mission, provide teachers with *essential criteria in both making sound pedagogical choices and in re-defining their own roles.* As the diagram below makes clear, conceptualising a Catholic pedagogy is no easy task. This is because a Catholic pedagogy sits at the confluence of a number of historically developed traditions, each of which has some impact in shaping the pedagogical choices open to teachers today.

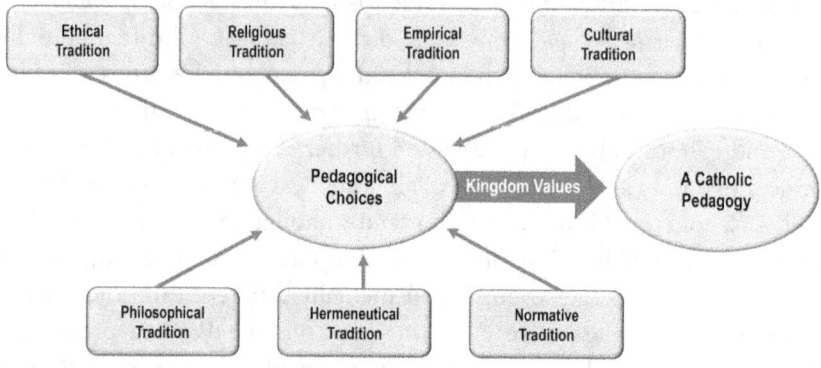

FIGURE 1.1: TRADITIONS IMPACTING ON PEDAGOGY IN CATHOLIC SCHOOLS

In concluding this chapter, we portray our working description — 'definition' being too constraining a term — of 'Catholic pedagogy' as follows:

Catholic pedagogy is a shared understanding that provides teachers with guidelines in their decision-making as to how best to advance the learning and development of their students.

This shared understanding is nourished by a community of educators striving to be faithful to the mission of Jesus in their time and place.

Enriched by the wisdom of both faith and culture, Catholic pedagogy advances the mission of the Catholic school community, and seeks the 'good' of each child.

Catholic pedagogy assumes sound analysis of the student's situation, and adequate understanding of what constitutes learning, including the conditions under which this occurs.

Catholic pedagogy engenders responsiveness to God's invitation to be co-creators of a more just and loving society and a flourishing natural world.

Catholic pedagogy is a profoundly ethical endeavour.

2

MISSION AND THE CATHOLIC IMAGINATION

Mission is a single but complex reality and it develops in a variety of ways
            Pope John Paul II, *Redemptoris Missio*, #41.

In order to keep focus in our exploration into pedagogy and the *Catholic educator*, we must also clarify how the Catholic community understands its religious purpose (mission), and whether this understanding has implications for the pedagogical choices educators must make.

'Mission' is often confused in its usage. Part of the reason for this is the rapid learning curve the Catholic community has been on in understanding its relationship with the world of which it is itself a part, and to which its mission is directed. Two questions must be explored:

- *How is 'mission' understood in contemporary Catholicism?*
- *What implications does this understanding now hold for Catholic educators?*

In this chapter we argue that the implications of an enlarged understanding of mission – particularly the multiple forms it can take – raises important pedagogical issues for education in general, and religious education in particular. This matter will be explored in more detail in subsequent chapters.

In answering the first question we employ two sources – the Church's normative documentation on mission, and the historical circumstances surrounding its development. The two need to be considered together to highlight the dynamic relationship between the Christian experience of mission 'on the ground' and the impact this has in shaping official teaching.

We approach this question of how mission is understood in contemporary Catholicism, by naming key themes and key 'moments' in the development of the Church's understanding of its mission. From there we examine how this understanding has been translated into pastoral practice, including Catholic schooling.

The fundamental goals of Christian mission always remain the same. In broad terms, the Catholic faith community has and always will be charged with:

- *Proclaiming*
- *Witnessing*
- *Dialoguing*
- *Actualising*

God's loving vision for creation. And this is always to be undertaken through humble openness and service, and in partnership with the Holy Spirit. This is a vision that was articulated by Jesus in terms of a metaphor, the 'Kingdom of God' that encompasses the entire cosmos, the earth, human history and all of God's creatures. It is the vision of the Gospel which, when actualised, is very good news.[1]

Church leaders previously interpreted this vision as something that *the Church* was responsible for implementing. They have subsequently learned that mission is something that God is effecting, and its role in this work is achieved *in partnership with the Holy Spirit, and with others.*

1. THE CATHOLIC IMAGINATION

Several times in this book we refer to the role 'imaginal horizon' plays in meaning-making. In simple terms, our imaginal horizon constitutes the limits of what we can 'see', and consequently act upon. Our imagination is always limited – we can imagine some possibilities and not others. Individuals think within a certain horizon, so too do members of a group. There is, for example, an imaginal horizon associated with 'being Catholic'. Imaginal horizons are rarely static. New circumstances throw up new challenges and force us to imagine new possibilities. Think of the advent of the motor car, or of the internet! Imaginal horizons are constantly being challenged and expanded.

Catholics have long been characterised by a *sacramental imagination*. Sacraments and sacramentals are often taken for granted as defining who we are as Catholics. We are baptised, confirmed, have sins forgiven, celebrate the eucharist etc. In recent centuries, much of Catholic life has revolved specifically around the seven sacraments as the principal means by which Catholics relate to God within their lives. As we shall see, Catholics today are called upon to develop a *missional imagination* which expands the 'sacramental imagination' which has characterised Catholics until recent

---

[1] The 'kingdom' of God is also translated as 'the reign of God'. We use these two terms interchangeably.

times. In fact *missional imagination* is the sacramental imagination in a new key.

Take for example the symbol at the centre of our eucharistic celebration, food. The extreme individualism that characterises most Western societies also impacts on the way many Catholics approach this sacrament. We tend to see it fairly exclusively as spiritual food for 'my' journey in such a way that we forget that the Jesus whose life we are sharing and celebrating actually fed hungry and vulnerable people. It is these actions which are used as the setting for his teaching about his relationship with his disciples (Jn 6: 5–58).

A highly personalised spirituality fails to pick up the force of Jesus' teaching in terms of both charity and justice, both touchstones of the authenticity of our eucharistic participation. Conversely, many of us engage in justice and charity, yet do not see this as eucharist-in-daily-life; but as simply a form of 'good works' that has lost its sacramental dimension. The Catholic imagination shrunk in response to the development of the dualism that distinguished the secular 'doing good' from the sacred 'eucharist'. This dualism tends to distort spirituality.

The sacraments we celebrate in our formal worship in the Church are an intensification of the broader sacramental reality of all of creation. All created things, by their very existence, speak of God to those so attuned. For them, the 'world is charged with the grandeur of God' as the poet Gerard Manley Hopkins famously attested.[2] How, then, can practising Christians unresistingly participate, albeit a little uncomfortably, in a culture that wreaks havoc on the natural world, that destroys capacity for food production, that wastes massively even as others are in need, and whose governments engage unchallenged (at least by many Christians) in unfair trade practices which harm the poor of the world? If, however, we are able to question, reflect, and then live within expanded imaginal possibilities, we find the *Catholic imagination*[3] morphs into a missional imagination and an accompanying *sensibility*.[4]

In moving more deeply into an exploration of the Catholic imagination, we review some thinking of Stephen Bevans SVD, a renowned systematic theologian, whose specialisation is the study of mission (missiology). Bevans

---

2 Joseph Martos, *Doors to the Sacred: Historical Introduction to Sacraments in the Catholic Church*. Missouri: Ligouri Press, 2014, explores the historical background to the sacraments as we know them today. While Catholics often assume that these have always been experienced in the way we experience them now, the sacramental nature of the Church has developed throughout two thousand years of history.
3 Andrew Greeley, *The Catholic Imagination*. Berkeley: University of California Press, 2000.
4 'Sensibility' as used here means adopting a characteristic stance to life that enables a person to address the complex emotional issues associated with social, religious and aesthetic experiences.

sheds light on the factors that make the shift to expand our imaginal horizon quite difficult.

2. MISSION AS MARGINAL TO THEOLOGY

Bevans sets out the requirements for developing a missiological imagination by focusing on *foundational theological ideas*. He approaches the subject from an historical/narrative perspective in two important papers.[5] He begins by pointing out that historically, Church thinking about mission has long been marginalised in theology, despite the fact that the history and theology of early Christianity is essentially 'mission history' and 'mission theology'. Christian theology began, Bevans states, as reflection on the lived experience of mission.[6]

The Gospels themselves are theologies that resulted from reflection on Jesus and his significance. They were written initially to nourish the faith of fledgling communities in the dynamic contexts of their time, when being a Christian meant being 'on the outer' and subject to sporadic persecutions. However, once Christianity began to find a privileged place in the empire, and later aligned itself with civic power as the era of 'Christendom' took shape, theology underwent a most significant change – it changed purpose and focus in becoming a reflection on the Church's life and on what constituted 'Christian faith'. In recent times, theologians shifting focus to the situations of marginalised people have called the Catholic community back, belatedly but quite urgently, to the style of mission reflection which characterised our beginnings and gave us the Gospels.

2.1 'Classicism' shrinks the Catholic imagination[7]

Given that theology had changed focus during the time of Christendom from 'reflection, in the light of faith, on the lived experience of Christians' to a somewhat disembodied 'knowledge of God and the things of God', it lost contact with missionary experience and the challenge of making present Jesus' vision and agenda. This shift would persist, in practice substantially unchanged, even as the Christian mission experience expanded first in

---

5 Stephen Bevans, *Wisdom from the margins: Systematic theology and the Missional Imagination*. Catholic Theological Society of America (CTSA Proceedings), 2001: 56, 21–41.
Stephen Bevans, 'Doing Mission Today: Where we do it; How we do it; What we do'. http://mohmv.com.au/Resources/Stephen%20Bevans%20Keynote%202.pdf
6 Part of the issue here is that, as a category, 'mission' does not appear in theological discourse until the 16th century and it undergoes major development in the 20th century.
7 The notion that ideas formulated in one culture should be taken as normative for all cultures is called 'classicism'. The development described above is an example of European classicism and the result was that theology continued to be characterised by a Eurocentric bias (to which theologians there were generally oblivious).

Europe itself, and in the 'New World' where Christians encountered a range of new situations and challenges.

The modern missionary era, corresponding to the first and second expansions of Europe into South America, Asia, Africa and Oceania (15th to the 19th centuries), threw up issues that required Christian responses. Today we identify these responses as *forms of mission* that now exist alongside the traditional mission activities of proclaiming the Gospel and forming faith communities. Examples include 'inculturation' (the Gospel taking root in a culture and being expressed in the images and thought patterns of that culture), and 'human rights' (rights which flow from people's very humanity, such as the right to physical security, to food, to education, to healthcare etc.).[8] Inculturation came into focus with the work of missionaries such as the Jesuits Matteo Ricci (1552–1610) in China, Roberto di Nobili (1557–1656) in India, and Alexandre de Rhodes (1591–1660) in Indo-China. Human rights issues arose in regard to the native South Americans.[9]

It was not until the work of Pope John XXIII (*Pacem in Terris* 1963)[10] and that of the Second Vatican Council (1962–5), that these would be recognised in the normative teaching of the Church as genuine *forms* that mission can take.

In the 17th and 18th centuries, Europe underwent major changes as 'Enlightenment thinking' gained ground. This placed a premium on rational thinking of a *deductive type* that reinforced the dominant method of theological reflection. As Western knowledge was differentiating into a variety of disciplines, European theology subdivided into specialities matched to the practical interests of priests and pastors. In this development, for example, moral theology was split off from doctrinal theology, with the latter becoming a technical and scholarly enterprise, a field for specialists only. Pastoral theology, the study of the lived Christian experience, was differentiated from fields such as Biblical exegesis, Church history and systematic theology, all of which were considered to be 'academic' disciplines. The result was the balkanising of theology as a discipline that now proceeded seemingly without a core holding it together conceptually.

In this context and despite the explosion of cross-cultural mission experience, 'theology' continued to be produced in Europe and exported. It was produced by theologians often ignorant of the evolving experience of

---
8 For a brief introduction see Jim & Therese D'Orsa, *Mission in Practice*. Mulgrave: Garratt Publishing, 2019.
9 Sabine Hyland, *The Jesuits in Latin America, 1549–2000: 450 Years of Inculturation, Defense of Human Rights, and Prophetic Witness*. Saint Louis: The Institute of Jesuit Sources, 2009.
10 Pope John XXIII *Pacem in Terris* (1963), # 9. http://www.vatican.va/content/john-xxiii/en/encyclicals/documents/hf_j-xxiii_enc_11041963_pacem.html

missionaries working in the societies and cultures of Latin America, Africa, Asia, and the Pacific. 'Theology' as formulated in European academies, both Catholic and Protestant, was presumed to be 'universal'. A by-product of this development was that sacramental theology became divorced from mission theology.

In the Catholic Church, European theology developed two major emphases: pastoring parishes and defending 'the faith' against the claims of other Christian denominations. The idea of reflecting on the lived experience of Church members who crossed cultural boundaries and encountered new developments remained largely foreign to European theologians. Such new developments included the emerging democratic consciousness, the effects of the industrial revolution, and European colonies' expanding sense of freedom from oppression while encountering people with different cultures, religions, and worldviews.[11] The interests that drove theological development had the unintended effect of shrinking the Catholic imagination so that Catholics came to live in a circumscribed cultural world.

2.2 Emergence of a new imaginal horizon in theology

Missiology, as an area of study, was initially confined to areas needed by those preparing for mission assignment in cross-cultural settings. It was established as a serious area of study only in the late 19th century. As it developed in the 20th century, missiology embraced reflection on the lived experiences of Christian mission considered globally. Employing an inductive methodology, it slowly began to affect the theological enterprise as a whole.

The first chair of missiology was established in Edinburgh and headed by Protestant missioner and theologian Alexander Duff.[12] Duff had the support of Protestant missionary societies, who funded missions and who saw the need to *prepare people adequately for work overseas*. Likewise, some European states with overseas colonies recognised the same need, because missions played an important role in colonial life. It was in this context that the first Catholic Chair of Missiology was funded at the University of Munster, Germany, in 1914.

---

11 The notion that ideas formulated in one culture should be taken as normative for all cultures is called 'classicism'. The development described above is an example of European classicism and the result was that theology continued to be characterised by a Eurocentric bias (to which theologians there were generally oblivious).

12 This was partly inspired by Propaganda Fide in Rome. See article by Andrew Walls on Alexander Duff (1806–1878), 187–8 in Gerald Anderson ed. *Biographical Dictionary of Christian Missions*. Grand Rapids: Eerdmans, 1998, 187–8.

In many Catholic seminaries the focus was on preparing priests for parish work so missiology, even when part of the curriculum, did not influence the theological imagination of the pre-Vatican II period. It was viewed, rather like anthropology, as a specialty for those serving as the Church's 'foreign affairs department' – exotic, and peripheral to mainstream theological education. This situation began to change only in the 1950s. The impetus for the change came from within the European theological community itself when theologians began to reclaim the doctrine of the Trinity in Christian theology, and draw out the connections between Trinity and mission.

This was significant because, across time, the Christian doctrine of God as Trinity had faded in the Catholic imagination. Karl Rahner's judgement on the lack of connection of the Christian doctrine of the Trinity with the rest of the theological enterprise is often quoted:

> *We must be willing to admit that, should the doctrine of the Trinity have to be dropped as false, the major part of religious literature could well remain virtually unchanged.*[13]

All that was about to change.

2.3 Mission as *'Missio Dei'*

In the 1930s the German Protestant missiologist Karl Hartenstein, reacting to the over-emphasis in Church circles on mission as *what Christians do*, reminded his colleagues that mission is essentially the *work of God* active within history. The phrase *'missio dei'* (God's mission) was thus coined.[14]

In 1952 Protestant theologian Wilhelm Anders proposed a theology of the Trinity which was to become very important in the development of mission theology in both Protestant and Catholic circles. He articulated a dynamic vision of the inner life of God which overflows in *loving, creative and saving involvement with all of creation*. This was God engaged in mission.

The impetus given to Catholic Biblical scholarship by Pius XII's encyclical *Divino Afflante Spiritu* (1943) led eventually to the recovery of the understanding that had faded from the Catholic imagination – the centrality of the Reign or Kingdom of God in Jesus' teaching and witness. While this had never been wholly lost, a Church-centred theology had seen the Kingdom of God become equated with the Church itself. Now came theological recognition that the Kingdom, for the coming of which the Church community prays daily, *is a larger reality than the Church*. The Church

---

13 Karl Rahner, *Trinity*. London: Burns & Oates, 1970, 10–11.
14 See entry on Hartenstein by Hans-Werner Gensichen in Gerald Anderson, 282.

is a community of people *intentionally committed to continuing the work of Jesus in bringing about the Kingdom or reign of God* in societies and cultures, and in the total earth community on which they depend. The recovery of the Biblical meaning of the Kingdom of God linked the mission of the Trinity to the mission of Jesus through the pervasive presence of God's Spirit in all of creation. In fact the Holy Spirit has been at work from the beginning and continues to guide the Christian faith community since Jesus returned to the Father.[15]

Catholic theologians also began to work with this insight, and the perspective became embedded in Vatican II's Decree on Missionary Activity (*Ad Gentes*) where we find the seminal passage:

> ... *the pilgrim Church is missionary by its very nature. For it is from the mission of the Son and the mission of the Holy Spirit that she takes her origin in accordance with the decree of God the father* (#2).

'Mission' was clarified and enriched through the 'rediscovery' of the theology of the Trinity. The Gospel motif of the Kingdom of God, far from being marginal or peripheral to theology, then moved quickly to become central to its content and process, and to how 'Catholic' can now be imagined. Mission, in the image used by the highly regarded Protestant missiologist, Andrew Kirk, consequently becomes the mortar that holds the theological building together.[16] A paradigm shift was occurring in the Church's understanding of itself and its mission from the mid-20th century.

Such leaps forward take time to make their impact on entrenched ways of thinking and doing theology. However, the shift was occurring, and it was accompanied by a renewed theological methodology, one which takes history, context, and human experience very seriously. This was liberating for the Catholic imagination.

For this imaginal leap to have a real impact, three obstacles had to be overcome:

- *Mission needed to be clarified as a theological concept*
- *Theologians had to understand the missional implications for their disciplines*
- *Catholics had to learn to think in terms of 'mission' rather than 'missions.'*

The first obstacle was removed officially for Catholics at the Second Vatican Council; addressing the second and third is still in process.

---

15 Ralph Del Colle. *Christ and the Spirit: Spirit Christology in Trinitarian Perspective*. New York: Oxford University Press, 1994 provides a highly regarded treatment of Spirit Christology.

16 J. Andrew Kirk. *The Mission of Theology and Theology as Mission*. Valley Forge PA: Trinity Press International, 1997, 51.

3. MISSION MOVES TO THE CENTRE

Foundational to a contemporary Catholic theology of mission is the work of the Second Vatican Council (1962–65). This created a platform from which further developments in mission theology would be launched. We will briefly summarise the emerging themes in the developing Catholic narrative of mission. Four key 'moments' in the Church's developing sense of its mission from Vatican II to the present provide a kind of navigational guide through this recent journey.

Contemporary mission studies place a deal of emphasis on what is called 'mission inter gentes',[17] which translates as 'mission between peoples'. The phrase recognises firstly that God is, and has been, at work in all people across human history, and that mission is very much a process of mutual openness and enlightenment in the search for truth, effected through dialogue between peoples and also between faith communities. Secondly, since each Christian community contextualises the Gospel in its own unique way, the mutuality between local churches also provides the means of accessing the truth for which we search and to which we are committed. It also helps communities to see the limitations in their own work, thereby learning from each other. This is a theme that Pope Francis returns to many times.

The four clear historical 'moments' in the unfolding of normative Catholic teaching on mission from Vatican II to the present are listed below. Associated with each 'moment' are a number of documents which frame discussion on the missional nature of the Church. Taken together they challenge Catholics to develop a missiological imagination.

3.1 First 'Moment': Vatican II (1962–5)[18] – 'The Church is missionary by its very nature' (*Ad Gentes* 2)

As we have indicated, theological development vis-à-vis mission began well before the Second Vatican Council. However, for Catholics, this event took the development onto another plane. The two great Council documents which dealt with the Church (*Lumen Gentium* and *Gaudium et Spes*) are, each

---

17 Jonathan Tan, 'Missio Inter Gentes: Towards a New Paradigm in the Mission Theology of the Federation of Asian Bishops' Conferences (FABC)', Mission Studies, Vol 21, No 1, 2004.
18 Key missional documents of the Council include:
- *Lumen Gentium (Dogmatic Constitution on the Church)*
- *Gaudium et Spes (Pastoral Constitution on the Church in the Modern World)*
- *Ad Gentes (Decree on the Church's Missionary Activity)*
- *Nostra Aetate (Decree on the Church's Relationship with non-Christian Religions).*

Other related documents include:
- *Dei Verbum (The Dogmatic Constitution on Divine Revelation)*
- *Dignitatis Humanae (The Degree on Religious Freedom).*

in different ways, profoundly missional in character. They also demonstrate clearly *that identity and mission are intimately linked* in the Church, as indeed they are in any institution or community.

Lumen Gentium (The Dogmatic Constitution on the Church), which dealt with the Church's identity, set a direction that was to continue to frame mission theology by utilising the graphic kingdom images found in the synoptic Gospels to describe the Church e.g. seed, little flock, salt, light, leaven (*LG* #5). This demonstrated very clearly that the Church is *at the service of the Kingdom of God*. Unlike *Gaudium et Spes,* however, *LG*'s theological methodology was traditional, that is, deductive.

Gaudium et Spes (The Pastoral Constitution on the Church in the Modern World) addressed the Church's relationship with the world in terms of identification with all that affects humanity, both its joys and sorrows (#1). Although designated a 'pastoral' constitution, *Gaudium et Spes* is, in its entirety, also a missional document, as is clear from its subject matter. It demonstrates that *the pastoral and the missional are not two distinct aspects of the Church's life*, but rather that they are complementary elements of the whole. Its theological methodology, 'discerning the signs of the times', is inductive, and this continues to be the modus operandi of mission theologians today. *Gaudium et Spes* also addresses the relationship between faith and culture, which remains a key challenge in bringing the Gospel to persons and societies. It is central to the meaning-making processes in which educators engage when they work in Catholic education.

The insight which summarised most succinctly the new trinitarian paradigm of mission already alluded to above, is found in the Council document dealing with what was called in the past the 'foreign missions' (*Ad Gentes*). We repeat it particularly for the purpose of drawing attention to the last part of the passage:

> *The pilgrim Church is missionary by her very nature, since it is from the mission of the Son and of the Holy Spirit that she draws her origin in accordance with the decree of God the Father ... This decree flows from the fount-like love ... of God the Father ...* (AG 2).

The second part of the sentence is vital in understanding the magnitude of the paradigm shift in regard to the Church's understanding of its mission. The document's indebtedness to the Protestant missiologists mentioned above is obvious. Mission comes from the very life of God, a life of overflowing love. The Church is not its origin; the Church community is its instrument.

The Council Fathers drew the attention of the whole Church to the fact that, since mission is first and foremost God's work, Church communities and individuals are privileged participants in what God is effecting in the world. *This understanding provides the basis for the Church's dialogue with the world.* The Church's role is to be at the service of the world and its people so that they may reach their destiny in God. And, since through baptism a person shares in the life of the Trinity, each of the baptised is called to share in God's work in the world.

In *Nostra Aetate*[19] the bishops also provided a perspective on a new and broader understanding of salvation. This perspective recognises that God has been at work in the world since the beginning of time, and so God has been at work among all peoples and all cultures. In this, the shortest of the Council's documents, the Church is specifically called upon to collaborate with members of other religions 'to preserve and encourage the moral truths' found among their adherents (*NA* #2). There is an implicit acknowledgement in this document that faithful adherents of other religions attain salvation through their religious traditions.

At the same time there is also a reaffirmation of the duty that Christians have to witness to their own faith. Two truths of faith are finely balanced here – God's universal and effective will that all be saved, and the unique role of Jesus as universal saviour. Theological exploration of these issues continues.

3.2 Second 'Moment': *Evangelii Nuntiandi* (1975) – Mission in its many forms is the Church's deepest identity

Evangelii Nuntiandi (*On Evangelization in the Modern World*), is the apostolic exhortation of Pope Paul VI (1975). This is the Pope's summary of the work of the 1974 world synod on evangelisation. Most importantly, Paul VI acknowledges the fact that mission has *many forms* i.e. there are, and can be, many expressions of the Kingdom of God in societies and cultures, particularly in the contemporary world with its varieties of human need to which the healing, teaching, and reconciling ministry of Jesus must continue to be addressed.

The 1974 synod on Evangelisation in the Modern World wrestled not only with the implications of the Council's teaching on mission, but did so in the light of a decade of experience in attempting to implement it. In the interim, traditional approaches in mission had proved problematic or too

---

19 The Second Vatican Council's document which deals with the relationship of the Church to people of other faiths.
https://www.vatican.va/archive/hist_councils/ii_vatican_council/documents/vat-ii_decl_19651028_nostra-aetate_en.html

limited. The roll-back of political colonialism in the sixties and seventies created confusion about the purpose and goals of missionary activity. This development, combined with the rapidly changing context and diminution of Christian life in the West, set the agenda for a deeper understanding of mission across the globe.

The issues covered at the 1974 synod were wide-ranging, and the bishops left the task of summarising discussions to Pope Paul VI. *Evangelii Nuntiandi*, released the following year, was his response to their request.

The document proved something of a watershed. Not without reason is it still termed a 'magna carta' of mission theology.[20] It re-affirmed the central missional insight of the Second Vatican Council, that mission is a sharing in the life of God, and acknowledged the insights of *Nostra Aetate*. It also clarified key elements in the emerging field of missiology, or mission studies as it is often termed, such as:

- *reclaiming the theology of the Kingdom of God as a basis for mission*
- *identifying conversion as vital for the evangelising church, as well as those to whom the good news is offered*
- *recognising that evangelisation applies not only to persons, but also to human institutions and cultures*
- *presenting mission as multi-faceted*
- *identifying the central place of proclamation through word and witness*
- *accepting that the unique way local people express their faith, 'popular religiosity', is to be not only respected, but also valued.*

Evangelii Nuntiandi continues to be regarded as a seminal document. It shows that a Gospel imperative such as justice in the world is an integral element of mission. Its influence on Pope Francis' approach to mission is obvious.

> Between evangelization and human advancement – development and liberation – there are in fact profound links. These include links of an anthropological order, because the man (sic) who is to be evangelized is not an abstract being but is subject to social and economic questions. They also include links in the theological order, since one cannot dissociate the plan of Creation from the plan of Redemption. The latter plan touches the very concrete situations of injustice to be combated and of justice to be restored. They include links of the eminently evangelical order, which is that of charity: how in fact can one proclaim the new commandment without

---

20 E.g., Peter Phan 'Proclamation of the Reign of God as Mission of the Church' in *In Our Own Tongues: Perspectives from Asia on Mission and Inculturation*. Maryknoll N.Y: Orbis, 2003, 39.

promoting in justice and in peace the true, authentic advancement of man (sic)? (Evangelii Nuntiandi #31).[21]

Evangelii Nuntiandi emphasised the need for Christians to speak to the hope that is in them on the grounds that witness must also be *articulated* if it is to be effective.

Always be ready to make your defense to anyone who demands from you an accounting for the hope that is in you; yet do it with gentleness and reverence (1 Peter 3:15).

As we will see later, being able to articulate what you know is central not only to being Christian, but also to effective understanding.

Because it was not a major theme of the synod, dialogue did not make an appearance in *Evangelii Nuntiandi*, despite Paul VI's earlier treatment of it in his first encyclical *Ecclesiam Suam* (On the Church, 1964).

3.3 Third 'Moment': (Redemptoris Missio 1990) – Mission is a central and permanent aspect of the life of the Church

Redemptoris Missio (*On the Permanent Validity of the Church's Missionary Mandate,* 1990) encyclical of Pope John Paul II. This work is a comprehensive discussion of mission. It devotes an early chapter (Chapter 2) to the Kingdom of God, and introduces a much-quoted discussion on the *importance of dialogue* in the Church's mission. Associated with this, *Dialogue and Proclamation* (1991) produced by the Pontifical Council for Inter-religious Dialogue, is noteworthy. Quite intentionally, 'dialogue' precedes 'proclamation' in its title.

Pope John Paul II's *Redemptoris Missio* (Mission of the Redeemer) was promulgated in 1990 as the change in human consciousness introduced by postmodern thinkers gathered pace, and in the context of a new phase of globalisation. There was an influential school of thought at the time which held that the era of mission 'ad gentes'[22] was over, on the grounds that Christian communities had been established in almost all countries of the world. The Pope reminded Catholics that this was not the case, and stressed the need to persevere in proclaiming the Gospel to all peoples.

---

21 Prior to the 1974 synod on evangelisation, the 1971 synod on justice also recognised the integral connection between evangelisation and one of its key forms:
'Action on behalf of justice and participation in the transformation of the world fully appear to us as a constitutive dimension of the preaching of the Gospel, or, in other words, of the Church's mission for the redemption of the human race and its liberation from every oppressive situation' (*Justice in the World* #6).
22 Translates as 'to the nations'. This is the phrase used of missionary endeavour directed to those who have not yet had the Gospel brought to them.

In devoting an entire chapter of *Redemptoris Missio* to the Kingdom of God, Pope John Paul II affirmed the earlier work of Paul VI. However, he set out to correct some mistaken emphases which had arisen in the interim. One was the equation of the Kingdom with earthly projects and struggles pursued within a horizon not open to the transcendent. Such a situation would reduce the Kingdom of God to an ideology (*RM, #17*).

Secondly, the Pope warned against detaching the Kingdom from Christ or his Church. In a beautiful and much-quoted passage, he reminded Catholics that Jesus is the perfect manifestation of the Kingdom:

> *The Kingdom of God is not a concept, a doctrine, or a program subject to free interpretation, but it is before all else a person with the face and name of Jesus of Nazareth, the image of the invisible God* (RM, #18).

Redemptoris Missio also sought to address inter-religious dialogue as the practice grew following the example set by the Pope himself.[23] His understanding of dialogue and the space given to it in *Redemptoris Missio* entrenched it as a *fundamental mode of mission*, complementing Pope Paul VI's emphasis on *proclamation through word and witness*.

As understood by Pope John Paul II, dialogue can take place at a number of levels (*RM #57*). *Dialogue of life* sees people living together amicably; *dialogue of action* sees people coming together around a common project such as work for justice and peace, or the education of young people; *dialogue of religious experience*, or what might be termed a dialogue of spiritualities, enables people to understand each other's experience in being people of faith, and in some cases this enables them to pray together; *dialogue of theological exchange* proceeds, both formally and informally, between those with theological expertise. Some of these forms of dialogue also apply to intercultural dialogue.

Redemptoris Missio called for a 'new evangelization' (*RM #3*), specifically naming three groups to whom the Gospel should be directed: those who have never heard the Gospel; those in whom the light of faith has grown dim; and the community of the faithful (*RM ##31–32*). Pope Benedict XVI called for a global synod on the new evangelisation before he resigned. Pope Francis had the task of presiding over it.

---

23 The great gathering of leaders of the world's religions at Assisi in October 1986, which Pope John Paul II initiated, stands as practical testimony to this commitment.

3.4 Fourth 'Moment': the work of Pope Francis – 'I dream of ... a missionary impulse capable of transforming everything'. *Evangelii Gaudium, #27*

Pope Francis' reflection on the synod on the new evangelisation, *Evangelii Gaudium* (*The Joy of the Gospel*, 2013), should be considered together with his landmark encyclical *Laudato si'* (*Care for our Common Home*, 2015) and the later *Gaudete et Exsultate* (*On the Call to Holiness in Today's World*, 2018). Building on the work of Pope Paul VI, Francis addresses the postmodern context, placing emphasis on a *new form of mission demanding attention in our time – care for the earth*. He also reiterates abiding themes such as the imperative of justice in the world. Like Paul VI and John Paul II, Francis presents an integrated and sophisticated vision of the Church's mission. A leitmotif in all of Pope Francis' communication is *dialogue* which he sees as vital *at every level of human life*. He calls all the faithful to holiness through their commitment to the Gospel in their own lives and in the world.

In the unfolding history of mission, the initial compelling form of Christian mission was *the quality of pastoral care* that Christians offered each other, and which made their communities so attractive in the brutal societies in which they first took life. This enabled people to make sense of the word being preached, and to be attracted to the eucharistic mystery. Pastoral care for our own members and those beyond our community continues to authenticate, or diminish as the case may be, the Christian message and way of life in our time. The point has already been made and bears repeating, the pastoral and missional aspects of the Church's life are integrally related.

The witness of faithful lives remains a pedagogical imperative for Catholic educators. Of course, the connection between life as lived and the message of God's love incarnated in Jesus *must be explained*, hence the teaching ministry of the Church and of each disciple. Dialogue between people at every level allows the process of making God's Kingdom continue. It provides the faith community with its core purpose and its most essential process.

4. MISSION – MODES, FORMS AND PEDAGOGICAL IMPLICATIONS

In the complex context of recent decades, various forms of mission have come into focus as faith communities have responded to human need. The central forms of pastoral care, liturgy and prayer, have been complemented by defence of human rights; human development and liberation; justice, peace and reconciliation; inter-religious dialogue; dialogue with truth-seekers; and care for the earth, etc. Each calls forth the missionary zeal of

Catholics in terms of the fundamental modes of mission – witness and word – pursued with and through dialogue.

Having acknowledged the unfolding narrative of mission through which our community has journeyed, and will continue to journey, it is timely to summarise consequential learnings that have surfaced.

i. The *formation* of teachers must be anchored in the Church's contemporary understanding of mission and the spirituality which enlivens understanding and brings it into the service of others. This formation must engender an integrated missional imagination.

ii. *The Gospel process of beginning with human experience* and then promoting a 'dialogue' with elements of our faith tradition has once again become a central method of theology. This process is central to sound religious education, both as a specific learning area and the religious education which occurs across the whole curriculum. The Catholic school, by its nature, is a laboratory of inter-cultural living and of dialogue in practice. At its best, it is an exemplar of learning by sensitive engagement.

iii. The Judeo-Christian understanding of God is as the Creator who continues to be active in history in a creative, saving and reconciling way. This understanding gives direction to *Christian discipleship* that, in partnership with the triune God, is oriented in mission to a similar creative, saving and reconciling involvement directed to the whole of creation.

iv. Because mission is a single, but complex reality, the Christian ministry of teaching promotes *an integrated view of faith* as a living and active force that helps students see connections between faith and life and between faith and culture (*The Catholic School* #57).[24] This presumes a sound understanding of mission in both its fundamental modes and its various forms on the part of the teacher.

v. Each form of mission has its own claim *on appropriate pedagogical methods* such as involvement in community liturgy and prayer; pastoral care; action directed towards a particular form of mission such as justice, peace, reconciliation, care for the earth, followed by serious reflection; the creative use of images and media; direct instruction; collaborative learning; and expressing faith in the

---

24 Congregation for Catholic Education, *The Catholic School*, 1977. http://www.vatican.va/roman_curia/congregations/ccatheduc/documents/rc_con_ccatheduc_doc_19770319_catholic-school_en.html

culture of a people. Each approach must be discerned on behalf of the missional partnership with God and God's people.

5. CONCLUDING REMARKS

In summary, at the beginning of the 20th century Catholics largely thought of the practice of the faith in terms of responding to the ministry that priests and religious offered to Catholics who lived in a more or less self-contained Catholic world. In this understanding, Catholic life centred on the sacraments – the liturgical and prayer life of the faithful who supported this interpretation of their Catholic faith. 'Mission' was separate and a specialist vocation. The Gospel was proclaimed, and the Church community expanded by 'converting' non-believers in foreign settings. In this paradigm, overseas 'missions' representing the Church's outreach held a special place in Catholic esteem, and were generously supported financially by the faithful. The pastoral and missional dimensions of the Church's life were experienced as two separate goods.

By the beginning of the 21st century, development in Catholic theology was shaped by 'missions' that became local churches as colonies achieved independence. In a largely European construction of mission, this has created limitations that became quite apparent. The Church's mission had come to be understood, at least officially, in much broader terms. These still included a pastoral ministry centred on the sacraments and the prayer life of the faithful, now integrated with the missional in one dynamic vision driving an orientation towards a globalised world with its vast human need both spiritual and material. Missional imagination did not replace the sacramental imagination but expanded and deepened it, providing a richer perspective on personal and communal faith, one of great consequence in meaning-making. 'Being Catholic' then implied a sacramental imagination in a missional key. Hence the shift toward a missional understanding that includes all aspects of pastoral ministry has great pedagogical consequences that must be seriously considered.

The challenge associated with this change in perspective is that theological insight has often run ahead of practical implementation. Lay people, clergy and religious, enculturated into an inward-looking Catholic world with its quite limited sacramental imagination, have struggled to deal with the personal and collective conversion required to think and act within the new possibilities offered by an outward-looking missiological imagination. In this new situation it is perhaps to be expected that questions will arise about the 'Catholic identity' of Catholic enterprises and what their fundamental purpose is.

Catholic educators are caught up in the institutional messiness associated with the paradigm shift vis-à-vis mission. The need for dialogue has never been more obvious. This process begins in the home but continues in Catholic schools. Understanding the need for dialogue, as well as managing it, are now crucial pedagogical skills that teachers must master in their service of God's mission. This is an important contribution that they can make to the good of the young people they educate. It opens the way for teachers to develop a Catholic imagination that is essentially *missional and sacramental* – missional because it is sacramental, and sacramental because it is missional – thus orienting them to the postsecular context and its effect on what 'being Catholic' means today.

Part A
CONFIDENCE BUILT ON FIRM FOUNDATIONS

Introduction

Catholic educators are part of a long tradition. Whether they realise it or not, they are influenced by the culture that this tradition has helped create in Catholic schools. Traditions do not emerge out of thin air, but are the product of reflecting on, and learning from, concrete historical experiences. They contain a wisdom that is hard-earned.

People tend to take the institutions they grow up with more or less for granted. This includes Catholic schools. People also tend to assume that institutions such as schools have always been around in much the same form. However, this is not the case.

The form schools take today is driven by the purpose that schooling serves in society, and this has changed over time. Changes in purpose have an impact on the curriculum – on what is deemed to be valuable knowledge. For example, 'STEM' (Science, Technology, Engineering, Mathematics) was hardly a curriculum designation at the turn of the millennium! Changes in the purpose of schooling also have an impact on pedagogy, particularly when it is understood in a narrow sense as 'what teachers do in the classroom to help students learn'. Currently, changes in the purpose of schooling are driven by a dynamic economic environment. This includes changes in the nature and availability of work and in the pace of technological developments. Taken together, these are reimaging what people see as valuable knowledge. The 'deep learning' and 'new pedagogy' movements seek to address this new situation.

What needs to be questioned now is how the present relates to the past in values and practices. Faced with the need for change, policy makers ask:

- *What are our options?*
- *Do we build on what is valuable in the past, or do we strike out in a new direction?*
- *If we take the first option, on what do we build?*
- *If we take the second, how do we determine the direction to be taken?*

These are questions that many Catholic school leaders are currently addressing.

In Part A we address the question: 'Where we have come from?' and explore the genesis of 'the big ideas' that gave Catholic schooling a value system and a sense of direction in the post-Renaissance world. We look specifically at the contribution of pioneer educators Ignatius of Loyola and John Baptist De la Salle whose foundational insights were carried not only by their own members, but by a multitude of other religious congregations around the world. The concern of Part A is to explore how these two pioneers:

- *framed the pedagogical relationship between student and teachers,*
- *created theological and spiritual foundations on which this framework could rest, and we ask:*
- *What relevance do their key insights have for us today?*

This 'return to the sources' helps us realise that today's Catholic educators are heirs to a most valuable legacy.

3

A HERITAGE OF GIANTS

Today's Catholic school educators belong to a tradition that dates back to the Renaissance, to a time when the elite in many societies began to appreciate the value of formally schooling the young. Prior to this, education was generally confined to those who wished to become clerics and to children of the wealthy who were usually tutored privately.

1. ORIGINS

Since Catholic schooling pre-dates public schooling, pioneer Catholic educators had to work through issues that only later claimed attention in the public sector. For example, the German educator Johann Friedrich Herbart (1776–1841) is credited with initiating the scientific study of pedagogy in much the same way as John Amos Comenius (1592–1670) is credited for his contribution to the development of curriculum. The Jesuits had been running schools for several decades in the case of Comenius, and in the case of Herbart, centuries!

In Christian experience, God's mission can take many forms and the Holy Spirit calls forth faith leaders who express their relationship with God through a particular service to others. The gift leaders receive to do this is called their *charism*. Charism *is given for the benefit of a community* and in the minds of most Catholics is associated with the founders of religious congregations. However, it is important to recognise that the Holy Spirit's gifts are given to a range of other leaders as well when the historical situation requires it. This is also the case in our own time.

In exploring the *origins* of pedagogical insight, we will deal in subsequent chapters specifically with the two pioneers who, in terms of education as we know it today, set the trajectory for a Catholic pedagogy – Ignatius of Loyola (1491–1556) and John Baptist De La Salle (1651–1719).[1] Ignatius of Loyola and John Baptist De La Salle developed a pedagogical vision for

---

1 This choice is not to underplay the contribution of women. Their pedagogical achievements in the history of Catholic education have been remarkable. However, in the early times women educational leaders were concerned principally with survival and the possibility of delivering a service to those in need, free from the restrictions of enclosure imposed on them by Church authorities. It would be only in later centuries that their talent as pedagogues would be enabled to flourish.

their immediate followers, one that would create a spiritual and theological path for later generations of Catholic educators, both women and men.

In terms of the Church's response to God's mission today, one of the most vital ministries is the education of the young. The history of Christian education is a long and complex one, and beyond the scope of this brief tribute. For many centuries the monasteries played the major role. Later the cathedral schools established by bishops in the Medieval cities educated not only young men preparing for clerical life, but also those being prepared for positions in the state and in commerce. Prior to the Renaissance which began in Italy in the 15th century and then spread across Europe, generally only the children of the wealthy were formally educated. Civic and religious leaders saw little point in educating the children of the labouring classes. Their role in life was to replace their parents as labourers.

With the Renaissance a new ambition arose – to advance human progress through education. The Jesuits came to see quite early the value of educating lay Catholics (male) to live in society and to contribute to public life. The early Jesuits were themselves very well educated by the standards of the day.[2] This contributed to the growth and prestige of Jesuit schools in Europe, a growth that was extraordinary and contributed significantly to providing the nascent education movement with its Christian humanistic orientation.[3]

The more ancient orders – Benedictines and later Carmelites, Dominicans and Franciscans, for example – had pursued education in various ways for hundreds of years prior to the work of Ignatius, but with Ignatius something new happened in terms of *education of the laity* – schools were founded specifically for their benefit, and to educate them for *life in the world*. Ignatius not only preceded the developments of public education, but he established something new – a pattern of education *in which life and faith were closely integrated* at a time when society was rapidly changing.

The economic development of Europe in the 16th and 17th centuries saw the emergence of a number of movements, secular and religious, that sought to make provision for the education of the increasing numbers of young people whose families flooded into the growing towns in search of work. Since many of these families lived at a subsistence level, any schooling on offer had to be gratuitous. In response to this the churches took up the challenge of educating the poor.

---

2   Ignatius of Loyola's initial group was formed from graduate students from the University of Paris where he was studying for his master's degree.
3   The Jesuits were founded in 1545 and by the time the society was temporarily suppressed by Pope Clement XIV (1773), there were approximately 700 Jesuits schools in Europe alone.

The leaders of the education movement were often inspired by the Enlightenment ideal of human progress, and what could be accomplished for young people through a humanistic education. It was in this milieu that the idea of *popular Catholic education* was born, and Jean Baptist De La Salle was its principal midwife. De La Salle was concerned with the education of working-class boys. Pioneer Catholic educators concerned with educating girls were forced to tread a more difficult path since they had to overcome the prevailing attitudes of Church leaders to 'women in mission'.[4]

2. WOMEN PIONEERS: ANGELA MERICI AND MARY WARD

Enlightened Catholic women leaders saw very early the need for girls to be educated, not least because of the powerful influence mothers have on their children. Later, as the modern period unfolded, public consciousness about the roles women might play in society shifted and it became clear that young women needed to be educated for roles other than motherhood. However, the women leaders of this movement faced a major obstacle – the attitude of Church leaders. The latter sought to control the efforts of women to educate young girls by requiring the sisters to become religious living in enclosed convents. The tradition that only religious living in this way were recognised as formal ministers of the Church was of long standing, but ill-suited to the needs of the times, particularly in the growing cities.

The idea that a group of women would come together and dedicate themselves to providing a service such as schooling to the Catholic community, outside some form of clerical supervision, was seen as impossible. The followers of Angela Merici (1494–1540), founder of the Ursulines, and a contemporary of Ignatius of Loyola, came under great pressure to conform to the prevailing Church code of enclosure as they battled hard to educate girls. Merici, however, wanted the same flexibility for her sisters that she saw the Jesuits enjoy in their educational endeavours.

In 1572 many of her early followers accepted enclosure and so lost this flexibility, particularly in meeting the needs of the poor. Sisters subject to enclosure could still provide education, particularly religious instruction, but only *to those who could come to a school within the convent walls*.[5] However,

---
4 For a detailed treatment of their difficulties see Susan Smith, *Women in Mission: from New Testament to Today*. Maryknoll N.Y: Orbis Books, 2007.
5 For an introduction to how Angela Merici sought to establish a way for devout women to live their Christian calling other than the two established options of marriage or life in an enclosed convent, see Querciolo Mazzonis, *Spirituality, Gender, and the Self in Renaissance Italy: Angela Merici and the Company of St. Ursula (1474–1540)*. Washington: The Catholic University of America Press, 2007. The Ursuline involvement in education developed after Merici's death, rather than during her lifetime.

some of Merici's followers did not accept enclosure, and continued to live as their foundress had intended.

Not only the early Ursulines, but a little later followers of the English woman, Mary Ward (1558–1645) founder of the Loreto Sisters, had to battle against the traditional prejudices of Church leaders hindering the ministry of women. This makes their achievements as educators all the more remarkable. Blocked at every turn in a deeply patriarchal, social and ecclesial environment, Mary Ward and other women religious pioneers adopted the *modus operandi* for running schools that had been developed by the Jesuits. Both the Ursulines and the Loreto sisters flourished in subsequent centuries when their contribution to women's education would be more readily accepted and appreciated both in Europe and in the colonies.

3. VISION IS INDISPENSABLE

De La Salle is the towering early figure in the development of formal schooling for children of the working poor in France. This was made possible by his farsightedness in insisting on the *lay identity* of his teaching brothers, an identity that brought with it the flexibility to train and deploy personnel free from episcopal interference. Because he was a priest, De La Salle was able to succeed where the women were frustrated. His foresight created the prospect of a Catholic system of free schools for the poor, something that had not existed previously in France.

De La Salle was outstanding not only in the clarity of his vision, but also in his ability to articulate this vision and translate it into action. While a pioneer in the development of 'Christian schools', he was not alone.[6] Like a carpet rolled out across history beginning during Renaissance times, running through the Enlightenment (late 17th and 18th centuries), and well into the 19th century, Catholic educators spread out as missionaries from Europe across the known world, often following their countrymen and women when they migrated to the colonies in providing education for their children.

---

6 In an insightful and challenging article, Herman Lombaerts traces aspects of the lay impulse in the life of the Church and the changing understandings and importance of what is known in the Church as 'the lay state'. He deals with this as a term implying relationships, within the context of institution, which of necessity change across time. He argues that these changing relationships are leading the transformations necessary within the Church community in our time. Herman Lombaerts, 'The Lay State' – an Indicator of the Transformations in the Church: The contribution of Brother Michel Sauvage', *AXIS Journal of Lasallian Higher Education* 5, no 3. Institute for Lasallian Studies at Saint Mary's University of Minnesota, 2014)

4. THE VISION SPREADS TO AUSTRALIA

Each country has its own variation on the story of the English woman Mary Ward, contemporary of Shakespeare and Elizabeth I, who wanted to do for girls what Ignatius' followers were doing for boys. She succeeded in her aim in Australia when her sisters, under the leadership of the great pedagogue, Mother Gonzaga Barry, made their way to Australia in 1875. The spiritual sons of John Baptist De La Salle (1651–1719) reached Australia thirty years later.

Seventy years after the death of De La Salle, Marcellin Champagnat (1879–1840), was born as the French Revolution swept across France. He and his Marist Brothers were to figure strongly in the rebuilding of the French Church and society in the wake of the Revolution. They continue to make a strong impact in Australia today, not least because of their formation of lay teachers and leaders who identify with the Marist charism.[7] The wider Marist family includes the Marist Fathers founded by Jean Claude Colin and the Marist Sisters who recognise Jean Claude Colin and Jeanne-Marie Chavoin as their founders. Both Fathers and Sisters have contributed significantly to Catholic education. Jules Chevalier's (1824–1907) Missionaries of the Sacred Heart and Daughters of Our Lady of the Sacred Heart make their way to our shores and continue to contribute generously.

Also, from France came the daughters of Marie-Madeleine d'Houet (1781–1858) – the Faithful Companions of Jesus – and also the spiritual daughters of Madeleine Sophie Barat (1779–1865), affectionately known as the 'Sacre Coeur nuns'. The Sisters of Our Lady of Sion, originally known as the Sisters of Notre Dame de Sion, came to the diocese of Sale in 1890 under the leadership of Mother Raphaela Cramoisi, and subsequently spread to the Melbourne archdiocese. They made a great impact on the young diocese of Sale through their preparedness to offer boarding facilities so necessary for those living in rural or regional areas.

The Church in Ireland sent forth a stream of educating orders – Nano Nagle's (1718–1784) Presentation Sisters; Catherine McAuley's (1778–1841) Mercy Sisters; and Mary Aikenhead's (1787–1858) Sisters of Charity. Bishop Daniel Delany (1747–1814) founded the Brigidine Sisters and Patrician Brothers, both of whom continue to contribute much in this

---

[7] See Br Michael Green's work on the importance of charism in understanding the graced contribution of 'spiritual families' to the mission of Catholic schools. Michael Green, *Now with Enthusiasm*. Mulgrave: Garratt, 2018. For a specific treatment on the Marist family with particular reference to its formational work directed to lay collaborators, see Michael Green and Darren McGregor 'Looking for New Wineskins: The Marist Experience' in Jim & Therese D'Orsa (eds), *New Ways of Living the Gospel*. Mulgrave: Garratt Publishing, 2015, 135–146.

country. Edmund Rice, (1762–1844) sent his Christian brothers to Sydney towards the end of his life. Although they withdrew to Ireland, brothers subsequently returned under the leadership of Br Patrick Ambrose Treacy and in 1869 established permanent foundations in Victoria and subsequently in other colonies.

From Italy came the Salesians, fathers and sisters, founded by the great pedagogue of youth, Don Bosco (1815–1888). These made their mark on many countries across the world, including Australia.

New religious families developed in many settings from the original Benedictines, Carmelites, Dominicans, and Franciscans. They worked in tertiary and school education in Europe and beyond, also establishing very successful educational enterprises in Australia. Australia's first bishop, John Bede Polding OSB, followed the Benedictine tradition of valuing education, residing over primary and secondary schools within his jurisdiction.

The above listing is far from exhaustive, and even for the purpose of acknowledging their work, there is a degree of risk of exclusion in specifically naming a selection from among the many who have served in this country. Early Australian bishops, totally convinced of the necessity of Catholic education, usually required any congregation seeking to make a foundation in Australia for whatever purpose, for example as a base for missions in other parts of Oceania, to contribute to Catholic education by opening a school. This was a condition of entry, and a key to the complexity of the story.

The Sisters of the Good Samaritan founded by Archbishop Polding and the Sisters of St. Joseph founded by Mary MacKillop and Julian Tenison Woods emerged as something entirely new. These were homegrown congregations that, like their predecessors, would take up the challenges of providing educational opportunities at home and missionary work overseas. Both groups were composed of women educators whose powerful pedagogy lay first and foremost in a deep spirituality made visible in the way they shared life with poor families. They educated young people and their families not least through improving the latter's sense of self-worth. They gave practical expression to the Kingdom value of 'solidarity with the poor'.

Both congregations expressed the free and adventurous spirit of a society whose aspiration was that things could be done better here than in the Old World, and that, given an excellent education, Catholics could play their part in building a society that would be the envy of the world.

5. KEEPING THE TRADITION ALIVE IN A NEW CONTEXT

Today many congregations are renewing educational practices by the serious formation of their lay colleagues based on the charism of their founding mothers and fathers. This project involves drawing out the *pedagogical implications* of that charism for the contemporary context.[8]

Several religious congregations are currently exploring or redefining the forms of relationship that can exist between members who are religious brothers or sisters and single and married people. They are seeking to ascertain what this change might mean for the nature of the group both now and into the future.[9]

6. FIDELITY TO AN ENDURING TRADITION

In the two chapters that follow, special attention is given to the *pedagogical legacies* of the pioneering founders of Catholic education as we know it today – Ignatius of Loyola and John Baptist De La Salle. These pioneers set a trajectory for Catholic pedagogy that has helped define the tradition to which, whether we realise it or not, we who educate belong. They influenced others in ways that were foundational in the development of a Catholic pedagogical tradition, as will become clear.

In making their impact, these pioneer educators have contributed

- *a spirituality that credibly translates into a vision of education capable of shaping a Catholic pedagogy*
- *key insights – theological and educational – capable of driving the developments they launched across time and across cultures.*

With each of these pedagogical pioneers there is a very clear correlation between *their spirituality and their approach to education*. In tracing these two issues, the focus is on their *pedagogical vision* and the principles underpinning that vision. The important issue is vision. Some of their pedagogical methods may endure, but most do not and should not, because techniques and practices are time and culture bound. In stepping behind and beyond

---

8 Some educators have pursued doctoral studies which delve into the nature and originality of the congregation's approach to pedagogy, for example John Braniff's *The Marist Brothers' Teaching Tradition in Australia: 1872–2000*. Ph.D. thesis. University of Sydney, 2005, and Christopher Hayes, *Paradoxes, parallels and pedagogy: A case study of Ignatian pedagogy and of teachers' perceptions of its implementation in Australian Jesuit schools*. Ph.D. thesis. Australian Catholic University, 2006.
9 Michael Green and Darren McGregor, 'Looking for New Wineskins: the Marist Experience' in Jim and Therese D'Orsa (eds), *New Ways of Living the Gospel.*

particular practices to the underpinning vision, the question we want to explore is:

- *What are the elements that gave their respective pedagogical visions enduring worth?*

4

SPIRITUAL LEADERSHIP AND THE THEOLOGICAL LEGACY OF IGNATIUS OF LOYOLA

In the previous chapter we acknowledged the wide-ranging heritage enjoyed by Catholic educators today, noting aspects of the unfolding narrative which helped shape the pedagogical power of so many educating communities. Moving from this broad overview, we focus more closely in this chapter and the next on two founding figures whose insights significantly shaped many of those who followed them. These two pedagogical 'founders' are Ignatius of Loyola and John Baptist De La Salle.

Inigo Lopez de Onaz y Loyola, known to most people as Ignatius of Loyola, was born in Spain's Basque country in 1491, a year before Columbus sailed on his epic voyage of discovery to what, for Europeans, was the 'New World'.

Ignatius was 'a child of the Renaissance' – leader, organiser, educator, spiritual guru, and eventually a much-loved saint of the Church. He was to influence the development of Catholic education in a variety of ways, not least because of his decision in the mid-16th century to establish schools for any boy or young man who wished to pursue an education, regardless of *what future he might aspire to.*

1. NEW DIRECTION: EDUCATING YOUNG PEOPLE FOR 'LIFE IN THE WORLD'

What Ignatius and his early followers offered was an education for *a lay Christian vocation lived out within society.* By doing so, the early Jesuits initiated a movement that would enable countless people across many generations to live out, within society, what the Second Vatican Council (1962–5) would later call the 'universal call to holiness'.[1]

---

1 Vatican II. *Lumen Gentium* (Dogmatic Constitution on the Church), Chapter V, 1964. https://www.vatican.va/archive/hist_councils/ii_vatican_council/documents/vat-ii_const_19641121_lumen-gentium_en.html

Even though Ignatius' own Christian vocation and that of his early companions was lived out within the parameters of a new religious order, he helped create broader possibilities for others. These possibilities are increasingly important in our own time when the lay vocation, lived out in various settings, is essential if the Gospel is to constructively bear on the society and culture in which we live. Today, as we are conscious of the call to mission of each of the baptised, we are also becoming aware that, in many areas of human life, only lay people can carry out that mission because only they operate in many workplaces. In other situations – education, health, media, and various social involvements for example – the collaboration of lay, religious and clergy is an important feature of mission. In terms of education, finding God in all things is an enduring challenge Ignatius has presented to all who take the Gospel seriously. It requires assiduous attention to the whole curriculum and to all pedagogical choices as young people are prepared for their lives and mission in the world.

1.1 Ignatius' pedagogical vision, a vision within a vision

The pedagogical vision of Ignatius and his early followers is the focus of this chapter. However, it is impossible to grasp the nature and shape of that vision without giving due attention to:

- *the context of the times in which it emerged, and*
- *the overarching religious vision that Ignatius developed.*

The pedagogical aspects of Ignatius' vision are *core elements in his spiritual vision itself.* It is the clarity of the elements that make up his spiritual vision, and their obvious and successful translation into the ministry of education, that provides the key to the authenticity and durability of the Ignatian pedagogical tradition.

In introducing *Ignatian Pedagogy – A Practical Approach* (1993),[2] Peter-Hans Kolvenbach SJ, speaks of the two roots of the genuine Christian humanism espoused and taught by Ignatius:

- *the distinctive spiritual experiences of Ignatius of Loyola himself*
- *the cultural, social and religious challenges of the Renaissance during the Reformation period in Europe.*

---

[2] *Ignatian Pedagogy – A Practical Approach,* 1993 is one of two documents resulting from a worldwide reflection on Jesuit education which took place in the 1970s and 1980s. The other is *Characteristics of a Jesuit Education,* 1986.
jesuitinstitute.org/Pages/CharacteristicsJesuitEducation.htm
The 2013 edition of *Ignatian Pedagogy* features enhanced footnotes and can be downloaded at www.sjweb.info/documents/education/pedagogy_en.pdf

The political, social and economic context in which Ignatius lived and worked is of vital importance in appreciating the significance and depth of his insights.

1.2 Unfolding of a spiritual vision

Ignatius' spiritual vision developed across his life. Trained as a courtier and soldier, his life's journey took him into combat, during which he was seriously wounded. While convalescing he had plenty of time to think deeply, and soon learned the value of reflecting on and seeking the meaning of his own experience.

Ignatius pioneered and perfected a kind of *reflective discernment* throughout his life and this shaped his approach to assisting others. Behind this concept of discernment stood a fundamental theological insight: *God is revealed and works through the circumstances of an individual's life.*[3] This insight shaped Ignatius' pedagogical approach once he and his followers became involved in schools.

After Ignatius' death, his early followers produced an important policy document to guide the conduct of Jesuit schools called the *Ratio Studiorum*. (1599). The document (written when John Comenius was a boy of seven) bears witness to the importance Ignatius placed on discernment.[4] He learned the importance of discernment because of his unique self-awareness. In many respects he was a pioneer of what in later centuries would be called phenomenology, the ability to process the data of immediate experience.

1.3 Discernment: finding meaning in immediate experience

English Catholic writer, Margaret Hebblethwaite, notes that as Ignatius whiled away the long hours during his convalescence from major leg injuries sustained in battle, he read what was to hand. This included *The Life of Jesus Christ* by Ludolph of Saxony. Ludolph's vision was of God's

---

3 Discernment is the art of discovering how best to respond to God in daily life. It is a process for coming to a good decision. In the language of the time it was discussed as 'the discernment of spirits'. There are many excellent introductions to the Ignatian practice of discernment. A well-regarded and popular introduction is that by James Martin, 'What Should I Do?' in James Martin, *The Jesuit Guide to (Almost) Everything*. New York: HarperOne, 2010, 305–338.

4 The *Ratio* encouraged the student's ability to reflect on experience and engage in discernment before acting. It is worth noting that the *Ratio* was the result of much discussion and reflection (discernment), by Jesuit educators over many years. The *Ratio* served as an educational primer until the suppression of the Jesuits in 1773. However, after their restoration in 1814, some regarded its degree of specificity in educational matters as limiting, given the change in cultural context as modernity began to emerge. The need to recapture the vision of Ignatius and to spell out its pedagogical significance was recognised in the post-Vatican II period resulting in the document entitled *The Characteristics of Jesuit Education* (1986) and *Ignatian Pedagogy: A Practical Approach* (1993). These documents are more suited to the Jesuits' very diverse educational apostolate conducted across many societies and cultures. It is important to note that, like the *Ratio,* both these documents have been produced through a process of discernment involving Jesuit educators from across the world.

action *in the world to come*. In contrast to this Ignatius came to realise that God's love is poured out in the world *in the here and now*. Its presence can therefore be sensed if people only know how to look. 'Discernment' names this form of 'looking'.

As a humanist, Ignatius appreciated the significance of human flourishing in the here and now. Hebblethwaite points to Ignatius' final reflection in *The Spiritual Exercises*, where he acknowledges 'life in this world' needs to be recognised as *an ongoing sign and expression of God's love*, a place where God is to be found. This was not the way many of Ignatius' contemporaries thought. For them, 'the world' was the enemy. Ignatius wrote:

> *God dwells in creatures: in the elements giving them existence, in the plants giving them life, in the animals conferring upon them sensation, in human beings bestowing understanding. So, he (sic) dwells in me and gives me being, life, sensation, intelligence; and makes a temple of me, since I am created in the likeness and image of the Divine Majesty (235).*

Underlining the realisation that creation and history are important to God, Ignatius' credo was that he should *'find God in all things'*.

1.4 Ignatius' Spiritual Exercises

Like most human beings Ignatius' life moved through several clearly defined periods. Once he had recovered from his injuries, he spent a considerable period of time in seclusion and prayer at Manresa, Spain. This was a testing time during which he experienced the full range of human emotions that might be expected in a time of profound personal transition. He learned a good deal about himself and human nature in this period.[5] His notes made at the time were later developed into his famous *Spiritual Exercises* which are precisely that, exercises of the spirit and the imagination designed to help a person grow in relationship with God, other people and God's creation.

Ignatius' spirituality placed great value on the use of the imagination in prayer and on the freedom of the human person in responding to God's invitation to conversion. As Ignatius came to see clearly, human freedom is a great gift that enables a person to enter into a loving relationship with God.[6]

Four important aspects of Ignatius' spiritual vision that in due course would also become recognisable elements in Ignatian pedagogy, are:

---

[5] In many ways Ignatius pioneered forms of intense introspection that would later come to characterise modern psychotherapy. His *Spiritual Exercises* form the basis of the thirty-day retreat that is still part of the training of all Jesuits and is used in spiritual formation by many other groups, religious and lay as well.

[6] It is important to note that Ignatius wrote the *Spiritual Exercises* while he was a lay man.

- *discerning God's spirit at work in one's personal life*
- *responding freely to God's invitation to a loving relationship*
- *finding God in all things*
- *using one's imagination.*

2. FOUNDING THE JESUITS

2.1 'Back to school'

At thirty-eight years of age, Ignatius found it necessary to face the fact that, if he wished to achieve anything for God, his education was woefully inadequate. So, although an adult, he went back to school. He made sufficient progress to pursue further studies at tertiary level. After a halting start to his studies in Spain, he found himself in trouble more than once for speaking about 'the things of God' without appropriate theological qualifications. Always a creative thinker, he ran afoul of the Spanish Inquisition.

Ignatius wisely made his way to Paris to study. He was impressed by the pedagogical approach used at the University of Paris, a pioneer in the sequencing of the learning process and in having a student progress through a series of grades when learning a new discipline. These features would become important aspects of the pedagogical practice adopted by the first Jesuit schools. Ignatius embraced good educational ideas and practices wherever they were to be found. For him, as for John Baptist De La Salle who would follow a century later, a good practice was a good practice and needed to be valued as such!

There is magnificent irony, considering Ignatius' impact on education in the century that followed, that having been awarded his Master's degree after five years of study at the University of Paris, he was not permitted to go on to doctoral studies because he was considered to be too old!

2.2 The First Jesuits

During his time in Paris, Ignatius became guide to a talented circle of friends who, with his help, sought to discern God's plan for them. They were all driven by a desire to be of help to the Church in very difficult times, wherever such help was needed. Theirs was a spirituality directed towards others.

While it seems clear that Ignatius did not initially see his calling as the ministry of schooling, later he would recognise the potential that this offered to both individuals and society. He would also see that this form of service had, potentially at least, an exceptional multiplier effect in terms of benefits that could flow on to the Church as it confronted the Reformers.

After exploring various directions in ministry, including attempting unsuccessfully to sail to the Holy Land, Ignatius and his circle of friends decided to put themselves at the disposal of the Pope who they believed was best placed to know where the Church's needs were the greatest.

To give form to this offer, Ignatius sought to found a new religious order as he was convinced that religious life offered the group the best way to ensure unity among themselves and stability in their work. Pope Paul III approved the order in 1540, and Ignatius led the group until his death in 1556.

2.3 Faith and culture in the Ignatian vision

The trajectory of Ignatius' spiritual vision lay in a direct line from the great theologian of the Medieval period, Thomas Aquinas. Aquinas saw nature and grace as perfectly reconcilable, so for him human cultures and faith could and should work together in leading people to God.

Ignatius displayed a similar expansive spiritual vision. The dichotomy between 'secular' and 'sacred' that influenced theology so disastrously up to the time of the Second Vatican Council, and continues to manifest itself today in a range of theological and practical ways, was foreign to Ignatius' worldview and spiritual sensibility. For Ignatius, such a dichotomy would have seemed entirely artificial.

The most well-known of Ignatius' spiritual and theological insights is the possibility of finding God in all things – events in one's personal life, one's reaction to them, and changes in the context in which people live. Ignatius had discovered for himself, and then taught, that *God is revealed to us in the circumstances of our lives.* This includes, obviously, our lives as educators.

Just as the people of the Bible came to know God as revealed to them in the circumstances of their earthly vicissitudes, that is in their physical, moral and spiritual journeys, this process is ongoing in history for every individual and community. Fundamental to Ignatius' thinking is that God has a purpose for each individual and that *the most important goal of discernment for each of us is to discover what that purpose is.*

Although Ignatius did not at first envisage that the Jesuits would be involved in education of the young, it is obvious that the main ideas that would drive the Jesuits' educational ministry across the following centuries developed during his lifetime.[7] Indeed, centuries later, it is easy to recognise something very Ignatian in the way the core project of Catholic schooling

---

[7] This theme is well developed by Chris Lowney in *Heroic Leadership: Best Practices from a 450-year-old company that changed the world.* Chicago: Loyola Press, 2003.

is expressed in the post-Vatican II magisterial document dealing with the identity and mission of a Catholic School:

> The task of the Catholic school is fundamentally a synthesis of culture and faith, and a synthesis of faith and life; the first is reached by integrating all the different aspects of human knowledge through the subjects taught, in the light of the Gospel; the second is the growth of the virtues characteristic of the Christian.[8]

3. JESUITS EMBRACE SCHOOL EDUCATION

When Ignatius received a request from the leading citizens in Messina, Sicily, to establish a school in the humanist mode for their sons, a number of stars aligned for the newly formed Jesuit group. They saw that education provided a means of enacting their spiritual vision among the young.

3.1 'Studia Humanitas'

Church historian John O'Malley SJ describes the way in which an educational theory compatible with the self-definition of the Society itself emerged among the early Jesuits.[9] He highlights their central desire to put their considerable talents at the service of the Church and of others.

As educators, the Italian humanists pursued the notion of upright living (*pietas*). Ignatius saw that 'right living' could, through schooling, be aligned with 'Christian living'. Schooling could therefore become a service that benefitted the individual, society and the Church, by promoting the 'common good'.

By agreeing to the request to open a school for boys destined for 'life in the world', Ignatius opened a new chapter in the history of education, not only in Messina, but worldwide. The chapter held much greater significance than those involved could possibly have imagined at the time.[10]

O'Malley also points out that the decision to establish a primary-secondary school inevitably brought the Jesuits *into a special relationship with cultures* since education in every society is a cultural institution. Education provides the primary mechanism through which culture is formally transmitted. The possibility of shaping or improving culture through the

---

8   Congregation for Catholic Education, *The Catholic School,* 1977, #37.
9   John W. O'Malley, 'How the first Jesuits Became Involved in Education' in George W. Traub, *A Jesuit Education Reader.* Chicago: Loyola Press, 2008, 43–62, especially 51.
10 By the time of Ignatius' death in 1556, the Jesuits were running 35 schools. By the end of the century the number had risen to 245.

power of the Gospel brought to bear in the process of Catholic schooling was as enormous in Ignatius' time as it is today.

What was unique about the Jesuit schools that began in Sicily and quickly spread across Europe? O'Malley makes three points in designating the difference that the Jesuits brought to education when compared with what was offered by established orders such as the Dominicans and Franciscans (who worked mainly in the universities):

- *The Jesuits decided quite formally that the staffing and management of schools was a true ministry of the order. This was the first time an order deliberately opted for schools as a primary ministry.*[11]
- *The Jesuits were proactive in establishing schools.*
- *Jesuit schools catered for those who were destined to live their Christian vocation in the world rather than in the service of the Church.*

Universities were well established in the Medieval period and professionalised higher learning. Unlike the universities, however, Jesuit schools did not take classical texts as the basis of their curriculum. Rather, they made contemporary works of literature the basis of the school curriculum – they developed their own version of the *studia humanitas*.[12] Poetry, drama, oratory and history were assumed to inspire noble and uplifting ideals. It was judged that these would, if properly taught, render the student *a better human being*, imbued especially with an ideal of service of the common good, in imitation of the great heroes found in literature.

The purpose of the new type of schooling was not the pursuit of abstract or speculative truth, which is what the universities pursued, but *the character formation of the student*, an ideal the humanists encapsulated in the word *pietas*. The genius of Ignatius lay in re-interpreting the purpose of schooling aimed at 'right living' in terms of Christian living – a synthesis in personal life that could influence the good of the individual, society and the Church.

3.2 Pedagogical legacy of Ignatius

The Ignatian pedagogical vision is set out in proposition form below:

- *God is at work in one's life journey and we have the freedom to respond to God.*
- *God has a purpose for each of us and the challenge of living well is to discover this purpose.*

---

11 O'Malley cites the figure of 800 schools being staffed by Jesuits at the time of their suppression in 1773 by Pope Clement XIV.
12 *Studia humanitas* 'the study of humanity' denoted the scholarly activities that humanists thought to be essential in promoting civilisation. It constituted the late-Medieval curriculum.

- *Personal and communal discernment is important in coming to decisions.*
- *Imagination plays an important role in human life.*
- *A Christian education nurtures the desire to emulate Jesus in being of service to others.*
- *Good educators have the capacity to recognise good practice wherever it is to be found.*
- *Through education the improvement of culture has an important place in the Church's mission.*
- *In Christian education there is an intrinsic connection between the secular and the sacred.*
- *Learning and Christian living need to be integrated in the educational process.*
- *Education can equip young people with the capacity for finding God in all things.*

A number of these elements are obviously inter-dependent.

4. RECONTEXTUALISING A TRADITION

Ignatius' legacy is particularly rich and is clearly delineated both in his writings and his practice. And it has been kept alive in Jesuit and other institutions. It is also very rich because of the worldview on which it is based. Ignatius' insights can be transferred to other times and places using the type of reflection that he pioneered: discernment. To access this tradition, contemporary educators have to do their own discernment!

In order to be useful today, the Ignatian legacy requires recontextualisation, which involves understanding the tradition in its original context, discerning what it might mean in the current context, and bringing the two into meaningful dialogue.

Although the social sciences and the human sciences were not available to Ignatius, Catholic educators of today need to access the findings of these in any credible discernment process capable of recapturing Ignatius' genius.

4.1 Recontextualising the Ignatian tradition

The first steps in recontextualising a tradition is *description* followed by *analysis*. Peter-Hans Kolvenbach, formerly a leader of the Jesuits, reminded Jesuit educators of the very challenging context in which they are now called on to educate in observing that:

> Since the Second Vatican Council, we have been recognizing a profound new challenge that calls for a new form of Christian humanism with a

distinctively societal emphasis. The Council stated that the 'split between the faith that many profess, and their daily lives deserves to be counted among the more serious errors of our age' (Gaudium et Spes, 43).[13] The world appears to us in pieces, chopped up, broken.

The root issue is this:

- *What does faith in God mean in the face of Bosnia and Sudan, Guatemala and Haiti, Auschwitz and Hiroshima, the teeming streets of Calcutta and the broken bodies in Tiananmen Square?*
- *What is Christian humanism in the face of starving millions of men, women and children in Africa?*
- *What is Christian humanism as we view millions of people uprooted from their own countries by persecution and terror, and forced to seek a new life in foreign lands?*
- *What is Christian humanism when we see the homeless roam our cities and the growing underclass who are reduced to permanent hopelessness?*

A disciplined sensitivity to human misery and exploitation is not a single political doctrine or a system of economics. It is a humanism, a humane sensibility, to be achieved anew with the demands of our own times and as a product of an education whose ideal continues to be motivated by the great commandments: love of God and love of neighbor ([as referenced in] Mark 12:30–31).[14]

Little has changed since 1993 when these words were spoken, except that the level of violence worldwide has worsened dramatically leading to more deaths, widespread poverty, destruction and displacement. It is not surprising then that one of the aims of Jesuit education as it is re-contextualised today is to produce graduates possessed of 'a faith that does justice'[15].

The pedagogical legacy of the Jesuit tradition to cultivate in young people 'a faith that does justice' challenges each Catholic educator:

- *to help young people develop a loving orientation to those who suffer*

---

13 Building on this expression of the need to link faith and life, the 'Magna Carta' on evangelisation of the post Vatican II period, *Evangelii Nuntiandi* (1975), spoke of the drama of the split between the Gospel and culture (# 20).
14 Peter-Hans Kolvenbach S.J. 'Ignatian Pedagogy: A Practical Approach'. Delivered to the Participants at the International Workshop on Ignatian Pedagogy, Villa Cavalletti, April 29, 1993 (formatting added). https://www.educatemagis.org/documents/ignatian-pedagogy-letter-from-father-general-kolvenbach-sj/
15 Roger Bergman, *Catholic Social Learning: Educating the Faith That Does Justice*. New York: Fordham University, 2011.

- *to expand the capacity for analysis in regard to the causes of suffering and its correlates, displacement and marginalisation*
- *to develop the character and will needed to respond as their circumstances allow. With Pope Francis, himself a Jesuit, the scope of this challenge has been broadened to include justice for all of creation.*[16]

These goals can be achieved only by utilising opportunities *present in all learning areas*. The serious Catholic pedagogue identifies opportunities and utilises them effectively. The purposeful creation of new educational opportunities such as exposure and service-learning programs, very much a feature of Catholic schooling today, helps young people develop the sensibility, understandings and values (worldview) that enable a heartfelt and intelligent response. This is vital work.

Re-contextualising the Ignatian pedagogical vision always places Jesus Christ – his person *and* his mission – at the imaginative heart of Catholic education.

Major efforts have been made to reclaim and re-translate Ignatius' vision within our contemporary context, and to share the results not only with the lay educators who comprise most of the staff of Jesuit schools, but with others as well.[17] Part of this process has been to critically assess the points of intersection between the Ignatian vision and understandings of pedagogy that are influential in our time.[18]

4.2 The uniqueness of each person

Ignatius' humanism includes both an appreciation of individual uniqueness and an understanding that this uniqueness finds expression only in and through the web of relationships through which our humanity is exercised – that is, relationships with God, self, our fellow humans, and the natural world. A Christian pedagogue of today, attuned to the Ignatian legacy, would readily recognise the necessity of *engaging all learning areas in developing that uniqueness*.

The 'secular' disciplines of learning, with their roots in human cultures, while having their own integrity, key understandings, and methods, can be made to work together for good by insightful teachers.[19] This is a

---

16 Pope Francis *Laudato si' (On Care for Our Common Home)*, 2015. http://www.vatican.va/content/francesco/en/encyclicals/documents/papa-francesco_20150524_enciclica-laudato-si.html.
17 The Lismore Catholic Education Office, for instance, has adopted Ignatian spirituality as their own and seeks to promote this in the schools of the diocese. See John Graham, 'Parish Schools Embracing Ignatian Spirituality' in Jim & Therese D'Orsa (eds and authors), *New Ways of Living the Gospel*. Mulgrave: Garratt Publishing, 2015, 183–191.
18 Christopher Hayes, *Paradoxes, parallels and pedagogy: A case study of Ignatian pedagogy and teachers' perceptions of its implementation in Australian Jesuit schools*. Ed.D. Australian Catholic University, 2006. https://researchbank.acu.edu.au/theses/174/
19 Congregation for Catholic Education, *The Catholic School*, 1977, 39.

fundamental Ignatian insight. In any Catholic education worthy of the name, every aspect of human life can and must be subject to the ethical dimensions arising from a true Christian humanism. It demands, therefore, that we place the humanity of the most marginalised at the centre of our social concerns, just as Jesus did.

4.3 Teacher-student relationship

No account of Ignatian pedagogy should omit the importance Ignatius placed on the character of the relationship between teacher and student. While the importance of the teacher might seem obvious, it is an importance to which only lip service is sometimes given. There are many gifted pedagogues in Catholic schools, and their contribution is enormous. However, even brief consideration shows that the most effective pedagogues are not necessarily those with the latest, or even the most creative techniques; rather they are those who can teach in their learning area in such a way that they take responsibility for *the personal growth of the student* and for implementation of the overall educational vision of the school – a vision hopefully shared by the community that nurtures the child or young person.

The student learns much from the respect shown her or him, from progress encouraged and acknowledged, and from creativity fanned into flame, so that growing in confidence, each student develops the capacity to translate what is learned into the betterment of the human and natural worlds. In Christian education, the best teacher *embodies his or her pedagogy.*

Ignatius' emphasis on and trust in human experience and the power of imagination shaped his contribution to pedagogy. However, the most fundamental aspect of Ignatius' approach lies in his insight that students are agents of their own learning because they are capable of creating knowledge by reflecting on their own experience, and that of others, in the light of their faith. His methodology for achieving this result is an educational transposition of the method of the *Spiritual Exercises*, and is given contemporary form in *Ignatian Pedagogy – A Practical Approach.*

4.4 Ignatian spirituality – a legacy for teachers

Ignatius' principal gift to Catholic educators lies in his demonstrating the possibility of *balancing interiority with the demands of mission.*[20] Today's Catholic educator would do well to look to the Ignatian legacy of reflective and discerning practice in establishing their own balance point between interiority and the demands of their mission to students (and through them to society and culture). This quest lies at the heart of the Ignatian legacy.

---

20 Ignatius of Loyola was the first to apply the terms 'mission' and 'missions', then in secular use, to the activities and posting of Jesuits. These terms were later adopted by the Church.

5

SPIRITUALITY OF TEACHING: ENDURING INSIGHTS OF JOHN BAPTIST DE LA SALLE

Teachers, as witnesses, account for the hope that nourishes their own lives ... by living the truth they propose to their pupils, always in reference to the one they have encountered and whose dependable goodness they have sampled with joy ...
(Educating Together in Catholic Schools: A Shared Mission Between Consecrated Persons and the Lay Faithful, #38).[1]

John Baptist De La Salle (1651–1719), patron saint of teachers, lived and worked at the beginning of what is known historically as the Enlightenment.[2] He enters the story of Catholic education a century and a half after Ignatius of Loyola. De La Salle was to have an extraordinary impact on the development of Catholic primary education at a time when, although the importance of primary schooling was widely acknowledged, in his homeland of France public resolve to fund it was lacking. Schooling, when it was available, was 'optional' and absenteeism a major issue.

1. AN 'ACCIDENTAL' EDUCATOR

The Church was to step into this funding vacuum by establishing 'gratuitous' schools. De La Salle's life's work helped shape the educational policies and practices of many other religious congregations, male and female, founded to teach primary children the four basics: reading, writing, arithmetic, and religion. He created something new in the Church – a group of laymen formed into a community of 'brothers', who were neither monks nor

---

1   Congregation for Catholic Education, *Educating Together in Catholic Schools: A Shared Mission Between Consecrated Persons and the Lay Faithful*, p 38 2007.
    http://www.vatican.va/roman_curia/congregations/ccatheduc/documents/rc_con_ccatheduc_doc_20070908_educare-insieme_en.html
2   The Enlightenment was an intellectual movement that dominated Europe during the period from roughly the mid 17th century to the early 19th century. It affected all areas of social life and culture including philosophy, politics, science, economics and religion. This movement manifested itself in different ways in different regions of Europe.

clerics, founded solely to educate boys drawn from the lower classes. He did this at a time when there was no such thing as teacher training and few effective models of how to run a primary school. A basic problem faced by educational leaders of his era was the lack of suitable male teachers. Primary school teaching was seen by men as 'the job of last resort' and so carried very little in the way of social status.

Our interest in this chapter is in the way in which De La Salle understood the pedagogical relationship between teacher and student, and how this influenced pedagogy in the system of Catholic schools he helped create. This relationship remains the interpretive key that makes his approach meaningful today.

1.1 Early life and education

John Baptist De La Salle was born at Reims in 1651, the oldest of eleven children, four of whom died at an early age. Like many boys from well-to-do families of his time, the young John Baptist was tutored at home until at ten years of age he was enrolled in the *College des Bons-Enfants* in Reims, from which he graduated eight years later.[3]

De La Salle decided quite early that he wanted to become a priest, and following his graduation from school studied theology at the University of Reims. A distant cousin, Canon Pierre Dozet, was chancellor of the University and also a canon of the cathedral. Deeply impressed with the personal qualities of his young cousin, Dozet resigned his position and privileges as canon in favour of Jean-Baptiste, who was duly installed as a lay canon in January 1667[4] (at age sixteen). As a consequence, De La Salle had to curtail his theological studies. The death of his mother, followed by that of his father a year later, meant that, at only eighteen years of age, De La Salle became the guardian of his younger brothers and sisters. His capacities as a leader and organiser became evident during this time. He continued his studies for the priesthood, as his circumstances allowed, eventually moving to the seminary of St Sulpice in Paris until his ordination in April 1678. Two years later, he completed a doctorate in theology. De La Salle clearly valued learning.

---

3   The College founded in the ninth century was then associated with the University of Reims and is now part of the University.
4   A canon in this period was a member of the cathedral chapter, a group advising the bishop and carrying out administrative and legal duties associated with the cathedral and/or the diocese.

1.2 Gratuitous primary schools for the poor

De La Salle's friend and one-time spiritual director, Canon Nicholas Roland, nominated him as executor of his will.[5] In executing the will upon the canon's death, De La Salle unexpectedly found himself establishing schools for the poor of Reims.

Canon Roland had himself attempted to organise a 'gratuitous' primary school for girls in Reims, but could not obtain the necessary civil permits. De La Salle resolved this matter, and soon girls were receiving free education at a school run by the newly established Sisters of the Child Jesus. The success of this venture led to a request by the girls' parents for him to provide a similar opportunity for boys. However, here De La Salle faced the problem of finding suitable teachers.

The initial challenge was to help those men who volunteered to staff his 'free' primary school for boys to learn how to teach. He also had to find housing for them. As he embarked on these ventures, De La Salle found himself increasingly sharing life with the teachers.

1.3 Forming a new type of religious community

As the movement to create Church-sponsored primary schools for the poor gained momentum, De La Salle saw that the training of teachers needed to be his top priority. Teacher training in this period followed the apprentice model, supplemented by other opportunities that De La Salle provided during holiday periods. He recognised that the quality of his teachers depended on their spiritual depth as well as their technical competence. This realisation became more important to him as his experience of running schools grew.

As this new form of Catholic apostolate took off, De La Salle was asked to train teachers sent to him by pastors from the rural towns around Reims.[6] He happily welcomed them into the schools and involved the newcomers in formation opportunities such as retreats that he provided as part of the teacher-training regime for his Brothers.

While volunteers accepted the challenge to become teachers of the poor, their enthusiasm often waned when faced with factors such as low remuneration, little personal support, the poor organisation of the schools, and limited resources. The situation in France was very similar to that faced by pioneering lay educators in Australia just over a century later.

---

5 Nicolas Roland was beatified in 1994 by Pope John Paul II.
6 In rural areas priests frequently took on the role of teacher, but without training their efforts soon came to naught. The alternative was to find a volunteer to take over the school and have him trained.

It seemed obvious to De La Salle that if the new primary schools were to survive, he had to address the situation of the teachers. His strategy was to establish a new form of religious community for men, an option that would provide its members with stability and community support, and ensure that their educational work was sustainable.

The custom of the time was that a cleric be in charge of any religious group of men. Initially there was no problem, as De La Salle was a priest. However, following the untimely death of the person he was preparing for the priesthood, and who was set to succeed him as leader of the first community, De La Salle decided that this arrangement was not workable for a group dedicated to teaching. Such communities needed leadership fully committed to educating the young.

When De La Salle took charge of free primary schools for the poor and artisan classes, several fundamental questions remained to be answered:

- *Would the children of the poor profit from education, given their family and social background?*
- *Was it possible to ensure that schools for the poor had good teachers, people who were competent, modelled good manners, were devoted to their task, and willing to stay in the profession?*
- *How would he develop teaching methods in keeping with the aims of this type of school?*[7]

These were all issues that De La Salle had to work his way through.

1.3 Band of 'brothers'

At the time teachers went by the title 'Master'. This did not accord with how De La Salle and the early members of his group saw their relationship with students. Members of the early community renounced the title 'Master' in favour of the term 'brother' by which they meant being *'brothers to one another, and older brothers to their pupils'*.

According to noted Australian De La Salle scholar, Gerard Rummery, this change reflected the pedagogical vision of De La Salle and his companions.[8] Rummery also notes that both elements were important: 'Both their identity as "Brothers to one another" and "their mission as older Brothers to their pupils" were complementary and inseparable.'[9] This was an altogether new way of formulating the pedagogical relationship between

---

7 Yves Poutet, *Origins and characteristics of Lasallian pedagogy*. Translated by Julian Watson FSC, Finian Allman FSC, Celsus Clark FSC, and John Walch. Manila: De la Salle University Press, 1997.
8 Gerard Rummery, FSC, 'The Coming of the Teaching Brothers' in Jim & Therese D'Orsa (eds), *New Ways of Living the Gospel*. Mulgrave: Garratt Publishing, 2015, 149.
9 Ibid, 150.

student and teacher and may have reflected De La Salle's experiences as an 'older brother' accepting responsibility, as guardian, for his younger siblings.

While De La Salle might be considered an 'accidental educator', his leadership, organising ability, and spiritual insight created something new in the Church – a teaching congregation made up of laymen dedicated to Catholic schooling.

2. DE LA SALLE'S SCHOOLS: INNOVATORS IN PUBLIC EDUCATION

Although De La Salle tried, he was at first unable to set up a school for poor students in Paris. Instead he obtained a property in Rouen that became the headquarters and formation house for his newly established religious congregation. Here the Brothers also established a secondary college that took boarders.

De La Salle also opened an academy for adults in the Paris parish of Saint Sulpice. Here geometry, architecture, and drawing were added to normal Sunday school activities.

2.1 Challenging established educational traditions

De La Salle's emphasis on training teachers stands as a major innovation in Catholic education. As a pedagogical innovator he saw that spelling and writing were best taught in conjunction with reading. This brought him into conflict with the 'Writing Masters' who at that time had a monopoly on the teaching of writing, (and who were losing pupils to De La Salle's schools).

De La Salle also insisted on teaching in the vernacular, as had others in both France and Germany, rather than in Latin as was customary in secondary schools. He recognised that most pupils could attend school for only a short time. If their education was going to be helpful in their life beyond school, then lessons had to be readily grasped. This would most likely be the outcome if they read and were taught in the language that they heard on a day-to-day basis. Latin was a luxury they could not afford.

De La Salle's schools popularised new teaching methods. He also opened schools that gave technical instruction, and boarding schools that allowed students to undertake a full secondary education. Providing adult education on Sundays so that parents and young people could learn together was another innovation. He even turned his attention to the reform of juvenile delinquents.[10]

---

10 George Van Grieken, *To Touch Hearts: the Pedagogical Spirituality of St. John Baptist De La Salle*. Doctoral Dissertation, Boston College, 1995, 239–240.

2.2 Setting up a viable organisational structure

De La Salle saw that the formation of stable communities of laymen, whom he named the *Brothers of the Christian Schools*, provided the foundation that made primary education not only viable, but also sustainable. The vision of education he shared with colleagues acknowledged the personal dignity of students drawn from a humble station in life, and this justified developing pedagogical practices suited to their needs, even though this brought the group into conflict with prevailing attitudes.

The Brothers had no hesitation in adapting the school curriculum to give it a 'local' character. For example, bookkeeping was introduced into the curriculum in Rouen where the pupils included the sons of merchants, and navigation was included in Calais for the children of fisherman.[11]

John Baptist De La Salle, like Ignatius before him, was able to *discern what was best in the prevailing culture of education*, and shape it to his immediate purposes. As Jesuit commentator Ravez notes:

> I am persuaded that in his pedagogy, as in his spirituality, [De La Salle] allowed himself to be inspired by his predecessors. He studied and followed their methods, and with the help of experience he adapted them little by little. The considerable reforms in scholastic matters effected by Peter Fourier, Demia, or Barre, proved an inspiration for De La Salle; gratuitous schools, open to poor children; the suppression of teaching Latin; the simultaneous method of instruction; manual training, and the first attempts at 'trade schools', Sunday Schools for youth and adults, attempts at starting 'Normal Schools' and so on ... John Baptist's share in promoting all these efforts remains immense.[12]

The freedom De La Salle's teachers enjoyed as members of a religious community enabled them to innovate because their schools were largely independent of municipal and ecclesiastical authority.[13]

3. THE CONDUCT OF THE CHRISTIAN SCHOOLS

De La Salle's legacy may be accessed in two major written sources: *The Conduct of Christian Schools (Conduite des écoles chrétiennes)*[14] which was to become a pedagogical classic of the 18th and 19th centuries, and *Meditations in Times*

---

[11] Rummery, 153.
[12] Andre Rayez, *Lasallian Studies*, 1952. Anonymous unpublished translation.
[13] Van Grieken, 239–40.
[14] John Baptist De La Salle, *The Conduct of the Christian Schools (Conduite des écoles chrétiennes)*. Landover MD: Christian Brothers' Conference, 1996.
https://www.lasallian.info/wp-content/uploads/2012/12/Conduct-2007-reprint.pdf

of Retreat, a selection of reflections De La Salle gave to his Brothers dealing with their unique vocation as teachers.[15]

The practicality of the *Conduite* led to its adoption or adaptation in Europe. From there it was subsequently carried around the world by members of religious congregations running schools for Catholics in European colonies during the 18th and 19th centuries.[16] The book provides detailed advice and direction on how to teach and organise lessons in a classroom. It doubled as a primer for training teachers and made a major contribution to the reform of primary education in France.[17]

De La Salle wrote the first version of the *Conduite* in 1706. The document existed only in handwritten form during his lifetime. It was published in book form only after his death as, during his lifetime, he was constantly revising it. The *Conduite* is the product of De La Salle's ongoing reflection on practice made in collaboration with Brothers teaching in schools and with those who supervised them. Within the Lasallian tradition, the *Conduite* came to be regarded as 'a work in progress' until advances in education and psychology eventually rendered its more prescriptive elements redundant.[18]

The *Conduite* was set out in three sections. The first dealt with the curriculum (reading, writing arithmetic and religion), the second with pedagogy (how to teach the 4 Rs), and the third addressed training new teachers. The text ran for some 200+ pages (depending on the edition).[19] The *Conduite* provided the detailed framework within which Lasallian schools functioned, and was supplemented by a set of readers matched to the three ability levels into which students were divided. De La Salle wrote these himself.

4. DE LA SALLE'S SPIRITUAL VISION

Like Ignatius of Loyola, De La Salle discerned value in the work of outstanding educators of his time in both the religious and public spheres. With the help of the early Brothers, he not only took the insights of these educators on board, he also adapted them in the light of the experience of his Brothers in teaching and running schools. *The Conduct of Christian Schools* was developed through *reflective practice* within a learning community, although those terms were yet to be formulated.

---

15 De La Salle regularly spoke to the Brothers in the context of the liturgy and during retreats. 206 of these reflections survive.
16 As part of their teacher training, members of De La Salle's communities personally copied their own versions of the *Conduite*.
17 For background to this important document see 'Introduction' in *The Conduct of the Christian Schools*. Lasallian Resources, 2007 edition, 20–32.
18 During the 18th and 19th centuries the *Conduite* went through 24 printed editions.
19 A translation of the original text is available at https://www.lasallian.info/wp-content/uploads/2012/12/Conduct-2007-reprint.pdf

In terms of other key themes of this book, De La Salle recognised that human experience and human ways of life (cultures) are important sources of wisdom for the Christian. However, in discerning the insights they offered, he realised that a Christian requires the light of faith to assist in separating the 'wheat from the chaff' (Matt 3:12). In other words, De La Salle was a man who, because of his fine intellect and deep faith in God's Spirit at work in a particular time and place, was well able to discern what to take on board, and what to reject.

4.1 Integration of the secular and the sacred

For De La Salle, all aspects of education, including religious education, potentially complement and support each other. The locus of De La Salle's discernment, and that of the first Brothers, was *learning*. The process of trial and error figured prominently in their learning. His school was the school of life, of 'hard knocks', and his teachers were not only schoolteachers, but also learners. His constant question to the Brothers was: 'Do the schools run well?'[20]

4.2 Vocation of the teacher

A key element in De La Salle's pedagogical vision was *the centrality of relationships*. Most obviously this began with relationships among the Brothers themselves, but also extended to the relationship of Brothers with students and relationships among the students. In his view, the notion of 'community' needed to extend from the religious community to the school community.

What makes De La Salle stand out dramatically from other religious leaders of his time is the unique way he viewed *the vocation of teaching*. It was not for him a matter of being a religious person first and secondarily being a teacher. For De La Salle, involvement in education *helped form a truly spiritual person*. This foundational conviction provided the essence of his spirituality and that of his Brothers. Whereas Ignatius articulated a more general Christian spirituality, De La Salle enunciated *a spirituality of teaching*. This he set out in later life in his formation guide entitled *Meditations in Time of Retreat*.

> *It is a great gift of God, this grace he has given you to be entrusted with the instruction of children, to announce the Gospel to them and to bring them up in the spirit of religion ...*[21]

---

20 Van Grieken, 223.
21 *Meditations*, # 9.1. Cited in Van Grieken's dissertation, section on De La Salle and the teacher. Published digitally through Lulu.com, 2011.

De La Salle saw the Brothers as following in the footsteps of the Apostles entrusted, with the gifts of instruction, exhortation and teaching – great gifts and a great responsibility.[22]

2.4 The centrality of the relationship of pupil and teacher

De La Salle had a profound sympathy for the difficult situation in which most of the boys attending his schools found themselves, with their burden of poverty and neglect caused by the long hours their parents worked (when they could find work). He referred to the students as 'weary and exhausted travellers'[23], who were at the same time intrinsically valuable because they were children of God and in this sense 'more valuable than children of the king'.[24]

Early Brothers understood their relationship with pupils as that of older brother, someone who took responsibility for their development. De La Salle refers to the pupils as 'disciples' – the terms 'student' or 'pupil' is rarely used in his writings.[25] There seems no doubt that De La Salle was evoking the image of Jesus and his disciples when he used the word 'disciple' to express the relationship between the teacher and his pupil.

De La Salle seemed well able to utilise his knowledge of scripture in negotiating a path through culture and human experience. His deep knowledge and love of scripture is obvious in his works. Just as in human life a disciple in any area of learning can one day become a master, the students in the schools were envisaged as one day being able to 'master' the teaching in hand – whatever the area of study may be – thus becoming masters themselves and so able to lead others in both the Christian community and in society. Van Grieken's words here are worth pondering:

> *Disciples are not taught in the ordinary sense. The concern is not simply for the passing on of knowledge. Rather, they are an extension of the teacher, taking on the teacher's convictions, commitments, and practices – in a word, taking on the teacher's spirituality. A teacher with disciples takes a personal interest in them, since they re-present all that the teacher imparts to them. By calling students your disciples, De La Salle, from the start indicates the kind of Christian relationship that he expects between teacher and pupil in a Christian school.*[26]

---

22 *Meditations*, ## 78.2, 145.3 & 193.2.
23 *Meditations*, # 37.1.
24 *Meditations*, # 80.3. The references above are taken from Van Grieken's discussion of De La Salle's approach to students, 241–250. A paperback version of these meditations was published by the De La Salle Brothers in 1994.
25 Van Grieken, 241.
26 Ibid, 242.

De La Salle structured classes in such a way that students progressed towards mastery often working in small groups in which students from higher levels monitored and helped the progress of students at the lower levels. In this way his 'disciple' theme melded into his aim of 'community building'.

2.5 The essence of teaching – to touch hearts

The central theme of De La Salle's *Meditations* is 'touching hearts'.

> *The life of the Brothers is to be a life characterized by prayer and study: Prayer gives a holy power ... the more prayer is practiced, the more God will help you find the skill to touch their hearts* (M, 148.2).

The 'touching of hearts' is a metaphorical way of referring to reaching the deepest aspects of a person's being, what they feel strongly about and value. 'To touch hearts' is to engage with people and provide opportunities for them to grow as persons, connecting their lives with those of Jesus. It is to help them shape their worldview and so their capacity to make sense of life in a way that is open to faith. This was De La Salle's ultimate aim.

3. PEDAGOGICAL SPIRITUALITY

In its essence, De La Salle's spirituality has something to offer all Christian educators. It is a spirituality that emerges out of the interplay of deep prayer and a pedagogical vision and practice. In the life of De La Salle, both pedagogical practice and prayer became fused into a discernible spirituality ideally suited to Catholic educators.

De La Salle's pedagogical spirituality set out in his *Meditations in Time of Retreat* is made concrete in *The Conduct of Christian Schools*.

3.1 Meditations in Time of Retreat

Meditations in Time of Retreat stands at the summit of De La Salle's spiritual legacy, yet for many years the document received limited attention. In the renewal prompted by the Second Vatican Council (1962–5), the De La Salle Brothers were asked to 'return to the sources' and so 'rediscovered' the spiritual heritage of their founder. Brothers undertook doctoral studies focused on the congregation's founding documents, and analysed their scriptural content. It was through a thorough study of these scriptural sources that the real significance of *Meditations in Time of Retreat* became clear.[27]

---

[27] See Miguel Campos' extensive introduction to *Meditations in Time of Retreat*.

By placing themselves and their ministry within the Lasallian story, those who follow a Lasallian spirituality today also open themselves to the Gospel call to mission. As noted earlier, for De La Salle there is *no distinction between a person's professional responsibilities as a teacher and those of a Gospel-based life*. This is a very innovative element in De La Salle's spiritual vision and cannot be emphasised too much as it is so often overlooked or simply misunderstood.

De La Salle's belief that technical competence in teaching and spiritual depth need to be developed *together* is worthy of much consideration in forming today's teachers, many of whom are lay people living in the world and dealing with secular and professional elements of Christian life in complex circumstances.

Catholic school teachers are people whose lives are lived predominantly in the world, rather than in religious communities. These teachers can benefit greatly from the distinctive insights and innovations of the highly educated, reflective and pedagogically pioneering patron of Christian teachers, John Baptist De La Salle.

Part B
KEY TOOLS FOR ANALYSING THE PEDAGOGICAL LANDSCAPE

Introduction

A starting assumption of this book is that a pedagogy that is 'Catholic' helps develop in students an imagination and a personal worldview that is open to faith, and to engaging with the world in which they live. This implies that the teacher has a similar worldview with similar assumptions. However, in a secular age this cannot be assumed. It takes a conscious decision on the part of the teacher to 'befriend' the Catholic tradition. This means that the teacher needs to be open to this possibility and aware of what a contemporary articulation of the faith tradition might be. However, the teacher also needs to be aware of its limits as a credible resource for making sense of life events. These are some of the issues pursued in Part B.

The contextual nature of all human knowledge

The development of human thinking and the concepts that underpin it are always *contextual*. In this respect, pedagogy is no different from anthropology, theology or any other academic discipline, including science. Important concepts arise at a certain point in human experience and provide an interpretive key to use in understanding past events, making sense of present events, or anticipating what might lie in the future.

The concepts of 'culture', 'worldview' and 'mission' fit this pattern, and to these we now add 'faith'. Concepts with significant interpretive power tend to expand in meaning as time passes and, in consequence, become increasingly difficult to define precisely. They can become so vague in meaning that they eventually lose their interpretive power. This is a real danger with all four words above. Hence our effort, with the assistance of some outstanding scholars, to present workable perspectives on them.

'Faith' in the context of 'worldview'

'Faith' has a history when attached to 'worldview'. The history of Christian faith in the Greco-Roman world of the first three centuries was not promising. Christians became convenient political scapegoats, particularly when the fortunes of Roman emperors waned. They were seen as 'different' and 'not one of us' because they rejected important Roman cultural norms, including worshipping the Emperor. They were easy targets for populist leaders since they did not take up arms; their interpretation of Christian faith did not permit this.

Pivotal moments in the development of the 'worldview of faith'

There appear to be six pivotal moments in the emergence of the worldview of Christian faith as we know it in the West today.

1. *When Christianity gained its freedom under Constantine, and then became the religion of the Empire under Theodosius I in 380*
2. *The final collapse of the Roman empire in the fifth century, leaving the Church as the most important civil organisation in Europe*
3. *The decision of bishops in the East to break away from the Church in the West in the eleventh century*
4. *The Protestant Reformation of the sixteenth century and its political, religious and economic impact on Western Europe*
5. *The Council of Trent (1545–1563) and the consequent reorientation of Catholic thinking and practice that followed*
6. *Vatican Council II (1962–5) and subsequent efforts to overcome some historical legacies of the previous 'moments'*

'Worldview of faith' and 'historic effect'

In making sense of the sweep of history, academics employ the notions of 'historical critical consciousness' and 'historic effect'. Historical critical consciousness refers to the ways in which past, present and future are interpreted as being connected. 'Historic effect' is an element of this. It refers to the way in which an event in the past can have effects that linger on and influence subsequent history, so throwing new light on the significance of an originating event in the process of making sense of what is happening in the present.[1]

Each of the events listed above has had an historic effect that sometimes enhanced the original intention, but also exposed flaws in what was intended – flaws that often have an effect which negates the original intention. For instance, after three hundred years of persecution, Christians must have felt vindicated when their religion was no longer persecuted and eventually became the religion of the Empire. However, the institutionalisation of the Church in this setting affected roles within the church. These tended to follow the pattern of the Empire; the Church had already begun to import the cultural values of patriarchy and hierarchy into its life. This tendency proceeded rapidly. The clear benefits of institutionalisation came with costs. The effects of institutionalism live on in history, and have now become dysfunctional in Church life in a very different time and culture.

The point being made here is that Christian faith *always exists in history* and is formulated against the background of human experiences as these unfold in time. The worldview of faith consequently develops within time. It has a history, and continues to evolve as history moves on. As both contextual and provisional, it is never final.

Phenomenology of faith

Such thinking has not always been clear to Catholic leaders who were trained to believe that faith existed as a set of revealed truths that are independent of history and culture – true in a particular form of expression for all people and all times. However, this is not how faith is experienced by individuals and groups within the Church. At the phenomenological level, faith is experienced as a living faith, a framework within which people can make sense of the events of their lives, whose meaning and significance might otherwise be opaque.

Re-contextualisation

As history unfolds and human experiences become more differentiated, what seems clear in the experience of faith today is that our understanding of what faith means and how it is practiced in day-to-day life needs to keep pace. The process by which this happens in known as *re-contextualisation*, where an older tradition is reinterpreted in the light of new experiences and understandings.

Each of the pivotal moments outlined above resulted in a re-contextualisation of the worldview of Catholic faith. Each produced a

---

[1] Jesus' resurrection from the dead comes to mind in this context.

historic effect that lives on, for better or worse, in the Catholic tradition as we know and experience it today. It is not possible to make sense of or interpret the worldview of faith independently of

- *the context in which this worldview is invoked in making sense of life events, and*
- *the story by which this worldview has come to take its present form (as the result of successive processes of re-contextualisation).*

Because we exist as persons-in-history, our grasp on the worldview of faith is both *contextual and provisional*. A common cause of conflict within a large-scale faith community such as the Catholic Church is for leaders or groups to take a particular re-contextualisation of the worldview of faith as its final and definitive form. This raises two questions for Catholic educators:

- *What does the worldview of faith look like in a postsecular age?*
- *What historic effects have to be recognised and dealt with in arriving at a post-secular understanding of the worldview of faith?*

Our hope is that key aspects of the first question emerge from this book. In Part C we explore the second question.

6

WORLDVIEWS AND THEIR ROLE IN MEANING-MAKING

A person or group's worldview plays constantly in their background shaping what they attend to, how they interpret events, what they value, and how decisions are made. For teachers this includes very obviously decisions about what and how to teach. Consideration of worldviews and their role in meaning-making is clearly of vital importance in education which is at the service of the Kingdom of God.

In this chapter the questions we address are:

- *What is a worldview?*
- *How do worldviews shape the work of educators?*

1. WORLDVIEW AS AN INTERPRETIVE FRAMEWORK

There are many definitions of worldview, just as there are many definitions of culture. The common dictionary meaning attached to 'worldview' is 'philosophy of life' which suggests that worldview is a cognitive category. This is a limited understanding. James Sire goes beyond the philosophical in defining worldview as follows:

> A *worldview is a set of presuppositions (assumptions which may be true, partially true or entirely false) that we hold (consciously or sub-consciously, consistently or inconsistently) about the basic make-up of the world.*[1]

Here the emphasis is on what people 'know and believe'.

Given the understanding of the human that we have adopted in this work, we find the concept of 'worldview' as proposed by anthropologist Paul Hiebert[2] to be more helpful than either of the above approaches

---

1 James Sire, *Naming the Elephant: Worldview as a Concept*. Downers Grove IL: Intervarsity Press, 2004, 19.
2 Paul Hiebert, *Transforming Worldviews: An Anthropological Understanding of How People Change*. Grand Rapids: Baker Academic, 2008.

because it is more comprehensive (see below). Essentially, our 'worldview' provides each of us with the *interpretive lens* through which we perceive our experiences, make sense of them, and respond to them. Our worldview determines the stance we, pre-reflectively, take on life. Hiebert's model conveys this understanding.[3]

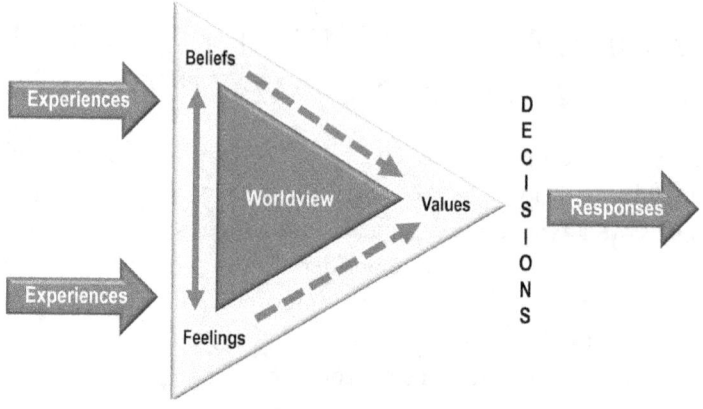

FIGURE 6.1: WORLDVIEW – A MODEL (HIEBERT)

Figure 6.1 suggests that our worldview acts as a buffer between experience on the input side of human consciousness, and decision and response on the output side. By acting in this manner our worldview conditions our response by taking into account what we *know and believe*, what we *value*, and the *sensibility* at play in processing experience. Sensibility refers to the more or less instinctive reactions we have to people and events. Sometimes these are emotional; at other times aesthetic. Some people, for instance, are naturally trusting of others; others are naturally suspicious. Some are extroverted; others introverted. Some process their thoughts internally; others like to talk them out in public. Such characteristics reflect a sensibility inherent in who we are. Sensibility manifests itself in how we 'feel' towards persons, events etc. It is worth repeating that a worldview determines the automatic stance a person *pre-reflectively* takes to experiences and situations. It is the 'something' that a person brings to making sense of the unfamiliar.

1.1 Personal worldview

A person's worldview is not simply 'a thing of the mind'. As a *stance to life*, worldview *encompasses the whole person*. The Bible repeatedly uses the synonym 'heart' to indicate a person's worldview.[4] Worldview is the *subjective*

---

3   Ibid, 28.
4   In an earlier study we devoted the final chapter to a discussion of worldview from this perspective. See Chapter 16, 'Catholic Curriculum: a Mission to the Heart of Young People' in Jim & Therese

framework within which we seek to make sense of our experiences and orient ourselves in the *objective world*.

How we make sense of events depends not only on what we (consciously or subconsciously) know and believe, but also on *what we value* and the *sensibility* that shapes how we react to and process new experiences. This is particularly the case when the new experience involves learning. Of the three – knowledge, values and sensibility – sensibility can be decisive in determining how a student approaches learning.

The way a student processes previous experiences of learning shapes the beliefs that they hold about learning, the value they place on it, and the way they feel about it. If a student's early experiences of learning are negative, this can shape how they think of themself as a learner, possibly leading to the 'I'm no good at maths', or the 'history sucks' syndromes.

In planning lessons, teachers overlook the sensibility that students bring to the classroom at their peril. This is one reason why the literature on 'good teaching' stresses the importance of creating a positive learning environment in the classroom and the importance of formative types of assessment.

1.2 Enculturation

We acquire our personal worldview in the process of growing up in a particular culture and community. This acquisition is a process that goes on largely outside of our awareness when we are quite young, and it is part of what cultural anthropologists call our *enculturation*.[5] Our personal worldview *determines what we choose to attend to when trying to make sense of our experiences*. It therefore controls the doorway to learning.[6]

Since there is so much in our daily experience that we could attend to, our worldview provides us with *a coping mechanism* enabling us to focus on some things at the expense of others. However, this selective form of attention *introduces biases into the process of meaning-making*. This bias needs to be acknowledged and taken into account by teachers in understanding how students process their experiences. Some of these biases are positive and some are negative.

As young people grow and develop, they gradually take (or should be encouraged to take) greater personal responsibility for *consciously* shaping their worldview. Schooling makes an important contribution to this process by helping students recognise and critique negative biases in their worldview

---

D'Orsa, *Catholic Curriculum*. Mulgrave: Garratt Publishing, 2012, 237–251. The work of David Naugle provided some key ideas featured in this chapter. See *Worldview: The History of a Concept*. Grand Rapids: Eerdmans Publishing, 2002, 267–274.

5 Social anthropologists call the process 'socialisation'.
6 Jim & Therese D'Orsa, *Leading for Mission: Integrating Life, Culture and Faith in Catholic Education* Mulgrave: Garratt Publishing, 2013, 144.

such as racism, sexism, ageism and so on. The hope of Catholic educators is that they can nurture into life a positive form of bias in the worldview of their students, one that also makes a space for faith.

As we pointed out in our earlier work on *Catholic Curriculum*[7], teachers today are in 'the worldview business' and this is something that they have to take into account in planning teaching and learning experiences for their students.[8] This realisation also needs to frame how they understand the pedagogical relationship that lies at the heart of good teaching.

2. COLLECTIVE WORLDVIEWS

Just as individuals have a worldview, so too do groups. One is inevitably the cause of the other. Canadian philosopher James Olthuis explains that worldview, while an individual construction, is influenced by the community to which a person belongs:

> *Although a vision of life is held only by individuals, it is communal in scope and structure. Since a worldview gives terms of reference by which the world and our place in it can be structured and illumined, a worldview binds its adherents together in community. Allegiance to a common vision promotes the integration of individuals into community. At times communality of vision not only binds people together, but also, ironically, provides them with the tools and vocabulary to advance with greater sophistication their internal differences.*[9]

Thus, it is possible to talk of 'the worldview of a community', 'the worldview of a faith community', 'the worldview of a culture', even 'the worldview of a profession'. Collective worldviews reflect the *selective attention* characteristic of groups and *the biases* that this selective attention often introduces into group life.[10]

2.1 Public worldviews

The collective worldviews we explore in the balance of this chapter are *public worldviews*, that is, they have a sponsoring community that maintains

---

7   Jim and Therese D'Orsa, *Catholic Curriculum: A mission to the heart of young people*. Mulgrave: Garratt Publishing, 2011.
8   Ibid, 4–6.
9   Quoted in Sire, 37.
10 'Bias' (also sometimes called 'prejudice') usually carries a negative connotation, but as used in this study it refers to the fact that individuals and groups are selective in what they attend to in trying to understand or interpret the world about them. Because our awareness is selective, our understanding is limited. 'Bias' or 'prejudice' refers to these limits in perspective. Not all biases have negative consequences, but many, such as those associated with racism, and forms of misogyny, most certainly do.

and oversees the development of traditions on which the worldview depends. Two important public worldviews are those of culture and of faith.

2.2 The worldview of culture

The worldview of a culture provides people in a particular cultural community with *a default frame of reference* that they subconsciously turn to in making sense of their experiences. Today we are living through a change of era, which means that the worldview of our culture is in a state of flux. We see major indicators of this change, for instance, in the re-definition of marriage and family, the quest for greater inclusivity in society, the emergence of social media as a new force in politics and social life, the cult of celebrity, the ubiquitous presence of the internet, the increasing secularity of society, and so on.

People today are living between a culture informed by the worldview of modernity and an emerging culture that is slowly taking shape and whose worldview will eventually supersede that of modernity.[11]

Anthropologists name a period in history such as ours a 'liminal era', a transition era in which the dominant culture slowly takes on a new form.[12] In such an era, very little seems stable as the traditions that define one culture seem to be fragmenting and the traditions defining the new culture have yet to take on a permanent form. While this is an exciting time to live in, it is also a very confusing time. Teachers charged with transmitting cultural traditions can interpret the liminal situation as either 'glass half empty' or 'glass half full'!

The sponsoring bodies for the worldview of culture include the academic communities that stand behind the disciplines of learning, and the media. Increasingly so, social media is becoming an important cultural force shaping what people attend to, what they value, and particularly their sensibility – how they feel about things.

2.3 The worldview of faith

The worldview of faith is an important public worldview. In the context of Catholic education, it is the worldview sponsored by the Church.

---

[11] The emerging era has a plethora of names: many look backwards such as 'post-modern', 'post-traditional', 'post-secular', 'post-Christian'; others look forward to a 'global era'. It will still be some time before the emerging era has an agreed name. Scholars, such as Charles Taylor, argue that the era of modernity is not over, but is being reconstructed on less ambitious assumptions.

[12] The concept of liminality was formulated by anthropologist Victor Turner as a stage of 'being in limbo', of being 'torn out of the familiar settings and relationships in which we live our lives'. (See Hiebert, 1994, 169.) The authors of this work see liminality as being the experience of the pilgrim, the pioneer, the missionary, or the person who crosses cultural boundaries.

In the frame of reference this worldview provides, people *choose* to attend to certain facets of their experiences and ignore others; they *choose* to accept certain beliefs, and they *choose* to develop a religious sensibility. Half a century ago this was not the case; people considered themselves 'Catholic' because they were 'born Catholic' and lived in a more or less Christian social world.

Unlike the worldview of culture, the worldview of faith no longer automatically functions as a default frame of reference in making meaning. In a secular culture, it is a frame of reference *that has to be consciously chosen* as a point of reference. People now have to *consciously make space for faith*. Charles Taylor calls this 'the condition of belief' in our present liminal situation.[13]

Taylor argues that for much of Western history the worldview of culture and that of faith overlapped so that the worldview of faith *was* people's default frame of reference in making sense of life. A change in outlook begun during the Reformation, accelerated with the Enlightenment period, and came to fruition in the modern era, whereby faith and culture became independent frames of reference in making sense of life. While the modern prediction was that religion would die out, this did not happen. The result is that culture and faith now exist in our postsecular world as *inter-dependent* rather than *independent* frames of reference in making sense of life.

Our liminal context has important ramifications for Catholic educators. Since our culture provides people with a default frame of reference in making sense of the world, and since this is secular, then we can expect that the majority of students, their parents, and a high proportion of teachers in Catholic schools, will make sense of life in a frame of reference that makes little or no reference to God or the transcendent. This will be the case 'across the curriculum' unless teachers make a conscious effort to change the situation.

The rhetoric used in Catholic schools to make sense of the new situation is that of 'bringing faith and culture into dialogue', and the essential pedagogical skill associated with this project is *being able to moderate respectful dialogue in the classroom*. While this is essential in religious education, it is also an important skill in other key learning areas. The task is made harder because of the secular bias students bring to class.

When dialogue occurs in a liminal situation, the teacher often realises that he or she is sailing in uncharted waters and that there are no simple answers to complex issues. The situation casts student and teacher in the role

---

13 There is a plethora of references to 'condition of belief'. See Charles Taylor, *A Secular Age*. Cambridge MA: The Belknap Press of Harvard University Press: 2007, 12, 25–28 etc.

of *co-constructors of knowledge within a community of learners*. It is a situation in which *a community of learners is needed* because the validity of what we claim to know always needs to be tested. Testing truth claims within a faith community is a long-established pedagogical principle within the Catholic tradition.

2.4 Worldview of faith: one option among many

The fact that our culture is secular, means that the worldview of Christian or Catholic faith is now *an option* open to students along with other religious and non-religious options. The pedagogical challenge for teachers in Catholic schools is to help students see that a choice 'for faith' is *reasonable, personally meaningful, and can feel 'right'* in today's cultural conditions – and to see this choice as *a meaningful stance towards life*. This is the goal, no matter what religious denomination or faith persuasion students belong to. It is a project that needs to be pursued 'across the curriculum' and not just in religious education classes.[14]

The modelling of teachers plays an important role in assisting students to see the Catholic worldview as a valuable resource in shaping how they see the world and how they approach life. If they are to be effective in this role, then teachers have to be able to recognise *an authentic presentation of the worldview of faith*.[15]

For a Christian, consciously shaping one's worldview, and bringing it into alignment with the values and relationships that characterise the 'Kingdom of God' revealed by Jesus, is a grace-shaped and life-long task. It is not completed during the school years. Assisting students to *set out on this journey* is a goal many teachers seek to achieve in a Catholic school. It is a goal that has consequences for how they see their role and interpret their identity as a teacher. It is the framework within which they understand the pedagogical relationship they have with their students and the responsibilities that flow from that relationship.

2.5 Critiquing the worldview of faith

The worldview of faith, like other worldviews, contains biases that need to be monitored and, where necessary, critiqued. This is part of the educational task of teachers in any authentic presentation of this worldview. Older students seem generally well aware of biases within the worldview

---

14 One of the major issues facing religious educators today is that the lack of inclusiveness in the Catholic Church does not 'feel right' for many young people. They have a sensibility that reacts to exclusion and so frames how they perceive the Church and its message.
15 As we will see later, there are several possible versions of this worldview that are authentic.

of Catholic faith, and sometimes regard them as a disincentive to their adopting it as a meaningful stance to life.

Most people today understand the worldview of faith *through the lens of their culture,* and from this perspective some elements of it do not always seem reasonable, meaningful, or 'feel right'.

The attitude of many Church leaders to the role of women in the Church, their perceived ambivalent attitude to LGBTQI people, and their equivocal attitude to those who are divorced, are stand-out issues for critique. Such issues highlight the ways in which the Catholic tradition can run up against the aspirations of our emerging culture. These matters can be resolved only through respectful dialogue resourced by prayerful and deep studies of the issues, and attentive listening to the experiences of people. This is the way the 'synodal church' that Pope Francis seeks to create necessarily functions.

2.6 The changing role of the teacher

Personal worldviews 'nest' within collective worldviews. For most people their personal worldview nests within the worldview of their culture. This is how culture works. If young people are to take their faith seriously in a secular society, then they have to choose, with assistance, to bring their faith into dialogue with their culture. This type of dialogue needs to be fostered in the classroom, and so it extends the role of the teacher into a new pedagogical role as *moderator of the dialogue between faith and culture.*

In the case of religious education teachers, the new role is extended to that of *moderator of dialogue among faiths, and also among faiths and secular worldviews.* Few teachers in Catholic schools have been trained for such a role, as until relatively recently the pluralism of belief found in most Catholic schools was largely ignored. The widespread adoption of the *Enhancing Catholic School Identity* (ECSI) project by school systems in this country has highlighted the pluralism in belief that exists in most Catholic school communities. It particularly challenges religious education teachers to understand their role as witness, expert and moderator (of dialogue). This development of the teachers' roles is significant in how they understand the pedagogical relationship they have with students and the ethical responsibilities that flow from it. These two issues will be taken up in more detail in later chapters.

7
CULTURE AND THE PEDAGOGICAL RELATIONSHIP

As John Baptist De La Salle saw so clearly, pedagogical practice ultimately comes down to how one conceives the special relationship between student and teacher. While it has deep roots in faith, elements of this relationship are always culturally situated. As cultures change, so too does people's understanding of the roles and responsibilities associated with pedagogy.

In terms of the sweep of history, in a short time the dominant 'jug to mug' transmission of knowledge from teacher to student has shifted to that of teacher and student being collaborators in meaning-making. What has occurred culturally to enable this shift? This and the following chapters will explore aspects of this change. This chapter puts the focus on the nature of culture itself. In the following chapters, aspects and consequences of the cultural movement – from pre-modern to modern, from modern to postmodern and from postmodern to postsecular – will be explored with a view to charting the resulting shift in pedagogical demands.

1.1 Culture

Today 'culture' is such a ubiquitous term that its meaning has become vague. For example, 'culture' is often seen as the culprit whenever an organisation becomes dysfunctional, be this a bank, school, cricket team, or church. In this chapter we seek to clarify what we mean by 'culture' and then explore the role that the 'worldview of culture' plays in how people, including teachers and students, make sense of their world. As we shall see, the worldview of culture plays a role of vital importance in shaping pedagogy.

Most people are so immersed in their culture that they do not notice it; they simply experience 'the way things are for us'. It is only when you encounter another culture that you realise that other people do things differently, see things differently, value things differently, and that, on some important issues, 'the way things are for them' diverges greatly from 'the way things are for us'.

This came home to one of us while studying in Rome some years ago. Jim was the victim of a home invasion and robbery. Waking up at 2:00 am with a knife at your throat and a torch blinding you is bad enough, but subsequently dealing with police authorities who did not speak English, and who worked in a system that they took for granted but you did not comprehend, was a total nightmare!

1.2 Culture as 'our way'

The experience highlighted just how different the Australian and Italian policing systems are, and how much we take our own system for granted. This is how culture works. It helps us define 'our way' or what we take as 'normal'. It provides us with a way of distinguishing 'us' from those who are 'not us'. It does this in a process that runs largely outside of our awareness. The fact that we take so much for granted relieves us of the need to think about a whole range of issues as we live our daily lives. A group's culture provides members with a critical coping mechanism.

In this chapter the questions we explore are:

- *What is culture?*
- *What is classicism?*
- *How does culture function in meaning-making?*
- *How do faith and culture interact in the process of meaning-making?*

1. THE MODERN CONCEPT OF CULTURE

Culture is the major topic studied in cultural anthropology. Within this discipline 'culture' has a variety of definitions depending on the perspective the anthropologist adopts. It has been suggested that there are as many definitions of culture as there are anthropologists, but this is an exaggeration.

The discipline of cultural anthropology is relatively recent. Pioneers in the field, such as Frank Boas and Edward T Hall, did much of their fieldwork in the early and mid 20th century. Cultural anthropology remained an obscure discipline until the outbreak of World War II, when American troops in the Pacific were forced to build a working relationship with local people whose cultures were different from their own. They soon found that treating local people as 'under-educated Americans' was very counter-productive. The situation became even more complex in the aftermath of the war when Japan and a number of countries in Europe had to be rebuilt. During this period the few US anthropologists available found themselves very much in demand, and when the rebuilding efforts were over, they returned to academic life with a host of experiences to analyse and learn from. In the 1940s and 1950s the study of cultural anthropology in the US and social anthropology in the UK gathered momentum.[1]

1.3 Mission anthropology's contribution

Mission anthropology uses the findings of cultural anthropology to analyse what has been learned from nearly four centuries of recent Christian missionary activity in cross-cultural situations.[2] Many missionaries, Protestant and Catholic, were trained to record local customs and languages. This was so that those who succeeded them in particular mission posts would know something of the 'way of life' and language of the peoples with whom they were working. The knowledge that accumulated from missionary experience formed the basis of 'mission studies' in many seminaries and universities.[3] On returning home, a number of missionaries went on to enjoy academic careers in cultural anthropology and made major contributions to the development of missiology. This has been a fairly recent development.[4]

As the world has become globalised and migration has increased, most Western societies have become more multi-cultural and multi-faith so that lessons learned from missionary experience have now begun to affect mainstream thinking in a variety of areas, such as theology and ecclesiology.

2. DEFINITION OF CULTURE

One of the most helpful definitions of culture we have encountered comes from mission anthropologist Louis Luzbetak SVD, who is regarded as 'the father' of mission anthropology. For Luzbetak culture is:

A people's more or less comprehensive, more or less successful, design (or plan) for living together peacefully in their particular environment.

---

[1] For a summary of the development of anthropology download *History of Anthropology* from Pearson Higher Education https://www.pearsonhighered.com/assets/samplechapter/0/2/0/5/0205738826.pdf

[2] For a summary of developments in Mission anthropology and the questions they raise for mission practice see 'Paul Hiebert *Mission and Anthropology*' at https://home.snu.edu/~hculbert/mission.htm

[3] In the colonial era, governments in Europe supported the development of mission studies, financially seeing the missionaries as an important and positive part of their colonising enterprises. The aim was to 'civilise' and 'Christianise' local people. This practice created a postcolonial legacy that mainstream Christian churches are still recovering from. In Belgium, for instance, the term 'mission' is rarely used in theological discourse because of its association with Belgium's colonial enterprise, and its unfortunate aftermath, particularly in Rwanda.

[4] Missiology is an inter-disciplinary area of study which includes mission theology and other sacred and secular disciplines. Its focus is the Church in mission. Missiology has developed significantly in the period since Vatican II.

To this understanding Luzbetak adds a number of qualifications:[5]

- *The 'plan' is seen as valuable and so is taught and learned.*
- *The 'plan' is dynamic in that it is able to be adapted as the environment changes.*
- *'The environment' has three principal dimensions: physical, social and ideational. Change can occur at any one of these levels, creating a need to adapt the 'plan'.*

It is also worth noting that:

1. *Culture is 'more or less successful' because cultures that do not adapt to changes in the environment eventually die. Archaeology is replete with examples of cultures that have failed to adapt to changes in the physical environment. Many Pacific nations face this prospect in regard to their physical environment at the present time due to climate change. Failure to adjust to changes in the social or ideational environments can be equally devastating – as Russian czars and French kings discovered too late!*
2. *Culture is 'comprehensive' in that the 'plan for living together' covers most aspects of life. A people's culture is not something that can be easily picked apart, as the whole is greater than the sum of its parts. Many Christians who are engaged in cross-cultural mission learn this lesson the hard way.*
3. *We are born into a culture and are well and truly enculturated before we reach school age. We acquire our culture by a combination of learning by trial and error ('do this, don't do that'), by observation ('this gets rewarded, that doesn't'), by imitating role models, and by listening to stories.*
4. *Culture has a provisional quality in that it is 'more or less' comprehensive and successful. Not everyone in a society necessarily agrees with 'the plan' as it is presented to them. But the existence of 'the plan' gives members of the group a common point of reference in discussing their differences.*
5. *Culture seeks to create conditions under which people are able to live together peacefully. It includes provisions and structures for dealing with various forms of conflict and tension.*
6. *Since 'success' is measured by survival in different environments, it is not usually helpful in comparing cultures.*

---

5 See Louis Luzbetak, 'The Nature of Culture' in *The Church and Cultures* (revised edition). Maryknoll NY: Orbis Books, 1988, Chapter 5, 'The Nature of Culture', 156–159.

An advantage of Luzbetak's definition is that it can apply to multiple entities: to a national group, an ethnic group, a church, a profession, a business organisation, a school, and so on.[6]

One of the major practical learnings of mission anthropologists is that culture is comprehensive: it cannot easily be picked apart and changed piece by piece. This is because, in its wholeness, culture provides people with *a default system for constructing meaning and so it is not surprising that they resist the tension, even chaos, that a significant change can make in their lives.*

Highly regarded mission anthropologist Paul Hiebert reports attending a Christmas celebration in India at which there was a nativity play. In the middle of the play Santa Claus and his reindeer suddenly appeared and gave the infant Jesus presents. He was at a loss to explain this until he remembered that in the West we make a distinction between what is secular and what is sacred. For us, Santa Claus belongs to the secular world, and the nativity belongs to the sacred world. In the worldview of the people with whom he was working, there was no division between the secular and the sacred. For them life is one. So, the apparent syncretism obvious in the actions taking place on the stage raised no issues for that particular audience.[7] A people's culture is built on a number of *unstated foundational assumptions*. Western cultures assume, for example, that there is a division between the sacred and the secular; the culture in which Hiebert's audience was immersed did not.

3. THE WORLDVIEW OF CULTURE

Drawing on our previous discussion of worldview, we can say that the 'worldview of culture' refers to what *a people* collectively knows and believes, the values they share, the common sensibility, all of which form a 'whole' in making sense of life.

3.1 Culture introduces biases

Culture is something that pertains to group life. As members of a group we each exist as a 'person-in-culture'. *There is no 'culture-free' position from which to make sense of life.*

---

6 Compare the above with the definition of organisational culture provided by Edgar Schein: The culture of a group is 'the accumulated shared learning of that group as it solves its problems of external adaptation and internal integration; which has worked well enough to be considered valid and, therefore, to be taught to new members as the correct way to perceive, think, feel, and behave in relation to those problems.
This accumulated learning is a pattern or system of beliefs, values and behavioural norms that come to be taken for granted as basic assumptions and eventually drop out of awareness.' Edgar Schein, *Organisational Culture and Leadership.* 5th ed. Hoboken N.J: Wiley, 2017, 6.
7 Paul Hiebert, *The Gospel in Human Contexts: Anthropological Explorations of Contemporary Missions.* Grand Rapids: Baker Academic, 2009, 11.

As the world and our own society become more pluralised, this situation becomes highly problematic. We think that our group's definition of what is 'normal' should be 'normal' for other groups, but this is not the case. For this reason, 'culture' has become an important issue in education. The classroom is increasingly a site for cross-cultural exchange and intercultural learning with the teacher expected to play the role of moderator, a role for which few have been prepared.

3.2 Culture and selective awareness

Without being aware of it, we pick up important elements in the worldview of our culture as part of our enculturation, through our early family and other experiences.

Culture provides us with a lens through which we see the world *in a selective way*. It always introduces a form of bias into meaning-making in that we attend to some things and not to others. Culture introduces untested assumptions about how we make sense of life, as in the Christmas celebration example above. As these assumptions are untested, learning to critique cultural assumptions is important in developing as a human being.

Young people in Australia grow up in a culture that is secular. This means that their default frame of reference in making sense of life is secular. As a result, people now take it for granted that 'faith' is one option among many when it comes to making sense of life. As an option, they can choose it, or ignore it. As Charles Taylor points out, this is now 'the condition of belief' in most Western countries. It is something that teachers in Catholic schools have to wrestle with both in their own lives and in helping their students learn.[8]

The secularity of our culture is an important facet of the *liminality* that characterises our present age. Liminality – that sense people have of pursuing life at an in-between time, on the threshold of something different and new – is a very important aspect of the experience of culture within which educators now teach.

4. CLASSICISM

In the 19th and early 20th centuries, Darwin's theory of evolution had a profound effect on the development of anthropology with the idea of the survival of the fittest being applied analogously to human cultures. 'Cultures' were assumed to exist along a continuum running from 'advanced' to 'primitive' with 'advanced' seen as being further along the evolutionary

---

[8] Charles Taylor, *A Secular Age*. Cambridge: Harvard University Press, 2007, 3.

path than the 'primitive'. An attraction for anthropologists in studying what they termed 'primitive cultures' was to track the stages they assumed human cultures passed through as they evolved. Within this perspective, European culture was viewed as providing the 'gold standard' against which all other cultures could be measured.

This approach to the study of culture was challenged in the post-colonial period when the overlay of European culture imposed on colonial peoples began to be rejected. In some instances, Christianity was seen as part of this overlay, and in many colonial settings the message for expatriate missionaries was simply 'Go home!'

4.1 Definition of classicism

The notion that one culture can be taken as normative for all other cultures is called 'classicism'. While far from unique to the West, in its most prevalent Western form classicism has been exemplified in recent centuries by European culture being taken as the norm in art, literature, science, architecture, and so on. This Eurocentric bias also found its way into philosophy and theology.

The advent of the empirical understanding of culture as 'the way of life of a people' challenged the basis of classicism. However, classicism is far from dead; it exists wherever 'our way' is taken to be normative for all others. It is alive within the Catholic Church when Western constructions of theology are taken as providing the norm for all people and all times.

4.2 A more global Catholicism

As the Catholic Church has become more global in composition, its leaders have had to deal with the impact of Eurocentric classicism on its teaching and self-understanding. This became an issue at the Second Vatican Council (1962–5) attended by bishops from all over the world, and it remains a matter of much controversy with the appointment of the first non-European pope for many centuries.[9]

Vatican II acknowledged the important role culture plays in shaping human understanding and sought to redefine the Church's relationship with the world's major faiths. As a consequence, the need for ecumenical and also interfaith dialogue was recognised and encouraged.

---

9   Vatican I (1869–70) had drawn about 700 bishops from many parts of the world, including Australia. However, it was dominated by Europe, and colonies were generally represented by expatriate bishops. Vatican II (1962–5) would be the first truly global council. For an authoritative study of Vatican I see John O'Malley, *Vatican I: The Council and the Making of the Ultramontane Church*. Cambridge MA: Harvard University Press, 2018.

This change in theological emphasis has corresponded to a major demographic shift in the students attending Australian Catholic schools. The shift has both cultural and religious dimensions. The student body is becoming more culturally diverse and the number of students from other religious backgrounds, and no religious background, is on the rise. As the demography of Catholic schools begins to look increasingly like that of public schools, the situation has led many people to ask: What is going on? Australian Catholic bishops have affirmed that Catholic schooling is *to be inclusive* and have resisted efforts to make the schools exclusive. The most often quoted document making this case is that of the NSW and ACT bishops, *Catholic Schools at a Crossroad*, 2007.[10]

The changes now underway require a *recalibration of the religious mission of Catholic schools* that includes reformulating the ways in which teachers deal with intercultural learning and learning at the interface of faith and cultures. The situation is relatively new. Many teachers are still learning how to address the challenges it poses not only for their role as teachers, but for their educational practice as well.[11]

4.3 *The ECSI* solution in religious education

The Enhancing Catholic School Identity Project (ECSI) in which several Australian school systems are engaged attempts to address these issues of intercultural learning and learning at the interface of faith and cultures. Its proponents suggest that teachers need to re-conceptualise their role in religious education to that of:

- *witness to Catholic faith*
- *expert in the Catholic tradition, and*
- *moderator of a dialogue among students of different faiths and worldviews.*

These three aspects of the religious education teacher's role have associated skills and understandings that need to be developed professionally if the ECSI project is to achieve its goals. This professional development is now a work-in-progress in many dioceses.

---

10 Catholic Bishops of NSW and the ACT, *Catholic Schools at a Crossroads* (2007). https://www.csnsw.catholic.edu.au/wp-content/uploads/2018/03/catholic-schools-at-a-crossroads.pdf
11 The Congregation for Catholic Education addresses some aspects of this challenge in its 2013 document *Educating to Intercultural Dialogue in Catholic Schools: Living in Harmony for a Civilization of Love*.
    http://www.vatican.va/roman_curia/congregations/ccatheduc/documents/rc_con_ccathe duc_ doc_20131028_dialogo-interculturale_en.html

We see the situation facing Catholic schools as having educational implications wider than ECSI envisages, and these educational implications *affect all teachers in a Catholic school* in their role as meaning-makers.

5. THE STRUCTURE OF A CULTURE

Not all aspects of a culture are of equal value. In analysing these and how they relate to one another, anthropologists refer to the various 'dimensions' of a culture.

5.1 Surface dimension: artefacts and norms

The most obvious dimension of any culture is what you can observe, its *surface dimension*. This includes what can be seen, such as artefacts, language, dress, patterns of behaviour, modes of communication, patterns of relationships, that which is celebrated, rituals of grieving, and so on. While someone can readily observe these, it is not immediately obvious to the observer *why things are the way they are*; the observations may be accurate, but the *meaning* for outsiders is unclear. The temptation for the untrained observer is to interpret what he or she sees from within his or her own cultural frame of reference. Early anthropologists soon learnt that such an approach does not yield accurate meaning.

If an outside observer asks a cultural insider why things are the way they are, the latter may struggle to give a clear answer because insiders take their culture for granted. However, insiders usually have access to cultural resources that enable them to find an answer.

It takes dialogue between an outsider asking questions, and an insider finding the answers, to uncover for the observer the meanings of what is being observed. In anthropology, reliable knowledge is therefore generated *intersubjectively*. Cultural knowledge cannot be generated objectively by an observer acting alone, as happens in fields such as physics or chemistry. Reliable knowledge in anthropology requires a different form of validation.

5.2 Values dimension: cultural values

Cultural values constitute the second dimension of a culture. Cultural values underpin what one sees at the surface level. They stand behind behavioural norms. They are celebrated in various forms of art, music and in ritual; they determine what is acceptable and not acceptable in communication and in human relationships.

Cultural values are *lived values*. They *characterise how people actually live*, not how they say they should live, or hope to live. The role of cultural values in underpinning norms of behaviour is important in all forms of group life, but particularly in organisations. Important cultural values often come to consciousness and have to be articulated when difficult decisions have to be made. Cultural values provide criteria in making key decisions.

The analysis of culture can be taken a step further if we ask: Why are some values in this culture seen as more important than others? Answering this question takes us to the final, or 'depth' dimension of the culture.

5.3 Depth dimension: cultural myth and worldview

The *depth or foundational dimension* of a culture is the level of *cultural myth and worldview*. As we have seen previously, a worldview embodies three components: what members of a group know and believe, what they value, and the sensibility (feelings) they bring to making sense of their life.

In cultural anthropology the word 'myth' has a technical meaning. This is a different usage from the way the word is used in common speech where it means 'something that is not really true'. In anthropology, a cultural myth holds the deepest truth about the group's identity. It is usually expressed as a narrative that combines historical facts with what a people hoped would be the case. Cultural narratives provide the means by which the worldview of culture is communicated within the group.

5.4 Structure and Australian culture

Australian culture rests on sets of cultural myths that establish its important cultural values. One set is associated with the early explorers and their efforts to cross the Blue Mountains, and to traverse the continent from north to south or east to west. This set also includes stories of the pioneers who cleared the bush in the face of great hardship and whose persistence eventually paid off. The myths convey the value of *'having a go'*. This particular set of myths is celebrated in the art of Frederick McCubbin, the stories and verse of Henry Lawson, the ballads of 'Banjo' Patterson, and is captured in the TV series appropriately named *Against the Wind*.

A second set of myths grew up around the Eureka stockade uprising and canonised the value that *'every man is entitled to a fair go'*.

A third series of myths relate to World War 1. in the events at Gallipoli, and later on the Western Front, the cultural value of *'sticking by your mates'* was born.

Finally, there are myths associated with migration to Australia that celebrate the value that *'everyone deserves a fair start'*, after which it is up to each person as to whether or not they succeed. Australians recognise that success takes effort and appreciate people making the effort, even when this does not result in success.

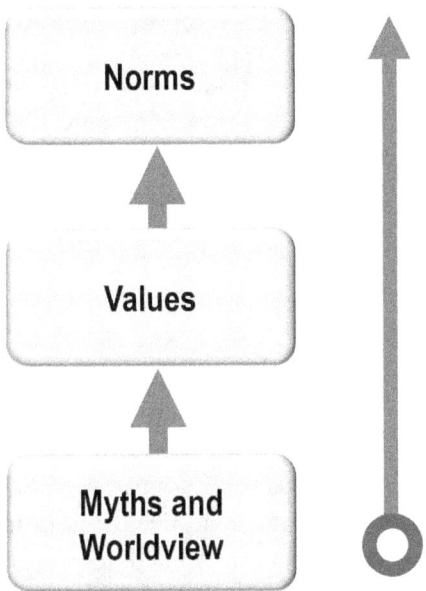

FIGURE 7.1: MYTHS, VALUES AND NORMS

As the examples above illustrate, cultural myths enshrine values conveyed through narratives. Cultural myths recount both elements of *what actually occurred and what people hope will be the case in the future*. That is, they embody their deepest aspirations. These aspirations underpin behavioural norms. This structure is set out schematically in the diagram above.

As times change, cultural myths are progressively updated and given a more contemporary 'spin'. For example, the stories of sporting heroes and heroines are often held up as contemporary parallels to much older stories. This process is known as *cultural recontextualisation*.

When people lose contact with their language and/or story, they soon lose a sense of who they are, and the social consequences can be devastating. This is why it is incumbent on leaders 'to keep the story alive'.[12] As an example, for Australian Aboriginal peoples 'the land' carries their story, so to dispossess them of their land is to rob them of their cultural identity. Unlike Europeans, Aboriginal peoples do not work from the cultural assumption that land is a private possession. For them it is a communal possession

---

12 Two volumes in the Mission and Education project which are relevant to this topic are Michael Green, *Now with Enthusiasm: Charism, God's Mission and Catholic Schools Today*. Mulgrave: Garratt Publishing, 2018, and Jim & Therese D'Orsa (eds and authors), *New Ways of Living the Gospel: Spiritual Traditions in Catholic Education*. Mulgrave: Garratt Publishing, 2015.

because their collective story is written on its features. A tragic situation has arisen in this country from the now long-standing clash of cultural worldviews in dealing with 'the land'.

Cultural narratives work most powerfully at the level of collective sensibility. People associated with a group strongly support actions that affirm their cultural values and react strongly to actions that seem to question these values. For instance, in Australian culture, anyone seen as 'not having a go' on the sporting field is held in contempt.

6. CULTURAL CHANGE

Since culture is conveyed through narratives, whoever controls the narrative controls the culture. In order to effect cultural change, it is often necessary to 'change the narrative'. This does not necessarily mean inventing a new story; it more commonly means reclaiming a narrative that has been lost, or some aspect that has faded from the collective memory. In recent Catholic experience, for example, we have reclaimed Jesus' teaching about the Kingdom of God.[13]

6.1 Charism and cultural change

Following Vatican II, religious congregations were asked to return to the charism of their founders. Many discovered that their knowledge of the founder was tied up in pious folklore and that it took some 'heavy lifting' by historians to reclaim the story of the founder.

The members of many congregations had lost track of the unique character of their founding mission. 'Renewal' for them has meant re-interpreting the charism of their founder and re-defining their specific mission in terms of contemporary needs. Catholic schools have benefitted greatly from these endeavours, and the focus that renewal has brought to shaping the value base on which schools work. This, in turn, has had important consequences for the culture of Catholic schools. The whole process has been an exercise in *re-contextualisation*.

6.2 Genesis story and renewal

A similar phenomenon occurs in the business world. People wishing to effect cultural change revisit the founding years of the organisation and reclaim the vision and values that drove the group at that time. In organisational

---

[13] Pope John Paul II devoted an entire chapter (chapter two) of *Redemptoris Missio* (1990) to a rich and important discussion of the Kingdom of God.
http://www.vatican.va/content/john-paul-ii/en/encyclicals/documents/hf_jp-ii_enc_07121990_redemptoris-missio.html.

life, *genesis stories* are seen as having particular importance. Genesis stories tell how the founder(s) overcame various difficulties to get the organisation functioning and set the trajectory for its growth.[14]

All groups have a 'genesis' story that they find necessary to return to from time to time. This helps to reorient the group and recapture the excitement that brought the group into being in the first place. All groups need 'renewal' strategies. These are important because of the way in which cultures are structured, and how they work as meaning systems.

It is worth remembering that the culture of any group always represents 'a success story'. The group's culture embodies a mythology of survival in the face of internal or external difficulties. Therefore, attempts to change the culture are usually resisted. Those leading them encounter, and generally have to develop, strategies to wear down what Michael Fullan names 'the impulse for rejection'.[15]

Faced with cultural change people quite validly ask: Why change a system that is working well for us? Without a good answer to this question, change goes nowhere.

7. TEACHER AS MEDIATOR OF MEANING

For the majority of our students, Australian cultural myths and values will feature strongly in the frame of reference they employ in making sense of life. While Australian culture is secular, it is not so in the sense of being necessarily anti-religious. However, its secularity includes the situation that faith now represents one option among the many available in choosing a frame of reference for making sense of life.

The aim of a Catholic school is to create learning conditions where students are *open to faith being an element in their personal worldview and, as a consequence, enabled to appreciate the relevance, and demands, of faith for their lives and their society's way of life (culture).* This is a more limited aim than once was the case, and reflects the change that has occurred in 'the conditions of belief' over the past five decades.

People today make *a conscious choice* when they include faith as an element in their personal worldview. Faced with growing pluralism in what people may believe, their choice goes beyond faith or no faith. Even if Christian faith is the option selected, there is the further issue of what kind of Christian faith will be fostered. The onus is on faith communities,

---

14   Edgar Schein *Organizational Culture and Leadership* (4th ed). San Francisco: Jossey-Bass, 2010, 210ff.
15   See Michael Fullan, *The New Meaning of Educational Change*, Fifth Edition. New York: Teachers College Press, 2016, 20. Fullan is quoting from the work of Peter Marris *Loss and Change,* London: Routledge and Kegan Paul, 1974.

including teachers in Catholic schools, to create the learning conditions in which students can make *informed choices* about what they believe and what they value from within the Christian tradition. The situation places considerable responsibility on all teachers in Catholic schools in their role as *mediators of meaning*.

8

THE WORLDVIEW OF FAITH

The consideration of worldview introduced in Chapter 6 raises a number of questions that need further exploration:

- *What do we mean when we talk about the 'worldview of faith' and say it can take multiple authentic forms?*
- *If a key pedagogical challenge now facing teachers in Catholic schools is to bring faith and culture into dialogue, what does this mean in practice?*
- *Against what back-story is this project taking place?*

The present chapter focuses on three things: general observations about the worldview of faith; the ways in which the worldview of faith can be understood; and the significance that pluralism in our faith understanding has for the way in which teachers in Catholic schools construe their authenticity as meaning-makers.

1. WORLDVIEW OF FAITH

The worldview of faith, like all worldviews, is made up of three elements:

- *what members of the faith community know and believe*
- *what they value, and*
- *the sensibilities they employ in making sense of their personal and collective faith experiences.*

This applies to all faiths, not just to Christian or Catholic faith. The worldview of faith can and does have multiple authentic forms within most faith groups. Our interest is the forms it can take within Catholic groups.

A compendium such as the *Catechism of the Catholic Church* is a formal statement of what the Catholic Church teaches on a comprehensive range of matters. It is not necessarily a statement of what individual Catholics know or believe. What people believe is shaped by their experience of living, and this often qualifies what they profess to believe.

Catholics exist as real persons living in concrete situations, and they are selective in what they choose to believe as well as in how they express their beliefs in daily life. Catholics in Kenya, for instance, express what they believe at Mass in a much more lively way than do Catholics in Australia. This is because they interpret what is happening from within a different cultural tradition.

Even within the same community, Catholics believe in ways that are different and selective. James and Evelyn Whitehead put the matter clearly in their seminal *Community of Faith* study when they state that no one believes it all, and no one believes all the time, but that is the task of the faith community.[1]

As a public worldview, the Catholic community sponsors the worldview of Catholic faith. In the final analysis, 'the faith' is what members of this faith community collectively believe. Catholic theology respects what is known as the *sensus fidei* – the intuitive sense that the global community has of what is correct belief. It is dialogue among local communities within the Church that refines this sense. Faith develops through a learning process of mutual self-correction carried out within a faith community. However, it develops from something, and that is an agreed set of foundational beliefs that are authoritatively taught. In Catholic education – schools, tertiary, parish etc. – teachers and leaders accept the responsibility to ensuring their educational processes take adequate account of the normativity of both Scripture and Tradition as a twofold witness to God's self-revelation in creation and salvation.[2]

Individuals and groups interpret the worldview of faith in different ways and two factors are important in making sense of this fact:

- *The teachings of the Church are not all of the same order. They exist in a hierarchy and people interpret the order within this hierarchy in different ways depending on their culture and experiences. Pope Francis interprets the worldview of faith through the lens of mercy and compassion. Others in the Church interpret it through the lens of Catholic social teaching, or a pro-life stance, or from the perspective of canon law.*
- *Even where there is agreement about beliefs and values, people bring different religious sensibilities to bear in making sense of their experiences.*

The consequence is that there is a variety of ways in which people come to understand the worldview of faith and incorporate this understanding into their personal worldview.

---

[1] James & Evelyn Whitehead, *Community of Faith: Models and Strategies for Building Christian Communities*. New York: Seabury Press, 1982, 10–13.
[2] There are a number of works which deal with the essence of the Catholic worldview, e.g. Thomas Groome, *What Makes Us Catholic: Eight Gifts for Life*. New York: HarperCollins, 2003, 133–168.

2. BRUEGGEMANN: PLURALISM WITHIN THE RELIGIOUS TRADITION

Highly regarded Old Testament scholar, Walter Brueggemann, explores an important aspect of pluralism within the Biblical tradition in his book *The Creative Word*.[3] He suggests that within this tradition there are three forms of religious knowing that ideally exist in creative tension with one another. In the following discussion we extrapolate from Brueggemann's work an awareness that, as the educational process proceeded within the communities of Israel, sensibilities associated with the three key forms of knowledge inevitably developed and deepened. It is these sensibilities that expressed individuals' worldviews, and continue to do so today.

2.1 Torah sensibility

The first sensibility is the *'Torah' sensibility*. People who view faith from this perspective are concerned primarily with what God has disclosed and how this is codified in law. Their sensibility determines what else they attend to in the tradition. Religion for this group is a matter of *correct beliefs, duty and obligation*.

In the cultural development of Israel this was the sensibility of its ruling elites – Israel's kings and its priestly class. The justification for a Torah sensibility is found in the first five books of the Old Testament, commonly named the Torah. While playing a vital role in the life of the community, when this sensibility runs unchecked, it provides a rationalisation for the abuse of power by religious elites, and marginalises ordinary people. This was the point in Jesus' critique of the Jewish elites in his time, and also one of the reasons he quickly gained popular support.

2.2 Prophetic sensibility

The oppression of the powerless by the powerful led to the emergence of a second form of religious knowing in the consciousness of Israel, referred to in the texts as 'a Word from the Lord' spoken by the prophets.

Prophetic sensibility, which is a sensibility of critique, developed in response to the suffering and marginalisation caused by those in power in Israel. Prophets reminded rulers that Israel had once been a captive people in Egypt and that God had liberated them from oppression, providing them with the chance to create a new social order.

---

3   Walter Brueggemann and Amy Erikson, *The Creative Word: Canon as Model of Biblical Education*. Second Edition. Philadelphia: Fortress Press, 2015. The first edition of this book (by Brueggemann) was published more than 30 years prior to the revised edition being prepared (1982). It remains a seminal work in Biblical education.

Prophets drew attention to the harmful effects economic decisions taken by Israel's elite had on the ordinary people, and pointed out the likely consequences of the king's flawed judgment. They challenged the uncritical way in which Israel's ruling class adopted the practices of neighbouring cultures, suggesting that by copying others uncritically, Israel was in danger of losing its distinctiveness as a covenant people.

Israel was a relatively small kingdom situated between the superpowers of the day. Its leaders had to walk a fine political line to ensure the kingdom survived. Prophets could foresee the consequences of poor political judgement and the suffering this would cause. When Israel was enslaved, it was the prophets who offered the people hope of a better future, a future stemming from authentically following the Torah. While being a prophet was not an enviable occupation, respect for the prophetic sensibility grew as Israel's history unfolded.

2.3 Wisdom sensibility

A third form of religious sensibility emerged as Israel encountered other cultures and came to appreciate the wisdom they contained. It developed as an additional 'mode of knowing' and grew out of the importance of Israel's location in the geo-politics of the day. Israel and its thinkers were exposed successively to Egyptian, Babylonian, Persian, Greek and Roman cultures during the years in which the Bible was being created and then compiled as literature. As inter-cultural learning occurred, the third form of knowing that developed was what Brueggemann calls a *wisdom* mode of knowledge. The sensibility associated with appreciation of this form of knowing provided an orientation to the values of other cultures. This led to a process of discernment of the wisdom found in cultures beyond Israel, followed by critical incorporation into Jewish religious tradition., It was a hotly contested sensibility, since sections of the Jewish community saw little value in integrating their faith with the wisdom of other cultures in this way.

For Brueggemann, it is no accident that the Old Testament is made up of collections of books known as the Torah, the Prophets and Writings (which include the Wisdom literature).[4] He suggests that not only is the *content* of the Bible revelatory, but so too is *the process by which it was created and organised*. God was, he contends, teaching the Jewish people that faith can be, and needs to be, approached from different standpoints. *Pluralism in religious understanding is evident in the very structure of the Bible.*

Brueggemann further suggests that if a faith community is to preserve its identity over time, it needs to keep these three forms of knowing in

---

[4] The Writings is a miscellaneous collection of literature which includes the Wisdom literature.

conversation and in balance with one another. This is a crucial *educational project* for any faith community to undertake if it wishes to survive beyond one generation.[5]

3. THREE TYPES OF CHRISTIAN THEOLOGY

Independently of Brueggemann, Protestant Church historian Justo Gonzales, and Catholic theologians Stephen Bevans and Roger Schroeder, consider that there are three types of religious sensibility found in the Christian theological tradition. They call these (somewhat unimaginatively) Type A, Type B and Type C theology.

3.1 Type A theology: faith is a matter of obligation

Type A theology interprets the worldview of faith from the perspective of *law, obligation and duty*. It initially developed in the Roman city of Carthage in Northern Africa and its principal exponent was Tertullian (155–220 AD), who may have been a lawyer by profession as he adopts a quite legalistic understanding of the Christian message. For Tertullian and his followers, Christian faith had little to gain from any encounter with culture, particularly Greek culture.

The strength of Type A theology is its insistence on clear teaching. The weakness of Type A theology is its tendency to interpret the faith in terms of doctrines and laws that are seen as unchangeable, leading to inflexible pastoral responses to concrete issues (such as divorced people approaching communion). Type A theology parallels Brueggemann's Torah sensibility.

3.2 Type B theology: faith as the search for truth

Type B theology developed in Alexandria in present–day Egypt. Its early proponent was Origen, who had been educated in Greek philosophy and culture. Origen (184–253 AD) was regarded as a brilliant teacher at the School of Alexandria, the major intellectual centre of the late Roman Empire.

Type B theology centres on faith understood *as a search for the truth*. Origen's major project was to show that Christian faith was compatible with Greek philosophy.[6] What these two intellectual traditions shared was a common search for the truth. Origen's work opened up a dialogue between

---
5 Brueggemann, 'Canon and the Educational Repertoire' in *The Creative Word*, 1–13.
6 Origen was influenced by the philosophy of Plato. The project he began was later taken up by St Augustine (354–450) who was a Neo-Platonist. Augustine was *the* theologian of the Catholic Church for a millennium.

Christian faith and Greek and Roman cultures. Type B theology shares much in common with Brueggemann's wisdom sensibility.

The strength of Type B theology is its unrelenting search for the truth. The weakness in Type B theology is that its proponents can become fixated on a particular version of the truth that, when applied to concrete pastoral situations, fails to understand the nuances of lived experience. As with Type A theology, this leads to intransigent and inflexible positions.

In the perspective of Type B theology, culture presents a challenge to Christian faith that must be addressed through dialogue. Seeking to respond to this challenge was integral to the pontificates of Popes John Paul II and Benedict XVI.

3.3 Type C theology: faith as pastoral response to the God of history

Type C theology originated in present-day Turkey. It was exported to Western Europe by Irenaeus. This occurred when he and some of his compatriots were forced to flee there during one of the many Roman persecutions.

Irenaeus (c125–c202AD) was elected as the bishop of Lyons in modern-day France. His experiences there led him to bring a *pastoral sensibility* to his understanding of Christian faith and the leadership of his growing community.

For Irenaeus, God is to be found in the events of human history and therefore in human cultures that are reshaped in response to these events. The 'seeds of the Gospel' are, for Irenaeus, to be found in every culture. The task of the faith community is to discover them and nurture them into new life so that insights found in the Gospel become incorporated directly into a people's way of life. In the perspective of Type C theology, the 'seeds of the Gospel' are sown by the Holy Spirit *creatively active in human history* and are found in the positive hopes and dreams that inspire a culture. Among these are hopes for peace and justice. Type C theology has much in common with Brueggemann's prophetic sensibility.

Of the three foundational theologians discussed above, Irenaeus was the only one who had any pastoral experience, and this shaped how he interpreted the worldview of faith.

The three orientations see the relationship between faith and culture in different ways. Type A's adherents see little need for any relationship. Type B's view both faith and culture as aiming at a common end, 'truth'. Type C, more strongly valuing history and human experience, accepts culture as having a religious dimension. Types B and C theologians therefore see great value in a dialogue between faith and culture.

3.4 Religious sensibilities in Church life

When we look at the various controversies running in the Catholic Church at any one time, it is possible to analyse them in terms of the types of theology (interpretation of the worldview of faith) that the participants espouse. For instance, Pope Francis seems to view the world from the perspective of Type C theology. His approach is clearly pastoral and his concern for the marginalised of the earth and the poor is unequivocal. He seems well aware that God's creative Spirit is at work in human history and that there are boundary questions in human life that cannot always be resolved quickly, but which must be resolved through ongoing dialogue and discernment.

The strength of Type C theology is its pastoral understanding of the complexity of human experience and its valuing of both history and culture as the loci of God's action in the world. Consequently, its proponents value salvation in history as well as beyond history. This stance brings them into dispute with those who see salvation as lying solely or mainly beyond history.

Coming predominantly from a Type C perspective, Pope Francis criticises those who make an idol out of 'truth' or 'law'. Consistent with this position, he has been conspicuous in downgrading the role of the Congregation for the Doctrine of the Faith and its pursuit of theologians exploring boundary questions in theology. In this respect he differs from his two immediate predecessors. His stance on issues such as refugees, the poor, and care for the earth is clearly prophetic.

3.5 Pluralism in the worldview of faith

The point to note here is that *the worldview of faith has no single or definitive articulation* even at the highest levels of the Church. It can be expressed authentically within any of the three sensibilities identified in this chapter. *None is inherently better than the others.* As a total articulation, each of the three is limited, as Brueggemann suggests. All three are needed to preserve the vitality of the faith community. All three are to be encouraged in the Church's educational endeavours and kept in appropriate *tension and balance*; it is through dialogue among them that the faith tradition develops and remains vital.

The notion that there can be pluralism *within* the Catholic tradition comes as news to many teachers in Catholic schools bought up to accept the now often rejected 'one way/our way or nothing' stance on the Christian faith tradition. Equally, many Catholics think of robust controversies among senior Catholic clerics as something of a scandal. The conservative Catholic press reports the situation this way. However, if we accept Brueggemann's argument, robust discussion is to be expected, and is a sign of life!

It is worth noting that all three modes of knowing outlined by Brueggemann in regard to the Old Testament *have the Torah at their core*. All three types of Christian theology *have the Gospel and its Kingdom values at their core*. In the Christian case, where the types differ is in the sensibility that people bring to interpreting the Gospel, and the way this plays out in determining what they value, what they choose to believe as a consequence, and how these together then shape what they choose to do and to become.

4. SOME PEDAGOGICAL IMPLICATIONS

Pluralism within the Christian tradition raises some important questions for teachers in Catholic schools and, in particular for how they see their role as meaning-makers and moderators in the dialogue between faith and culture. The following questions bear thinking about:

- *What sensibility shapes how I understand the worldview of faith?*
- *What faith beliefs do I really hold?*
- *What Christian values do I see as really important?*
- *How does it feel to be Catholic? How do I wish it felt?*
- *How does my religious sensibility impact on what I think is important in student learning?*
- *How does my religious sensibility shape my understanding of culture and its importance in the life of my students?*
- *How does my religious sensibility shape my pedagogy?*

In exploring these questions. it is useful to reflect on when important choices have had to be made and how you made them, the beliefs that were in play then, the values that justified what you chose, and so on. This enables you to identify *lived values* (the values that do shape your life) as distinct from *espoused values* (the values that people suggest ought to shape your life or that you say shape your life).

Some of the above questions will be new to teachers, but this does not make them any less important. They challenge stereotypical ways in which the worldview of Catholic faith has been presented. Teachers in Catholic schools have to come to grips with their own understanding of the worldview of faith and how they choose to access it if they are to be authentic as meaning-makers for their students. In a liminal era, when what is considered 'normal' is being re-defined, the personal authenticity of teachers is crucial.

Faith is something that people grow into and this growth parallels and feeds off other human experiences, so one size does not fit all. While people can grow in faith, they can also grow out of faith as life unfolds. This is why a pastoral approach is needed in understanding the complexity of human life and living.

9

THE CHANGING RELATIONSHIP BETWEEN FAITH AND CULTURE: FROM CHRISTENDOM TO VATICAN II

A major aim in building a pedagogical relationship with students in Catholic schools is to help them bring faith and culture into dialogue in making sense of their lives. This is a necessary step in being able to see the worldview of faith as a plausible framework for meaning-making, one that they can 'befriend' and in which they can feel at home.[1]

Culture and faith play complementary roles in helping young people make sense of life because they draw on vital but different sources of wisdom. In a Catholic pedagogy, teachers seek to draw together these two sources of insight in coming to decisions about how best to help students learn, and flourish as individuals and as members of their civic and religious communities.

Since the beginning of the modern era, culture and faith have existed in an uneasy tension. In everyday life, culture and faith exist in an *interdependent*, rather than an independent relationship. For instance, faith needs both the symbolic and linguistic resources of a culture to find meaningful expression. Most Western societies and cultures still opt for an implicitly Christian value system, even while many distance themselves from the faith that stands behind such a system. As a consequence, both faith and cultural communities share common values, hold in common a number of assumptions about what it means to be human, and share a common language.

The task of bringing faith and culture together in making sense of life for students is ongoing. Teachers participate in this task at a certain, very influential, point in students' life journeys, and so it is helpful for them to know why the present situation is the way that it is.

---

1 In their seminal text *Methods in Ministry*, James and Evelyn Whitehead propose a model of theological reflection that brings faith and culture together in making sense of life. They suggest that, for this to happen, it is necessary to 'befriend' both faith and culture. By this they mean adopting a critical, but empathic, stance to both. When we 'befriend' someone we do not expect them to be perfect. We accept them for who they are, aware of their limitations as well as their attractive strengths. James & Evelyn Whitehead, *Method in Ministry*. Revised edition. Kansas City: Rowman and Littlefield, 1995.

In this chapter and the next we explore the currents of thought that have led Catholics to where they are now, providing something of a backstory to the present relationship between faith and culture. Our questions are:

- *Where are we in the unfolding story of how faith and culture relate in Western societies?*
- *How does knowing where we are help or hinder teachers in Catholic schools in supporting students to become meaning-makers?*

1. AN EXCLUSIVE FRAMEWORK IS SHATTERED

1.1 Social imaginary of Christendom

From the 4th to the 16th centuries, the Catholic faith was such an integral aspect of European cultures that it is difficult to speak of faith and culture as separate entities. The influence of the Christian faith in the era known as *Christendom* was all-pervasive. The intellectual world of Europe in this period was dominated by 'truth' as defined by the Catholic Church. This made Church leaders incredibly powerful, so much so that they could use civic power to enforce Catholic beliefs and practices and, to their own advantage, negotiate Church exemptions from various imposts placed on other civic organisations.[2]

Long before the Reformation, Catholicism had become the established religion of Europe. This meant that it became integral to political and intellectual life. Catholic leaders came to take this position as normal and did not see it as problematic. Why would they? They lived in what Charles Taylor calls *a social imaginary*, a view of society that very much favoured the Church in general, and them personally.

In the social imaginary of Christendom, order on earth was presumed to reflect the order existing in heaven, with the king or pope at the top of a hierarchy of social orders that defined people's position in society.[3] The majority of people interpreted this social order as willed by God.[4] In the worldview of Christendom you were born into a social order and

---

2   The situation we know as 'Christendom' was not as monolithic as we may tend to think when we consider its legacy from a distance. The work of Church historian John O'Malley, in his *Vatican 1: The Making of the Ultramontane Church.* Cambridge MA: The Belknap Press, 2018 provides a view of the pluralism characterising the Church. An example of this lies in the relationships between Church and state, pre and even post the standardising that the Council of Trent attempted to achieve.
3   The term 'holy orders' is a linguistic remnant of this era.
4   During Christendom the matter of who was at the top of the social hierarchy, king or pope, was never quite resolved. In consequence, popes saw it as important to control people and territory in much the same manner as kings, and kings saw their role as God-given and carrying religious responsibilities. Some kings were crowned by popes, and some popes were, in effect, the appointees of kings.

took your place in that order for granted. You did not challenge it. During Christendom, faith was understood as legitimating this social imaginary.

1.2 Cracks appear in the social imaginary of Christendom

In the 16th century, the faith tradition as then understood spread to what became known as the 'New World' where explorers from a largely Catholic background encountered peoples who were radically different from themselves and had a totally different design for living (culture). So different were they that many Europeans wondered if these new peoples were really human! The championing of indigenous people's full humanity by missionaries stood in stark contrast to the attitudes and behaviour of European colonists.[5] The 'new world' experience alerted many people in Europe to the possibility of non-Christian civilisations.

1.3 The Reformation: a new form of religious consciousness in Europe

The Reformation (early 16th to mid 17th century) saw a decisive break within the Christian world of Europe. Firstly, it generated cultural and religious fault lines, and then fractured the worldview of faith as it had been understood in Christendom. This cultural change was aided by the advent of a new technology – the printing press – that facilitated the rapid spread of new ideas.

Protestants not only held different beliefs from Catholics, they pioneered a different way of life from that experienced in so-called Catholic countries. As a result of the Reformation *new forms of critical consciousness became possible.*

Catholic leaders faced serious problems as the Reformation took shape. Church life and governance had deteriorated. Church leaders were roundly criticised for their inaction and this was bound to produce an overreaction, which it did.

To respond to the reformers, Pope Paul III convened an ecumenical council and bishops, mainly from Europe, assembled at Trento in Northern Italy. The Council of Trent ran from 1545 until 1563, the extended timeframe being due to interruptions caused by the political upheavals of the period. The dual purpose of the Council of Trent was to condemn the theological errors of the reformers and to initiate reforms within the Roman Catholic Church. Catholics at the time, including the clergy, had very limited theological training; there were few guidelines for the selection

---

5 While Catholic missionaries agitated for the rights of indigenous peoples in 'the New World', they generally did not at the time carry this through to agitating against the slave trade from Africa which was then in full swing.

of clergy; and sacramental theology was rudimentary. All of this changed as a result of the Council of Trent. As an outcome of this Council, ordination to the priesthood became *the* source of status, power and authority in the Catholic Church and the role of the non-ordained was diminished in consequence – a situation that would remain largely unchallenged for the next five centuries. Catholic leaders had 'reformed' the Church by turning it into a clerical institution.

1.4 Separation of the Christian worldview from public life

If the aim of the Catholic counter-reformers was to halt the spread of Protestantism as a religious and cultural movement in Europe, it failed. In the 17th century religious divisions assumed even more disastrous proportions during the Thirty Years' War (1618–1648). A long, very complicated, and brutal, series of conflicts was fought along religious and political lines. Due to its tragic consequences – huge loss of life, the devastation of vast areas of central Europe, and economic depression – the worldview of Christian faith, in its now multiple and competing formulations, was discredited. It was now no longer viewed as the primary interpretive framework for making sense of life. The notion that religion was divisive and should be excluded from civic affairs slowly gathered support, as thinkers in Europe began to formulate a new social imaginary, one quite different from that of Christendom.

Other circumstances that gave impetus to this development included the emergence of 'Enlightenment thinking' (see below), increasing world trade, the economic development of city-states, and the emergence of a new merchant class (including bankers). These had no place in the old social imaginary.

1.5 Emergence of the Enlightenment

The chaos and trauma of events in Europe in the 17th century led to the emergence of Enlightenment thinking in the 18th century. As the name suggests, thinkers of the period posed radical new questions such as:

- *Can we organise society in another way?*
- *On what value base should this re-organisation proceed?*
- *How can we do it?*

These thinkers argued that such questions should be answered on purely *rational grounds,* without appeal to the contested religious beliefs that had led to the undoing of Europe and untold human suffering. If culture is understood as 'a people's, more or less comprehensive, more or less successful, design for living together peacefully in their particular environment',[6] then the Enlightenment project sought to establish culture in Europe on a new basis. This would be done by changing the ideational environment and denying validity to dogmatic religious beliefs. They wished to change the basis on which truth and knowledge depended.

Catholic Church leaders of the period had become so incorporated into the *ancien regimes* of Europe, and also into a political *status quo* which they regarded as God-given, that they rejected the Enlightenment project outright. This reaction left the Catholic Church in a weak position when an era of change initiated by the French Revolution (1789–1793) swept across Europe.

Ordinary people, yearning to be free of the corruption and mismanagement that characterised the *ancien regimes* in their respective countries, perceived the Church as siding with their oppressors and as the enemy of 'progress'. This became the catch-cry of *modernity*. Church leaders were on the defensive, and found themselves condemning modernity's positions on human rights, freedom of religion, freedom of conscience, separation of Church and state – all of which would later be adopted at the Second Vatican Council (1962-5)! Catholic leaders trapped faithful Church members into a very conservative stance because they did not read the signs of the times in which they lived. As a consequence, they were oblivious to the better aspirations of what was threatening.

The Catholic Church's position of political privilege made it an easy target for modern states seeking to finance political change and promote the new secular ideology among their people. They simply confiscated Church property and sold it.

Growing differences between the Christian churches and modern states contributed to the emergence of a new worldview, *the worldview of modern culture* as a novel and powerful interpretive framework for making sense of life. The modern period's new 'plan for living' diverged sharply from that envisaged by Catholic leaders. The division between faith and modern culture opened the pathway to secularisation. This pathway would develop several discernible 'faces'.

---

6 This is the definition of culture offered by Catholic mission anthropologist Louis Luzbetak. See Chapter 7 above.

2. SECULARISATION AS A FEATURE OF MODERN CULTURES

2.1 Secularisation of 'truth'

The sociological and economic developments noted above coincided with the rise of science. Scientific truth depended on experiment, accurate observation and measurement. Its method was seen to provide legitimation to its findings, which therefore did not require legitimation from other authorities. This was a new development in Christian Europe, the importance of which could scarcely be overestimated.

Faith and science were initially viewed as complementary by both Church leaders and early philosophers such as Francis Bacon. This position was expressed as the 'two books' theory of revelation, holding that God had revealed Godself through both the 'Book of the Bible' and the 'Book of Nature'. Church leaders supported this theory until 'science' was applied to the study of human beings in an attempt to discover 'the laws of human nature'. When these were proposed as alternatives to the 'laws of God', as understood in the Judeo-Christian tradition, trouble was inevitable.

In the 17th and 18th centuries, for an increasing number of educated people, the notion that an *exclusively* Catholic worldview had any mortgage on 'truth' became increasingly implausible. While many agreed that the laws of human nature were set in place by God and that humans could discover them through science, they also believed that, if God did create these laws, it would be contradictory for God to interfere with how they worked in practice. They further argued that events specific to the Christian narrative, such as the virgin birth and Jesus' resurrection, could not have happened. Neither could Jesus have worked miracles since a miracle, by definition, means that God would be countermanding God's own laws. This particular worldview is known as Deism. It developed in early modernity and played a powerful role in the political developments in Britain and the United States. As a philosophical position, it rejected revelation altogether and saw reason as the only necessity in establishing the existence of a supreme being. As Charles Taylor points out, the emergence of Deism was the last stop on the route to asking: is the concept of God really necessary?[7]

As the modern period unfolded, science was seen as providing the new basis for truth, and the role of Church leaders as arbiters of truth was largely disregarded. *Secularisation had become a part of modern life and an assumption on which modern culture increasingly depended.*

---

7   See Charles Taylor's 'Providential Deism' in *A Secular Age*, 221–269.

2.2 Secularisation of government

The response of successive popes to the emergence of the new culture in Europe was essentially to 'circle the Catholic wagons' and reaffirm the worldview of faith as it had existed in Christendom, ignoring the cultural changes that had taken place, and the aspirations and thinking that lay behind them.

As modern states were created, a new social imaginary developed, based on democracy, liberty and equality. People aspired to govern themselves rather than to put their trust in a social order controlled by kings or popes. The level of organisation required to run a modern state now lay beyond the competence of a single person and his/her group of advisors.

Modern states met the challenges of popular government in different ways leading to a differentiation in national cultures and a differentiation of social and political institutions within each state. To keep the peace, modern lawmakers determined not to endorse any faith position as normative. Thus, politics in Europe was secularised during the 18th century. In the 19th century this development quickly spread to European colonies around the world, including Australia. As one of the major institutions created in the modern period, and regarded as the responsibility of governments, public education was also made compulsory and secular.

2.3 'The long 19th century'

Successive popes of the 19th and early 20th centuries saw what was happening around the world as unholy and an unmitigated disaster for the Church[8]. Popes of this period, that Church historian John O'Malley SJ calls 'the long 19th century'[9], were drawn from the Italian nobility and shared the sensibilities of that class. They still interpreted the worldview of faith in terms of Christendom, despite the cultural changes occurring about them (and from which they were largely insulated). The division between faith and culture that began with the secularisation of knowledge, grew wider with the secularisation of government.[10]

---

8 A form of secularisation in the 18th and 19th centuries that we do not experience today is the secularisation of church property. In many European countries church property, particularly that owned historically by monastic orders, was effectively 'nationalised' without compensation and orders disbanded by government decree. In Italy, this form of secularisation applied to the Papal States that at the time made up one third of present-day Italy.
9 John W. O'Malley, 'The long nineteenth century' in *What Happened at Vatican II*. Cambridge Mass: the Belknap Press, 2008, 53–92. O'Malley is using an idea utilised by others such as Eric Hobsbawn in analysing the history of ideas from the French Revolution to the outbreak of World War 1. Others had used similar terminology in identifying other historical periods.
10 This division would grow even wider in the 19th and 20th centuries with the secularisation of services previously supplied by the churches such a health, education, social welfare and aged care.

If at the Council of Trent in the 16th century, the Catholic Church 'circled the Catholic wagons', the circle was drawn even tighter at the first Vatican Council (1869–70) where the doctrine of papal infallibility was proclaimed.[11] In uncertain and ungodly times the bishops saw that the solution lay in re-establishing certainty through strong leadership centred on the authority of the Pope.[12]

2.4 Catholic reaction to modernity

The popes of 'the long 19th century'[13] (1800–1918) condemned a world 'gone wrong' and condemned the 'injustices' visited on the Church. As modernity took shape, they rejected it, unable to separate the worthy aspirations in its worldview for human betterment, democracy and freedom, from the excesses and shortcomings that had characterised its beginnings. Any suggestion *from within the Church* about the need to re-contextualise the worldview of faith in order to take account of the cultural transition underway was condemned and the protagonists persecuted.

Church leaders seemed to find it hard to comprehend *that there had been, or indeed could be, a split between faith and culture*. Their understanding of the worldview of faith did not allow for a possibility that later generations of Catholics would take for granted. For example, many Catholic bishops initially interpreted the emerging demand for human rights, central to the modern secular mindset, as an attack on the established order of society, rather than as a cry to recognise the dignity of all people.

Some Catholic leaders did recognise that the hopes of modernity could be aligned with Jesus' Kingdom values. They saw the broader need for the Church to enter into dialogue with modern thinking and culture. These leaders had great sympathy for the many educated Catholics who now found themselves living within the orbit of competing worldviews. These competing worldviews are perhaps best expressed as those of Church leadership with its social imaginary drawn from Christendom, and those of the modern social imaginary within which people now made sense of their day-to-day lives.[14]

In the mid-20th century a number of these leaders became the driving force behind many of the 'progressive' positions adopted at the Second

---

11   *The Catechism of the Catholic Church*, 889–891, explains the meaning of Church teaching about the infallibility of the Church as a whole, and that of its leader, the Pope, when, by virtue of his office, he teaches at the most official level ('ex cathedra') about faith and morals.
12   Not everyone at the time agreed with this view including the recently canonised John Henry Newman and a number of the bishops attending from the US.
13   O'Malley, 2008, 53–92.
14   There is irony in the title of Australian theologian James McEvoy's book *Leaving Christendom for Good: Church-World Dialogue in a Secular Age*, the implication being that weaning Church leaders from the worldview of Christendom represented a positive development.

Vatican Council (1962–5).[15] Pope John XXIII called the Council. Drawn from peasant stock, he was the only pope of the modern era who did not belong to the Italian nobility. In the period following the Council, some theologians who had been influential in its deliberations played a key role in the development of theologies that sought to open up a dialogue between faith as it had been articulated in the Council's documents, and the culture of modernity.

---

15 Historians often refer to the 'long nineteenth century' in regard to the period from 1800–1914. Here, highly respected Church historian John O'Malley SJ refers to the period from 1900 to the mid-20th century as 'the long 19th century', so little did Catholic thinking change in this period. The clericalism that characterised Church culture in the 'long 19th century' remains largely in place to this day as Australian bishops appearing before the recent Royal Commission into Institutional Responses to Child Sexual Abuse have freely admitted (2013–2017).

10

THE CHANGING RELATIONSHIP BETWEEN FAITH AND CULTURE: VATICAN II TO THE PRESENT

In the previous chapter we traced the changing nature of the relationship between faith and culture from Christendom to the Second Vatican Council. In this chapter we continue that exploration. We begin by focusing in on the Council and its work in forging a relationship with modernity. However, the rapid societal and cultural changes which have occurred across the half-century since the close of the Council have resulted in a series of world synods dealing with various topics. Held at regular intervals, these have become a major way of continuing the theological developments initiated at the Council.

1. VATICAN II: THE WORLDVIEW OF FAITH BECOMES MORE INCLUSIVE

Events of the early to mid-20th century – the experience of living through two world wars with their accompanying horrors, the Cold War, and the struggles of colonised peoples to gain their independence – slowly brought about a major change of consciousness in Church leaders. This was the historical and cultural context in which Pope John XIII decided to call the Second Vatican Council (1962–5).[1]

1.1 A Global Council

Over two thousand bishops attended this Council, and their final reflections are recorded in the sixteen official Council documents that remain normative for the Church. The bishops acknowledged the divisions emerging between the worldview of Catholic faith in areas of the world where the Church was long established, as well as issues relating to faith and culture in the many societies and cultures in which the Church was more recently established.

---

[1] Pope John XXIII was the first pope for over 100 years who was not a member of the Italian nobility. He was the son of peasant farmers and rose through the Church's hierarchy as a diplomat. He had an understanding of the world shaped, among other influences, by his experiences of living outside Europe, for example in Istanbul.

Vatican II was the first Church Council at which there was a *global representation* of bishops. This meant that, for the first time, the Eurocentric thinking that had dominated Catholic theology and the Church's pastoral ministries for centuries, was challenged by the presence and input of those who participated.[2] And, since many peoples of the world do not think within a European framework, nor operate according to European sensibilities, nor readily adopt European values, the bishops also acknowledged the need for faith and cultures to be brought into serious dialogue. A major change in perspective is evident in the Council's *Pastoral Constitution on the Church in the Modern World (Gaudium et Spes)* that has a large section devoted to the relationship between culture and faith.[3]

While progressive in their understanding of the important role culture plays in how humans make sense of life, many bishops attending the Council did not seem to recognise that *the Church itself has a culture*[4]. So they did not anticipate the challenges that lay ahead in making changes to a Church culture that had remained largely static for many centuries. Nor did they anticipate what would be involved in making changes to an interpretive framework that many Catholics had been wrongly taught was unchangeable.

In any cultural change, those with much to lose are those in power. As a result, they are usually the first to oppose cultural change. As an institution, the Catholic Church proved little different from other institutions in this respect. In consequence, the implementation of the decrees of Vatican II has been a long, selective, and painful process still very far from completed.

1.2 Calls for 'dialogue with the world' and for the 'evangelisation of cultures'

Pope John XXIII died during the Council and was succeeded by Pope Paul VI. In 1964 Paul VI issued an encyclical (*Ecclesiam Suam*) setting out his strategic priorities for the benefit of the whole Church (and, pointedly, for the bishops attending the Council). One of these priorities was to open up a dialogue with the modern world. Expressed in a rather quaint language style this priority reads as follows:

---

2 This challenge came as a major shock to leaders of the Vatican bureaucracy who had supervised preparations for the Council. A number of the documents they prepared for discussion were rejected, including the document on Catholic schooling. Many of these departments assumed they spoke with the authority of the Pope. At the Council they found out that this was not the case.
3 *Gaudium et Spes* (The Church in the Modern World), 53–62.
4 The insights of cultural anthropology translate quite closely to the 'way of life' of organisations and institutions, so the term 'culture' is widely used in connection with both.

> But it seems to Us that the sort of relationship for the Church to establish with the world should be more in the nature of a dialogue ... We do not mean unrealistic dialogue. It must be adapted to the intelligences of those to whom it is addressed, and it must take account of the circumstances. Dialogue with children is not the same as dialogue with adults, nor is dialogue with Christians the same as dialogue with non-believers. But this method of approach is demanded nowadays by the prevalent understanding of the relationship between the sacred and the profane. It is demanded by the dynamic course of action which is changing the face of modern society. It is demanded by the pluralism of society, and by the maturity man (sic) has reached in this day and age. Be he religious or not, his secular education has enabled him to think and speak and conduct a dialogue with dignity.
>
> Moreover, the very fact that he engages in a dialogue of this sort is proof of his consideration and esteem for others, his understanding and his kindness. He detests bigotry and prejudice, malicious and indiscriminate hostility, and empty, boastful speech.
>
> If, in our desire to respect a man's freedom and dignity, his conversion to the true faith is not the immediate object of our dialogue with him, we nevertheless try to help him and to dispose him for a fuller sharing of ideas and convictions.
>
> Our dialogue, therefore, presupposes that there exists in us a state of mind which we wish to communicate and to foster in those around us. It is the state of mind which characterizes the man (sic) who realizes the seriousness of the apostolic mission and who sees his own salvation as inseparable from the salvation of others. His constant endeavour is to get everyone talking about the message which it has been given to him to communicate.[5]

Following the Council, Pope Paul VI developed these comments further in his apostolic exhortation *Evangelii Nuntiandi* (1975). This is his summary of the outcomes of the 1974 world synod on evangelisation. It is highly regarded on many counts, not least for its discussions about faith and culture. In it Paul VI noted that: 'The split between the Gospel and culture is without a doubt the drama of our time ...'[6] He argued that the Church needed to expand its concept of mission to include 'evangelizing cultures', a task that should go hand in hand with the Church's 'evangelizing herself'. As he wrote:

> The Gospel, and therefore evangelization, are certainly not identical with culture, and they are independent in regard to all cultures. Nevertheless, the

---

5 Paul VI, *Ecclesiam Suam*, ## 78–80.
6 Paul VI, *Evangelii Nuntiandi*, # 20.

kingdom which the Gospel proclaims is lived by men (sic) who are profoundly linked to a culture, and the building up of the kingdom cannot avoid borrowing the elements of human culture or cultures. Though independent of cultures, the Gospel and evangelization are not necessarily incompatible with them; rather they are capable of permeating them all without becoming subject to any one of them.

The split between the Gospel and culture is without a doubt the drama of our time, just as it was of other times. Therefore, every effort must be made to ensure a full evangelization of culture, or more correctly of cultures. They have to be regenerated by an encounter with the Gospel. But this encounter will not take place if the Gospel is not proclaimed.[7]

The teachings of Vatican II and its immediate aftermath provided important guidelines for recontextualising the worldview of faith in the modern era, that is, for working out how faith might legitimately permeate modern culture 'in depth and down to its very roots'.[8]

2. POSTMODERN CRITIQUE OF MODERNITY

Vatican II took place in the mid-1960s, just prior to the time when a number of the fundamental assumptions on which modernity was built came under sustained scrutiny from scholars known as the postmodern critics.[9]

The catalyst for postmodern critiques of modernity was human suffering, that of the vast numbers of people forced to rebuild their lives after World War II, and that of the many victims created during the great political upheavals that occurred as people in colonised territories broke free of their overlords. These events fuelled a search for radical alternatives to the 'way of life' long taken for granted by people in the West.

The Church teaches that the Holy Spirit is creatively at work in the whole world, that is, in all people and in all cultures. The lesson from the struggles and failures of the modern period was that this presence is encountered in the best aspirations of a society and culture and that Church leaders need to discern what these are. Failure to do this simply exacerbates tensions between faith and culture and fails to acknowledge where the Holy Spirit is at work.

Vatican II emphasised the importance of baptism in the life of the Christian and the responsibilities that go with it. It encouraged a greater

---

7 Ibid.
8 Ibid.
9 Jean Francois Lyotard in 1979 wrote *The Postmodern Condition: A Report on Knowledge* in which he coined the term 'postmodernism' in a philosophic context.

role for all the baptised in the Church's mission.[10] Its teachings often ran counter to the *prevailing Church culture* built around an exclusively male clerical leadership that showed a degree of degeneration into the self-serving culture known as clericalism.[11]

2.1 Paul VI's call for 'Church renewal'

In *Ecclesiam Suam* Pope Paul VI had set a second goal for the Council – renewal of the Church. He saw the need for all Church members to refocus on the core mission of making Jesus and his message known, and of continuing Jesus' healing ministry. In practice, this meant reclaiming Jesus' teaching about the Kingdom of God, a teaching that scripture scholars agree is central to the way Jesus understood his mission.

When we talk about the worldview of faith, we are talking about Jesus' vision of the kingdom of God that should be present not only in the lives of individuals and of groups, but also embedded in the Church's own culture. Further, one of the vital ministries of the Church is to make present the kingdom of God wherever possible in all human cultures.[12] The Kingdom of God has both material and spiritual dimensions. It embraces relationships, social structures, and the natural world. It does not exist in history in any final form; rather, in this changing world its presence is always provisional. The Kingdom of God provides a transforming goal for all Catholic education, and thus for the kind of pedagogies which will enable students to commit to its agendas.

2.2 'Postmodern' has multiple meanings

Vatican II sought to create a new dialogue with modern culture. Today, however, Catholics live not only with the cultural realities of modernity which continue to exist, but with what is termed 'postmodernity' and also 'postsecularism', and this adds an overlay of complexity to the relationship between faith and culture. However, what postmodernity means precisely is highly contested, the term 'postmodern' being used in a number of ways.

---

10 *Lumen Gentium*, 10.
11 *Lumen Gentium*, for example, emphasised the call to holiness of all the faithful (Chapter V). This call to holiness was again taken up by Pope Francis in 2018 in *Gaudete et Exsultate*.
12 The Church was slow to recognise the contribution the social sciences could make to an understanding of the functioning of organisations, including the Church. The notion that the Church itself has a culture and that this functions much like any other organisational culture took a good deal of time to germinate as Church leaders had thought of the Church as a perfect society (that is having within itself all that was needed for its own life). This belief led to an over-emphasis on the holiness of the Church and the authority of its leaders. The formation of the *Pontifical Council for Cultures* in 1982 represented a marked change in direction and opened up a range of conversations between Church leaders and social scientists.

As an *intellectual movement*, a postmodern stance is concerned to critique some of the assumptions on which modern culture rests, particularly its construction of knowledge and power. Modernity heralded a time when confidence in the power of human reason as the basis of progress seemed almost unbounded. Scientific progress in terms of technology seemed to be taking humanity on an ever-upward journey of greater human achievement and comfort. However, the twentieth century was a time of profound disillusionment. Its ideologies of Nazism, fascism and communism that enslaved vast populations, two world wars, the Great Depression, the Cold War, a nuclear arms race, the degradation of the planet, and the growing gaps between rich and poor within and between societies, left faith in modernity's exaggerated claims in tatters.[13] While the best of modernity's hopes, aspirations and possibilities remain, as do its positive achievements, humanity is beginning to learn that these must be actualised in a spirit of humility, and in awareness of the limitations in the assumptions and claims on which much of modernity's endeavour has proceeded.

Central to the postmodernists' critique of modernity is their critique of the primacy of reason to produce the kind of human progress promised by modernity, building on the aspirations of the Enlightenment. Theirs is a profoundly pessimistic outlook[14] that needs to be recognised by educators, not least because of its influence on young people.

Postmodern critics, such as Jean Francois Lyotard, called into question the 'meta-narratives' of modernity. Metanarratives are 'universal truths' that in modernity were taken as self-evident. A metanarrative proposes that some truths apply to all people for all time, that is they claim to reflect the 'structure' of what it means to be human. Narratives of this kind in the form of communism, Nazism and fascism have proved disastrous for vast numbers of people. Capitalism is another example of a modern metanarrative which must be judged to have brought a mixture of blessing and misery to many.

Postmodern critics include Christianity in the category of metanarrative. Certain approaches to Catholicism, which represent it as a 'closed' narrative, do indeed merit the descriptor 'metanarrative'. There are, however, other very different ways of being a Church community and constructing the

---

13 There are many helpful treatments of modernity and its shortcomings. One which we have found particularly insightful in terms of modernity's weaknesses, but also its strengths and ongoing potential, is John Thornhill's *Modernity: Christianity's Estranged Child Reconstructed* (Grand Rapids: Eerdmans, 2000). A summary of Thornhill's work on modernity can be found in Jim & Therese D'Orsa's *Catholic Curriculum: a Mission to the Heart of Young People*. Mulgrave: Garratt Publishing, 2011.

14 In *Catholic Curriculum*, we devote two chapters to postmodernism – Chapter 11, 'The Post-modern Critique: Prophets of Deconstruction', and Chapter 12, 'The Postmodern Critique: The Prophets of Reconstruction'. The first features Nietzsche, Lyotard, Foucault and Derrida; the latter Taylor, Habermas and Thornhill. These chapters may prove a useful introduction for those who wish to examine postmodernity in terms of ideas and as a sensibility.

Gospel in our time and place. These are properly described as 'open' narratives, open to responding to whatever challenges fidelity to the Kingdom of God may require. These are diametrically opposed to the designation of metanarrative in the above sense.

Thankfully, the 'deconstructionists' do not have the stage all to themselves. In our final chapter, for example, we feature a contemporary 'prophet' of reconstruction – Lieven Boeve and his treatment of Christianity as an open story. Boeve's work provides an essential perspective on a central goal of Catholic pedagogy, that of making present God's saving mission in a time of confusion. It seems a most appropriate theme to utilise in drawing this study to a close, and for that reason will not be repeated here, but simply acknowledged. The discipleship of scholars who in our era, as in every era, provide renewed insight into Christian faith, undertake a profoundly missional endeavour. It is such scholars that Catholic education seeks to form and encourage.

As a *sensibility*, postmodernism also has a positive element, one with which Christians resonate strongly. We refer to a form of critical consciousness open to the 'voices' of those silenced by the operation of political, social and religious power and its capacity to create 'victims'. As with the liberation theologians before them, the postmodern ideal is 'to give a voice to the voiceless'. Thus, in the postmodern period *a new sensibility re-emerged* with respect to difference and diversity as these exist within any group or society. Early beneficiaries of this change of sensibility have been members of the LGBTQI communities, women, indigenous peoples, and people with 'disabilities.' whilst still a work in progress, their voices are now heard, and their rights affirmed through various forms of affirmative action and anti-discrimination legislation.

3. LIVING IN A POSTSECULAR AGE

'Postmodernism' as an intellectual movement was short-lived not least because it was self-referentially incoherent. In denying the validity of metanarratives, postmodernity was in fact creating its own metanarrative. If all metanarratives are to be regarded with suspicion, then this must also apply to the metanarrative of postmodernity itself! Like modernity, however, many aspects of the postmodern sensibility do persist.

An important assumption of modernity was that 'modernisation' would prove to be the nemesis of faith. Faith and modernisation were seen as locked in a zero-sum game; as one increased, the other must necessarily decrease. However, this did not happen. While secularisation increased its scope across the modern period aided by globalisation, religion in the West did not disappear; rather, *it changed form.*

Support for institutional religions such as Catholicism and mainstream Protestantism did decline (depending on how 'decline' is understood), but the influx of people from other parts of the world through migration, as refugees, or as students studying in the West, saw a flowering of other forms of religion. This helped people in the West in their search for new expressions of the 'spiritual' both within and beyond mainstream religion. For these reasons, our current age is sometimes described as 'postsecular'. This does not mean that secularisation in its major forms no longer exists. It does. 'Postsecular' means that modernity's assumption that modernisation would lead to the demise of religion has proven false.

A plurality of religions and life-options has become a characteristic of our present age. The worldview of Catholic faith is now one option among many. In a postsecular culture which continues to be influenced by postmodernity, people *piece together their worldview* from among the many options open to them. The age of cultural Catholicism, so much a part of Catholic life in this country in the 1950s and 1960s, is over. While many aspects of society – for example, the relationship between Church and state – had long moved beyond Christendom, the cultural Catholicism experienced by those growing up at that time shared much in common with Christendom. Accepting the positive features of moving beyond this experience, with the new and enriching forms of dialogical encounter now available to Catholics, Australian Catholic theologian James McEvoy speaks of Christendom and its worldview (which characterised cultural Catholicism) having been 'left behind for good'.[15] The recognition of the rich possibilities of living the Gospel in the contemporary era has provided McEvoy with his ironic but optimistic theme and title. His work is a local contribution to those who seek to understand the elements of the 'open story'. It is this which the Second Vatican Council in its dialogical approach to the world introduced Catholics, and which scholars such as McEvoy and Boeve have developed further in the contemporary situation.

A pluralisation of worldviews is one important consequence of living in the cultures impacted by globalisation. According to Boeve, pluralisation leads to *individualisation*, the possibility of each person being able to choose his or her interpretive stance to life.[16] Perhaps it would be better to recognise that the individualisation accompanying modernity also drives globalisation,

---

[15] James McEvoy, *Leaving Christendom for Good: Church-world Dialogue in a Secular Age.* New York: Lexington Books, 2014.

[16] Lieven Boeve, *Interrupting Tradition: An Essay on Christian Faith in a Postmodern Context.* Louvain: Peeters Press, 2003, 52.

and that both processes now proceed together. The consequence of both processes is that young people will generally choose their own stance in life which means that tradition, in its various forms, no longer plays the same role it did in passing on either culture or faith.

Globalisation affects culture in another way. As people from different parts of the world intersect on an ever-increasing basis through travel, migration, study, work and so on, and as people visit the world vicariously via television and the internet, the value placed on difference and diversity in postsecular culture rises. Difference and diversity are no longer something we encounter once in a while; they are now the stuff of life, and we have to deal with it whether we want to or not. Confronted with the changing mix of students in their classes, teachers are familiar with this phenomenon and the demands it makes in terms of both curriculum and pedagogy.

Central to Christian mission amid today's pluralised world is dialogue which, like Pope John Paul before him, Pope Francis sees as always central to the proclamation of the Gospel (see Chapter 24). Pope Francis' approach to dialogue is heartfelt and practical. It is coupled with discernment, not surprisingly given the depth of his formation as a son of Ignatius of Loyola. He calls for theological education to be renewed according to the criteria of dialogue and discernment in order for the Kingdom of God to be proclaimed, and recognised and supported.[17] His 'dialogical way' applies equally to Catholic education at all levels in terms of both process and goals.

> *The dialogical way of proceeding is the way to arrive where paradigms, ways of feeling, symbols, representations of people and peoples are formed. To arrive there – as 'spiritual ethnographers' of the soul of people, let's say – in order to be able to dialogue in depth and, if possible contribute to their development by announcing the Gospel of the Kingdom of God, whose fruit is the ripening of an increasingly broad and inclusive fraternity.*

3.1 Educating in a postsecular age

Living in a postsecular age in which both modernity and postmodernity continue to make their impact poses unique questions for Catholic educators such as:

- *How do we help students position themselves to develop a coherent worldview when the culture requires them to choose its key elements from among a sea of possible options?*

---

17 See for example Pope Francis' remarks at the *Theology After Veritatis Gaudium Encounter* in Naples, Italy, 21 June, 2019. Zenit, June 24, 2019. https://zenit.org/articles/popes-full-remarks-at-theology-after-veritatis-gaudium-encounter-in-naples-italy/

- *How do we help them see Christian faith as worth including in their interpretive framework, when there is considerable 'evidence' readily available to them, channelled via the media, suggesting this is not a good idea?*
- *How do we assist students to negotiate the challenges posed by the need to deal with difference and otherness?*
- *Very specifically, how does this task fit within my conception of the pedagogical relationship I have with my students?*

Clearly, teachers cannot help students deal with such issues if they have not carefully thought through the issues themselves.

4. DEALING WITH THE WORLDVIEW OF THE AGE

4.1 Acknowledging plurality

The worldviews of Christendom, modernity, postmodernity and of the postsecular era, are each examples of an overarching worldview that crosses a range of societies and cultures. This is referred to as the 'worldview of the age'. The media plays a powerful role in disseminating the worldview of the age. The rapidity with which, in recent times, the predominant worldview of the age has moved from modern to postmodern to postsecular has meant that many, even in the one society, often continue to adhere to a particular version of it when others have moved on to embrace a different version.

Consequently, one of the difficulties faced by school leaders is that teachers, students and their parents often live today in different, or indeed multiple, cultural worlds *even when they belong to the same national grouping*. Some brought up during modernity still operate according to its assumptions about knowledge. Others influenced by the postmodern critique of the late 20th century carry with them a deep suspicion of institutions, and have little time for institutional values or practices including Church values and practices. As a result, their identification with the community of faith is often tenuous at best.

The Church itself has been slow to address the issues of difference and otherness that are a growing feature of Western societies. There is, however, some documentation providing guidance, for example *Educating to Intercultural Dialogue in Catholic Schools: Living in Harmony for a Civilization of Love* provided by the Congregation for Catholic Education in 2013. This important document makes the case that the Catholic school through its community, curriculum and pedagogy has significant capacity to promote appreciation and harmony among people. It provides a useful theological underpinning to the case it makes. An often-quoted passage provides a clue to its direction:

> *The love for all men and women is necessarily also a love for their culture. Catholic schools are, by their very vocation, intercultural.*[18]

4.2 Reading the signs of the times

Many Church leaders seem at a loss in knowing how to read the signs of the times and in so doing make sense of the present pluralist cultural situation. Among Catholic educators the approach seems somewhat more assured. A number of systems and schools have embarked on the *Enhancing Catholic School Identity* (ECSI) project. This project is predicated on an analysis of the place of faith in a postsecular culture provided by theologians and researchers from KUL.[19] A basic assumption of this analysis is that it is through encounter with the person who is 'other' that we establish our own religious identity. In part this happens because the 'other' forces us to look at what is *particular* in our own religious positions (so the better to critique it and arrive at a 'post-critical faith').

4.3 Identity formation among young people

Identify formation involves two complementary dialogues. The first is a *dialogue with 'the one who is different'* and the second is a *dialogue with our own tradition*.

The dialogue with one's own faith tradition involves two essential tasks:

- *developing an understanding of the tradition so that it becomes possible to distinguish authentic representations from stereotypes that distort it,* and
- *critical appraisal of the tradition so as to appreciate the biases inherent in it.*

The dialogue with 'the other' requires that we encounter the person 'who is other' seeking to *understand their worldview* as a framework that makes sense of life for them, even though it may not have the same meaning for us. This latter position is new for some Catholics brought up to think that they have direct access to 'the truth' and so do not need such encounters. It

---

18 Congregation for Catholic Education, *Educating to Intercultural Dialogue in Catholic Schools: Living in Harmony for a Civilization of Love*, 2013 #61.
 http://www.vatican.va/roman_curia/congregations/ccatheduc/documents/rc_con_ccatheduc_doc_20131028_dialogo-interculturale_en.html.
19 Many Australian educators have become familiar with the richness of theological work feeding into the ECSI project through their visits to KU Leuven and other studies. Boeve's work on the options facing a Catholic institution in a pluralising context is among those that remain influential, for example, on the development of the typologies of the Melbourne scale.

is here that the Enhancing Catholic School Identity (ECSI) project has run into difficulty with critics who fear that abandoning an exclusive Catholic claim to 'truth' relativises all truth. These critics are of the view that ECSI, rather than strengthening Catholic identity, diminishes it.

The KUL response is that religious truth, and therefore the worldview of Catholic faith, does not exist in any absolute or uncontextualised sense. Catholic faith has always been understood and lived in a contextual manner. As the context changes – whether it be historical, cultural or linguistic – so too does the way in which faith is understood, articulated and practised.

4.4 Re-contextualising Christian faith

People who see faith as unchanging are simply taking a particular understanding and articulation of Catholic faith (a specific contextualisation) as definitive for all people and all times.

For Boeve and the KU Leuven scholars associated with the development of the ECSI project, the challenge for Church leaders in our postsecular age is to recontextualise Catholic faith so that it is meaningful for people, is responsive to their best aspirations, and is true to the dynamic Catholic tradition. In practice, this means developing a theological framework that can deal with difference and diversity within the Church, as well as speak meaningfully to people faced with the pluralism, in both faith and life options, that characterises our times.

This is also a challenge for Catholic educators. The ECSI project stands as a valid attempt to address this challenge. By highlighting the need to re-contextualise the worldview of faith, ECSI represents a first step in what is likely to be a long, and hotly contested, pathway to the future. While it points in a helpful direction, there are few specific guidelines that tell Catholic educators (or bishops for that matter) what the outcome of re-contextualisation will be or how it is to be achieved in practice. Both would seem to depend, ultimately, on the Holy Spirit at work in human history.

5. THE WORLDVIEW OF FAITH AS PERSONAL

The 'worldview of faith' is not a thing, nor is it a set of teachings. It exists as the possession of a people, and of each individual. While we share a worldview with other people of faith, our personal appropriation of the worldview of faith is *a framework that we construct for ourselves to make sense of our world in religious terms*. However, the only guarantee that we are on the right track is that we find the broader faith community is journeying with us.

The way in which faith is incorporated into our personal worldview admits to many possibilities, depending on whether our starting assumptions are modern, postmodern or postsecular. If modern, a person sees faith as largely unnecessary; if postmodern, they interpret faith as a metanarrative to be treated with suspicion; if postsecular, they see faith as one of many options open to them.

The approaches taken by Pope Francis and his two immediate predecessors highlight the pluralism that now exists in how the worldview of faith can be constructed. For Popes John Paul II and Benedict XVI, the worldview of faith is constructed on the basis of tradition, wide scholarship, and carefully reasoned arguments that respect the value of truth. For them, the worldview of faith presents very much 'a thing of the mind'. Pope Francis, however, constructs the worldview of faith on a very different basis. For him, the challenge is to locate people's individual stories within the narratives of Jesus. This is a project requiring memory, imagination and critical judgment, and it presents as a project of the heart.

To be able to see one's story as significant in relation to another's, is to approach the deep mystery of love. When this also involves viewing the world from the perspective of a loving and merciful God, then new light is thrown into some of the dark places that exist in Church life and in the Catholic tradition.

Pope Francis sees through the eyes of married people who do not share the same faith, but wish to participate in the Eucharist together; he looks through the eyes of the many divorced and remarried Catholics, and initiates changes in the way the Church ministers to them; he sees the world through the eyes of the marginalised and refugees and becomes an advocate on their behalf; he sees through the eyes of Amazonian people whose world is threatened by greed. The list goes on, but the approach is consistent. *Placing yourself in the position of another brings their story and yours into conversation. From the new understandings that this generates, growth and change become possible.*

There is a profound pedagogical principle being modelled here, one that should shape the way in which Catholic educators understand and interact with students in all their rich diversity.

To some of Pope Francis' clerical colleagues, his way of constructing the worldview of faith is 'completely incomprehensible'.[20] As with the apostle Paul, Pope Francis does not seem to see 'law' or 'abstract truths' as having the last word in the way we understand or practise our faith. This is not in any way to deny that there is a set of teachings that the Catholic Church

---
20 Words of Dutch Cardinal Eijk reported by James Roberts in *The Tablet* May 7, 2018.

takes as definitive. However, very few Catholics ever get to know what these teachings are in full.[21] Most rely on a *working knowledge of faith* that they can apply to their concrete lives and relationships. And Catholics collectively have a 'sense of faith' (*sensus fidei*) that shapes an authentic following of Jesus.

So, our questions to teachers in Catholic schools are:

- *What is important to you in the worldview of faith?*
- *What interpretive power does faith have for you as a framework in making sense of your life as a teacher?*
- *How does faith impinge on the decisions you make when planning, learning, and working with your students?*

In a context where the official school curriculum is at best neutral towards faith, the scene is set for students to take the secular worldview of their culture as the *sole* framework in making sense of life. The Catholic school offers an alternative, a choice to bring the worldviews of faith and culture into conversation in making sense of life. This cannot happen, or is very unlikely to happen, in cases where teachers do not see the worldview of faith *as an interpretive framework that is important in their own lives.*

6. BRINGING THE PIECES TOGETHER

Chapters 9 and 10 have traced the narrative by which faith and culture took divergent paths in modernity. In these chapters we and outlined efforts to work out how to bring them into conversation in a postsecular culture. The story is outlined schematically in the diagram below.

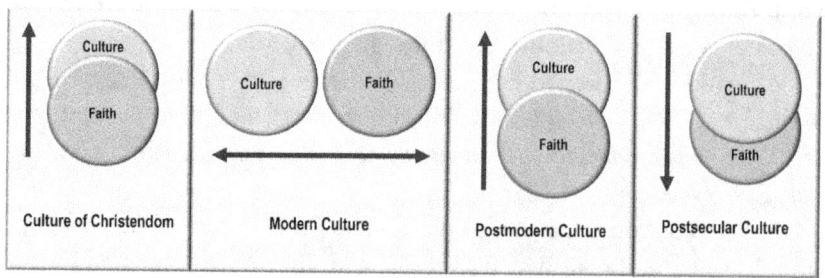

FIGURE 10.1: CHANGES IN RELATIONSHIP BETWEEN FAITH AND CULTURE ACROSS TIME

During Christendom, faith overshadowed culture as a source of personal and collective meaning. During the modern period, people rejected this way of constructing meaning, but in the process introduced an alternative

---

21 These teachings are set out in the *Catechism of the Catholic Church* which is a reference document that runs to 800+ pages. https://www.vatican.va/archive/ENG0015/__P9V.HTM.

series of biases into the way in which knowledge is created by maintaining that faith had no place in the creation of knowledge. These biases were called out in the postmodern period when postmodern philosophers and many people of faith began to find common ground, sharing a new respect for the victims of power (including the earth itself), with the result that postsecular culture does allow a place for faith in its public square.

A present danger is that the assumptions that underpin our secular culture simply dominate all meaning-making. Given that faith is now very much a matter of personal choice, this danger has major implications for how faith is presented to young people if it is to have a chance of being a meaningful element in their personal worldview. The role of the faith community becomes paramount in making this possible.

The faith community offers individuals *a plausibility structure* supporting the choice for faith and a practical means to give expression to that choice. As part of the faith community, Catholic schools are a major means of offering this support. The responsibility of Catholic educators is *to frame their pedagogical relationship with students in a manner that takes into account the cultural situation in which the latter form their personal identity*. This realisation now has an important bearing on how Catholic schools frame their mission and ministry of education.

Part C
CONTEMPORARY PERSPECTIVES ON PEDAGOGY

Introduction

In Part C the focus in on pedagogy and the meanings this term has today. There seem to be two distinct approaches: the one most people are familiar with is the pragmatic approach that interprets pedagogy narrowly as 'what happens in the classrooms to advance students' learning'. The pragmatic understanding exists in two research-based forms. The first depends on quantitative research into 'what works in the classroom' and the exemplar of this approach is found in the mega-studies of John Hattie and his notion of 'deep learning'. A second tradition depends on qualitative research as exemplified in the work of Michael Fullan who is also committed to deep learning via the 'new pedagogy' movement. These two pedagogical traditions seem to dominate discussion about pedagogy in the English-speaking world. Each tradition, in its own distinct way, seeks to establish 'what works in the classroom' and develop teaching strategies matched to research-based understandings.

Continental educators offer an alternative approach that focuses on the special relationship that exists between adults and young people in learning situations. In this perspective pedagogy describes the particular relationship between an adult and learners directed in age-appropriate ways to promote a learner's growth to maturity, as well as the responsibilities this relationship entails for adults. Here we are talking about an ethical understanding of pedagogy that covers parenting, teaching, youth work, counselling – any relationship in which an adult interacts with a vulnerable child with the aim of helping the child grow and develop towards maturity.

The ethical approach to pedagogy revolves around the questions:

- *What is the 'right thing' to do by this child in this situation?*
- *What 'good' do I seek to achieve for this child or this group of children?*

The ethical approach explores the subjective meaning that teaching has for teachers and the subjective meaning that learning has for students. This involves quite a different form of research from that undertaken in the pragmatic tradition where the aim is to establish 'scientific' results with universal validity. The ethical approach draws its inspiration from European phenomenology – the study of subjective meaning that an event or experience has for the participants. Phenomenology is not concerned with analysing experience after the fact, as happens in reflective practice. It is concerned with the meaning practice has for participants *in the act of practice*. Put simply, the questions it raises are:

- *What meaning do teachers give to their actions when teaching?*
- *How do they make sense of the situations in which they find themselves in the classroom?*

Alternatively,

- *What meaning do parents give to their actions in parenting?*
- *What is the experience of parenting like for parents? How do they make sense of it?*

This form of analysis which deals with pre-reflective accounts of human experience leads to somewhat different conclusions from those derived in other forms of research that claim to be objective, whether based on quantitative or qualitative studies. In reflective practice accounts, the meaning of an experience is often mediated by the models used to analyse it.

In Part C we consider ethical approaches to pedagogy, drawing on the phenomenological approach of Canadian educator Max Van Manen, and the complementary philosophic approach of US educator Robert Starratt. This is followed by exploration of 'values pedagogy', before moving on to address the pragmatic tradition as found in John Hattie's studies and in Michael Fullan's 'new pedagogy'. The pragmatic tradition in pedagogy now seeks to promote 'deep learning' which is understood in a variety of ways. We seek to clarify this concept by appealing to the work of the US Centre for Research.

The section concludes by asking the questions:

- *What insights do the approaches outlined offer teachers in a Catholic school?*
- *How might these be incorporated into a 'Catholic pedagogy'?*

A common weakness in all the approaches is that, while each seems to recognise the need for teachers to have a theory of 'what learning is', most fail to articulate such a theory. This then becomes the topic explored in Part D.

11

PEDAGOGY AS ETHICAL ENDEAVOUR: ROBERT STARRATT AND MAX VAN MANEN

This chapter aims to open up important aspects of the contemporary field of pedagogy with the assistance of significant and accessible contributors – Robert Starratt speaking out of the US tradition, and Max Van Manen speaking out of the European tradition. Knowledge of their work helps educators to evaluate what is essential in making wise pedagogical choices aimed at successful learning and personal development that are constitutive of the 'good' of each student.

1. TWO COMPETING PARADIGMS OF THE HUMAN

Respected US educator Robert Starratt points out that educational thinking is caught between two conceptions of what it means to be human, that is between the two competing paradigms which follow.

1.1 Atomistic and relational paradigms

This older paradigm derives from the Enlightenment thinking of the 18th century. It furthers an *atomistic view* of the human person which promotes the concept that society is comprised of *self-interested individuals* who are able to live together via a *social contract*. In this contract they choose to curb their self-interest in order to respect the right of every other self-interested person to pursue his or her self-interest, thus promoting the *common good*.

Within this perspective, human societies should be governed by *rational principles and laws* discovered through the sciences of politics, economics and sociology. These principles and laws should be applied by elected governments so as to govern according to the terms of the social contract as set out in the constitution of the state.[1]

The atomistic paradigm was challenged in the mid-20th century by an alternative view, one that understands reality in dynamic and fluid terms in

---
1 Robert J Starratt, *Cultivating an Ethical School*. New York: Routledge, 2012, 10–11.

which every created thing is related to everything else – relationality. This view considers that it is *relationality* that defines what is. This paradigm, first developed in the natural sciences, was then applied to human and social reality. Under its influence humans are understood not as atomised self-interested individuals, but *as essentially social and relational.*

Starratt notes that 'the realities of globalisation and the risks facing the global community appear to be underscoring the necessity of recognising the relationality view of how the world *must* work if the human race is to have a viable future'.[2] How people in a society understand what it means to be human shapes what they see as the goals of education, what they construe as good pedagogy, and what they deem to be worth teaching young people in the various contexts in which learning happens, in the home, the school, the sports club, the dance group, and so on. In the West, decisions about 'how the world works' and 'what is worth teaching' are embodied in the traditional curriculum that is often formulated quite independently of 'how children learn' and 'what is of interest to them'.

1.2 Pragmatic and ethical understandings of pedagogy

The concept of 'pedagogy' is understood in different ways. These understandings can be broadly classified as lying along a spectrum from 'narrow' to 'broad', or from 'pragmatic' to 'ethical'.

In the English-speaking world 'pedagogy' is generally understood in the narrow, pragmatic, instrumental sense of 'teaching practice'.[3] 'Pedagogy' is equated with 'teaching young people in school settings'. Little distinction is drawn between 'pedagogy' and 'teaching practices' and, in consequence, the word 'pedagogy' has tended to fall into disuse in favour of the latter phrase.

In the European tradition pedagogy is understood as referring to *the special relationship that exists between an adult and a child in the context of learning*, where the adult may be a parent, a teacher, a psychologist, a youth worker etc., and the learner is a child or young person.

This relationship is special because of:

- *the asymmetry between the adult and the child in the relationship, and*
- *the responsibilities the relationship imposes on the adult in helping a young person to grow towards maturity.*

In this perspective the term 'pedagogy' implies that the act of helping a child to learn occurs within *ethical boundaries*.

---

2   Ibid, 11.
3   In Europe the process of learning how to teach a particular subject is given the general name *didactics*. In English this word carries the negative connotations of rigidity and inflexibility.

When used in the narrow sense, 'pedagogy' carries the restricted meaning of 'teaching school children to learn'. When used in the broad sense, it includes all the contexts in which children learn. It is in this broad sense that 'pedagogy' enters theological discourse.

'Divine pedagogy' is a phrase sometimes used in Catholic catechetical discourse to describe the ways in which God reveals Godself to humans through human experience and through action within history, and so invites persons and communities into relationship. Response to this call to relationship teaches human beings about *who God is*, and who they are in relation to God, one another and the natural world.[4]

Most teachers, in religious education as well as in general education, employ an understanding of pedagogy that sits somewhere on the 'narrow' to 'broad' spectrum. In exploring this understanding further, we are indebted to the work of Canadian educator Max Van Manen.[5] Our argument is that a broad or ethical understanding is essential in formulating pedagogies that are Catholic.

For Van Manen pedagogy is ethical because:

> ... *it is pedagogy that makes the crucial difference in a child's life. Pedagogy involves us in distinguishing actively and/or reflectively what is good or right and what is life enhancing, just, and supportive from what is not good, wrong, unjust, or damaging in the ways we act, live and deal with children.*[6]

Elsewhere he observes:

> ... *pedagogy can generally be described as distinguishing what is good and right from what is bad and wrong (not good or inappropriate) in our ways of acting and interacting with children. Of course, in our everyday living with children we do not always know how to distinguish actively and reflectively what is good from what is not good (or is less good) for children. In certain situations, and predicaments, we may question and doubt ourselves or admit that we may not know what is best for this child or these children.*
>
> *But the point is, that this doubt and uncertainty belongs to pedagogy and shows us the profoundly ethical nature of pedagogical thinking and acting. Without this ethical uncertainty pedagogy would be reduced to a set*

4　See the following magisterial documents for references to 'divine pedagogy' – *Dei Verbum*, 15; *General Directory for Catechesis*, 112, 129, 132; *The Catechism of the Catholic Church*, 53.
5　Born and raised in Holland, Van Manen migrated with his family to Canada where he became Professor of Research, Pedagogy and Curriculum Studies at the University of Alberta. Van Manen has been responsible for translating the works of European authors such as Martin Langeveld into English, thus making them available to an English-speaking audience, and also exposing readers to continental thinking about pedagogy.
6　Max Van Manen, *Pedagogical Tact: Knowing what to do when you do not know what to do*. New York: Routledge, 2015, 19–20.

of techniques, recipes or rules. Teaching, parenting and caring for children are never simple affairs that can be handled by means of rules and recipes ... pedagogy is both the tactful ethical practice of our actions as well as the doubting, questioning, and reflecting on our actions and practices.[7]

Pedagogy, as used here, is ethical because *it is primarily relational.* Teachers are ever haunted by the question: am I doing the right thing by this child or group of children? In the adult-child relationship that characterises pedagogy, the adult must acknowledge and respect the vulnerability of the child still in the process of maturing. Abuse of the pedagogical relationship between adult and child can arrest the development of the child because it erodes the trust that children must have in adults if they are to learn how the world works and their place in it.[8]

1.3 The phenomenological approach to pedagogy

Max Van Manen adopts a phenomenological approach to pedagogy. That is, his research interest is in *the lived experience of people engaged in teaching, parenting, youth work and so on, and in helping children and young people to grow towards maturity in age-appropriate ways.*

Phenomenologists pursue detailed accounts of human experiences in order to understand what the experience means subjectively for the participants. It is an approach to human experience that developed out of European philosophy in the 19th and early 20th centuries, partly in reaction to attempts to study human experience using the 'objective' methods of the natural sciences.[9]

For Van Manen, pedagogy has to do with the personal, relational and ethical aspects of teaching and bringing up children.[10] It involves the attempt to see and understand the complexity of life in the classroom and in school experiences considered more generally, as well as exploring the ways in which these contribute to the growth, learning, and development of young people.

The aim of pedagogy goes beyond imparting knowledge to children, and involves *creating the conditions that make learning possible for them.* Imparting

---

7 Ibid, 33.
8 This was made evident in the harrowing testimony of witnesses appearing before the Australian Government's Royal Commission into Institutional Responses to Child Sexual Abuse (2013–2017).
9 The natural sciences study objects that are incapable of exercising agency. This is not true of human subjects. When a rock is observed, it remains unchanged. When a human subject is observed, the fact that he or she knows they are being observed can change the way they behave. This is particularly true when people are being tested. The human sciences therefore need to develop methods of study that take human agency into account.
10 In all that follows the reference is to 'children and young people'. However, endlessly repeating this phrase makes for awkward reading, so the reference in future will be to 'children' or to 'child' but this should be understood as including young people as well.

knowledge is simply one way of helping students to learn, and not necessarily the most effective way. Making a shift in the understanding of pedagogy as pragmatic to pedagogy as ethical redefines the role of a teacher. Teachers now need to be more aware of *what it takes for students to learn*.[11] In other words, they need *an explicit theory of learning*, an issue we take up in Part D.

2. RESEARCH TRADITIONS AND PEDAGOGY

This shift in understanding has proved problematic. Teachers operate in a 'real' world that does not easily accommodate the controls commonly needed in experimental research, and so they tend to be resistant to its conclusions. *The classroom is a world in which theory and practice are co-constitutive of one another.* The progression from theory to practice has not always proved helpful in improving practice.

2.1 A critique of traditional approaches to educational research

As a phenomenologist, Van Manen is critical of research into teaching because he believes it tends to underestimate the complexity of life in a classroom. He sees the classroom as providing an environment in which *theory and practice rarely exist in a causal relationship*, but are co-determinate of one another within a process that is iterative – a process of design, test, analyse, redesign, retest, report and so on.

Van Manen maintains that the *practice of teaching has developed more or less independently of research knowledge*. This is also why researchers such as Hattie complain that teaching is too little influenced by research findings, and Fullan can demonstrate that most educational projects fail.[12]

We believe the position accorded teachers in educational research places them in a *passive position,* one of 'recipients of research knowledge' that often fails to take into account what teachers know *as a result of their own experiences*. The consequence is that *teachers are rarely the drivers of new knowledge about teaching and learning*. As a result, the knowledge they acquire is often deficient.

This historical legacy has left teachers in a relatively weak position in regard to critiquing the advent of technology in schools, a development that is also redefining their role. In an increasingly technologically mediated world, the vital importance of the personal and relational dimensions of teaching and learning are thrown into sharp relief, rendering a narrow,

---
11   Van Manen, 11.
12   See John Hattie, *Visible Learning: A synthesis of over 800 meta-analyses relating to achievement,* New York: Routledge, 2009, and Michael Fullan, *The New Meaning of Educational Change.* New York: Routledge, 2015.

pragmatic and instrumental understanding of pedagogy increasingly problematic.

Much of what teachers learn about teaching is sourced in 'reflective practice'. However, this is reflection carried out *after the fact* and, given the way classrooms function, usually well after the fact. However, *the act of teaching occurs in the here and now* and the art of teaching lies in the myriad decisions that teachers make on the run in the various 'pedagogical moments' that present themselves in their interactions with students in the classroom. In these moments the teacher makes split-second decisions about what is in the best interests of the child, as far as learning is concerned. Failure to act means that the moment passes, and a learning opportunity is squandered.

2.2 The pedagogical dilemma

As Van Manen notes, a major difficulty for many teachers is that they are called on to act when they are often unsure about what the right action actually is. It is this facet of teaching, and how teachers make sense of it, that interests Van Manen as a phenomenologist. He suggests that, over time, teachers develop *'pedagogical tact'*, by which he means that they develop a unique form of *pedagogical judgment* that enables them to respond reflexively to 'pedagogical moments' in the seemingly chaotic circumstances that often exist in a normal classroom.

Teachers are able to develop this tact if their focus remains on 'the good of the child'. The key question guiding the pedagogical relationship is therefore: What serves 'the good' of this child, or this group of students? How a teacher construes 'the good of the child' is therefore critical to how they understand pedagogy and how they enable learning. Living with children, whether in the home or in school, prompts a particular form of reflectivity centring on the question: Am I doing the right thing? This question highlights the ethical nature of the relationship between adult and child in learning. It brings home to adults that children are naturally vulnerable and need proper care.

2.3 Providing proper care

Adults are, or should be, aware that children who do not receive a minimum of 'proper care' tend to do poorly in life because deep down they seem to have a sense that the 'the game of life is not worth playing'. This sensibility becomes embedded in their developing worldview as it takes shape. Effective pedagogy seeks to prevent this happening, and to work with the young person to develop a very different worldview, one that is transforming in terms of their own life and their impact on the world.

Pedagogy embraces something that is primordial in the adult-child relationship – doing right by the vulnerable child or young person. It involves an ethic that is *relational* and intends a caring responsibility on the part of the adult for the child. The way people interpret this ethic is shaped by the cultural context in which it takes place.

The way parents and teachers understand this context and the pedagogical ethic *depends therefore on the worldviews they themselves bring to the task.* This, in turn, depends on the worldview of their culture which provides them with the default frame of reference they employ in making sense of their task. Faith may also play a part in this process, but this can no longer be assumed to be the case. Faith perspectives *must be consciously included.*

Pedagogy is concerned with the formative experiences of children and young people, but these have to be understood in the context in which they occur. School pedagogy depends on how well teachers understand:

- *the developmental realities associated with children's learning*
- *the lived experiences of children as learners*
- *the context in which learning occurs*
- *the impact these factors have on how teachers construe what is good for the child.*

3. UNDERSTANDING THE CONTEXT OF LEARNING

The pedagogical relationship fostered in a Catholic school aims to assist the child to develop towards maturity within a particular cultural and religious context. How the teacher understands this relationship depends on how he or she understands these contexts.

There are many analyses describing the transitions now occurring in Western cultures.[13] We find Starratt's analysis helpful. He analyses the cultural shifts in terms of four 'megatrends' and highlights their impact on school education.[14] These megatrends are detailed below.

---

13 See, for instance, Charles Taylor *A Secular Age*. Harvard University Press, 2007; Jonathan Sacks, *The Dignity of Difference: How to avoid a clash of civilizations*. London: Continuum, 2003. For an analysis within a qualitatively larger (cosmic) frame see Ilia Delio, *Making All Things New: Catholicity, Cosmology, Consciousness*. Maryknoll N.Y: Orbis, 2015. Pope Francis' 2015 encyclical *Laudato si' (On Care for Our Common Home)*, contains much useful analytical material as well as references to analyses given in magisterial documents by recent popes.
14 Robert Starratt, *Cultivating an Ethical School*. New York: Routledge, 2012, 6–11.

3.1 Megatrends impacting on how teachers assess 'what is right for the child'

Globalisation

As a result of the migration that is a spinoff of current globalising trends, schools are becoming multicultural, or much more multicultural as the case may be. In consequence, they have to make rapid accommodation for the newcomers, leading in many cases to a renewed understanding of 'the good' that teachers seek to achieve for their students.

In its 2013 document, *Educating to Intercultural Dialogue in Catholic Schools Living in Harmony for a Civilization of Love*,[15] the Congregation for Catholic Education argues for an *anthropological* approach to inter-cultural learning that can and must occur as students from many different cultures rub shoulders in the school. The learning must involve a sound anthropology because inter-cultural learning is fundamentally between 'two flesh-and-blood individuals'. Furthermore it claims:

> *Cultures take on life and continually redraw themselves starting from the encounter with the other person. To go out from oneself and consider the world from a different point of view is not a denial of oneself, but, on the contrary, is necessary for enhancing one's own identity* (# 38).

A further important element of globalisation, namely the flow of information, throws into relief another aspect 'the good' teachers seek to achieve in regard to students. This information flow shrinks the psychological distance between people of different nationalities. Authorities are also finding it increasingly difficult to censor ideas and values flowing through global communication portals. Constructively discerning and utilising this information flow for 'the good' are challenges for both teachers and students.

Environmental Degradation

Global warming is now recognised as a major international threat. Schools cannot solve environmental sustainability problems, but they have a responsibility to help the younger generation understand what is at stake and to help cultivate gifts which can be used for earth sustainability. Failure to do so would constitute a form of moral neglect.

Learning to Navigate the Information Speedway

Digital technology is globalising the consciousness of children as is evidenced by the recent international movement of school students inspired by the leadership of Swedish student and climate activist, Greta Thunberg. This

---

[15] This document is an essential source in regard to several themes of this chapter.

has happened so fast that increasingly there is a disconnect between student consciousness and teacher awareness. As Starratt observes:

> ... by grades six or seven students may have acquired a larger mental encyclopedia of information than some of their teachers who find themselves too busy correcting homework or grading quizzes to surf the web for anything remotely connected to what they are teaching.[16]

Teachers would seem to have an ethical responsibility to stay at least as current as their students. The information highway (or 'speedway' to use Starratt's term) also provides opportunities to diversify the way students learn by connecting their learning to 'real world' issues and to their interests.

Digital developments are now challenging the traditional 'one size fits all' approach to teaching with its over-reliance on textbooks to promote student learning and a curriculum that no longer seems to reflect *the way the world works now*. In doing so, they ask teachers to rethink their answers to the question: 'What is good for students?'

The Relationality Shift

The shift from individualism to understanding one's identity in terms of membership in various communities, corresponds to other shifts:

- *from seeing knowledge in objective or absolute terms, to seeing it in more provisional terms*
- *from seeing humans as having power over the natural world, to seeing humans as being part of an endangered natural world*

These shifts in perspective have important educational consequences in learning how the world works and finding one's place in it.

Reflexive Modernity

As has been noted earlier, postmodern critics have challenged many of the assumptions on which the culture of modernity depended, with the consequence that people are now suspicious about traditional sources of knowledge be they scientific, philosophical or religious. A *'hermeneutic of suspicion'* pervades the academic world and this becomes transposed into the world of school learning. It can undermine students' confidence in what they know, leading to forms of relativism that hinder their taking an ethical stance to life.[17]

---

16   Starratt, 2012, 9
17   An ethical stance to life means that the young person accepts certain positions on the basis of principles or beliefs that they have personally appropriated, not because some authority declared them to be 'normal'. Relativism as developmental psychologist James Marcia points out is an immature stance to identity formation in that it enables people to 'sit on the fence' in negotiating

To these four megatrends a fifth needs to be added that is specific to Catholic schooling.

A Shift in Interpretive Authority within the Catholic Church

US sociologist Michelle Dillon points out that, within the Catholic community, a shift in interpretive authority is underway from the clergy to the Catholic community.[18] When it comes to what to believe and how to practise their faith, Catholics increasingly look to their own consciences, rather than to formal religious authorities.

Today, Catholics raised from birth to understand that in matters of faith the Pope has the last word, find that even senior cardinals are challenging Pope Francis because they disagree with him. The clear message they send is that the Pope only has the last word *'provided he agrees with me'*. In other words, my conscience is the ultimate determinant of what to believe. Ordinary Catholics have concluded that, if this approach is okay for the cardinals, it is okay for them!

Dillon points out that the transfer of interpretive authority currently underway finds justification in the teachings of Vatican II.[19] Pope Francis' advocacy of a 'synodal church', and his encouragement to bishops to listen to their people, also support a trend towards having confidence in the religious experience of the community, and what such listening might be calling the Church to.

3.2 Determining 'what is right by students'

For Starratt, each of the above trends raises pedagogical issues for teachers confronted with the question: 'What is 'right' for these students?' And they pose a further question: 'What is the teacher expected to do?'[20] This question takes on added significance in the changing context of the Catholic Church and the implications this is likely to have for Catholic schooling. If teachers in the public system often find themselves faced with the dilemma of 'knowing what to do when they don't know what to do', as Van Manen contends, then this dilemma is amplified for teachers in Catholic schools, particularly those involved in Religious Education.

Starratt is critical of both the process and content of traditional pedagogy. For him, the traditional learning process is, as Paulo Freire describes it, a

---

the crisis of identity in adolescence. Marcia is a Canadian psychologist whose work extends that of Erikson. Although his work is widely quoted, it is most accessible through presentations and summaries, e.g James Marcia's *Adolescent Identity* https://www.academia.edu/12364473/ADOLESCENT_IDENTITY_JAMES_MARCIA eadedn21

18   Michele Dillon, *Postsecular Catholicism: Relevance and Renewal*. New York: Oxford University Press, 2018. See also Michelle Dillon, *Catholics in Transition*. Maryland: Rowan and Littlefield, 2013.
19   Ibid.
20   Starratt, 14.

'banking' process whereby learners deposit information in their memory vaults to be taken out to buy their way into a successful score on a test. The traditional curriculum expects that students acquire the knowledge judged legitimate by the state and conform to the state's general interpretation of how the world works. This tends to be a distortion of how the world actually works, because it is focused on how the world worked in the past.

A similar critique could be made of the traditional approach to pedagogy and curriculum in Religious Education in many Catholic schools. This approach, particularly in the area of the curriculum, contains what the local bishop sees as an interpretation of how the world of faith works, and this may be a distortion of how it works today given the changes underway. As a consequence, many bishops have become open to drawing insight from other dioceses' curricula, and to diocesan personnel working together on aspects of curriculum development in Religious Education, while accepting that the final responsibility rests with themselves.

Commenting on the most significant of these megatrends Starratt writes:

> *A relationality view of pedagogy (with space and with past, present and future)*
> *… not only positions the learner in relationship to the curriculum as emerging in the past as an historical interpretation of the world then, of how it worked, of its possibilities and challenges, but also how the knowledge of the curriculum positions us for an interpretation of the world now, of how the residue of the past still lingers (for better or worse) in present day, social, political and cultural life.*
> *… The pedagogy and curriculum of the school will <u>either</u> express an ontology of possessive individualism … that separates the individual from the world he (sic) seeks to master, as well as an epistemology of knowledge as revealed in a curriculum of already obsolete facts, <u>or</u> an ontology of relationality and an epistemology of knowledge gained through a mutual dialogue about intelligibility and significance within a relational, globalized world of both the subject being studied and the learner doing the studying …*[21]

The above observation also highlights one of Van Manen's main points: *pedagogy requires of the teacher the ability to distinguish what is good and what is not so good in their interactions with children for whom they carry responsibility.*[22] Ultimately, this ability will be dependent on the worldview that the teacher brings to the task. Therefore, it follows that teachers carry an ethical

---

21 Starratt, 16–17.
22 Van Manen, 25.

responsibility for how they form their own worldviews and for ensuring, in the context of Catholic schooling, that this remains open to faith.

4. UNDERSTANDING THE WORLD OF THE TEACHER

One of the problems teachers face in dealing with parents and the public generally is that, since everyone has attended school, people think that they know what the world of the teacher is like. However, knowing what it is like to teach is something that only becomes real in the experience of being responsible for the learning of a specific group of students. In much the same way, knowing what it is like to be a parent becomes real in the act of parenting.

While the essence of good pedagogy might lie in knowing what is good for the child, this is never a simple affair. Teachers do not always know the answer to the question this poses in every situation, but they are expected to provide an answer in the immediacy of the circumstances in which it arises. This situation highlights the real dilemma of teaching – being called on to do something when you do not know what to do!

Van Manen suggests that pedagogy in schools requires a combination of *thoughtfulness and judgment* that has much to do with *who the teacher is*. It is this that helps the teacher negotiate 'pedagogical moments'. This is a form of knowledge that issues from the heart (sensibility, beliefs and values) as well as the head (knowledge), and for which there is no easy substitute.[23]

In the pedagogical relationship the adult needs to realise that *the children are not there for them; they are there for the children*.

Children are children because they are caught up in the primal process of becoming. They are still able to experience life as possibility and this renders them vulnerable. Teachers (and parents) act pedagogically when they consciously show the child *possible ways of being in the world*. They are able to do this if they realise that adulthood does not represent a finished state. This is so because life forever puts the questions to adults:

- *Is this how I should be living my life?*
- *Is this how I should be spending my time?*

There is always more to learn if, as adults, we reflect on these questions.

These are phenomenological questions and Van Manen observes 'no one awakens these questions in an adult more powerfully, or more disturbingly,

---
[23] Ibid, 77.

than a child'.[24] Few teachers have not had to wrestle with them. In consequence, many teachers do their utmost to understand what it is like to live in the world of a child. This enables them to develop a special empathy for their students without which teaching can seem akin to hell.

In sharing their lives with children, teachers cannot help becoming an example of *what it means to be an adult*. In the process they often become aware of new possibilities in their own development. Children open a doorway to hope for teachers by creating 'adult pedagogical moments' for them. The converse is also true. When a teacher loses interest in the development of children or what interests them, he or she loses the empathy essential to pedagogy and, with this, the pedagogical relationship begins to break down. Mutual learning in the classroom dies, and pedagogy morphs into instruction.

An ethical understanding of pedagogy resists this form of pedagogical degeneration in teachers.

---

24 Ibid, 36.

12

VALUES PEDAGOGY: EVALUATING APPROACHES

One of Catholic education's major goals is the integration of life, faith, and culture. The other is the formation of virtue and a Christian character.[1] Values play a vital role in achieving both of these goals. In this chapter, we introduce three values projects which have featured in Australian schools and reflect on the learnings they offer Catholic educators in the matter of pedagogy. Each country will have its own experiences of such endeavours. The important issue for leaders is to analyse and reflect on what has been learnt from the experiences of 'values pedagogy' in terms of achieving Catholic education's major goals.

1. CATHOLIC SCHOOL TEACHERS AND VALUES FORMATION

Children and young people acquire values within the pedagogical relationships that they form with their parents and teachers. This occurs through formal and informal learning, as well as through explicit teaching. The role modelling of teachers and parents is demonstrably important in how students learn what 'being in the world' can mean.

1.1 Historical shifts in teacher formation

For most of the past three hundred years in the West, Catholic education has been in the hands of religious. Their training began with a novitiate experience that was specifically aimed at spiritual and character formation rather than training directly appropriate to 'being in the world'.[2] The formation religious received assumed the continued existence of a public Catholic culture shared with students and their families that justified and supported the value emphasis they brought to the classroom.

---
1 Congregation for Catholic Education. 1977. *The Catholic School*, ## 12, 37.
2 Most novitiate experiences occurred in situations where novices were intentionally isolated from 'the world'.

Today Catholic education is predominantly in the hands of lay people. Public Catholic culture is weak, and the character of teachers in Catholic schools is formed in a quite different time and manner, so the witness they offer of 'being in the world' is necessarily very different from that of their religious predecessors. This change raises the question: *What is appropriate in formation for those teaching in Catholic schools today?* This is an important values question, since values shape not only the *what* of Catholic schooling but also the *how*.

Several diocesan and congregational school systems, together with the National Catholic Education Commission (NCEC) in Australia, have recently attempted to address the question above by developing frameworks to guide formation[3] and putting in place a suite of formation processes.[4]

1.2. Personal worldview as an important 'good' in Catholic schooling

The 'good' that we have proposed in earlier chapters as fundamental to Catholic education in a postsecular world is needed *to assist students to develop a personal worldview that is open to faith* (understood as both the faith of the community and as relationship with God). Such an openness to faith then allows for, and requires, *formation* as a person of faith. In the case of Christian students this openness to relationship with God is coupled with positive relationships with others and with the natural world, and is expressed in their growth as disciples of Jesus.

As was pointed out earlier, a personal worldview is a 'whole' made up of three interacting parts:

- *what the student knows and believes*
- *what they value*
- *a sensibility that determines the emotional and aesthetic dimensions of living with others*

In this perspective, 'worldview' is not tied exclusively to the cognitive (what students know and believe).

---

[3] These are generally accessible on the website for the particular Catholic school system. A recent offering is NCEC (2017), *A Framework for Formation for Mission in Catholic Schools*. This document opens with the statement:
For the Catholic school to achieve its objectives, it needs people who are ... confident in their understanding of the Christian faith as it comes to expression in the Catholic tradition and eager to do their best to help their students grow in their own understanding of the presence of God at work in their lives. This Framework for Formation for Mission in Catholic Education has been developed to assist our teachers and other staff in their understanding of the awesome responsibility they have accepted, mindful of the old Latin tag: 'nemo dat quod non habet' – no one can give what he or she doesn't have.

[4] Formation, in terms of both theory and practice, has been a major focus of the Mission and Education project. See Jill Gowdie, *Stirring the Soul of Catholic Education: Formation for Mission* (Mulgrave: Garratt Publishing, 2017); Michael Green, *Now with Enthusiasm*. Mulgrave: Garratt Publishing, 2018, and Jim & Therese D'Orsa, *New Ways of Living the Gospel*. Mulgrave: Garratt Publishing, 2015.

1.3 Acquiring values within a personal worldview

In building a pedagogical relationship capable of handling the challenges of living in a postsecular world, it is necessary to address the matter of *personal and communal values* and the processes by which these are acquired and transmitted. In this context pedagogy aims to help young people develop their sense of what 'membership in the world' means for them (to re-use Starratt's phrase as introduced in Chapter 11).

In the last chapter the focus was on the *ethical nature of pedagogy*. This drew us into discussion about *ethical understandings* that stand at the heart of the pedagogical relationship (Van Manen), and the *ethical framework* within which the pedagogical relationship stands (Starratt).

The phenomenological approach to pedagogy already discussed can be distinguished from approaches to pedagogy that *directly address values issues*. The latter are the focus of the present chapter that has its origin in Australian educational approaches linking values with pedagogy.

2. APPROACHES TO 'VALUES PEDAGOGY'

In Australia, 'values education' approaches to pedagogy have been employed in both Catholic schools and the public sector. In consequence, this country is recognised as a leader in the field of 'values pedagogy'.[5]

2.1 Values education and pedagogy

At the national level, between 2003 and 2010 the Australian Government sponsored a large-scale project designed to promote values education in all Australian schools. Across the decade the project had a number of names and was supervised by different government bodies. The initial motivation for the project was political concern about the transmission of 'national values' as Australian society became more multicultural, and as concerns were raised about the place of moral education in public education. The Australian Values Education Program (AVEP) was a large-scale, well-resourced project that involved some 100,000 students, 5000 teachers, 312 schools and 50 University researchers.[6] AVEP aimed to explore:

- *the utility of values education within the national goals of schooling*
- *what could be learned about best practice pedagogy in values education*

---

5 Terence Lovat, 'Values Education as Good practice pedagogy: Evidence from Australian Empirical Research'. *Journal of Moral Education* (2017) Vol. 46, no. 1, 88–96.
6 Ibid, 89. Schools formed themselves into clusters of four to ten for the purpose of seeking grants. Twenty-five clusters were selected for stages 1 and 2, and 15 for Stage 3, although the number of applicants was much higher than those selected. Successful applicants received up to $50,000 to implement their programs. The 312 schools were a representative sample of Australia's 9000 schools.

Two decades previously, and in the aftermath of the Second Vatican Council (1962–5), the National Catholic Education Association (NCEA) in the US developed its *Vision and Values in Catholic Schools* project. This initiative sought to promote 'Gospel values' in Catholic primary schools as a means of securing their Catholic identity. Teachers from Australia attending the annual NCEA conference in the US were exposed to this program and subsequently the Catholic Education Office Sydney decided to adopt and adapt the program. Brother John Cleary FSC, was among the leaders in this project resulting in its being widely adopted in NSW Catholic primary schools and beyond in the 1980s.[7]

Many secondary school teachers in Catholic schools at this time were familiar with *values infusion* as a pedagogical technique through its use in environmental studies and peace education. Values infusion was used to bring selected values into play in addressing topics in the formal curriculum. Environmental, peace and justice concerns were not specifically addressed in the curriculum at the time and this was of serious concern to some educators.

Values infusion was subsequently adopted as the pedagogical strategy in the development of Sydney Catholic Education's *A Sense of the Sacred* project which ran predominantly in secondary schools across the 1990s and well into the 2000s. This project sought to *make explicit* the values orientation of the NSW secondary curriculum and provide a critique of it from a Catholic perspective.

Values education has resurfaced in more recent times as an issue in the *Enhancing Catholic Identity* project (ECSI) whose proponents from the Catholic University Leuven (KUL) offer a severe critique of 'Christian Values Education' *as this has developed in Europe*.

Our experience has been that many Catholic school teachers fail to distinguish between 'values education' as used in Australian educational discourse and 'Christian Values education' as used by the proponents of ECSI. Australian educators have been pioneers in values education and their experience of it seems very different from the experience in Flanders. The critique offered by the KUL people leading the ECSI project, a critique arising from a very different approach and experience, has tended to confuse thinking about the issue in many Catholic schools in this country, resulting

---

7   In the 1970s and early 1980s professional development carried out by Catholic systems in NSW depended to a considerable extent on the initiatives mounted in the largest Catholic school system in the state, that of the Sydney archdiocese, which was supported by the Catholic Education Office. As a consequence, the *Vision and Values* program was widely implemented in NSW Catholic primary schools.

in a negative impact on the place of values in pedagogy in some Catholic schools.

In the balance of this chapter we use the term 'values pedagogy' to include pedagogical approaches associated with 'values education' and offer some perspectives on this form of pedagogy. We proceed in three steps:

- *Values pedagogy in the Catholic domain*
- *Values pedagogy in the public domain*
- *Values pedagogy: the KUL critique*

3. VALUES PEDAGOGY IN THE CATHOLIC DOMAIN

3.1 Vision and Values in a Catholic School

If you drove past a Catholic primary school in Sydney in the mid 1980s, you would generally have found a large sign outside the school announcing that this was 'Community' or perhaps 'Justice' week. This indicated that the school was participating in a local version of the *Vision and Values in a Catholic School* program.

3.1.1 Background to the program

The *Vision and Values* program, as it was known, was a national project developed by the NCEA in the US to build Gospel values explicitly into the school curriculum. In the process, the hope was to raise awareness among students, parents and staff about 'Gospel values' in a rapidly secularising world. The project also served as a formation opportunity for many teachers working in Catholic schools.

The program was trialled in the 1970s before being formalised and published by the NCEA in 1981, with Sr Carleen Reck SSND as its principal author.[8]

3.1.2 Methodology

Vision and Values was published as two resources: a *Participant's Guide* and a *Leader's Guide*. Its methodology borrowed heavily from the *values infusion* pedagogy being pioneered in environmental education and peace studies.

3.1.3 Aims of the project

The aim of the *Vision phase* of the project was to establish the *Gospel identity* of the school. The aim of the *Values Phase* was to reinforce this identity by 'infusing' eight 'Gospel values' into the life of the school, including its curriculum and its pedagogy. This was to occur through a systematic process

---
8   Carleen Reck, *Vision and Values in a Catholic School*. Washington: NCEA, 1981.

of reflection by the staff and students on selected Gospel values and their place in school life. It should be noted that the program also sought to include parents by inviting them to introduce the same values into home life. *Vision and Values* adopted nine 'working principles' that had emerged during the trial period. These, instructive even today, are:

1. *Renewal programs are built on the past.*
2. *A staff has the responsibility to improve the school every year.*
3. *Staff members should be involved in plans and decisions related to a school program.*
4. *The total school community should participate in every important school program.*
5. *A school should be able to adapt a program to meet its own needs.*
6. *A leadership team can facilitate initiation and adaptation.*
7. *A consultant can be a strong support.*
8. *Successful projects have a broad scope.*
9. *Decisions by consensus unify rather than divide.*[9]

The *Vision Phase* of the project drew its inspiration from the normative *documentation* on Catholic schooling, in particular the Congregation for Catholic Education's texts *The Catholic School* (1977) and *To Teach as Jesus Did* (US Catholic Bishops' Conference 1972) which were taken as normative for the project.

3.1.4 The values phase

The *Values phase* followed a set pedagogy involving five stages, all of which were supported by resources provided in the *Leader's Guide*:

1. **Selecting a value.**
2. **Reflecting on the value** (*reading about the value; dialoguing with others about the value; thinking about how to implement the value*).
3. **Applying the value** to school (*whole school and department including curriculum planning*) *and home life.*
4. **Evaluating together** (*identifying what has been learned and what has been achieved*).
5. **Celebrating together** (*that a Gospel value has been brought to personal and communal awareness; that new things have been learned; that obstacles have been overcome and achievements realised in promoting the value*).[10]

---

9 Carleen Reck, *Vision and Values in the Catholic School. Leader's Manual.* Washington: National Catholic Educational Association, 1981, L2–4.
10 Carleen Reck, *Vision and Values in the Catholic School Participant's Guide.* Washington: NCEA, 1981, 4–11.

The values chosen were community, faith, hope, reconciliation, courage, service, justice and love. A criterion used in selecting them was that they have *both a personal and a communal dimension*. For instance, 'service' at the personal level was taken to mean:

- *Persons who live the Gospel value of service as disciples of Jesus, the servant, consider themselves to be called to a life of service evidenced by giving their time, talent and money to persons within and beyond the school community.*

At the school community level, it was taken to mean

- *Members of the school community are convinced that service is an integral part of Christian social living evidenced by seeking and offering service to others through special programs and informal opportunities.*[11]

The *Vision and Values* project did not take its choice or delineation of the eight 'Gospel Values' as being definitive. It invited participants to adapt this aspect of the program to make the selection more relevant to a particular context.

3.1.5 Implementation in Australia

When it was implemented in NSW Catholic primary schools, the project was adapted to more specifically include the home. So, for example, when 'service' was the value being taught and practiced at the school, it was also being encouraged in the home.

Catholic primary schools in NSW put their own interpretation on 'Gospel values' and it is not uncommon to walk into an Australian Catholic primary school, even today, and see banners with the names of values hanging on the walls – a legacy of the original *Vision and Values* project.

The resources provided to guide reflection on the values chosen in the *Vision and Values* project were strongly influenced by, and linked to, the Gospel text and included stories of people who provided notable examples of living particular values. These links sometimes became more tenuous in local adaptions of the project as secularisation advanced in this country.

3.2 *A Sense of the Sacred* Project (SOS)
3.2.1 Background

The SOS project had its origins in two sources: Fordham University's *Leaven Program* developed under Sr Loretta Carey RDC, and the Australian National Catholic Missionary Council (NCMC)'s *Mission and Justice program*.

---
11 Ibid, 6–7.

Both programs developed resource kits for secondary schools. These kits focused on applying values, that were explicit in Catholic Social Teaching and normative Church teaching on mission, to major social, political and economic problems of the era (1970s and 1980s). Both programs were targeted at secondary students and adults.

In 1992, the Religious Education and Curriculum Directorate was formed in the Catholic Education Office Sydney with the mandate, inter alia, to bring a faith perspective into all teaching and learning areas in Catholics schools. Along with a revamping of the secondary Religious Education curriculum (the primary curriculum having been recently renewed), *A Sense of the Sacred* would become the vehicle to achieve this objective.[12] It aimed to infuse a set of Catholic values into all major areas of the curriculum, starting with secondary science. Over the following years, resource kits were developed and trialled for use by secondary teachers in other key learning areas.

3.2.2 Aim of the project

This aim, as set out clearly in each kit, follows:

> *This project is for school leaders and the teachers in their departments. It is an invitation to look at those places where learning and values come together (which is virtually everywhere). It seeks to promote exploration of the questions:*
>
> - *what does it mean to know?*
> - *what does it mean to value?*
> - *what does it mean to create meaning?*
>
> *within the framework of the shared values and assumptions which hold us together as a particular group of Jesus' followers.*[13]

The document continues:

> *Meaning-making is an important goal of the teacher in guiding the learning process. There is no doubt that we continually create meaning in response to what we perceive. The meaning we create depends on many things, the most telling being the world view we bring to our perception. There is, however, an important process in all this. Human beings not only perceive, but we have the capacity to imagine. What we imagine is fed not only by what we see, but also by our previous experiences, and our values.*

---

12 One of this book's authors, Therese D'Orsa, was appointed first Director of the combined unit.
13 Catholic Education Office Sydney, *A Sense of the Sacred: Science*. Sydney: CEO, 1993, 1.1.

> *Since we can imagine, we can also create cultures. Because we can reflect, we can alter and improve cultures. In his teaching process, for example, Jesus encouraged people to think about and to question and challenge their cultural assumptions, even some of the most entrenched.*
>
> *... The outcomes on which we focus ... in this project are associated with the development of a critical consciousness.*
>
> *Such an awareness is facilitated by teachers whose pedagogy focuses on experiential learning that is meaning-centred and which encourages an appreciation of human knowledge as a truth to be discovered ... Critical skills need to be applied to society as well. The transmission of culture, a very important part of education, must be balanced by processes that are 'critical and evaluative'.*[14]

3.2.3 Catholic 'meta-values'

The project operated on the assumption that there are five interrelated Catholic meta-values:[15]

- *Sacramentality of all creation*
- *Dignity of the human person*
- *Communion – past, present and future*
- *Cultural transformation*
- *Reconciliation and Hope*[16]

These values are sourced in scripture, tradition and the lived experience of the Catholic community. Each exists, in practice, as a constellation of more narrowly focused human and religious values, which surface in all forms of human action. As *A Sense of the Sacred* notes:

> *The learning of values relates to the formation of conscience and moral development. It prepares for an affective maturity that enables the person to perceive the world with sensitivity and compassion leading to active concern.*[17]

The links to 'forming a worldview open to faith' seem obvious. The document continues:

> *In a Catholic context, Values Education involves an introduction to a worldview that seeks to ensure the Gospel message of Jesus Christ puts down deep roots within contemporary society ...*

---

14 Ibid.
15 A 'Catholic meta-value' refers to an undisputed Catholic value shared by Catholics worldwide.
16 *A Sense of the Sacred: Science*, 1.2–1.3.
17 Ibid, 1.7

A *'Sense of the Sacred'* is about integration of the teaching of the Key Values within the Key Learning Area of Science.[18]

3.2.4 Project methodology

The project methodology accepted that students develop values using a number of processes:

- *values clarification*
- *values analysis*
- *values acquisition*
- *values judgement*

and that these processes need to be kept in balance in planning learning experiences, otherwise values may be accepted uncritically. Values infusion was seen as the most adequate process for meeting these criteria.

As a pedagogical practice, values infusion is summarised in the tables below. The model involves consciously changing the paradigm that teachers use in lesson planning.

Value infusion Model (Peace Studies)	
Original Aim	Original Activity
Look at the aim of the lesson and the concepts to be introduced.	Review suggested activities.
Infused Aim	Infused Activity
Include a related justice/peace concept.	Reframe activity to achieve both original and infused objectives.

TABLE 12.1: NCEA, *INFUSION LEADERSHIP WORKSHOP MANUAL*, 22 (RONEOED MATERIAL UNDATED)

As used in *A Sense of the Sacred*, this model was adapted as follows and applied to a topic in the school curriculum.

Value infusion Model (Sense of the Sacred)	
Original Aim	Original Activity
Look at the aim of the lesson and the cultural concepts or value to be introduced.	Review suggested activities.
Infused Aim	Infused Activity
Introduce a related faith concept or value.	Reframe activity to include an infused activity to achieve both original and infused objectives.

TABLE 12.2

---

18 Ibid

In environmental education, peace education and in the approach used in *A Sense of the Sacred,* the aim is to expand the student's imaginal horizon from a focus on the immediate, to recognising that 'being in the world' has not only a personal dimension, but also an interpersonal, cultural, global and structural dimension.[19]

With a clear objective in mind, Catholic secondary teachers set about re-mapping the NSW curriculum in terms of values associated with all major topics. They then prepared lesson plans using the values infusion method to teach the topics. Resources supporting *A Sense of the Sacred* were developed to cover all major key learning areas. The materials developed were disseminated in a set of Teacher's Manuals that had a distribution well beyond the Sydney archdiocesan schools.

Three factors led to the demise of the project. The first was the release of the Australian National Curriculum. This document would have required a complete reworking of the project. Secondly, *A Sense of the Sacred* relied on printed manuals, and by 2006 its ageing resources not only needed to be upgraded, they also needed to be put online. Finally, changes of leadership in the Sydney archdiocese and the Catholic Education Office resulted in Curriculum and Religious Education again becoming separately managed units within the Catholic Education Office, so *A Sense of the Sacred* became an orphan in distress. Neither the *Vision and Values* nor the *Sense of the Sacred* initiatives were ever formally evaluated.

4. NATIONAL VALUES EDUCATION PROJECT

Concern about the place of values in education and pedagogy was not only one for Catholic educators in the 1990s and early 2000s, but also for the national Government as the country became increasingly multi-cultural and social cohesion emerged as a societal and political issue.

4.1 Framework for Values Education in Australian Schools

In 2005 the Howard Government published the *National Framework for Values Education in Australian Schools.* The *Values Framework* was the culmination of a three-year study which came to the conclusion that:

- **education is as much about building character** *as it is about equipping students with specific skills*

---

19 When *A Sense of the Sacred* was first introduced, some members of the clergy were concerned that it was to replace the formal Religious Education curriculum, whereas the aim was to complement it, so enabling students to bring faith, life, and culture together in making sense of life in all their learning. Once this matter was clarified, it gained clergy support.

- ***values-based education can strengthen students' self-esteem**, optimism and commitment to personal fulfillment; and help students exercise ethical judgment and social responsibility*
- *parents **expect schools to help students understand and develop personal and social responsibilities**.*[20]

The 2003 *Values Education Study*, carried out as part of this initiative, identified that values education was on a sound footing in Australian schools, but that a number of challenges lay ahead. These included:

> ... *improving whole school cultures, developing school mission statements incorporating a set of values, including values in key learning area programs, increasing student engagement, belonging and connectedness to schooling, fostering student empowerment and encouraging youth civic participation, improving student and staff health and wellbeing, promoting improved relationships, tackling violence, anti-social and behavior management issues, and building student resilience as an antidote to youth suicide and substance abuse.*[21]

With these in mind, the government allocated $30m over four years to continue the *Values Education Study* (VES) and identify 'best practice' in values education and values pedagogy.

4.2 Goals of the Australian Values Education Study

The intention in developing the *National Values Education Framework (NVEP)* and supporting the *Values Education Study* was to ensure that schools provide values education in a planned and systematic way which would enable them to:

- *articulate, in consultation with their school community, the school's mission/ethos*
- *develop student responsibility in local, national and global contexts and build student resilience and social skills*
- *ensure values are incorporated into school policies and teaching programs across the key learning areas*
- *review the outcomes of their values education practices.*[22]

---

20 Taken from Commonwealth of Australia *National Framework for Values Education in Australian Schools*. Canberra, 2005, 1.
http://www.curriculum.edu.au/verve/_resources/Framework_PDF_version_for_the_web.pdf
21 Ibid, 3.
22 Ibid

The NVEP proposed nine national cultural values to be promoted in Australian schools:

1. *Care and Compassion: care for self and others*
2. *Doing Your Best: Seek to accomplish something worthy and admirable, try hard, pursue excellence.*
3. *Fair Go: Pursue and protect the common good where all people are treated fairly for a just society.*
4. *Freedom: Enjoy all the rights and privileges of Australian citizenship, free from unnecessary interference or control and stand up for the rights of others.*
5. *Honesty and Trustworthiness: Be honest, sincere and seek the truth.*
6. *Integrity: Act in accordance with principles of moral and ethical conduct, ensure consistency between words and deeds.*
7. *Respect: Treat others with consideration and regard, respect another person's point of view.*
8. *Responsibility: Be accountable for one's own actions, resolve differences in constructive, non-violent and peaceful ways, contribute to society and to civic life, take care of the environment.*
9. *Understanding, Tolerance and Inclusion: Be aware of others and their cultures, accept diversity within a democratic society, being included and including others.*[23]

These emerged in the 'national conversation' held as part of the 2003–5 *Values Education Study (VES)*. This also yielded a number of guiding principles to be adopted in taking the project to a further two stages:
Effective values education:

1. *helps students understand and be able to apply values*
2. *is an explicit goal of schooling that promotes Australia's democratic way of life and values the diversity in Australian schools*
3. *articulates the values of the school community and applies these consistently in the practices of the school*
4. *occurs in partnership with students, staff, families and the school community as part of a whole-school approach to educating students, enabling them to exercise responsibility and strengthening their resilience*
5. *is presented in a safe and supportive learning environment in which students are encouraged to explore their own, their school's and their communities' values*

---

23 Ibid, 4.

6. *is delivered by trained and resourced teachers able to use a variety of different models, modes and strategies;*
7. *includes the provision of curriculum that meets the individual needs of students;*
8. *regularly reviews the approaches used to check that they are meeting the intended outcomes.*[24]

The 'guiding principles', set out above, reflect what had been learnt about best practice in values education and values pedagogy in the initial stage (2003–2005) of the VES. There would be two more stages in what was renamed as the *Values Education Good Practice Schools Project,* and which we are referring to as the *Australian Values Education Project (AVEP).*

Each of these stages involved 25 clusters of schools whose projects were closely monitored through internal reports and external observation. Schools participating in the project were *free to choose their own projects and pedagogical approach.* At the end of each stage (2006 and 2008) a formal report was prepared so that learning across the project was cumulative. Due to limitation of space, we comment only on the findings of the Stage 2 and Final reports.

4.3 At the Heart of What We Do (2008)[25]

This report prepared by the Curriculum Corporation for the Australian Government details the learning and experiences of the 310 schools in 25 clusters taking part in the search for 'good practice' in values education. 'Good practice' was taken to be 'a school-driven, ground-up approach to exploring values education practice in local school contexts'. In Stage 2 of AVEP some schools were selected specifically to 'focus on the implementation of values education across all key learning areas' (thus providing a public secular model parallel to Sydney Catholic Education's *A Sense of the Sacred* project).

While SOS used a values infusion methodology, in implementing the *National Values Framework,* schools were free to develop their own methodologies which included:

- *student action groups preparing for community events*
- *'kids teaching kids' in the context of 'school community capacity building'*
- *Vision projects creating a sustainable vision for the future*

---

24 Ibid, 5.
25 Curriculum Corporation, *At the Heart of What We Do: Values Education at the Centre of Schooling.* The Final Report of the Values Education Good Practice Schools Project, Stage 2. Report commissioned by the Australian Government and prepared by the Curriculum Corporation, Carlton, 2008.

- *service learning embedded across key learning areas*
- *restorative justice initiatives*[26]

These methodologies were reported as case studies, phenomenological case writing, and reports from University observers, education officers, and mentors acting as consultants to particular initiatives. This mountain of qualitative data was aggregated by the Curriculum Corporation to identify two general conditions necessary for values education and values pedagogy to be effective:

- *Values education is sustained over time only through a whole school approach that engages all sectors of the school community.*
- *School leadership is critical in developing values education as a core part of schooling.*[27]

The data also yielded 10 principles of good practice that are set out below:

1. **Establish and consistently use a common and shared values language across the school.**
2. **Use pedagogies that are values-focused and student-centred within all curriculum.** *(Effective values education used pedagogies that mirrored the values being taught)*
3. **Develop values education as an integrated curriculum concept, rather than as a program, an event, or an addition to curriculum.** *(Values education as a central principle underpinning the school curriculum offerings, the curriculum design, pedagogy and assessment)*
4. **Explicitly teach values so students know what the values mean and how the values are lived.** *(Values-based schools live and breathe a values consciousness)*
5. **Implicitly model values and explicitly foster the modeling of values.** *(Once values are explicitly established within the school, the modelling implicitly reinforces the values learning)*
6. **Develop relevant and engaging values approaches connected to local and global contexts and which offer real opportunity for student agency.** *(Effective values education is not an academic exercise; it needs to be deeply personal, deeply real and deeply engaging the student's heart mind and actions)*

---

26 *At the Heart of What We Do*, 7.
27 Ibid, 9.

7. **Use values education to consciously foster intercultural understanding, social cohesion and social inclusion.** *(Values education provides a context for positively engaging with diversity and difference)*
8. **Provide teachers with informed, sustained and targeted professional development and foster their professional collaborations.** *(Professional learning can be a critical factor in developing sustainable value-based schooling)*
9. **Encourage teachers to take risks in their approaches to values education.** *(Successful values education initiatives are positively disturbing and disruptive in nature. They can challenge familiar and traditional notions of curriculum and the teacher's role, the way schools operate, student-teacher relationships, and the very nature of schooling)*
10. **Gather and monitor data for continuous improvement in values education.**[28]

A general conclusion from AVEP is that *learning is a mediated process*. It is mediated by classroom teaching strategies such as collaborative learning, carefully crafted experiences outside the classroom, social networking through ICT, enhanced learning materials, or a combination of these. Service learning and storytelling were other strategies widely used.[29] (In the case of the EREA cluster, service learning was 'decoupled' from the presumption that service 'belonged' only in religious education.)[30]

4.4 Giving Voice to the Impacts of Values Education (2010)[31]

As stages 1 and 2 of AVEP unfolded, reporting processes and outcomes took a phenomenological turn, focusing on the 'story' of individual projects and how they were experienced by participants. Each story represented the storyteller's interpretation of the impact the project had in a particular context. In Stage 3 these were collected and sorted to arrive at a set of stories that seemed to condense the major learnings from AVEP about the impact of values education and values pedagogy. These cases were reported in the AVEP final report which also outlines the six major impacts of a decade's work. The findings related to:

---

28 Ibid, 9–12.
29 Service learning featured prominently in reports from the EREA and WestPEERs clusters which were both composed of Catholic schools.
30 EREA – Edmund Rice Education Australia – is the body responsible for the governance of a network of Catholic schools which operate across Australia within the tradition and spirituality of Blessed Edmund Rice.
31 *Giving Voice to the Impacts of Values Education: The Final Report of the Values in Action Schools Project.* Carlton: Education Services Australia, 2010.

1. **Values Consciousness.** *(There was an increased consciousness of the meaning of values and the power of values education to transform learning and life.)*
2. **Student Well-being.** *(Values education improved student well-being through the application of values-focused and student-centered pedagogies that allowed students to reflect deeply on the nature of values and what these mean to them and others.)*
3. **Student Agency.** *(Agency refers to the capacity of individuals to act independently and to make choices and act on them. The VEP indicated that student agency is facilitated through outreach, community projects and service learning. These have to be approached in ways that [encourage students to feel] safe and supported in their values learning.)*
4. **Connectedness.** *(The VEP highlighted the value of a 'community of practice' in learning. This is a group of people who share a concern and passion for something they do, and who learn how to do it better as they interact regularly.)*
5. **Transformation.** *(Change was at the heart of the VEP. This was promoted by the use of the action research cycle. Numerous reports focused on communal and personal change that happened during the VEP. It highlighted what good values education and good values pedagogy are and the sorts of difference this can make to students, teachers and whole school communities.)*[32]

Clearly, Australian educators have built up a significant amount of evidence regarding what is effective in values pedagogy both in the Catholic sector and the public sector.

5. KU LEUVEN CRITIQUE OF CHRISTIAN VALUES EDUCATION

Christian values are important human values. The Leuven critique is that when they become the focus of instruction in Catholic schools, they can lose their Christian meaning and revert to a solely secular meaning. This effect has been noted in Australian Catholic schools in projects aimed at helping the marginalised through social justice involvement.[33]

One issue here is that 'Catholic values' are often presented to students as *abstract,* independent of the 'story' that gives them both significance and a particular character for members of a faith community. That students are often more attuned to the secular 'story' associated with these values is

---
32 Ibid, 5–10.
33 Joan Daw, *Young People, Faith and Social Justice.* Box Hill: Yarra Institute Press, 2013, 125.

not surprising. This is because secular culture acts as a kind of default in the meaning-making process when one lives in a secular society. It takes a conscious effort on the part of teachers and leaders to make the connections with the journey and story of the faith community. The eight values that feature in the *Vision and Values* project all have secular equivalents. The meta-values used in the *A Sense of the Sacred* project are similarly abstract and require translation through 'story'. So, there is some substance to the ECSI critique. It stands as a necessary caution, one based on real and saddening experience. In some situations a values education process has eventually *substituted* for a thorough program of Religious Education.

In our view it is important not to 'throw out the baby with the bath water'. All three projects outlined above contain important lessons for teachers to aid them in understanding their role and their relationships with colleagues, parents and students in the process of teaching and learning. It is important to be aware of the potential pitfalls in dealing with value issues in Catholic schooling, but these have to be weighed against the very considerable benefits. The KU Leuven critique is directed at forms of Christian values education that do not 'start with why'.[34] Examples of this are a *Vision and Values* program minus the vision, *A Sense of the Sacred* program that did not see the integration of faith and culture as its objective, or an Australian Values project that lost its connections to what makes Australians Australian.

In regard to AVEP, a major insight to emerge from the study was that the values have to be 'modelled in the pedagogy', not seen as distinct from it. As a consequence, schools were given *freedom* with respect to the *How* of the project and were grouped together to *collaborate* on dealing with the *What*. Put in other words, students and teachers came to realise what being Australian meant actually being Australian *by living the values* as they went about their engagement in education!

In the Australian experience of values education as featured in this chapter, whether in the Catholic sector or in the public sector, the *medium became the message*, and all three projects *began with why* and never lost sight of this. This does not appear to have been the way things were done in Flanders, and KU Leuven leaders are correct in severely criticising those developments. The issue for them is not to assume that the European experience defines values education in Australia; the cautionary tale for educators here and elsewhere is to ensure that it does not.

An irony of a values-driven pedagogy in Australia, as Lovat points out, is that the Government that signed off on the Australian Values Project

---

34 See Simon Sinek, *Start with Why*. London: Penguin, 2009.

also signed Australian schools up to NAPLAN[35] as a way of improving the country's international competitiveness, as measured by national PISA[36] scores. While this choice dramatically changed the approach to school pedagogy in many Australian schools, NAPLAN has not resulted in better PISA scores. In fact the reverse is true! On the other hand, countries such as Turkey, that stayed with a values pedagogy as developed in Australia, have been the big improvers according to PISA rankings.[37]

Catholic schools stand in a deep and long-standing faith tradition played out in many key areas, as we acknowledged in the early part of this book. The values grounded in this tradition have extraordinary potential to shape pedagogy and draw out the potential of every young person.

Leaders are invited to ponder the various experiences touched on in this chapter and the lessons they offer for transforming young lives through successful values-based learning.

---

35 An Australian national Government-sponsored assessment regime which, since 2008, has tested students in years 3, 5, 7, and 9 in the areas of reading, writing, literacy, and numeracy.
36 Program for International Student Assessment (OECD).
37 Terence Lovat, 'Values education as good practice pedagogy: Evidence from Australian empirical research'. *Journal of Moral Education*, 46, 2017, 94.

13

THE EMPIRICAL RESEARCH TRADITION: THE QUANTITATIVE APPROACH OF JOHN HATTIE

Education has a substantial research tradition focused on 'what works in the classroom'. This is particularly the case in the English-speaking world. Such a research emphasis is an empirical tradition that is essentially pragmatic. And it has both a *qualitative* and a *quantitative* base. In this chapter we focus on *quantitative research* on pedagogy as exemplified in the work of well-known researcher John Hattie. This tradition takes a 'narrow' view of pedagogy, as discussed in Chapter 1, equating it with the work of teachers.

1. COMMON SENSE VERSUS SCIENTIFIC APPROACHES TO LEARNING

There are two broad approaches to 'what works' in the classroom. The first focuses on the *'common sense' reflections of teachers*; the second is the systematic attempt to *bring science to bear on the practice of teaching*. These two approaches can be complementary, as illustrated in the following exchange between researcher John Hattie and a teacher reflecting on her 'common sense' experience of teaching smaller classes:

> *As a teacher, I have on the ground experience that tells me that class size can impact teaching and learning in negative ways. If push comes to shove, my experience is more valuable to me as a teacher because I see it and I live it over and over again [more] than any research that tells me I'm wrong about class size. This is not to say that I'm going to toss my hands up in the air, say that it's because I have a large class, and just give up. Absolutely not! However, I do know, again from experiencing large, medium and small class sizes, that class size does matter. Furthermore, a complete reliance on quantitative studies really does not provide a whole picture of 'what works' in education.*
>
> Eliza Waingort, July 23, 2018.

I agree that all appearances and reactions are that smaller classes make a difference – although the research is reasonably systematic that these differences while positive are very small. And relative to spending our educational resources on one of the more expensive interventions we might be wise to invest elsewhere (provided we are given this option).

There is evidence that a major reason why the effects are small is that teachers do not change how they teach to optimize the opportunities of small class size. Also, class size is often a proxy.

- **For parents** *it is a proxy as they believe smaller classes mean more individual attention to their child (but there is no evidence this happens).*
- **For principals** *it is a proxy for staff-student ratios as this is a major factor in most school funding models.*
- **For teachers***, it is a proxy for removing the most disruptive students – and these disruptive students do take much time, attention and can detract from other student learning. Let me ask you – would you rather have 40 students who want to be in class, or 20 who do not? Would you rather me come and remove randomly 10–12 students, or you pick the 5 you do not want in class?*

Yes, there is more to the world than quantitative studies, but they can make us think, question our assumptions, and should be part of the story. [Formatting added.]

John Hattie 26 July 2018[1]

The *Ratio Studiorum* developed as a guide for Jesuit schools, to which we referred in Chapter 4, and St John Baptist De La Salle's *The Conduct of Christian Schools* referred to in Chapter 5, both reflect the *common sense tradition* – what lived experience tells us about what works in classrooms and schools. The hope is that quantitative research would confirm this tradition but as the above exchange indicates, there are good reasons why this may not be the case.

John Hattie's synthesis of quantitative research in his 2009 book *Visible Learning,* and in later publications, provides a widely quoted summary of 'what works' in helping or hindering student achievement.[2] The tradition is not without its critics as we saw in the last chapter, particularly when test results are taken as the measure of 'student achievement', since learning

---

[1] Corwin Connect website, https://corwin-connect.com/2018/06/clearing-the-lens-addressing-the-criticisms-of-the-visible-learning-research/ accessed 12 July 2019.
[2] Achievement is commonly measured by standardised tests in literacy, numeracy and science.

happens at a number of levels.³ 'Achievement' can be an ambiguous measure given that how it is being assessed is not always specified in the research. This raises the important question: How does student achievement, as measured by tests, relate to student learning?

2. CHANGING CONCEPTIONS OF 'SUCCESS' IN SCHOOLING

How people assess 'what works' in enhancing student achievement depends on their conception of what 'success in learning' looks like, either for students individually or for the school collectively. How 'success' in construed also changes as the context of learning changes.

In John Baptist De La Salle's era, the parents of his pupils generally had no formal education themselves and so placed little value on an experience that had eluded them, so success for school leaders in that age meant getting the young people to actually attend school. This was still the situation more than a century later in the early days of Catholic schooling in Australia, and remains the case, for instance, in some developing countries such as East Timor.

In the early Ignatian educational tradition, the targeted clientele was different, and this led to a different definition of success. Jesuit schools aimed to prepare young people from the emerging middle classes to take up responsible positions in their society, so 'success' was quite 'visible' in the sense in which Hattie uses the term.

In post-World War II Australia, 'success' in Catholic schooling was measured in terms of two major parameters:

- *passing on 'the faith' (understood as propositions to be believed and practices to be followed)*
- *creating 'life chances' for students.*

Until the 1970s these remained realistic goals. Two changes then made it necessary to re-define what constitutes 'success' in Catholic schooling:

- *Following the teachings of the Second Vatican Council, many Catholics no longer understood faith in propositional terms, but rather in relational*

---

3   Hattie identifies three levels of learning: *surface learning* associated with mastering the basics of a particular field; *deep learning* which requires higher order thinking enabling the student to make connections and see relationships between what were initially disparate concepts; and *transfer learning* that enables concepts to be applied to new problems or situations. Hattie's contention is that students move between these three levels in learning, and whether or not a particular teaching intervention works depends on where students are at in this learning process. (John AC Hattie & Gregory Donoghue, 'Learning Strategies: A synthesis and conceptual model'. *Science of Learning*, 23 May 2016, 1.

terms. *In the same period, and in a separate development, traditional Catholic practices fell into decline.*
- *Economic changes in Australia meant that schooling ceased to provide a direct entry to the world of work. Its role became preparatory for the majority of students.*

These changes caught out people who had come to take the immediate post-war context as 'normal'. Expectations for Catholic schooling that had historically been taken as 'givens', could no longer be realised. Measured against the old criteria of success, Catholic schools were now seen as failing. Such beliefs still prevail in sections of the Catholic faith community.

Today there remains a good deal of confusion about what constitutes 'success' in Catholic schooling. However, the new parameters of success seem to be coalescing around three interrelated goals:

- *Maximising achievement in student learning, relative to the students' abilities*
- *Accompanying young people as they construct a personal identity open to faith*
- *Helping young people bring the insights of faith and culture together in making sense of their life experiences.*

Defining 'success' in this way poses a range of questions:

- *How do we assess student learning?*
- *How do young people establish their identity?*
- *How do teachers view the relationship between faith and culture in making sense of their own lives?*
- *How do school leaders indicate to teachers and parents that the context for learning in Catholic schools has changed?*
- *How do Catholic systems and schools prepare teachers, parents and students to work within the emerging definition of 'success'?*

These are all questions that have an important bearing on the *pedagogical outlook* that teachers use with young people in Catholic schools. In the remainder of this chapter our aim is to explore the strengths and limits of the pragmatic approach to pedagogy in the changed context of Catholic schooling.

3. ACHIEVEMENT AND LEARNING: FINDINGS OF THE QUANTITATIVE TRADITION

There is a substantial database on 'what works in promoting student achievement' largely in the US and associated with innovations by teachers, schools, school systems, and governments. The quantitative research-base is large, varies in quality, and has now cumulated over several decades. As a consequence, making sense of it has proved difficult and the impact of research in changing pedagogical practice remains limited.

The general conclusion would seem to be that: *In the hands of some teachers, some practices, in some contexts, work for some students!*

4. VISIBLE LEARNING (2009)

The work of John Hattie[4] and his associates in New Zealand and Australia has proved instrumental in bringing some clarity to an otherwise confusing situation, but not without a degree of controversy.[5]

The sheer volume of educational research since the 1970s on factors that influence student achievement led to meta-studies being undertaken to draw together the findings of individual research projects. Hattie's innovation was to synthesise these meta-studies into what might be described as a mega-study. His intention is obvious in the title of his acclaimed book, *Visible Learning: A synthesis of over 800 meta-analyses related to achievement.*[6] This was no small feat and his research, which remains ongoing, has received international acclaim.

4.1 'Effect Size' as a metric of impact

The challenge facing Hattie in dealing with the mountain of data he sought to analyse was to develop a *metric* that would allow the results of studies, that often used different statistical approaches, to be legitimately compared. He accomplished this task by adopting the notion of *'effect size'*.

'Effect size' *for a class* can be calculated using the following formula:

---

[4] At the time of his original research Hattie was Professor of Education at the University of Auckland. He was subsequently appointed Professor of Education and Director of the Melbourne Education Research Institute at the University of Melbourne and is currently chair of the Australian Institute for Teaching and School Leadership (AISTL). Since 2009 Hattie's database has expanded to 1200 meta-studies.

[5] Hattie analyses the results of meta-analyses. This means that his analysis is 'second-order', once removed from the original research. Hattie acknowledges that the quality of these original studies varies considerably in terms of their design and method of analysis. This would suggest the need to view his conclusions with some caution.

[6] John Hattie *Visible Learning: A synthesis of over 800 meta-analyses related to achievement.* London: Routledge, 2009.

$$\text{Effect size} = \frac{\text{Mean (post intervention)} - \text{Mean (pre intervention)}}{\text{Standard deviation for the class}}$$

The formula can be equally applied to an *individual student* in the form:

$$\text{Effect size} = \frac{\text{Score (post intervention)} - \text{Score (pre intervention)}}{\text{Standard deviation for the class}}$$

The formula means that 'no change' has an effect size of 0. Effect size can be positive or negative (indicating that a factor or intervention is counter-productive). Positive effect sizes can be misleading as a student's score on most tests will reflect *developmental maturing*. The effect size of most interventions will include this maturing effect and not necessarily be entirely due to the impact of the intervention.

4.2 Finding the 'hinge point'

Hattie and his colleagues identified a very large number of factors that influence student achievement and calculated their effect size. The results turned out to be normally distributed, centring on a mean of .4. Hattie calls this the 'hinge point'. In Hattie's research an effect size greater than .4 indicates a positive impact on student achievement.

In Visible Learning and Hattie's subsequent publications, effect size is presented in schematic form as illustrated below. Hattie estimates that the typical maturation effect is .1 and the typical 'teacher effect' is between .2 and .4. By this he means that if there is a live teacher in front of the class, student achievement will usually advance by .4 during the intervention, all other things being equal!

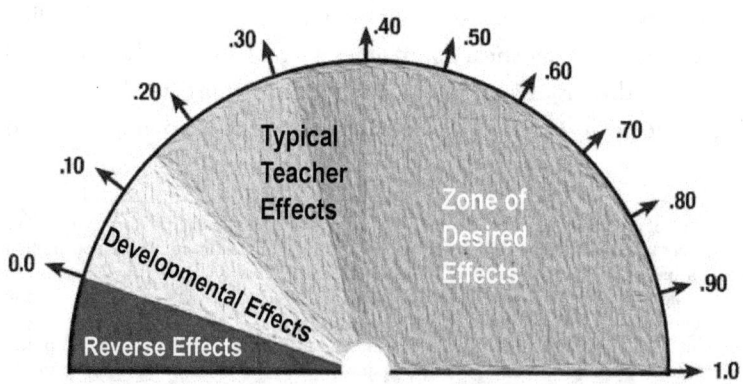

FIGURE 13.1: HATTIE'S TEMPLATE FOR ILLUSTRATING EFFECT SIZE[7]

---

7   *After Hattie*, 2009, 43.

What Hattie and his team sought to identify were factors and interventions that produced an effect size greater than .4. This placed the interventions in what he calls the 'zone of desired effect size'. In other words, these factors had such a positive effect on student achievement that the impact on learning should be clearly 'visible' to both the teacher and the learner.

4.3 Factors impacting on student learning

Hattie's methodology enabled him to test the impact of multiple individual factors and interventions on student achievement. He divided the results into six categories. These categories concerned:

- *the student*
- *the home*
- *the school*
- *the curriculum*
- *the teacher*
- *teaching approaches*

The table below summarises some of the notable influences on student achievement with (in some cases) their corresponding effect sizes as found throughout Hattie's text.

The Child	The Home
• Prior knowledge and Learning (.67)	• Parental expectations of the child
• Student expectations	• Parental involvement in learning (.51)
• Openness to experiences	• Socio-economic status (.57)
• Student beliefs about the value and worth of material learned	
• Student engagement in learning	
• Student's sense of self-worth as a learner (.43)	
The School	**The Teacher**
• Climate in the classroom (.52)	• Quality of teaching (as seen by students) (.44)
• School size (.43)	• Teacher expectations (.43)
• Class size (.21)	• Teacher-student relationship (.72)
• Peer influences (.53)	• Teacher's clarity in articulating criteria of success (.75)
	• Professional development (.62)

The Curriculum	Teaching Approaches
• Balance of surface and deep learning • Learning strategies to construct meaning • Deliberate strategies to teach skills and understanding	• Setting challenging tasks • Providing multiple opportunities for practice • Knowing when one has attained the goal • Metacognition • Planning and talking about teaching • Seeking feedback from students about the success of teaching

TABLE 13.1: NOTABLE INFLUENCES ON STUDENT ACHIEVEMENT (HATTIE)[8]

4.4 Signposts to successful learning.

Hattie synthesises the general findings of the *Visible Learning* study by nominating six *signposts toward excellence in education*, all of which have implications for teaching and many of which were highlighted in the previous chapter dealing with the ethical approach to pedagogy. His six 'signposts' are as follows:

1. *Teachers are among the most powerful influences in learning.*
2. *Teachers need to be directive, influential, caring, and actively engaged in the passion of teaching and learning.*
3. *Teachers need to be aware of what each and every student is thinking and knowing, to construct meaning and meaningful experiences in the light of this knowledge, and have proficient knowledge and understanding of their content to provide meaningful and appropriate feedback such that each student moves progressively through the curriculum levels.*
4. *Teachers need to know the learning intentions and success criteria of their lessons, know how well they are attaining these for all students and know where to go next in light of the gap between students' current knowledge and understanding and the success criteria of: 'Where are you going?', 'How are you going?', and 'Where to next?'.*
5. *Teachers need to move from the single idea to multiple ideas, and to relate and then extend these ideas so that learners construct and reconstruct knowledge and ideas. It is not the knowledge or ideas, but the learner's construction of the knowledge and ideas that is critical.*
6. *School leaders and teachers need to create school, staffroom, and classroom environments where error is welcomed as a learning opportunity, where discarding incorrect knowledge and understandings is welcomed, and where participants can feel safe to learn, re-learn, and explore knowledge and understanding.*[9]

---

8   Material drawn from Hattie, 18.
9   Hattie 2009, 238–9.

The last four 'Signposts' on this list move from teaching to learning and suggest elements in a theory of learning that are needed to support effective teaching.

4.5 *Start with Why* – Simon Sinek

Hattie takes his idea of 'signposts' further in *10 Mindframes for Visible Learning: Teaching for Success*,[10] a book he co-authored with Klaus Zierer. The theme of this book is summed up in the title of its preface: '*How we think* about the *impact* of what we do is more important than *what* we do'. The authors suggest that the most important criterion of 'success' in teaching lies in *knowing the impact of interventions* in promoting student learning. In effective interventions the impact on learning *is visible* to both the student and the teacher.

Hattie acknowledges the influence of leadership guru Simon Sinek on his thinking. Sinek proposes that there are three questions that leaders need to answer: 'Why?' 'How?' and 'What?' Too many leaders mistakenly start with 'What needs to be done?', he argues, adding that good leaders start with the question: 'Why are we doing it?'[11]

Hattie applies this thinking to teaching where he argues the 'Why?' question needs to come before the 'How?' question in shaping the way teachers engage with their students. Being clear about 'Why?' enables a teacher to bring passion and impact to the task of making those crucial moment-by-moment decisions essential in effective teaching in the classroom.[12] This is his answer to 'the dilemma of pedagogical tact' discussed in Chapter 11. Teachers know *'what to do when they do not know what to do because they know why they are doing things the way they do!'*

4.6 *Teaching for Success* (2018)

Hattie & Zierer outline ten 'mindframes' that teachers need to bring to pedagogical decision-making based on their studies of 'effect size'.[13] The mindframes are set out in a somewhat cryptic form in this work and are expanded here for the purpose of clarity.

1. *I evaluate my impact on student learning.*
2. *I see assessment as informing both how I evaluate the impact of my*

---

10 John Hattie & Klaus Zierer, *10 Mindframes for Visible Learning: teaching for success*. London Routledge, 2017.
11 Simon Sinek, *Start with Why: How Great Leaders Inspire Everyone to Take Action*. New York: Penguin, 2009.
12 Hattie & Zierer, xiv.
13 The justification offered for some of these mindframes seems slim on the evidence provided in the text.

> *teaching and how I plan the next steps in advancing student learning.*
> 3. *I collaborate with my peers and students in developing my conceptions of what constitutes 'student progress' and my own impact on student learning.*
> 4. *I am a change agent and believe all students can improve.*
> 5. *In planning my lessons, I strive for real challenge and do not settle for simply 'doing your best'.*
> 6. *I give and help students understand feedback, and I interpret and act on feedback given to me.*
> 7. *In teaching, I balance dialogue with monologue.*
> 8. *I explicitly inform students as to what success in learning looks like from the outset.*
> 9. *I build relationships and trust so that learning can occur in an environment where it is safe to make mistakes and learn from others.*
> 10. *I focus on learning, the language of learning, and learning how to learn.*[14]

Implicit in this list is a conception of the pedagogical relationship central to an ethical approach to pedagogy.

Hattie and Zierer emphasise the importance of teachers being able to:

- *take on board a range of clues provided by students in assessing the impact of their teaching on student learning*
- *be humble in admitting 'I got it wrong' when planning specific lessons*
- *be willing to reframe the approach.*

Taken together, these three factors constitute a 'response to intervention'. This factor has an effect size of 1.07 and suggests that the effectiveness of an intervention depends *on the teacher's ability to give and receive feedback*. While the first of these factors in unsurprising, the second was unexpected since few teachers seem to seek direct feedback from their students. Mostly this happens informally.

5. CENTRALITY OF FEEDBACK IN LEARNING

Given the important role feedback plays in advancing student learning, and therefore teacher impact, Hattie and Zierer deal with this issue in some depth[15], distinguishing three types of feedback which correspond to the three questions:

---

14 Adapted from the chapter headings in Hattie and Zierer, v–vi.
15 They make the point that feedback given in the wrong way, or at the wrong time, or at the wrong level, can be counterproductive in student learning.

- *Where am I going?*
- *How am I going?*
- *Where to next?*

5.1 Levels at which student feedback can be given

The above questions highlight the three levels at which feedback can be given:

- *the learning task*
- *the process of learning central to completing the task*
- *how the student invests in the task and the process (i.e. their capacity for self-directed learning)*

These three levels are interrelated. If students are clear about the task and *what success looks like*, they become more engaged in the learning process, and eventually take ownership of the task and of their own learning. It is therefore possible to provide students with feedback at each level.

Feedback on the third factor, self-directed learning, seeks to encourage students to make their own judgements, choose their own directions and make improvements as the task proceeds (and check these with the teacher).[16]

5.2 Teacher stances on feedback

Hattie and Zierer suggest that a teacher can adopt one of three stances on feedback:

- *'feedback' comparing present performance with past performance*
- *'feed up' commenting on present efforts*
- *'feed forward' relating present efforts to future goals*

The authors summarise the differences between these forms of feedback in the table below. In summarising the important role feedback plays in learning, they note:

> Discussions on feedback are regularly dominated by the notion that the feedback should be directed from the teacher to the learner. The teacher is said to be responsible for giving students detailed and comprehensive feedback on their learning as often as possible. As important as it is, it is but one of many forms of feedback – and if overdone, it can overload students and degenerate into a pointless exercise ... Teacher-to-student feedback may be important, but learner-to-teacher feedback is just as, or even more important. After all,

---
16 Ibid, 86–89.

the teacher cannot answer the questions of whether the students achieved the goals, whether they understood the content, whether the methods were useful, or whether the media were helpful. These are questions only the learners can answer. The teacher's role is to elicit, listen and then react (and) engage in dialogue (with the student on these matters).

Successful feedback is thus a cyclic process involving two forms of feedback: <u>feedback from the teacher to the student</u> and <u>feedback from the students to the teacher</u>. Since these two forms of feedback are also structurally related and mutually dependent, it is justified to speak of an endless dialogue process that starts with correctly understood feedback.[17] [italics added]).

Hattie and Zierer summarise their suggestions on feedback in the following table[18]:

	Level of Feedback		
	Task	Process	Self-Regulation
Past (**Feedback**)	What progress has the learner made on goals and content?	What progress has the learner made on task completion? Is there evidence of improvement?	What progress has the learner made on self-regulation strategies?
Present (**Feed up**)	What goals did the learner reach? What content did the learner understand?	How did the learner complete the task? Is there evidence of how the learner worked?	What self-direction strategies did the learner successfully apply?
Future (**Feed Forward**)	What goals should be set next? What content should be learned next?	What tips on task completion should the learner be given next?	What self-direction strategies should the learner apply next?

TABLE 13.2: FORMS OF FEEDBACK (HATTIE AND ZIERER)

For Hattie, the important learning from his study of meta-analyses is that, while many factors impinge on achievement in student learning, *the role of the teacher is critical.* This role includes such factors as building teacher-student relationships (SE=.72), being clear (SE=.75), providing feedback (SE=.73), using formative types of evaluation (SE=.90), employing metacognitive strategies (SE= .69).[19]

---

17 Ibid, 89–90.
18 Ibid, 89.
19 Hattie, 118, 126, 173, 181, 189.

In evaluating Hattie's research, it is important to note that his studies focus on interventions and factors *individually*, whereas in the classroom several run concurrently. It is their *cumulative impact,* rather than their individual impact, that has to be taken into account, and this issue qualifies any individual findings.

6. HATTIE'S MODEL OF LEARNING

With the above qualification in mind, *Visible Learning* throws some light on the question: 'How should teachers teach?' In doing so, it raises further questions: How do students learn?' and 'Why is it that some forms of intervention have a better impact than others?'

In *Visible Learning* Hattie identifies important elements in 'what works' in promoting student learning, but *offers no theory of learning* that explains 'how children learn'. If teachers are 'to begin with Why?', then this omission reveals a serious gap in Hattie's project. He attempts to address the matter in a 2016 paper co-written with Gregory Donaghue that matches learning strategies identified in the *Visible Learning* study to stages in what the authors propose as 'the learning cycle'.[20]

The general conclusion of the paper is that interventions are most effective in improving student achievement when *they are matched to the phase the student has reached in the learning cycle*[21] which helps explain why learning strategies that have a high effect size may not produce good results in particular classes or for particular students.

Hattie and Donaghue acknowledge that while it has been possible to investigate some 400+ learning strategies as if they were independent, in fact they are not. If learning is considered as a process, then strategies need to be matched to where the student is at in the process. It is, therefore, important to develop a model of the learning process itself.

They suggest that learning occurs in three major phases. In their model, surface learning and deep learning each has two sub-stages: an acquisition stage and a consolidation stage. They contend that without deep learning – the ability to recognise relationships and make connections – little transfer of learning can be expected and the ability to apply what has been learned to new situations remains limited.[22]

---

20 John Hattie and Gregory Donoghue, 'Learning strategies: A synthesis and conceptual model'. Science of Learning Research Centre: Graduate School of Education, University of Melbourne, 2016.
21 Ibid, 1.
22 Figure 13.2 simplifies Hattie's discussion.

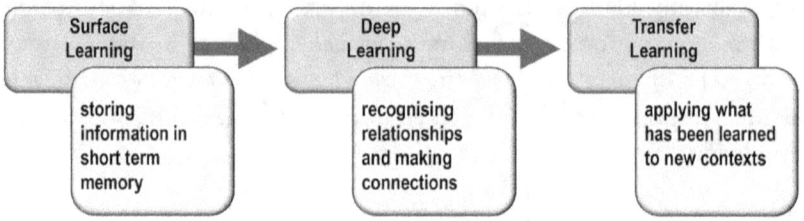

FIGURE 13.2: PHASES OF LEARNING (HATTIE AND DONAGHUE)

7. CONCLUSION: A QUANTITATIVE APPROACH TO PEDAGOGY

The research of Hattie and colleagues summarises the many factors that can impact on student learning and that therefore might, individually or collectively, shape pedagogy. His approach is pragmatic, and he is aware of the limits that apply in depending on quantitative data, particularly when student achievement is measured solely by test results. He encourages researchers to undertake meta-studies based on *qualitative research,* expecting that these will complement his findings.

Hattie's identification of 'effect sizes' as an important metric in assessing and comparing the findings of quantitative studies has been a significant development in making sense of the mountain of data now available. He acknowledges that, while it is possible to identify the salience of particular interventions through focused research, *these interventions often work in combination in the actual classroom situation,* so teachers would be wise to take this into consideration in planning their teaching.

It needs to be recognised, however, that educators who pursue qualitative research into student learning, and so into 'what has an impact in the classroom', may have different objectives from those of Hattie et al, and see the challenge of improving student achievement as being met using a quite different approach. Michael Fullan is a prominent advocate of the pragmatic approach to teaching and learning using *qualitative research methods.* In Chapter 14 we review his work in relation to the 'deep learning' and the 'new pedagogy' movements.

John Hattie has made a very valuable contribution to the empirical-pragmatic approach to pedagogy that dominates discussion in the English-speaking world. Implicit in his work is an understanding of the pedagogical relationship, but this remains undeveloped. His work points to need for a coherent theory of learning to underpin good pedagogy and he proposes a model that serves this purpose. We will return to this issue in Part D.

14

'DEEP LEARNING': QUANTITATIVE STUDIES

The three previous chapters raised important issues relating to the present state of pedagogy. Chapter 11 argued that pedagogy specifies the ethical boundaries of the special relationship between an adult and child, as this pertains to teaching and learning, raising the question: How do I do the right thing by this child, or group of children? Chapter 12 examined what we termed 'values pedagogy', focusing on specific programs developed to inculcate values in de-traditionalising societies such as our own. Chapter 13 was concerned with 'what works in the classroom in promoting student achievement' and the research reported isolated a number of factors that affect student achievement, chief among them being the role of the teacher.

While not explicitly addressing ethical issues, Hattie et al raise the important ethical question: What is a teacher expected to do in promoting student learning? This question focuses the efforts of those pursuing the pragmatic approach who are advocates of 'deep learning'. In this chapter we explore the concept of 'deep learning' and the research base on which it depends, and in the next we review attempts to integrate deep learning within teaching practices.

'Deep learning' has become something of a catchcry for those who have argued for the 're-purposing' or 're-culturing' of public education over the last decade. However, there is limited consensus about what constitutes 'deep learning', how it can be measured, or its pedagogical implications. What do they mean by the term and to what extent does it align with 'deep learning' as used by Hattie?

1. MEANING OF 'DEEPER LEARNING'

'Deeper learning' is a term associated with '21st century learning skills' and the ambiguity this created led to the National Research Council (NRC) in the US being tasked with giving definition to the terms 'deep learning' and 'deeper learning' in order to provide much needed clarity to research on both topics.

1.1 Education for Life and Work (2012)

In 2012 the NRC published the results of its detailed study in a report titled *Education for Life and Work: Developing Transferable Knowledge and Skills in the 21st Century*.

Models of Learning

This report begins by outlining two models of learning: the *cognitive model and the sociocultural* model. The cognitive model distinguishes between *the processes* of individual learning and the acquisition of knowledge and skills seen as the *products of this learning*. The sociocultural model focuses on the *social context* in which learning takes place and in which knowledge and skills are generated. The authors' observation of this perspective is that:

> The sociocultural perspective emerged in response to the perception that research and theory within the cognitive perspective were too narrowly focused on individual thinking and learning. In the sociocultural perspective, learning takes place as individuals participate in the practices of a community, using the tools, language, and other cultural artifacts of the community. From this perspective, learning is 'situated' within, and emerges from, the practices in different settings and communities.[1]

Socio-cultural learning results from an individual being *embedded in a cultural community*. This form of learning happens largely out-of-awareness and so outside of a person's conscious control and capacity to critique. Children learn 'our way of doing things' long before they go to school. As we pointed out in Chapter 7, one of the functions of schooling is to help students identify the biases usually present in knowledge acquired socio-culturally, and therefore pre-critically.

Socio-cultural learning happens in all forms of group life including in professions such as teaching. Schools, and school systems, develop a construction of pedagogy that is then passed on through discussion (cognitively), but also through imitation and observation (socio-culturally). This is the pedagogical situation in many Catholic schools.

Meaning of 'Deeper Learning'

The NRC Report links 'deeper learning' and '21st century skills' using the notion of 'transfer', which is understood as 'the ability to use prior learning to support new learning or problem-solving in culturally relevant contexts'. This enables the authors to make a meaningful distinction between 'deeper learning' and '21st century competencies', as follows:

---

[1] National Research Council, *Education for Life and Work*, 2012, 73.

> We define deeper learning not as a product, but as <u>processing</u> – both within individual minds and through social interactions in a community – and 21st century competencies as <u>the learning outcomes</u> of this processing in the form of transferable knowledge and skills that result.[2]

Expanding on this comment the report also notes:

> We define "deeper learning" as the process through which an individual becomes capable of taking what was learned in one situation and applying it to new situations (i.e., transfer). Through deeper learning (which often involves shared learning and interactions with others in a community) the individual develops expertise in a particular domain of knowledge and/or performance … The product of deeper learning is transferable knowledge, including content knowledge in a domain and knowledge of how, why and when to apply this knowledge to answer questions and solve problems.[3]

This understanding differs from that offered by Hattie in the last chapter where deep learning was presented as *a condition for transfer learning to occur.*

21st Century Competencies

Education for Life and Work categorised '21st century skills' into three domains: the *cognitive*, the *intrapersonal* and the *interpersonal*, as set out in the table below.

The term 'competency' refers to the items in each domain as each *involves some combination of knowledge and skills.*

Domain	Clusters of Competencies
Cognitive	• cognitive processes strategies • domain specific knowledge • creativity
Intrapersonal	• intellectual openness • work ethic • conscientiousness • positive self-evaluation • self-regulation
Interpersonal	• collaboration • responsibility • conflict resolution

TABLE 14.1: DOMAINS AND COMPETENCIES (NRC *EDUCATION FOR LIFE AND WORK*)

The authors point out that there is very little that is '21st century' about this list, as it represents competencies that have long been in demand. What

---

2 Ibid, 74
3 ibid, 5–6

has changed in the 21st century is 'society's desire that *all* students have attained levels of mastery – *across multiple areas* of skill and knowledge – that was previously unnecessary for individual success in education and in the workplace.'[4]

2. NRC'S MODEL OF LEARNING

Since 'deeper learning' is associated with 'transfer', it poses the question:

- *What is happening in people's minds when transfer occurs and under what conditions does this occur?*

In addressing the 'processing that is central to deeper learning' the NRC summarises existing knowledge from cognitive psychology to outline a model of learning summed up schematically in the diagram below.

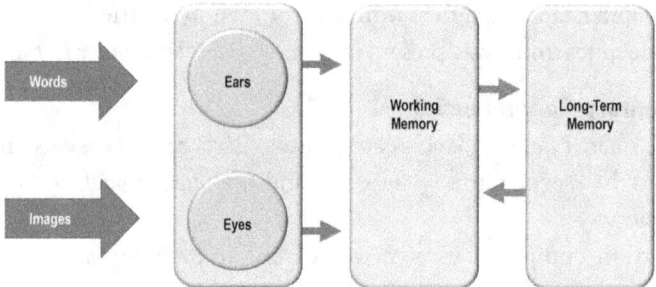

FIGURE 14.1: NRC MODEL OF LEARNING

There are four elements to the model: external stimuli, sensing, short-term memory and long-term memory. The conscious mind *buffers* external stimuli (words and images) by attending to them selectively. In doing so, it filters out extraneous information preventing this from reaching the *working memory*.

2.1 Working Memory

Research has demonstrated that working memory, the third element in the model, is strictly limited both in terms of how many pieces of information it can hold at any one time and for how long this can occur. Despite this limitation, working memory serves the important role of enabling us to locate ourselves in place and time and so provides us with a sense of personal continuity.[5]

---

4 Ibid, 3.
5 The films *Memento* (2000) and *Before I Go to Sleep* (2014) explore (rather dramatically) what life can be like when a person loses his or her working memory.

Working memory (also called short-term memory) is *what we use to process information immediately in front of us*. The conscious mind also attempts to *organise the incoming data in line with concepts and principles already stored in the long-term memory*. These two forms of memory exist in dynamic relationship and feed our imagination with images.

2.2 Long-term Memory

Unlike working memory, long-term memory seems *almost unlimited* in its capacity to store information.

Current theories suggest that long-term memory has two major divisions: content memory, also known as *semantic memory* ('How the world is') and *procedural memory* ('How things are done') that records processes.

In addition, there are two less well-researched aspects of memory. The first is *emotional memory* that ties specific feelings to events recorded in the long-term memory. We can often recall not only an event, but also the feelings we had at the time it occurred. The second, *kinaesthetic memory*, ties specific muscle movements to events ('muscle memory'). This is important in playing sport because it enables the athlete to react to a stimulus without thought since he or she has dealt with this stimulus previously. Think, for instance of a batsman faced with a short-pitched ball during a cricket match, or a netballer passing the ball.

The process by which information is moved physiologically from short-term to long-term memory is not well understood, nor is the way in which the long-term memory integrates knowledge and reorganises itself.[6] However, sleep seems to serve an important function in both these processes. The old adage 'I will sleep on it' contains a good deal of practical wisdom! Exercise plays a role as well.

2.3 The Problem of Transfer

Studies of expertise suggest semantic and procedural memory restricts mental 'processing' to the discipline-based domains in which knowledge is stored. They also suggest that *learning in one domain* (say, literacy) *is not easily transferred to another domain*. That is, being good at solving problems in maths (because you have deep content knowledge and strong procedural knowledge in this domain) may not transfer to solving problems in the humanities and vice-versa.

Research quoted in the NRC report notes that the ability to solve problems tends to be *domain specific*. The report acknowledges that people

---

[6] Much of what science knows about the operation of the brain comes from studies associated with people who have suffered some form of brain trauma.

do have 'general methods' for solving problems, such as trial and error or using analogy, but these tend to be quite inefficient when compared to domain specific methods.

2.4 Neuroscience: Memory and Learning

Neuroscience has made considerable advances in locating where in the brain specific acts of memory occur. The findings from this research have some significant implications for improving student learning, both in terms of what they affirm and what they discount.[7]

Brain research currently affirms that humans are not good at multitasking, so in learning situations it is important to *avoid distractions* that impact on the student's ability to attend to the task in hand. Secondly, it suggests that catering for different 'learning styles' is something of a myth in the commonsense usage of the term, a result also identified by Hattie. The research affirms the importance of active recall, of 'chunking' learning, interleaving tasks, using advance organisers and scaffolding new work, all of which are learning strategies familiar to teachers.

A major problem faced by neuroscientists is that, while they can locate where brain activity occurs, they have, as yet, no definitive way of tying their knowledge to activities of the human mind. 'Mind' and 'brain' are not the same thing, although they are clearly related. Neuroscience studies the human brain; philosophers study the human mind. A challenge for teachers in interpreting neuroscience's claims is to avoid forms of reductionism that equate 'mind' with 'brain'.

The following exercise is instructive in seeing how the working memory and the long-term memory interact in problem-solving. Consider the following code:

1	⌟	6	⌈
2	⌞⌟	7	⌉
3	⌞	8	⌈⌉
4	⌝	9	⌈
5	□	0	○

Look at it for 30 seconds and then use it to write down your mobile phone number.

This problem requires using your working memory. The challenge level drops considerably if the task is moved to the long-term memory by

---

[7] For a recent summary of these findings and the research that underpins them see *The Brain: Learning and Memory: From Research to Practice* Queensland Brain Institute, 2017, available at URL https://qbi.uq.edu.au/learning.

accessing an idea firmly embedded thereby setting the numbers in a pattern with which we are familiar.

1	2	3
4	5	6
7	8	9

Now it becomes clear that we are not dealing with a random set of symbols, but with a pattern used in the familiar game of noughts and crosses. Once you have this insight, the task of encoding your mobile number can be carried out with ease. The lesson from this exercise is that *it is preferable to solve problems by accessing long-term memory*, rather than overloading the working memory. For this reason, teachers attempt to connect new work to 'big ideas' already known by students.

2.5 Memory schemas

Cognitive psychologists recognise that ideas are organised by the brain into wholes, called *schemas*. 'A schema is a previously learned and somewhat specialised technique for organising knowledge in memory in ways that prove useful in problem solving.'[8] Schemas provide the building blocks of memory organisation and we need to access them in understanding or interpreting new information.

Schemas play a key role in enabling thinking to move from working memory to long-term memory as well as in enabling us to recognise new situations as instances of ones that are already known, which is something essential to knowledge transfer. A situation becomes meaningful if we know the general principles or procedures to apply from previous experience, and therefore which strategies are most likely to work effectively in a new situation.

In summing up the research on schemas, the NCR report concludes:

> As learning occurs, increasingly well-structured and qualitatively different organizations of knowledge develop. These structures enable individuals to build a representation or mental model that guides problem solution and further learning, avoid[s] trial and error solution strategies, and formulate[s] analogies and draw[s] inferences that readily result in new learning and effective problem solving. The impact of schematic knowledge is powerfully demonstrated by research on the nature of expertise.[9]

---

8   Ibid, 78.
9   Ibid.

Experts are not good 'in general' but are good *at something*. The expert has organised his or her knowledge (semantic and procedural) in a way that is *readily retrievable* and so is useful. They often do this by organising new information into well-connected schemas before they commit it to memory. Teachers attempt to do this for their students when they scaffold new content.

In learning new content, *the law of practice* applies. In acquiring a new skill, early performance requires effort *because it is dependent on working-memory*. Repetition moves the skill into the long-term memory, by-passing the working-memory. As this happens the skill becomes automatic, no longer requiring further conscious attention.

To develop a skill, *students need to know they are progressing, so formative feedback* is important. Without this the research indicates there is little learning.[10] This result is also confirmed by Hattie's study as we saw earlier.

3. DEEP LEARNING: OPPORTUNITIES AND LIMITS

The NRC study proved to be an important step in the emergence of 'deep learning' as an educational imperative. It sought to provide a conceptually sound foundation for the movement by setting out a clear understanding of what 'deep learning' means (the learning process) – and by distinguishing this from '21st century skills' (the content of this learning process).

The authors aligned 'deeper learning' with Hattie's notion of 'transfer learning' and identified the conditions under which transfer occurs,[11] drawing on the limited research available on cognitive functioning. In doing so, they established a number of key findings with implications for pedagogy:

1. Deep learning appears to be **domain specific**.
2. There is a limit to how far knowledge and skills developed through deep learning can transfer because of **the domain specific nature of learning**.
3. There are **effective instructional methods** that make deep learning possible.
4. Deep learning involves **well-organised knowledge in a domain** that can be **readily retrieved and applied** to new problems in that domain.
5. Deep learning requires extensive practice backed up by **formative feedback** so that students know where they are going wrong.

---

10   This result is confirmed independently in Hattie's *Visible Learning* study.
11   Note the distinction here between the NRC's understanding of deep learning and that of Hattie and Donaghue discussed in the previous chapter.

6. It is possible to distinguish between rote learning and meaningful learning. **Meaningful learning makes transfer possible**.
7. It is more appropriate to talk of '21st century competencies' rather than '21st century skills' since 'competency' embraces both the skill and knowledge needed for successful performance.
8. '21st century skills' are competencies that have long been seen as valuable, what makes them '21st century' is that **they are now required of most students**, whereas formerly they were required of a few.
9. '21st century competencies' fall into three domains: cognitive, intrapersonal and interpersonal. The task of the school and the teacher is to equip students with these basic competencies.

The pragmatic research tradition throws up many key findings with respect to pedagogy, much of it based in quantitative studies. However, when the context of learning changes substantially, which the NRC report takes as a given, then there is need for a more holistic (qualitative) approach to research as many interrelated factors have to be identified and distinguished before more focused research can occur. This has been the case with deep learning and the development of pedagogical practices to implement it, as we will see in the next chapter.

15

THE QUALITATIVE RESEARCH TRADITION: MICHAEL FULLAN

The pragmatic approach to pedagogy follows two *traditions*. The first tradition is *quantitative* and has two strands – that concerned with *what works in the classroom* epitomised in the work of John Hattie, and that concerned with *how students learn* as captured in the National Research Council (NCR) report.

A second tradition is based in *qualitative research* – detailed accounts of how schools function and how teachers engage with students in promoting learning. This tradition also has two strands: a *phenomenological strand* which deals with the lived experience of teaching and learning – and the *reflective practice strand* that is concerned with what can be learned from reflectively analysing the experiences of teaching and learning. This latter strand is the subject of this chapter.

1. THE CONTRIBUTION OF MICHAEL FULLAN

The qualitative tradition is well captured in an international project headed by well-known Canadian educator Michael Fullan, and in research sponsored by the Hewlett Foundation in the US. Both projects seek to promote 'deep learning'. As we noted earlier, 'deep learning' has become something of a catchcry for those who have argued for the 're-purposing' or 're-culturing' of public education over recent years, with many claims made for its effectiveness in improving student outcomes. Fullan has been at the forefront of this endeavour.[1]

1.1 Michael Fullan

Fullan came to international prominence in 1982 with the publication of

---

1 Michael Fullan is Canadian-born (1940). He studied at the University of Toronto (UoT) and worked on the staff from 1970 to 1988 following his doctoral studies. He became the Dean, a position he held after UoT amalgamated with the Ontario Institute for Studies in Education in 1996, and held this appointment until stepping down in 2003. For the next decade Fullan served as policy advisor on education to the Premier of Ontario. Currently, he is the Director of New Pedagogies for Deep Learning: Global Partnership.

The Meaning of Educational Change[2], a meta-study of educational change and the factors that shape it. As Fullan suggests in the title, in order to be effective, educational change (including pedagogical change) has to be *meaningful* for those involved. Fullan has been a passionate advocate of reform in education and has advised many groups on school and system reform.[3]

Since the early 1990s Fullan has published a book almost every year on the educational issues of the day.[4] While cynics may claim that Fullan does not have an unpublished thought, his writings record the trajectory along which educational thinking has evolved in recent decades.[5] In more recent books he has brought into sharper focus a lifetime's experience of working on system reform.[6]

As an educational practitioner, Fullan promotes a praxis-oriented methodology in which people learn by reflecting after the fact on their experiences of engaging in the process of change. His books are laced with case studies of individuals and groups leading various forms of change and learning from the experience.[7]

For Fullan, effective reform of the education system is a matter of changing the culture of school systems so that they better serve the purpose of promoting student learning of a type that will enable students to survive and thrive in a rapidly changing social, economic, political and technological environment. He is dismayed by the high level of student disengagement in traditional schooling now conveyed in numerous research reports from Western countries. The situation provides educational reform with an ethical imperative.

1.2 Deep learning: competing conceptions

In Fullan's view, the essential condition of educational change is that students master the competencies of 'deep learning'. In suggesting this, he engages with the wider debate about the meaning of 'deep learning', and what this entails for teachers. We have seen, for example, that for Hattie 'deep learning' is 'a phase in the learning process'. It constitutes the precondition

---

2   Michael Fullan, *The Meaning of Educational Change,* Toronto: OISE Press, 1982.
3   Fullan's conception of how an effective school system works is set out in his 2015 book *Coherence,* co-authored with Joanne Quinn, where he brings together the results of a career spent dealing with educational reform issues.
4   In addition to this, Fullan has a formidable list of articles that he has written, many of which he generously makes available on his website.
5   Fullan has 36 titles currently in print. He has won the Education Book of the Year Award four times.
6   For example, see Michael Fullan and Joanne Quinn, *Coherence: the Right Drivers in Action for Schools, Districts and Systems.* London: SAGE, 2015.
7   Fullan uses a reflective practice approach to research. This differs from the phenomenological approach used by Van Manen who is interested in the meaning that teachers give to the lived experience when engaging with students in the process of learning.

for 'transfer learning' – the ability to apply what has been learned to new contexts. This is *one* interpretation of 'deep learning'. The NRC report spoke of 'deeper learning' rather than 'deep learning' (without explanation) and associates this with a wide range of competencies.

2. 'DEEPER LEARNING': FROM THEORY TO PRACTICE[8]

As a consequence of the NRC report, a number of foundations in the US sponsored research initiatives aimed at fostering 'deeper learning' based on the findings of the report. Among them was the Hewlett Foundation that set out to discover which teaching strategies produced deep learning, and to assess the impact these strategies had on student learning, if used in a sustained way.[9]

This project, that began in 2010, equates 'deeper learning' with 'acquiring the 21st century competencies'. The project places emphasis on the 'domain specific' nature of 'deep learning'. The Hewlett Foundation adapted the NRC's 21st century competencies to arrive at the modified set as depicted in the table below.[10]

	Cognitive (thinking and reasoning)	Intrapersonal (self-management to reach goals)	Interpersonal (expressing information to others and interpreting others)
Deeper Learning Competencies	Thinking critically	Learning how to learn	Working collaboratively
	Mastering rigorous academic content	Developing academic mindsets	Communicating effectively

TABLE 15.1: DEEPER LEARNING COMPETENCIES
(HEWLETT FOUNDATION'S ADAPTATION OF NRC'S 21ST CENTURY COMPETENCIES)

In this table, 'developing academic mindsets' means developing a positive attitude to oneself as a learner. The Hewlett project was evaluated in 2015. Interim results from a number of New York high schools seem encouraging.[11]

---

8   The Hewlett foundation is supported by the owners of the Hewlett Packard company.
9   For an account of this project see 'Deeper learning: for every student every day' at https://hewlett.org/wp-content/uploads/2016/08/Deeper%20Learning%20for%20Every%20Student%20EVery%20Day_GETTING%20SMART_1.2014.pdf
10 Adapted from 'Deeper Learning for Every Student Every Day', 9.
11 See *Charting the Progress of the Hewlett Foundation's Deeper Learning Strategy, 2010–2015* available at https://hewlett.org/wp-content/uploads/2017/04/Deeper-Learning_2017_RTI-.pdf

3. 'NEW PEDAGOGY' AND 'DEEP LEARNING'

In another major project, a consortium headed by Michael Fullan is carrying out a large-scale project to promote 'Deep Learning' under the title *New Pedagogy for Deep Learning* (NPDL). This project, begun in 2013, involves, at the time of writing, over 1400 schools, mostly primary, in seven countries.[12] In 2018 Fullan, Quinn, and McEachen published an account of the project in *Deep Learning: Engage the World, Change the World*.[13]

3.1 The NPDL model of deep learning

Fullan employs a particular construction of 'deep learning' and advocates a specific approach in helping students succeed in achieving it. In *Deep Learning* he and his colleagues outline the organising ideas needed *in developing a pedagogy capable of producing deep learning* which the authors acknowledge presently exists only in embryonic form.

The NPDL project seeks to develop exemplar schools within a school system in order, in Fullan's words, 'to seed whole system change'. The aim of the NPDL project, as set out on its website, is expressed as follows:

> We work alongside educators to change the role of teachers to that of activators of learning who design learning experiences that build on learner strengths and needs, create new knowledge using real-life problem solving and help all students identify their talents, purpose and passion.[14]

For Fullan, 'deep learning', equates to acquiring six 'global competencies': character, citizenship, collaboration, communication, creativity and critical thinking, that he refers to as the '6Cs'. He links these with an approach to teaching that encourages students, to 'engage the world change the world'.

The NPDL project postulates that students acquire the 6Cs, as set out in the table below, in a process *that passes through identifiable stages*. Details of these stages can be accessed on the NPDL website.[15] The assumption is that the NPDL stages framework will enable teachers to assess students' progress in deep learning.[16] What is not made clear from *Deep Learning: Engage the World Change the World* is how this framework was developed and the assumptions on which it rests.

---

12 The consortium includes over 100 Australian schools from Victoria, Tasmania and Queensland, as well as schools in Canada, New Zealand, Uruguay, Finland, United States, and the Netherlands.
13 Michael Fullan, Joanne Quinn, and Joanne McEachen, *Deep Learning: Engage the World Change the World*. London: Sage Publications, 2018.
14 See the homepage of npdl.global.
15 Ibid, 17.
16 The progressions are based on 'evidence of learning' and move from 'limited evidence' to 'proficiency' in five steps. See Fullan et al, 2018, 20.

Global Competence	Dimensions
Character	• Learning to learn • Grit, tenacity, perseverance, and resilience • Self-regulation, responsibility, and integrity
Citizenship	• Thinking like global citizens • Considering global issues based on deep understanding of diverse values and worldviews • Genuine interest and ability to solve ambiguous and complex real-word problems that impact human and environmental sustainability • Compassion, empathy and concern for others
Collaboration	• Working interdependently and synergistically in teams • Interpersonal and team-related skills • Social, emotional, and intercultural skills • Managing team dynamics and challenges • Learning from and contributing to the learning of others
Communication	• Communicating effectively with a variety of styles, modes and tools including digital • Communication designed for different audiences • Reflection on and use of the process of learning to improve communication
Creativity	• Having an "entrepreneurial eye" for economic and social opportunities • Asking the right inquiry questions • Considering and pursuing novel ideals and solutions • Leadership to turn ideas into action
Critical Thinking	• Evaluating information and arguments • Making connections and identifying patterns • Problem solving • Constructing meaningful knowledge • Experimenting, reflecting and taking action on ideas in the real world

TABLE 15.2: NPDL – 6 CS.

3.2 Comparing understandings of deep learning

There is considerable overlap between the elements in the deep learning models offered by the NRC (and also the adapted form used by the Hewlett Foundation), and the NPDL project. There are also significant differences, indicating that there is still lack of clarity as to how 'deep learning' is understood. For instance, while 'creativity' is a major category in Fullan's list of global competencies, it is a component of 'critical thinking' in other models. The NRC framework places emphasis on the academic disciplines as the context in which deep learning occurs (i.e. emphasising the cognitive domain). This emphasis is missing in Fullan's framework where a stress is placed on the use of problem-based learning and inquiry-learning in exploring 'real world issues' relevant to students and the world in which they live. The approach accentuates what 'membership of the world' means.

Fullan's thinking seems aligned with that of Starratt, discussed in Chapter 11, seeing the goal of pedagogy as learning 'how the world works and finding one's place in that world'. Those advocating for deep learning through the NPDL project seek to *redefine the way in which 'success' is understood in student learning and how this change transforms the pedagogical relationship.*

A problem with the NPDL model is that *it is not underpinned by an adequate theory of learning,* an issue given considerable emphasis in the NCR report.

3.3 Co-opting a theory of learning: SOLO Taxonomy

Some schools participating in the NPDL project address this lack of an adequate theory of learning by adopting the SOLO (Structure of Observed Learning) taxonomy. This taxonomy, developed by Biggs and Collis, proposes that human understanding develops in five stages ranging from *not understanding* to *deep understanding*. The model is outlined in the diagram below.[17]

Levels of Understanding				
Pre-Structural	Uni-Structural	Multi-Structural	Relational	Extended Abstract
I don't really know anything about this	I know one thing about this	I know a few things, but I am not sure when or how to use it	I understand there are relationships among the things I know	I can explain what I know to others and can apply what I know in new contexts
	Surface Understanding		Deep Understanding	

TABLE 15.3: SOLO TAXONOMY (BIGGS AND COLLIS)

The taxonomy utilises the surface understanding/deep understanding dichotomy identified by Hattie. It envisages deep understanding as having two components as implied in the NRC model, moving from deep understanding (relational) to deeper understanding (extended abstract).

A virtue of this taxonomy is that it enables students to monitor their level of understanding and it enables teachers to plan lessons based on an assessment of their students' understanding. The goal of teaching is to assist students to arrive at 'deep understanding' (which is equated with 'deep learning').[18]

---

17 John Biggs and Kevin Collis, *Evaluating the Quality of Learning: the SOLO Taxonomy*. New York: Academic Press, 1982. While the original work is now out of print in English, its ideas can be accessed through various articles e.g.
https://www.johnbiggs.com.au/academic/solo-taxonomy/

18 For an example of this model in practice see http://www.myrossbush.school.nz/solo-taxonomy.html

3.4 Problematic of the 'new pedagogy'

Fullan's 'new pedagogy' advocates both problem-based learning and inquiry-based learning. Hattie notes that these strategies have only a limited 'effect size' in advancing student learning (ES=.31). He suggests this is because teachers use these strategies before students have the knowledge base needed to engage in this type of exercise. He contends that at some point students have to 'do the hard yards' associated with mastering the content and procedures to become deep learners. Against this critique, Fullan quotes multiple (primary school) examples highlighting the effectiveness of his approach.[19]

The present state of play would suggest that the evidence from studies taking a pragmatic approach to deep learning, whether quantitative or qualitative, is stronger in delineating the 'what' of deep learning than in defining the 'how'.

4. 'NEW PEDAGOGY' INVOLVES MORE THAN 'TEACHING PRACTICES'

The 'deep learning' frameworks explored in Part C seek to re-purpose schooling and introduce new pedagogical thinking. In the case of the NRC, and also the Hewlett Foundation, the drive for change in pedagogical approaches arises from the ethical demands of *living in a new social and technological context*. In Fullan's case, the driving force is the *increasing level of disengagement reported of students in traditional classrooms and an ethical imperative* to address this matter, both for society's benefit and for the benefit of the students themselves.

However, as Fullan notes, little can be achieved without changing the outlook of teachers and the mindsets they bring to teaching, and without critiquing the ways in which they make pedagogical decisions. The issue is not *what to teach* (this is covered by curriculum guidelines) but *how to teach, and how the role of a teacher is construed*.

4.1 Four factors shaping deep learning

Fullan suggests that 'deep learning' results from a confluence of the four factors – pedagogical practices, learning partnerships, learning environments, and levering digital.[20] This means that not only does 'deep learning' require new pedagogical practices, it also requires that schools create *learning*

---

[19] A number of these (all primary school projects) are featured as video clips on the npdlglobal website.
[20] Taken from the NPDL framework reproduced in Michael Fullan, Joanne Quinn, and Joanne McEachen, *Deep Learning: Engage the World Change the World*, 34.

partnerships with parents, with the community, and *within the teaching staff itself.* Schools must also make better use of the digital resources at their disposal.

If students are to 'engage the world' in which they live, they have to understand its problems and challenges *through reflecting on personal experience accessed via life in the home and in the community.*

'Deep learning' also requires a major change in the way the *learning environments* are created in classrooms and in schools. If students are to master the intrapersonal and interpersonal competencies essential to deep learning, then teachers will need to create opportunities for this to happen within their lessons. Learning occurring within the *process* of a lesson becomes as important as learning associated with the *content* of the lesson. Specifically, students need *to learn how to learn* if they are to become better learners.

Today's students are 'native' to the digital world, and the 'new pedagogy' needs to utilise the *educational opportunities* that now exist in that world. Fullan suggests that these must be leveraged *to make learning relevant and effective.*[21]

> *We use the term leveraging digital in place of technology to signal that we are not discussing devices, software, or apps of the day, but rather focusing on the role that interaction with digital can play in enhancing the learning. Effective use of digital facilitates deep learning partnerships with students, families, community members, and experts regardless of geographical location and supports student capacity to take control of their own learning both within and outside the classroom walls.* [22]

The pedagogy needed to address deep learning will require not only rethinking traditional practices, but also better collaboration between teachers, between teachers and students, among students, and with parents and the local community. In meeting these conditions, new traditions will be established, particularly with respect to the interpersonal and intrapersonal domains identified as '21st century skills'.

Fullan understands that at present there are few examples of 'the new pedagogy' and that 'lighthouse projects 'need to be created to make this more 'visible' (Hattie's term). The NPDL website now provides a digital platform for disseminating best practice, but only among members of the NPDL consortium.

---

21 Ibid, 80–82.
22 Ibid, 81.

5. 'NEW PEDAGOGY' AND CATHOLIC EDUCATION

The pedagogical thrust of the various models of 'deep learning' discussed above sits comfortably with Catholic teaching. 'Engage the world, change the world' aligns with the imperative of Catholic social teaching. It also aligns both with Ignatius' insight that God is to be found in all things and his goal that the students being educated in Catholic schools have a transforming impact on society – a Jesuit ideal in education that has become a normative ideal in all Catholic education.

5.1 Repurposing of pedagogy

Repurposing pedagogy to deal with a changed social, technological and economic context is something that Catholic educators cannot ignore. While the parameters of deep learning remain contested, what is clear from research on pedagogy, at least as this term is understood in the English-speaking world, is that *teachers play an indispensable role in student learning.*

However, success in schooling can no longer be defined solely in terms of cognitive achievement, but also has to address the ethical imperative to include the intrapersonal and interpersonal domains of learning as well. This change makes demands on teachers to rethink their pedagogical practices and their role in a way that:

- *is more attentive to the relational dimension of pedagogy*
- *encourages students to become active agents (individually and collectively) in their own learning*

The role for teachers is morphing from that of 'expert' to that of 'learning partner', 'model', and 'mentor' who can accompany students on their journey to deep learning. Phenomenological research is called for that explores the lived experience of teachers living through this transition so that they can make better sense of what is happening.

The pragmatic research tradition seems to have arrived at the conclusion that deep learning is now an essential element in how we define success in schools. However, the tradition has not yet arrived at an adequate conception of the pedagogy needed to produce deep learning. In part this is because, methodologically, pragmatic research isolates individual factors affecting learning and assesses their contribution, whereas in reality it is *the confluence of these factors that is decisive.*

5.2 Bringing pedagogical traditions into conversation

Pedagogy, as Van Manen points out, is essentially ethical and relational, not only in terms of how ideas are connected, but in how people are connected. This aspect of pedagogy, essential to the phenomenological tradition, is often missing once pedagogy becomes narrowly focused on 'what works in the classroom'. The pedagogical thinking of Catholic educators needs to maintain a wider focus if it is to remain Catholic and also true to the legacy they inherit from John Baptist De La Salle and Ignatius of Loyola.

The pragmatic and the ethical understandings of pedagogy need to be brought into close conversation in the English-speaking world, for the benefit of both. This is surely possible because the pragmatic approach has an implied ethical understanding and the ethical approach has an implied theory of what works in the classroom!

5.3 Pedagogy needs a theory of learning

A weakness in the various initiatives to promote 'deep learning' discussed in the last three chapters is that they lack a coherent understanding of what learning involves. Hattie offers a simple model of learning. The SOLO taxonomy offers a somewhat more comprehensive model. The NRC also offers a model based largely on the role memory plays in learning. All three initiatives agree that *pedagogy needs to be underpinned by a theory of what is going on in students' heads in the process of learning*. Every teacher has some insights into what this theory might be. For the most part these seem intuitive. In Part D we examine the important contribution philosophy makes to a theory of learning.

Part D
LEARNING AND PEDAGOGY: ESSENTIAL VOICES

Introduction

In Part C we saw that it is not possible to discuss pedagogy coherently without a theory of learning. This need arises in all five approaches to pedagogy explored in the last section. In the pragmatic tradition the need is sometimes met by reference to the insights of brain science. In the ethical tradition it arises as a consequence of seeking to do 'the right thing' by the student within the pedagogical relationship. In 'values pedagogy', the medium becomes the pedagogical message.

Part C also drew an important distinction between 'brain' and 'the human mind'. How the human mind works is the territory of the philosophers and here there are two, more or less distinct, traditions. The older tradition is epistemology, that explores the nature of knowledge and what we mean when we say, 'we know something'. The newer tradition is hermeneutics and is concerned with how we interpret or make meaning, where the medium can be texts or events etc.

In Part D we approach the task of developing a theory of learning to underpin pedagogy in two steps. The first step is to explore what the philosophers have to say about how the human mind functions. This usually provides a picture of how the *adult* human mind functions.

Pedagogy is concerned with how the human mind works in *a developing person* and the stages it passes through in this development. Teaching plays an important role in this. It is therefore necessary to place *a development overlay* over the considerations of the philosophers to arrive at an adequate theory of learning applicable to school-age students. This overlay mediates what 'doing the right thing' by this student, or this group of students, means in the various stages of their development when the objective is learning.

Part D therefore unfolds in five sections outlining:

- *the epistemology of Bernard Lonergan*
- *the moderate hermeneutics of Hans Georg Gadamer and Paul Ricoeur*
- *insights about student learning from developmental psychology as found in the work of Jean Piaget and his successors*
- *a theory of learning consistent with these three sources that can underpin pedagogy*
- *an exploration into mission, dialogue and pedagogy acknowledging the essential place of 'dialogue partners' in making present the Kingdom of God. It proceeds utilising perspectives drawn for normative Catholic documentation, the Tony Blair Institute for Global Change (TBIGC), and the Enhancing Catholic School Identity Project (ECSI) which features the Hermeneutical-Communicative (HC) approach to Religious Education.*

The assumption of this section is that teachers have some notion of what is happening in students' heads in the process of learning. This is often implicit but is influential in shaping how they teach. The aim of the section is to bring these implicit notions to consciousness so that they can be critiqued, and their strengths and weaknesses identified.

16

INSIGHT INTO KNOWING: CONTRIBUTION OF BERNARD LONERGAN, PART 1

In Part C we looked briefly at the contribution that 'brain science' has so far made to education and to a theory of learning (Chapter 14). The challenge for the brain scientist is to design experiments that relate brain activity to the mental acts of the subjects that they are testing. The nature of these mental acts depends on the *subjective accounts* of the people being observed. Brain activity, however, is assessed *objectively* using various types of scanning. Aligning the two creates significant challenges, not least because the English language provides us with a cornucopia of words to describe mental activity – paying attention, thinking, knowing, puzzling, explaining, understanding, imagining, dreaming, judging, problem-solving, deciding, remembering, planning, to name but a few!

All of these activities have *common sense meanings*, most of which overlap, so isolating one in the design of an experiment is far from easy as the attempt to do so raises questions about which activity is actually being tracked in an experiment.[1] This situation opens up the wider philosophic question about whether or not it is possible to learn about 'the mind' in the same way that we might seek to understand how a car works – that is, by examining its parts! The whole here is clearly greater than the sum of its parts!

1. LIMITS OF HUMAN KNOWING

The distinction between 'mind' and 'brain' is an important one. Science has made significant progress in exploring where things happen in the brain and how memory works, and can provide insight into general brain functioning, particularly with reference to its malfunctioning. However, it has been the philosophers who have explored the notion of the 'human

---

1 As an example of the crossover in meanings, we know from common experience that remembering plays a role in dreaming (as does imagination).

mind' and how it works. As recorded historically, this began with Aristotle in the 5th century BC.

The works of Aristotle were lost to the Western world during the so-called Dark Ages (Early Medieval period) mainly because few could read the Greek in which they were written. They were reclaimed in the thirteenth century. Thomas Aquinas (1225–1274) used these 'rediscovered' works and laid down the philosophic foundation on which Christian doctrine was formulated in the centuries that followed. The influence of Aristotelian philosophy on theology was normative in Catholic theology up to the Second Vatican Council.

1.1 Descartes and the 'method of doubt'

The rise of science in the 17th century, and the challenge it offered to theology as *the source* of human knowledge, led René Descartes (1596–1650) to endeavour to put human knowledge on a firm foundation. This was in the face of challenges offered by sceptics who doubted the human capacity to arrive at true knowledge.

Descartes was a polymath whose interests lay in the field of mathematics, science, theology and philosophy. He was also a devout Catholic and strongly influenced by the new scientific approach in the construction of knowledge advocated by his contemporary, Galileo (1564–1642). His endorsement of the latter put him in conflict with Catholic Church authorities in France, forcing him to flee to Protestant Holland for his own safety.

Descartes thought of the human person as a machine designed by God and controlled by the human mind. His anthropology is often parodied – humans are 'minds on legs'.

In response to the prevailing scepticism of his age, Descartes wanted to find a foundation on which true knowledge could reliably be built. To do this he employed 'the method of doubt'. That is, he called into question all 'received opinions', including philosophic and religious insights, to see what was left of human knowledge when this was bracketed out. The one thing he found that he could not call into question was his awareness of himself as thinking. This led him to his famous conclusion 'I think, therefore I am'. Starting from this premise he went on to argue to the existence of God and to justify the philosophic and religious conclusions that the sceptics were questioning. In doing so, Descartes opened up a new chapter in philosophy because he was in effect saying that the foundation of truth does not lie in an objective 'world out there', but in the subjective understanding of the person doing the thinking. This shift in perspective gave Descartes a claim on the title, 'father of modern philosophy'.

Descartes was not without his critics who pointed out that in arguing for a new foundation for true knowledge, he often assumed many of the philosophic principles that he had called into doubt. However, by identifying the need to *justify knowledge in order for it to the accepted as true,* he won his place in the history of ideas.

1.2 Immanuel Kant

The German philosopher Immanuel Kant (1724–1804) took the insights of Descartes further, arguing that what we know is not an exact reflection of 'the world out there', but is determined by *the way in which the human mind is structured and the way it processes information.* That is, we employ notions like 'time' and 'cause and effect', not because these exist in nature, but because this is how the human mind processes data.

Kant distinguished between the world of 'phenomenon' – the world out there – and the world of 'noumenon' – ideas in the mind. What humans have access to is the latter, not necessarily the former. Kant's philosophic approach is known as *idealism*. Its premise is that human knowledge is captive to the structure of the human mind and is limited by this structure. Its grasp of 'the world out there' is thus always limited.

1.3 Critical realism

Catholic and other philosophers challenged Kantian idealism arguing that we do know 'the world out there', but our knowledge of it is provisional. This position is known as *'critical realism'*. 'Realism' because we have knowledge of the real world: 'critical' because we are aware that there are limits to what we know. These are imposed by the nature of the human mind and how it works, and by limits in the different ways in which we justify what is known, such as the scientific method.

2. ENTER BERNARD LONERGAN

Bernard Lonergan (1904–1984) made a significant contribution to the debate about the nature of knowledge and human knowing in his seminal study, *Insight*.[2] It is the outline of *cognitive functioning* as presented there, and its pedagogical implications, that we explore in this and the next chapter. Lonergan is an important thinker because he provides *a missing element* in contemporary pedagogical thinking: viz a coherent outline of what is involved in human knowing (and therefore in learning). Lonergan's outline

---

[2] For a wide-ranging discussion of this topic see Robert Henman, 'Can brain scanning and imaging techniques contribute to a theory of thinking?' in *Dialogues in Philosophy, Mental and Neuro Sciences,* 2013: 6(2), 49–56.

of cognitive functioning provides a challenge to some of the pedagogical approaches discussed in the two previous chapters.

All teachers operate from at least an implicit theory of how children learn. This is often based on what Lonergan calls *'common sense knowledge'*. Such knowledge is concerned with the here and now and avoids academic pretensions. Common sense knowledge represents 'what works for me' (or for us), not what works for everyone.

2.1 Bernard Lonergan – biography

Lonergan (1904–1984) was a Canadian Jesuit and is regarded, according to *Time* magazine, as one of the most distinguished thinkers of the 20th century.[3] He was also a polymath who sought to reconcile modern thinking in science, history, economics and philosophy with Christian thought. His most famous work is *Insight: a Study of Human Understanding*. Running for some 800 pages of closely argued philosophy, this book is not for the fainthearted. It is in two parts. In the first 10 chapters Lonergan explains what is involved in human knowing. In the balance of the book he uses his outline of cognitive functioning to revisit the big philosophic and theological questions.

2.2 A phenomenological approach

Lonergan takes a *phenomenological approach* to the study of human knowing beginning with the question: What do we mean when we say we understand something?

He uses the *data of human consciousness* as the basis of his analysis. Put another way, in attempting to understand what it means to 'understand something', it is important not only to focus on what we are trying to understand (*contents of understanding*), but we also need to keep track of our mental activity in trying to understand (*process of understanding*). This is the essence of the phenomenological approach. This is, however, a major problem for English-speakers. In English we use the same word 'understanding' to refer to both the process and the product of understanding. This creates problems for a philosopher.

2.3 The human cognitive dynamism

Lonergan's core insight is that any productive method of reflection has to take note of the *cognitive dynamism at work in the human mind* since this dynamism stands behind all mental acts.

---

[3] *Time*, April 20, 1970. Lonergan held teaching positions at the University of Toronto and the Pontifical Gregorian University in Rome. He later served as Distinguished Visiting Professor at Boston College and as Professor of Divinity at Harvard.

While the dynamism can be analysed as a sequence of stages, in reality there is a continual interaction among the stages. Lonergan argues that his outline of the human cognitive dynamism *is not a model*; rather it is something that *exists prior to all models* because you have to employ the dynamism to formulate any model! This means the dynamism is invariant across cultures and times. It is a characteristic of 'being human', something shared by all people in all times. As such, it stands as the foundation on which all knowledge rests.

3. WORKING WITH THE DATA OF HUMAN CONSCIOUSNESS

As a prelude to exploring Lonergan's thought, it is helpful to reflect on how we process data in coming to know something, and what steps are involved.[4] We ask you to attempt to solve the problem below and keep track of the mental processes you used before reading any further.

3.1 A phenomenological experiment[5]

Consider the two parts of the following problem
4 5 9 13 17 X
5 3 7 11 Y
Problem 1.1 What is (X) the next number for the top line?
Problem 1.2 What is (Y) the next number for the bottom line?

FIGURE 16.1: A PHENOMENOLOGICAL EXPERIMENT

Problem 1.1

To resolve this problem the first mental act is to *focus* on the data in the table. The next step is to *ask questions about it* such as:

- *Is there any relationship between the numbers in the top row?*

Some will quickly see (i.e. understand) that there is a pattern. With the exception of the first number, each successive term is four more than the previous term. So, X would be 21.

Others will recognise the numbers as forming an *arithmetic sequence*. Here they are *recalling a concept* stored in their long-term memory as a consequence of studying mathematics previously. They see the sequence has the form

$$a, a+d, 2a+d, 3a+d \text{ and so on}$$

---
4 We are indebted to Henman quoted above for the approach taken in this section.
5 Henman, 50.

where, d, known as the *common difference,* is four and so X will be 21.

There are *two* sets of data being generated in solving this problem. The first is that associated with *solving a numerical problem* by attending to the data in the shaded box and putting questions to it (or, for some, *accessing memory* to make sense of the problem). The second data set is that of our consciousness, i.e., the mental acts we employ in solving the problem. The latter Lonergan terms 'the data of consciousness'. We are aware of ourselves as attending to the given data, putting questions to it to discover any relationship, and having the insight that there is a relationship. Of course, in problem-solving we do not normally attend to our mental acts, but if asked to do so, we certainly have this capability.

Problem 1.2

Here we begin again by attending to the data in the box and putting a question to it

- *Is there a pattern to the numbers in the bottom row?*

In attempting to answer this question many people argue *by analogy* – since the numbers in Problem 1.1 constituted a sequence, common sense suggests that Problem 1.2 might follow a similar pattern. The additional mental acts involved here are:

1. *Formulating a hypothesis (the numbers form a sequence)*
2. *Testing the hypothesis*

People soon find that in this case arguing by analogy does not work. So, they have to look for other possibilities.

Their thinking has moved through the sequence:

- *attending to the data*
- *putting questions to the data*
- *forming a hypothesis*
- *testing the hypotheses*
- *making a judgement (i.e. drawing a conclusion) based on the data.*

A negative conclusion means that we are forced to return to the starting point of the process, to the original data. When we do this, the insight might arise that *'maybe we have to consider all the data'* in solving this problem, and not just some of it (as in Problem 1.1).

So, a new question arises:

- *Are the numbers above the line related to the numbers below the line?*

To answer this question requires some *trial and error experimentation* that soon reveals that there is a pattern. Some people will work this out 'in their heads, others will use their mathematical knowledge to recognise the pattern.

If terms in the top line are numbered t_1, t_2, t_3 etc., and the terms in the bottom line s_1, s_2, s_3 etc., then

$$s_2 = 2t_1 - s_1,$$
that is, $3 = 2 \times 4 - 5, 7 = 2 \times 5 - 3$ and so on.
So, Y will be $2 \times 13 - 11 = 15$.

Again, it is important to distinguish *the content* of the problem (finding Y) from *the processes used* in arriving at the answer (bringing to consciousness the mental operations being carried out in finding Y).

4. THE PROCESS OF HUMAN COGNITION

4.1 Stage 1: attending to the data of experience

Lonergan takes it as axiomatic that *the desire to know* is fundamental to the human condition and this distinguishes humans from other animals. This desire finds expression in *inquiry*. From the earliest age children want answers to the questions: What is it? Why? How? and What for?

To answer such questions, we must attend to the sense data available to us. That is, we need to *assemble the data*. Our experience of doing this happens at two levels: *the level of fact and the level of consciousness*.

Not only do we attend to the matter in hand (data of fact) but we also have an awareness of ourselves as attending (data of consciousness). Schematically we can represent the situation as follows:

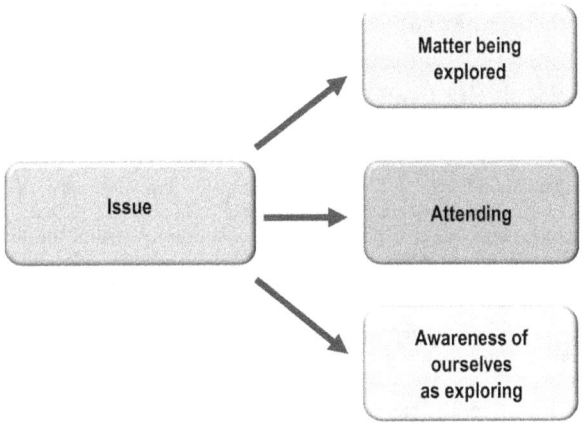

FIGURE 16.2: ATTENDING TO THE DATA OF EXPERIENCE

4.2 Stage 2: understanding experience

The second stage in the cognitive dynamism is our attempt to understand the data. At the level of fact, we put what Lonergan calls *'questions for understanding'* to the data:

- to identify any possible relationships that exist
- to recognise the categories the data falls into
- to see if this particular set of data possibly fits into a wider pattern

Memory and imagination play an important role in answering questions for understanding. When we can answer these questions (What? Why? or How?), then we say, 'we understand' (as you would have experienced in solving the problems above). You will note that the answers to 'questions for understanding' are usually provisional – they *identify what is possibly the case*, not necessarily what the case is. This is because *our understanding can be wrong*, i.e., we can misunderstand the issue at hand.

The process and product of understanding

Lonergan distinguishes *the process* of finding possible relationships from *the outcome* of this process. Seeing patterns or making connections he terms 'gaining an insight'. In his terminology, *insight is the product, 'understanding' is the process*. This distinction is important since in common language we use the word 'understanding' to cover both the process and the outcome of the process, and this causes considerable confusion.[6]

Culture and insight

In exploring a new topic or issue, we are aware of ourselves as understanding or, as the case may be, not understanding, something new. Understanding occurs within the imaginal horizon that we bring to the process and this is determined in large part by our culture. As someone brought up in a Western culture, one's understanding is necessarily limited by the imaginal horizon associated with that culture, which limits what we take for granted as 'normal' or 'natural'.[7]

---

6 There is less confusion when it comes to another synonym for 'understanding' and that is 'interpreting'. In the act of interpreting a poem, for instance, I know that this is 'my interpretation' or some critic's interpretation and that other interpretations might be possible. The distinction between process and outcome here is clearer.

7 At the time of writing, democracy protests in Hong Kong are occurring. Here, two understandings of what constitutes 'normal' are in conflict, those of mainland China and those of the democratic West, at odds over the place that the rule of law has within their respective traditions. In one country the legal system is an arm of the government, and in the other it is independent of government. The protestors want to maintain their democratic freedoms under the 'rule of law' and the Chinese authorities want to maintain the access that Hong Kong gives Chinese businesses to Western banking and investment. The latter are both likely to be severely restricted as long as there is uncertainty about the rule of law in Hong Kong. Both sides face a dilemma as each operates from a different (and apparently) incompatible conception of what is 'normal'.

When issues are explored collaboratively, the resultant dialogue often widens the horizon within which people come to understand an issue, and so allows them to imagine additional possibilities. This can make the resolution of conflict possible. Culture (and faith, in some cases) plays an important role in determining the horizon within which insight occurs.[8]

Common sense and scientific ways of understanding

Since most issues are dealt with in the here and now, people first employ 'common sense' understandings and language in dealing with the matter in hand. This seems particularly true of teachers in the classroom. This form of understanding tends to close off theoretical perspectives that *explain why things happen the way they do* and thus go beyond common sense. In a common sense understanding the sun revolves around the earth; from a scientific perspective this is not the case.

Understanding and intelligence

In developing awareness of ourselves as understanding, we become aware of the various forms that our intelligence can take. According to Lonergan, the more intelligent a person is, the more likely he or she is *to raise the right questions* in processing the data of experience. In the first part of *Insight* Lonergan gives multiple examples illustrating the different ways in which people have arrived at important insights in different domains of knowledge. Most of these insights seem reducible to *putting the right questions to experience*.

Schematically the situation is set out below.

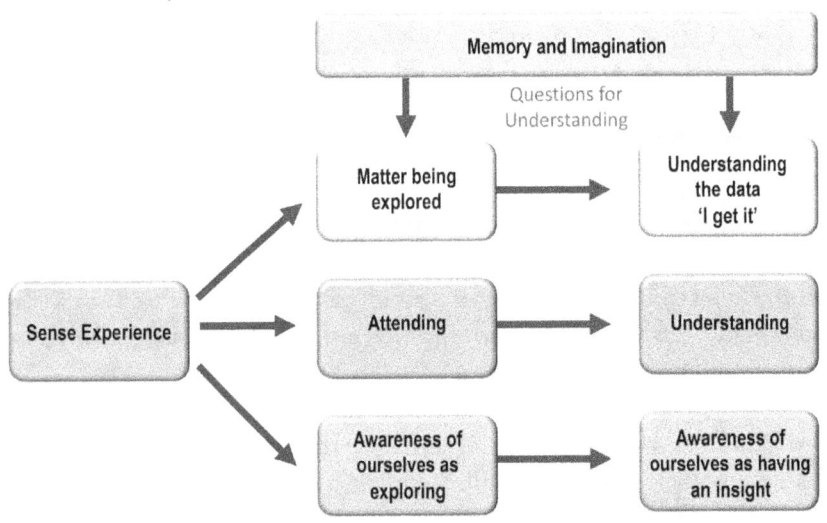

FIGURE 16.3: UNDERSTANDING AND AWARENESS (LONERGAN)

---

8   Culture's important role is acknowledged in the *socio-cultural approach* to learning. It is less obvious in the more individualistic *cognitive approach* to learning.

Memory and imagination play an important role in determining what we attend to in sense experience, as well as the questions we ask ourselves in seeking to understand. Our attention, as discussed above, is necessarily selective.

4.3 A second phenomenological experiment

To reinforce what has been said above, we introduce Problem 2 and ask you to track your mental processes in arriving at a solution.

A B C D E K L O

F G H I J M N P?

2.1 What is the rule for determining which letters are below the line?
2.1 What is the next letter below the line?

FIGURE 16.4: A SECOND PHENOMENOLOGICAL EXPERIMENT

Because Problem 1 was worked out using numbers, the temptation is to argue by analogy that Problem 2 can be worked out similarly. (To avoid much frustration, we provide the hint that *this is not the case*.) So, it will be necessary to change the domain of knowledge in which a solution is sought and *focus on the letters*.

Here we already know that letters are used to make words. If we look at the letters below the line, they contain one vowel and seven consonants. Again, we know from experience that this combination is unlikely to make up a word. By a process of elimination, we find that the solution must lie in putting questions to the data above the line. Here the letters are in alphabetical sequence and contain both vowels and consonants. So, the question to ask is:

- *Do the letters above the line form an anagram for some known word?*

We can hypothesise that this is the case, and use trial and error to discover that the letters are an anagram of the word 'blockade'. When we look at the letters below the line, we find that they too are in alphabetical sequence, but none appear in the word 'blockade'.

So, the 'rule' we are looking for is: 'The letters below the line are vowels and consonants **not** found in the word 'blockade". The next letter in sequence below the line will therefore be Q which is not found in 'blockade'.

Again, the problem itself is not important; what is important is tracking the way in which we use mental processes to arrive at the solution. In doing this we have to access the procedural knowledge that we have previously stored in memory, (i.e. use the 'general problem-solving methods' referred to in Chapter 14).

5. THE INTELLIGENT PROCESS OF INQUIRY

In addressing the first two stages in Lonergan's analysis of cognitive functioning we have asked readers to attend to the way in which they go about the process of solving puzzles, and particularly to reflect on how they attend to the data of their own consciousness and put questions to it in the process of trying to understand something.

5.1 The process of inquiry
The process at work seems to be:

Step 1. Being aware of ourselves as trying to understand the data ...
by asking questions relevant to understanding the data, such as:

- *What is to be discovered here?*
- *How will I go about it?*
- *Why are the numbers or letters organised the way they are?*
- *What is the pattern?*

These *Questions for Understanding* generate a tension within us that motivates us to try to solve a problem, understand the pattern at work, discover the rule, and so arrive at a correct answer.

Step 2. Seeing patterns not only in the data, but also in our mental acts
In solving problems, we access general problem-solving strategies stored in memory such as trial and error, arguing by analogy, process of elimination. That is, we recall *procedural knowledge* from our previous experiences. We also recall *content knowledge* stored in long-term memory that is (usually) domain specific. We are able to imagine new ways in which the data can be assembled. Our questioning enables us to see parallels between what we are attempting to understand and previous experiences. We can also see that we are trying to understand the present case as an example of some more general principle or category that we have previously understood.

Step 3. Arriving at an insight
Insight corresponds to the experience 'I get it. I can see what is going on here'.

The result of questioning our own mental acts is to see, perhaps for the first time, that 'this really is how my cognitive processes seem to work' when trying to understand something new. A few minutes reflection indicates that the above three-step process happened irrespective of which puzzle you were working on.

For Lonergan, being intelligent means 'being able to ask the right questions' so that the process of understanding can proceed *at pace*. He notes that intelligent people seem to 'get it' before others, whether this be responding to puzzles, exploring new topics, picking up social cues, responding to social situations, being empathetic, learning a new role, playing a new piece of music and so on. Intelligence can have a number of different forms. People who are strong in one form (solving technical problems) are not necessarily strong in other forms (dealing with people).

Understanding begins with the *intelligent process of putting questions to the data of experience* to arrive at an insight (by asking What? Why? How?). This process is spontaneous, driven by the inherent desire to know, and results in *common sense forms of knowing* – i.e. knowledge with practical application in the 'here and now'. Learning can also result in disciplined inquiry that leads to a *scientific form of knowing* where there is an interest in ideas for their own sake, not just in terms of their immediate practical value.

Commenting on the process of intelligent inquiry Lonergan observes:

> *The light and drive of intelligent inquiry unfolds methodically in mathematics and empirical science. In the human child it is a secret wonder that, once the mystery of human language has been unraveled, rushes forth in a cascade of questions. Far too soon the questions get out of hand, and weary adults are driven to ever more frequent use of the blanket, 'My dear, you cannot understand that yet.' The child would understand everything at once. It does not suspect that there is a strategy in the accumulation of insights, that the answers to many questions depend on the answers to still other questions, that often enough advertence to these other questions arises only from the insight that to meet interesting questions one has to begin with quite uninteresting ones. There is, then, common to all men (sic) the very spirit of inquiry that constitutes the scientific attitude. But in its native state it is untutored. Our intellectual careers begin to bud in the incessant What? and Why? of childhood. They flower only if we are willing, or constrained, to learn how to learn. They bring forth fruit only after the discovery that, if we would really master the answers, we somehow have to find them out ourselves.*
>
> *Just as there is spontaneous inquiry, so too there is a spontaneous accumulation of related insights. For questions are not an aggregate of isolated monads. Insofar as any question is followed by an insight, one has only to act, or to talk, or perhaps merely to think, on the basis of that insight, for its incompleteness to come to light and thereby generate a further*

question. Insofar as the further question is in turn met by the gratifying response of a further insight, once more the same process will reveal another aspect of incompleteness, to give rise to still further questions and still further insights. Such is the spontaneous process of learning. It is an accumulation of insights in which each successive act complements the accuracy and covers over the deficiency of those that went before. Just as the mathematician advances from images through insights and formulations to symbols that stimulate further insights, so too the spontaneous and self-correcting process of learning is a circuit in which insights reveal their shortcomings by putting forth deeds or words or thoughts, and through that revelation prompt the further questions that lead to complementary insights.[9]

Questioning the data of experience enables us

- *to form concepts*
- *to categorise data*
- *to see relationships within the data*
- *to organise data and store it in memory*
- *to apply what we know to new situations.*

Questioning the data of experience Lonergan calls 'being intelligent'. 'Being attentive' and 'being intelligent' are the first two stages in the dynamism of knowing (and therefore of learning).

5.2 Common sense and scientific understandings

Lonergan illustrates the distinction between common sense and scientific ways of understanding using Charles Goodyear (1800–1860) as an example.

Goodyear hoped to devise a way of treating rubber that would make it more useful for practical purposes. He was not alone in this endeavour as a number of scientists, some with considerable corporate backing, had been treating rubber with various chemicals in the hope of finding commercial uses for it.

The cost of Goodyear's experiments was so high that he bankrupted his hardware business which, considering he had a large family, was not an outcome his wife appreciated. Tekippe takes up the story:

One day he (Goodyear) was trying still another mixture of sulphur and rubber when his wife came to the door from the market. He had not expected

---

9   Bernard Lonergan, *Insight* (Vol 3, of the *Collected Works of Bernard Lonergan*, edited by F.E. Crowe and R.M. Doran). Toronto: University of Toronto Press, 2013, 196–7.

her so soon, so surreptitiously he stuck the mixture in the oven and went out to meet her. Later he came back to retrieve the mixture and found, to his astonishment, that it had changed. It was more pliable but had not melted in the heat; it held up even under the test of cold as well. So that was the answer: sulphur plus heat! He named the process 'vulcanization', after the god of the smithy, Vulcan.

What is notable here is the element of serendipity... Here it appears to take centre stage: the breakthrough is almost entirely by accident. Nevertheless, such an insight is not altogether accidental: the result, no matter however happenstance, can only be recognised by a person who is prepared for it; and that expectation is set by the question that had dominated Goodyear's days and nights for years. If his wife, for example, had discovered the pot, she would probably have thrown it out as just another of her husband's impractical messes.[10]

It was the disciplined nature of Goodyear's inquiry that enabled him to recognise that he had stumbled on a way to treat rubber that would enable practical uses for it (for which all motorists today are very grateful).[11]

Had Goodyear's wife thrown his mixture of rubber and sulphur out, she would have been using a 'common sense' approach to knowing, as she could see no practical use for the 'smelly mess' in her oven.

5.3 Nature of insight

The forming of an insight is rarely an isolated event. Inquiring intelligence works spontaneously

- *to integrate insights*
- *to organise them into schemas*
- *to relate them to one another*
- *to apply them in new situations*

In this way, insights into a particular topic *cumulate over time* and provide a degree of mastery over a particular field. This then serves as the basis for further inquiry into the field.

Gaining insight is not just the work of individuals. The development of understanding is often a collaborative endeavour. As Tekippe observes:

A *person with an insight spontaneously wishes to share it with another.* "Let me tell you what I have found out!' Teachers do it more formally in the

---

10 Terry Tekippe, *What is Lonergan up to in* Insight? Collegeville: The Liturgical Press, 1996, 42.
11 Unfortunately, Goodyear was not able to capitalise on his invention as some of his competitors claimed the patent. He died seriously in debt, but is remembered for his contributions, whereas those who made his life miserable are not!

classroom, but parents, siblings, friends, neighbors may be at it in practically any conversation. Knowing the insight already, it is as if a path has been trod; the learner walks in the footsteps of the knower, who points out the landmarks to follow, the obstacles and snares to avoid.[12]

The SOLO model of learning, dealt with in the previous chapter, saw understanding operating at three levels, 'no understanding', 'surface understanding', and 'deep understanding'. 'Surface understanding' equates to acquiring information, ('attending to the data' in Lonergan's frame of reference). 'Deep understanding' comes closer to the intelligent inquiry underpinning the development of insight.[13]

---

12 Terry Tekippe, *Bernard Lonergan: An Introductory Guide to* Insight. Mahwah N.J: Paulist Press, 2003, 47–48.
13 The SOLO model assumes that people begin learning new work 'from scratch'. Such a position is hermeneutically naive since it ignores the role culture plays in all learning.

17

INSIGHT INTO KNOWING: CONTRIBUTION OF BERNARD LONERGAN, PART 2

In this chapter we continue with our exploration of a theory of learning drawing on the contribution of Bernard Lonergan, particularly on his treatment of human knowing.

1. UNDERSTANDING IS NOT KNOWING

In common speech we often confuse the mental activities of 'remembering' and 'understanding' with 'knowing'. For Lonergan, remembering and understanding are important elements in the process of knowing, but they are not the same thing. The reason for this is that our understanding or interpretation[1] of events *can be wrong*. We can misinterpret things, or we can simply choose not to understand if this means going against our own interests. *Something more than understanding is involved in knowing.*

1.1 Meaning of 'knowing something'?

Here we run into a second semantic problem with the English language – the different ways in which the words 'knowledge' and 'knowing' are used.

When we look at something, there is a sense in which we can say we 'know it' because we know the category into which it fits. In education this is called 'surface learning' and the knowledge involved falls into the category of 'information'. We all have a great deal of information stored in our memories and, as we have shown previously, this plays an important role in learning, but information by itself explains very little.

Lonergan distinguishes between 'knowledge' understood as 'information' and knowledge that has 'a claim on truth' and so has explanatory power. The latter is associated with 'deep learning' because it is an abstract form of knowing that enables us to explain why things are the way they are or how

---

[1] 'Understanding', 'interpretation' and 'insight' are terms referring to the same reality – the product of the process of understanding. The fact that in common speech we use the word 'understanding' to indicate both a process and its outcome is confusing.

things work. This is also the transferable form of knowledge deemed essential for learning to be considered 'deep'. Insight of its nature is provisional. It tells us what possibly is the case, not what is the case.

2. MOVING FROM UNDERSTANDING TO KNOWING

This brings us to the third stage in the process of knowing. Having gained insight into a situation, the question arises:

- Is my insight correct?

2.1 Question for reflection

To answer this question, we are forced *to weigh the supporting evidence* and to question its quality, before making a judgement about what is true or false. So, a new set of questions arises such as:

- Is the explanation credible?
- Am I sure?
- Is it true?
- Is it just highly probable?
- Is it true only in some cases? and so on.

To each of these questions the answer is a simple 'Yes' or 'No'. This is a characteristic of what Lonergan names a *'Question for Reflection'*.

Questions for reflection, unlike 'questions for understanding', do not lead to further insights, but follow on from insight revealing, as Tekippe points out, that insight is 'less than the whole story of human knowing. Rather, it is in the nature of a hypothesis that must still be verified.'[2]

A *Question for Reflection* implies *making a judgement* based on criteria capable of establishing the truth of things once the evidence is weighed. Any question for reflection must therefore be preceded by the mental acts of *reflecting on our understanding and assessing its worth in verifying this understanding.*

Part of this reflection process involves exploring the implications and the possible consequences of acting on what we understand to be the case. This requires both imagination and analysis. It is the territory explored in crime fiction and in popular TV detective series' such as *Vera, Endeavour,* or in a lighter vein, *Father Brown.*

People are convicted of a crime on the basis of the available evidence, and not on a detective's hunches. (Such hunches often raise questions about

---

2   Terry Tekippe, *Bernard Lonergan: An Introductory Guide to* Insight. New York: Paulist Press, 2003, 61.

where pertinent evidence might be found.) Very often crime dramas hinge on the fact that the lead detective has to account for an anomalous piece of data, something that does not fit the pattern that the common sense interpretation of his or her colleagues or superiors indicates, and which usually points to one suspect as the guilty party.[3] (*Death in Paradise* makes an art form of this dramatic device).

Crime dramas, as well as our own experience, illustrate the fact that the reflection based on the intelligent process of inquiry needs to continue until *all the facts* are accounted for, *and there are no more pertinent questions to be asked*. At that stage, and only at that stage, is it possible to affirm whether a correct judgement can be made. If this is not the case, then clearly the process of inquiry needs to continue.[4]

In testing whether our insight is correct, we need to be aware of *the criteria we are employing in making judgements* about the truth of things. This is important in all forms of learning as the criteria are different in different domains of learning.

2.2 Domain-specific criteria used in affirming what constitutes knowledge

Physical, medical and social scientists respond to the questions posed in intelligent inquiry by developing a hypothesis and then devising, or getting someone else to devise and carry out, an experiment to test whether the hypothesis is correct or not. Here *evidence validates understanding* and so we say science 'knows' something. Knowledge developed in this way is provisional, since a later experiment may call the results of an earlier one into question.[5]

The physical and medical sciences provide us with *one model* for validating knowledge. However, this method does not work as well in the human sciences, such as anthropology, sociology or psychology where knowledge is often *validated through inter-subjective dialogue*.[6] In theology a key means of validation of knowledge is reference to sacred texts. Such

---

3 This is usually put forward by a 'detective plod' who acts as a patsy for the lead detective. Dr Watson serves this purpose in the case of the famous Sherlock Holmes.
4 Many books explaining Lonergan's account of human cognition turn to detectives as illustrative of his approach. For instance, Peter Beer uses the lead detective in the Hitchcock film *Dial M for Murder* as a case study in the way human cognition functions. See Peter Beer, *An introduction to Bernard Longeran: exploring Lonergan's approach to the great philosophic questions*. Sid Harta Publishing: Victoria, 2010. Tekeippe (2003) uses Sherlock Holmes in a similar manner.
5 The international community of scientists ultimately affirms what can be held as scientific knowledge.
6 Theology appeals to a third way of knowing, one based on correctly interpreting religious traditions. The criteria for making correct judgements about a religious tradition are themselves part of the tradition. As a consequence, religious traditions are often incompatible with one another since they operate on different understandings of what is true. A purpose of inter-faith dialogue is to find common ground and common purpose among the adherents of different faiths given these differences.

texts underpin particular religious traditions and play an important role in their worship rituals. In Catholicism, it is important to note that scripture is faithfully interpreted within the framework of the *total tradition* of the faith community.[7]

Lonergan terms the process of weighing the evidence and critically examining the criteria used in answering the question for reflection as *'being rational'*.

2.4 Knowledge and culture

The process of knowing does not happen in the abstract, but always within a particular historical and cultural situation. In the reflection phase of knowing, as in the understanding phase, the criteria used to assess the evidence are influenced by the culture in which we live, and these will vary across time.

In the Middle Ages *theological criteria* dominated the construction of knowledge. Copernicus's astronomical data was discounted because it seemed clearly to contradict the Bible. Almost by definition, it could not be true within the dominant worldview. In the modern period, *scientific criteria* came to dominate the construction of knowledge as these were thought to establish 'objective facts', whereas theological and philosophical positions were discounted as 'subjective opinions'. Again, within the prevailing worldview they could not be held as true.

In Soviet Russia *ideological criteria* determined what constitutes knowledge. This approach came unstuck badly when the Chernobyl disaster of 1986 occurred, and it was impossible to cover up the scale of the damage done. Something similar seems to be happening on a global scale at present with respect to climate change and in China in respect to the outbreak of the coronavirus.

In pre-modern times theology established what could be considered 'public knowledge' and so could be taught, while in the next era science came to take on this public role. Today we have a more nuanced understanding of the limits of both science and religion in determining what might be considered 'public knowledge'. We also have a better understanding of the role that culture plays in any determination of what is 'true'. However, what is held to be knowledge is still prone to ideological manipulation by those in power whether in the US, China, Australia or elsewhere. The problem with the ideological manipulation of knowledge is that sooner or later truth

---

7   A helpful guide is the post-synodal apostolic exhortation of Pope Benedict XVI, *Verbum Domini* (*On the Interpretation of Sacred Scripture in the Life of the Church*), 2010. Also, from the Pontifical Biblical Commission there is *The Interpretation of the Bible in the Church*, 1993. These and similar documents are downloadable from the Vatican website.

catches up with those in power, usually with devastating consequences, as the Chernobyl experience clearly demonstrates.

2.5 Fitting the pieces together

Lonergan's picture of the dynamism of human cognition is illustrated schematically in the diagram below.

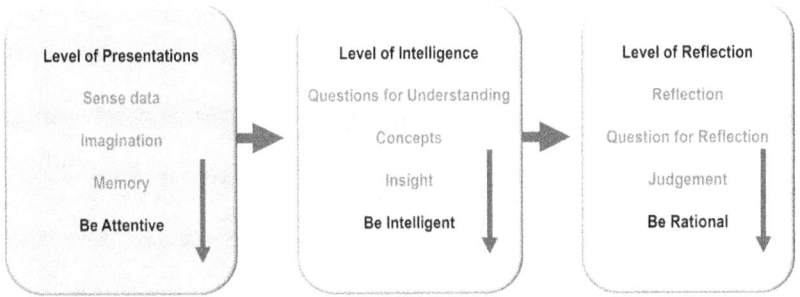

FIGURE 17.1: DYNAMISM OF HUMAN COGNITION – LONERGAN

The judgement that something is true or false marks the end of the knowing process. At that point we can say we 'know' something as being true and so it is applicable in multiple situations. This is a different form of knowing from that involved in acquiring information, even though in common speech we use the same word 'knowledge' for both forms.

Lonergan distinguishes between 'simple knowing' and 'compound knowing' where the first refers to surface knowing and the second to 'deep' knowing.

Of the three elements in the Level of Reflection, the last – making a judgment – is clearly the critical one.

- *How do we make good judgements about our insights?*
- *How do we know if our understanding is correct?*
- *Using what scales do we weigh the evidence?*

These are questions central to reflection, to knowing, and, by extension, to both teaching and learning.

2.6 Being balanced in judgement

Lonergan argues that *balanced judgement* is required in knowing. How does a person acquire balanced judgement so that he or she can have confidence in the value of their insights? Lonergan does not answer that question directly, but instead proposes four conditions that must be met. A person with balanced judgement:

- *habitually seeks to gain knowledge (he or she is a learner)*
- *views mistakes as a chance to learn (he or she learns from experience)*
- *is committed to developing expertise (learning aims at mastery)*
- *is sufficiently self-aware to counter the influence that personal and cultural biases have in making a judgement (learning involves self-knowledge)*[8]

The originality of Lonergan's approach to knowing lies in his use of the data of consciousness to explain how human cognition functions. He appeals to the data of the reader's own consciousness to validate the positions he takes.

It is important to note that Lonergan, unlike Hattie or the National Research Council, is not proposing a model of learning. He is outlining what he sees to be *the foundations on which all learning and knowledge rest*.

2.7 Lonergan and 'deep learning'

Our previous experiences, as recorded in memory, are a vital resource in arriving at an insight. Lonergan, who was writing in the early 1970s, reinforces three issues highlighted by Hattie in *Visible Learning*. These issues have also been stressed in the discussion of 'deep learning' in the previous chapters, and they seem central to 'the new pedagogy':

- *In learning, what is important is not the questions the teacher asks the students, but the questions that students are encouraged to put to their own understanding. If a teacher asks questions of students, these ought to challenge students to question their own understanding.*
- *It is important that students have the opportunity to test the accuracy of their insights by articulating them in a group so that the spontaneous process of self-correction inherent in understanding can unfold. This requires a classroom environment that is relatively safe so that students feel secure enough to speak out.*
- *It is important that students learn how to learn and that they understand the mental processes at work in learning, as well as the relationships that exist among them. In particular, they need to be aware of the criteria that apply in determining what constitutes knowledge in the various domains of learning. Confusion between the knowledge acquired in surface learning and in deep learning often confound this issue. Without some guidance here, students unwittingly apply scientific criteria inappropriately to other domains. This is sometimes the case in Religious Education.*

---

8 Summarised from Tekippe 2003, Chapter 8, 'How Does One Become a Person of Good Judgement?', 67–77.

As we noted at the outset of the previous chapter, all teachers have at least an implicit theory of 'how students learn' or 'what is going on in students' heads when they are being taught'. Lonergan tends to make explicit what for many teachers is only implicit. In doing so he provides a scaffold for planning lessons by providing a coherent framework outlining what is central to knowing, and so to both teaching and learning. His work gives explicit form to that of Hattie and Fullan by putting 'deep learning' on a sound epistemological footing.

In conclusion, Lonergan's 'transcendental precepts' are worth repeating.[9] In both teaching and learning it is necessary to:

- *be attentive*
- *be intelligent*
- *be reasonable*

as Lonergan defines these terms.

2.8 The fourth transcendental precept

If we learn in order to act, there is a further imperative. In applying what we know, it is necessary to *'be responsible'*, by which Lonergan means to *act in accord with what you know to be true*. But this takes us into the field of ethics and that is beyond the scope of this chapter, which has been to provide a coherent account of what is involved in knowing and drawing out some of the implications of this for both teaching and pedagogy.[10]

---

9   'Transcendental' in this context means 'true for all cultures and all times'.
10 Lonergan relates stages in the dynamism of human cognition to stages in the transformation of human consciousness, each of which involves a form of 'conversion'. For a discussion of this aspect of his thinking see John Collins and Sandra Carroll, 'Teaching Practical Theology: Implications for Theological Education with Reference to Lonergan's Theoretical Framework', *Australian eJournal of Theology*, Vol 18, no 2, 166–174.

18

INTRODUCING THE HERMENEUTICAL TRADITION

In the previous two chapters we have looked at understanding and knowing from an *epistemological perspective*. In this and the succeeding two chapters we view understanding from within the *hermeneutical tradition*. Whereas epistemology is the study of the origin, nature and limits of human knowledge, hermeneutics is concerned with interpretation and the construction of *meaning*. 'Understanding' is a central concept in both disciplines.

One of the joys of teaching is experiencing the moment when the light in a student's eyes 'goes on' as he or she finally 'gets it'. All teachers know the thrill of that moment! But what does the student actually 'get', and what process is going on in the student's head when she or he 'gets it'? Put another way, *when we say a student 'understands' something, what exactly do we mean?*

As we noted previously, all educators work from at least an implicit understanding of what is going on in students' heads when they are learning, but this implicit understanding is based on assumptions.

- *But are these assumptions correct?*

This is the question we explore in this chapter.

1. INSIGHT, INTERPRETATION AND UNDERSTANDING

We use the word 'understanding' in a variety of ways. Consider the following:

- *Sahr has a very limited understanding of English.*
- *I fully understand your situation.*
- *Clare has an intuitive understanding of music.*
- *I do not understand what you are saying.*
- *You have no understanding of how that makes me feel.*
- *Don't misunderstand me.*

- *Roger has an uncanny understanding of people.*

The examples above make it clear that, as used in common English, 'understanding' can be full, partial, lacking, intuitive, interpretive, or completely missing. The word is used as a noun and as a verb, as the destination and as the journey that takes us to the destination. It is not surprising that a good deal of misunderstanding exists about understanding!

1.1 Insight

Bernard Lonergan skirts some of this confusion by reserving the word 'insight' to mean *the product of understanding*. In his frame of reference 'to understand' *means to have insight into*. Insight can be personal, or it can be shared and so become collective. It can be partial, arrived at intuitively or as the result of teaching, or the product of experience. Understanding can also mean *a way of interpreting events*. Insight can be right or it can be wrong. It can be missing. Lonergan draws a distinction, like all good philosophers, between *understanding as process and understanding as product*, between the journey and the destination.

Gaining insight is a necessary step in all learning whether this involves learning a text, the sequence of steps in a dance routine or the notes in a musical score, making an entrance in a drama production, juxtaposing elements in a work of art, mastering algorithms in maths, creating code on a computer, experimenting in science, applying a moral principle, or figuring out the game plan in a sporting event.

The process by which insight comes about is inherently mysterious.[1] For some people understanding comes quickly; for others it develops over time. Teachers are well aware that some students understand what they are trying to convey well before they have even completed their presentation. For other students, insight arrives laboriously and only after several presentations of the same material often using different methods.

Students *make mental connections* – an essential step in gaining insight – in different ways and at different speeds depending on their stage of development. In the classroom situation many understand after a clear presentation of material, while others make connections visually via diagrams or mind maps that provide them with scaffolds. Some students respond to a narrative approach, discovering where key ideas come from, while others make the connections only in discussion with fellow students or by asking questions. Some make connections in maths, sport, and the

---

[1] Canadian philosopher and theologian Bernard Lonergan S.J. whom we met in the previous chapters, wrote a famous book called *Insight* that deals with human understanding. It is over 800 pages long indicating that the topic is far from simple.

expressive arts only through practice. Sometimes it requires a combination of these approaches before a student finally 'gets it'.

Using language in this familiar way highlights three important things about human understanding:

- *Understanding always involves a content; we gain insight into 'something'.*
- *Understanding is the process of linking the unfamiliar to the familiar so that new patterns are created that include both.*
- *Understanding arrives in many ways and the speed at which this happens is unpredictable.*

1.2 Insight, learning and prior understanding

We have to understand in order to know.[2] Insight can be right or wrong; not only can students understand what the teacher is saying, they can also misunderstand it as well. Teaching aims to assist students create alignment between what they already understand and what is presented for them to understand, to make links between the familiar and the unfamiliar – in Gadamer's words to create 'a fusion of horizons'[3]. When it comes to learning something new, prior understanding (right or wrong) stands in the background of the students' attempts to understand, but as we shall see, it does not stand there alone!

2. MIND, BRAINS AND LEARNING

To say that something 'is going in on in a student's mind' is to unconsciously buy into a philosophic position – that humans have 'minds'.

2.1 Mind and brain

'Mind' is usually the focus of philosophic enquiry, while 'brain' is the focus of scientific enquiry. You can put a brain under an MRI scanner and locate where particular brain activities are located, something that is not possible with the human mind. Using technology, we can view the brain and learn how its parts work. It is not possible to see a mind. 'Mind' is a concept that belongs *to a different order of analysis.*

Science tells us important things about the brain. 'Brain science' can tell us *where* various functions associated with 'mind' take place, such as memory, logical thinking, aesthetic appreciation, and so on, but it is quite limited in what it can say about *how* these functions take place. Both disciplines,

---

2 We 'know' something when our insight about it is validated in some authoritative way.
3 Hans-Georg Gadamer, *Truth and Method*, 2nd Rev. Edn. London: Sheed & Ward, 1989, 306–7.

philosophy and science, are needed to explore the nature of the human mind.[4]

2.2 Mind as a product of culture

In this chapter we introduce a third partner to science and philosophy in a conversation about the human mind – cultural anthropology. In doing so we expand our focus from 'mind as an individual possession' to include 'mind as the product-of-culture'.

Learning takes place in real people, not in abstractions. Real people live in communities, cultures and a particular historical context. The interrelationships that exist among the three C's – community, culture and context – are the particular concern of cultural anthropology. These shape not only *what people* learn, but also *how they learn and why they choose to learn particular things*. Considering mind in isolation from the contexts, cultures and communities in which the human person functions, can distort from the outset any attempt to 'understand understanding'.

Concepts from cultural anthropology such as 'worldview', 'context' and 'tradition' play an important role in all forms of human understanding. Since, as we saw in the last two chapters, understanding provides the doorway to learning, community, culture, and context shape learning. Any notion of 'mind' that omits these concepts fails to make essential connections in attempting to gain insight into how we create meaning, and so make sense of the world in which we live.

The question of how we understand the world around us has perplexed philosophers and educators since at least the time of Plato and Aristotle. Philosophy offers limited, if real, insight into human understanding, as do science and cultural anthropology. Science is limited because it is not possible *to objectify* the human mind.[5] Cultural anthropology contends that educational theories are deficient when they focus too sharply on the individual, thought of implicitly as 'a brain on legs', and when they do not take into account that education is directed to *real persons who live in communities and cultures embedded in history*. Teachers educate the 'real people' of cultural anthropology, not the 'brains on legs' of modern philosophy.

Before proceeding further, in the remainder of this chapter we introduce hermeneutics for those unfamiliar with the field. We start our exploration of hermeneutical principles in the context in which they were first developed

---

4 An important conclusion from brain science is that the brain cannot multi-task when it comes to human awareness. We cannot focus our awareness on two things at the same time, so driving and texting are inherently dangerous for mere mortals. Neither can students learn if their attention is somewhere else.

5 We have to use our minds to understand the human mind. There is no 'mind-free', objective position from which to interrogate human understanding.

– *textual hermeneutics,* the interpretation of texts. As a discipline, hermeneutics came to prominence as the 'rules for interpreting texts'. However, in the 20th century it was realised that there are many forms of 'text' that require interpretation. This led to the evolution of *philosophical hermeneutics*.

3. SOME BASIC HERMENEUTICAL PRINCIPLES[6]

By the mid-20th century, philosophers such as Hans-Georg Gadamer, Paul Ricoeur, Jurgen Habermas, and Jacques Derrida, realised that all life-events constitute a form of 'text' that people interpret. This understanding finds its expression today, when we say we can 'read people', or 'interpret their body language'. Footballers are valued for their capacity to 'read the play'. Businesses collapse when leaders fail to 'read the writing on the wall'. Church leaders are expected to 'read the signs of the times'. Teachers 'read things into' what principals do or say, and so on. All these forms of 'reading' or 'interpreting' have nothing to do with texts as we usually use the term. They all indicate that *understanding involves interpreting, and this can happen in a number of real-life contexts.*

The process of understanding engages us as persons with minds, values and sensibilities, all of which shape our capacity to make linkages between *what we already understand and what remains to be understood.*

To explore the pedagogical significance of hermeneutics we will use the *Letters of Paul* as an example of 'ancient text'. By examining the issues that understanding this text raises, it is possible to draw out some of the basic principles in hermeneutics.[7]

In the next two chapters we bring these principles together in developing a 'working model' of human understanding that can be applied in pedagogical decision-making.[8]

3.1 Textual hermeneutics: the starting point

Two 19th century German scholars, Friedrich Schleiermacher and Wilhelm Dilthey, are regarded as the 'fathers' of hermeneutics. They were the first to systematically explore the rules that apply in understanding (interpreting) written texts.[9] The question they attempted to explore was:

---

[6] In the balance of this chapter and the ones that follow we are heavily indebted to the work of Shaun Gallagher as set out in *Hermeneutics and Education*, New York: The University of New York Press, 1992.
[7] While we say 'understanding the Letters of Paul' we could equally say 'interpreting the Letters of Paul'. In hermeneutics 'understanding' and 'interpreting' are used interchangeably.
[8] It bears repeating that a working model is a simplification of a more complex reality that throws light on a topic and enables testable predictions to be made.
[9] To understand a text, it is necessary to make sense of what is on the pages. Each page contains symbols that are unintelligible unless you are familiar with the language and linguistic system that stands behind the symbols. Understanding a text involves interpreting the symbols.

- *Is it possible to arrive at an authoritative understanding of a text when you can no longer use the author as a point of reference in determining its meaning?*

Schleiermacher and Dilthey gradually systematised the rules for interpreting ancient texts as they wrestled with this question.

If the author and reader *live in the same culture, context, and community*, the task of understanding what the author meant is fairly straightforward since there are many common points of reference. The task becomes much harder when the reader and the author are separated by several centuries.

When reading a text, we unthinkingly interpret what it says *within the horizon of our own culture*, even when we know the writer was seeking to communicate with people living in a very different historical and cultural situation, and often employing another language with a different linguistic structure. This form of reading is called *naive literalism*. The potential for misunderstanding in reading a text in this way is very high.

3.2 Why interpret ancient texts?

For most people, the first question to be addressed in understanding an ancient text is:

- *Why bother (trying to make sense of ancient texts)?*

Put in a more concrete way,

- *Is there any purpose in knowing what Romans took away from listening to Cicero's speeches?*
- *Does this have any relevance today?*

The same questions can be put to the *Letters of Paul, The Gospels, The Iliad, Hamlet, the American Declaration of Independence*, etc. The basic answer to such questions is: Because they tell us something significant about the human narrative and who we are! Of course, for those who approach such texts as the Gospels and the Letters of Paul as *sacred scripture,* these are both ancient texts and *much more than ancient texts.*

This brings us to a first principle in hermeneutics.

- *All human understanding has a narrative quality.*

In human understanding, present, past, and future are interwoven. We gain insight into the present by making linkages to our past and by looking to a hoped-for future. Understanding orients us to the past, to new experiences in the present, and to a hoped-for future. It locates us within a *particular unfolding story.*

World of the text

Ancient texts are relevant to the extent that they encompass important aspects of *the human story* and reveal the hopes that drive the evolution of that story. An ancient text brings together four major elements for the reader:

- *the actual historical and cultural context in which the text was written*
- *the writer's understanding of that context*
- *the audience's understanding of the context*
- *the writer's intention*

All four factors shape the sense that a contemporary reader can make of the text.

Authors write out of a particular historical context. How the reader understands this context in large part shapes whether or not the author's aim in writing is realised.

World behind the text

To understand an ancient text requires knowing something about the historical context in which the text sits and how the author and his audience understood this. It is impossible, for instance, to understand *Emile,* Rousseau's ground-breaking book on education, without knowing something of the context in which it was written and the ideas that had currency at the time. Rousseau also made a number of assumptions about what readers who shared his context and culture already knew. When we read the text today, we can only *infer* what Rousseau wished to convey from *what is in the text and our understanding of its context.*

To approach the text without understanding the writer's context is foolhardy, but unfortunately, that is the way in which many people interpret the Bible. Furthermore, since our understanding of the original context *is an interpretation*, our insight into the meaning of an ancient text is always limited, so the text's exact intended meaning for the writer's audience often eludes us. *It is not possible to recreate the world of the author, as the author experienced it.* This is to seek a form of objectivity that simply does not exist.

By exploring the four factors above we *can partially reconstitute* the author's frame of reference, and the source of his insights. The relevance of the text for us today depends *on the value we place on insights communicated in the text.*

Historic effect

Important texts, such as the Gospels, have *an historic effect*. That is, they have had an effect in shaping cultures. A contemporary reader is aware of this effect to some extent, so they read the text in the light of their appreciation of this historic effect. Thus, there is a sense in *which a text can take on a meaning of its own,* independent of what the original author had in mind. In this way important texts become *the source of traditions* and these become incorporated into a people's or community's 'design for living together' – it becomes part of their culture.

World in front of the text

We make the effort to understand a text when we judge that it contains insights that can make a valued contribution to the unfolding of the narrative to which we belong and the notions of human flourishing and human possibility embedded in that narrative.[10] *Important texts speak to the future.* Thus, we still study the ancient Greek tragedies, but we do not study ancient Greek science. Aeschylus, Sophocles, and Euripides still have something to say to us today about the human condition; ancient Greek science does not.[11]

4. LETTERS OF PAUL: A CASE STUDY IN TEXTUAL INTERPRETATION

The Letters of Paul[12] illustrate how the four factors outlined above, the world of the text, the world behind the text, historic effect, and the world in front of the text, all come together in making sense of what Paul has to say.

4.1 World of the text

Paul wrote in the early first century for people living under Roman rule. He also wrote in the context of faith communities that expected the return

---

10 Richard Tarnas, *The Passion of the Western Mind: Understanding the Ideas that Have Shaped Our World View,* explores the narrative of human possibility, as does Charles Taylor in *A Secular Age.*
11 This is a summary introduction to an area of particular interest to Christians for the assistance it provides to their encounter with the Bible which for them is sacred Scripture. One of the most widely respected Catholic scholars dealing with Biblical interpretation is Sandra Schneiders, as in *The Revelatory Text: Interpreting the New Testament as Sacred Scripture.* Revised Edition. Wilmington: Michael Glazier, 1999. The great scripture scholar Raymond Brown (1928–1998) credited Schneiders with distinctions made in her work which influenced developments in his own insight into hermeneutics and the Bible. (See Donald Senior, *Raymond Brown and the Catholic biblical Renewal.* New York: Paulist Press, 2018, 277). Paul Ricoeur's narrative hermeneutics stands behind the work of most mainline scholars dealing with Biblical interpretation.
12 Paul authored letters in the period prior to AD 66. Scholars agree that there are a number of letters included in the Pauline corpus attributed to Paul but that either he did not write (the style is not his) or could not have written (they were composed after his death). These are not fakes but follow the cultural custom of a disciple writing in the style and with the authority of his leader.

of Jesus in the near future. In advising communities about Christian life in his time and circumstance, Paul did not intend to overturn the existing social order. Both he and his audience took many things as givens that are totally unacceptable to a 21st-century sensibility, for example, slavery and patriarchy. Within the existing social order, however, Paul saw all humans as equal before God and treated women as colleagues – fellow workers in advancing his mission.

Paul was a contemporary of Jesus although he lived considerably longer. He grew up in Tarsus now part of the city of Mersim in south-central Turkey. Paul's worldview was shaped by both his Greek education and his Jewish upbringing. We do not know why Paul came to Jerusalem, but his knowledge of Judaism enabled him to join the influential Pharisee group once he arrived there.

Jesus grew up in predominantly Aramaic-speaking Galilee. His target audience was mostly illiterate Jewish peasants living in an oral culture, so he used immediate and down-to-earth language when speaking to them. Paul's major audience was Greek-speaking gentiles, so he had to recontextualise Jesus' teaching into categories that Greeks and other gentile audiences could appreciate and understand.[13]

Paul's strategy in spreading Jesus' message was to create small communities committed to living 'the Way'. He was able to check his interpretation of 'the Way' against that of Jesus' immediate followers. Despite this, Paul's work among non-Jews created suspicion among the Jewish Christian community in Jerusalem. Leaders from there sent emissaries to check up on what Paul was doing, a development that created considerable friction within early Pauline communities.

When he embraced Christianity, Paul brought formidable energy, imagination and intellectual firepower to the movement. Besides Greek, he seems to have been fluent in several languages. Jesus spoke in Aramaic, not Greek, so there were some inherent challenges for Greek speakers in understanding his message since the linguistic structures of Aramaic and Greek are quite different.[14] Where Jesus' style of communication was concrete, direct and appealing to the imagination, Paul's style is often rhetorical and conceptual, appealing to the mind.

---

13 Paul lived and died in the period before the Gospels were written, and so had no access to them in the form with which we are familiar.
14 Aramaic had a much more limited linguistic structure than Greek. It was spoken within a community that was largely illiterate and very down-to-earth. Aramaic is read right-to-left like Hebrew or Arabic and not left-to-right as with European languages. Greek provided Paul with a more complex vocabulary and with well-credentialed literary forms. Paul rarely refers directly to Jesus' actual teachings, he writes within his own theological constructions of what Jesus meant.

Paul wrote for audiences that were largely non-Jewish, but for whom religious issues were important. The majority of his audiences spoke or understood Greek. In re-contextualising Jesus' message for his audiences, Paul employed a range of Jewish concepts. His creative understanding of the *significance of God's revelatory love at work in Jesus and his teaching* was formulated in a frame of reference that was often foreign to his audience, but one that Paul with his Jewish background took for granted. This created some confusion as to what he actually meant. Because Paul took a deep personal interest in the communities he helped establish, he wrote to reassure, but also to inform and correct both understandings and practices. Another reason for writing was to counter the influence of emissaries from Jerusalem who were sent to check up on him, and in doing so were undermining his influence and teaching.

In summary, we can say that Paul's insights into Jesus and his message were worked out in the process of re-contextualising the significance of Jesus' life for people who spoke a different language and made sense of life within a different frame of reference from the Christian community in Jerusalem. When this challenge is appreciated, we can see that Paul's task has many parallels with those facing Catholic educators today.

When we bring these factors together, we arrive at a second principle of hermeneutics:

- *All understanding is shaped by language.*

Every language imposes its own constraints on meaning. We can understand only when we are able to articulate what it is that we seek to understand.

This principle has important pedagogical significance. It is the reason why many teachers say that they *really* understand something only when they have taught it. In the act of teaching they have to articulate for others what it is that they have been trying to understand for themselves. Similarly, many students understand something only in the process of articulating it within a group discussion.

While Paul faced problems in his own time, these are exacerbated when we read him today. Most Catholics encounter the Letters of Paul as short excerpts read at Mass on Sunday. They have little or no knowledge of Paul's context or the concerns that caused him to write, so they interpret what they hear from within their 21st century Western context, concerns and sensibilities. Not surprisingly, for many in the congregation these readings have quite limited meaning.

This brings us to a third principle in hermeneutics:

- *We always bring something to the task of understanding.*

There is no such position as *tabula rasa* when it comes to understanding something new. While we may say we are 'clueless', in fact we are not! Even when students have no prior knowledge of what a lesson is about, they do not arrive empty-handed. The 'something' they bring are biases and preconceptions (good and bad) that they have absorbed through being part of a context, culture and community. These biases and pre-conceptions are usually held subconsciously and constitute what is known in hermeneutics as the *fore-structure of knowing* and in cultural anthropology as one's *personal worldview*. In the next chapter we will explore the nature of this 'fore-structure' in more detail.

Our personal worldview *orients us towards the unfamiliar*. It determines the questions we put to the unfamiliar, and even our willingness to engage with it. If students come from homes in which religion is looked on with suspicion and distrust, they subconsciously pick up from the family 'vibes' that religion is unimportant. Thus, they have few questions to ask about it, may even be hostile to it, and see religious education classes as a waste of time. Religious education teachers often have a hard time overcoming this form of bias. They can choose to blame the students for their poor attitude or lack of interest, but often this means misinterpreting the students' situation, one that is more often than not dictated by their home context rather than by their actual intent.

When we take the words of an ancient text at face value, we are reading from the perspective of *naïve literalism*. In terms of our discussion, naive literalism ignores *the distance between Paul's context, culture and community and our own. Naïve literalism also ignores the historical effect that Paul's writing had as it has worked its way into the Christian tradition and through this into Western culture*. All this has an impact on how we make sense of what he says.

Naive literalism was the stance to the Bible adopted by most theologians and Church leaders throughout much of the history of Christianity.[15] It still haunts Catholic theology (and many homilies). The development of what is known as the *historical critical method* takes the hermeneutical principles outlined above into consideration in making sense of biblical texts.[16]

A fourth principle of hermeneutics requires us to:

- *Appreciate the tension that always exists between the familiar and the unfamiliar.*

---

15 Naive literalism means reading the Bible at face-value, as if it were happening in the here and now. Any distance between the context of the ancient text and the present context is largely ignored.

16 This important method must be complemented by other valuable methods, for example narrative criticism, in helping communities benefit from engagement with the Bible as sacred scripture.

Understanding involves *bringing the unfamiliar into the orbit of the familiar. It also involves an appreciation of difference.* Understanding is a process that puts questions to difference, in search of answers. This is how linkages between the familiar and the unfamiliar are made. Naive literalism ignores this difference and therefore frustrates understanding and learning. The questions a teacher puts to the learner play a secondary role in the development of understanding. Sound pedagogy seeks to elicit questions *on the part of the learner.*

From a theological perspective, Paul's insights are revelatory in that they throw light on God's vision or dream for humankind which Jesus described as the Kingdom of God. As we gain insight into this vision, we develop the norms and values that guide our actions. The insights encountered more generally in the New Testament become normative *to the extent that they give direction to our hopes*. How we, in the 21st century, interpret these hopes opens up new possibilities for us, particularly in how we understand human flourishing. We respond to the hopes embedded in ancient texts to the extent that we recognise the wisdom they contain. *Understanding provides insight into new possibilities.* It orients us to the future.

A fifth principle of hermeneutics is:

- *All understanding is ultimately self-understanding.*

Through the process of questioning we position ourselves in *the web of relationships that defines our life-world*. This web includes relationship to self, family and peers, community and society, the created world, and ultimately our relationship to God. As the latter develops, we find ourselves seeing all other relationships in a new light. This change in perspective we call 'conversion'.

In the process of understanding, we put questions to the unfamiliar and so open up new possibilities. Hope is normative in human understanding because it keeps us open to these new possibilities.

4.2 Human understanding is always incomplete

Paul's teaching as we have it in his letters raises challenges; so too does that of Jesus in the Gospels. The four canonical gospels were written at least forty years after Jesus' death. We know little about the historical authors (beyond pious legends). What we do know is that the they wrote for *particular communities* and sought to interpret what they knew about Jesus and his teaching *in a way that was meaningful for these communities.*

The *Gospel* authors had to re-contextualise the meaning of Jesus' message, not only for a new audience, but also for a new generation.[17] They did so, not by writing histories,[18] but by constructing *unique theological narratives* sometimes borrowing from one another, sometimes using unique memories and sources, *but always with the circumstances of their own community in mind*.[19]

As with the letters of Paul, the central issue in understanding a gospel is to recapture the hopes to which it speaks, to re-interpret these in terms of our own context, and then to respond. This requires *imagination as well as memory*.

A sixth principle of hermeneutics is:

- *Human understanding is never complete.*

One example is when an author has an insight about the human condition developed in a particular context that she wishes to communicate. The insight endures in other contexts to the extent that *it speaks to the human aspirations and seeking expression in that context* and provides some direction in how these aspirations can be realised.

Literary classics, and great works of music or art, have the capacity to *transcend the contexts* in which they were created in this way. People living in another context *appropriate* the insights that master works contain because they remain meaningful and relevant.

In this section we have explored a number of basic insights in *textual hermeneutics* by considering the issues that arise in the *Letters of Paul* and the *Gospels*. These insights all have a bearing on what constitutes sound pedagogy. We conclude by setting them out in summary form below:

- *Understanding provides the **pre-condition for knowing**, but is not to be confused with it. Understanding can be right or wrong!*
- *Understanding is an **activity of real people**, not 'brains on legs'.*
- *Understanding is the process of making connections; insight is the outcome.*
- *Understanding unfolds in time and has a narrative quality. We always understand things from a particular position because we are embedded in a culture, context and community.*

---

17 They could have had no idea that their writing would come to be treated with the reverence given to the Hebrew Scriptures.
18 Well into the 20th century it was fashionable to write a Life of Christ that took the four Gospels as quasi-historical works, the contents of which could be compiled into a single story. The Gospels were seen neither as unique, nor as theological works in their own right, works which explain Jesus' significance and the significance of his mission and message. This aspect of the Catholic tradition has been deconstructed by modern biblical scholarship.
19 This theme is well developed in Raymond Brown's, *The Churches the Apostles Left Behind*. New York: Paulist Press, 1984.

- *Understanding **is shaped by language**. We understand when we can articulate what we understand.*
- *People always bring something to the task of understanding – **their personal worldview**.*
- *Understanding is mediated by the questions that people put to themselves when confronted with the unfamiliar.*
- *All understanding is ultimately **self-understanding**, an opening up to new possibilities.*
- *Understanding **engenders** hope since it opens us up to the future.*
- *Understanding **is never complete** because further insight is always possible.*

In this chapter we have endeavoured to explore important aspects of human understanding, what it is, and how it works. The aim has been to 'ground' the implicit pedagogical theories that many teachers draw on in teaching and promoting learning in the classroom. We have further developed ideas initially presented by Lonergan. In addition, we have explored basic principles in hermeneutics as they apply to making sense of texts. We have highlighted the fact that understanding does not happen in the abstract, but is embedded in a culture, context and community and all three influence the process and content of understanding.

In the next two chapters we develop a model of understanding based on the principles set out above. The model suggests why traditions play an important role in learning.

19

UNDERSTANDING FROM A HERMENEUTICAL PERSPECTIVE

As we saw in the last chapter, hermeneutical principles justify many of the pedagogical choices that teachers make, even if these choices are made more implicitly than explicitly. While early scholars involved themselves in the interpretation of written texts, in due course scholars have come to expand the notion of what constitutes a 'text' to include events and all forms of human expression. Two seminal thinkers in this field are Hans-Georg Gadamer and Paul Ricoeur.[1]

1. GETTING A 'FEEL' FOR THE SUBJECT

In writing a book, the chapter that presents the most difficulty for authors is generally the *Introduction*. In the introduction an author endeavours to provide the reader with a broad understanding of the areas to be covered, the questions to be addressed, and some indication of why these might be worth exploring. The aim is to present the 'big picture' before the reader engages with the detail.

The problem is that, at the outset, an author is often not entirely clear what 'the big picture' actually is. So, as his or her research proceeds, the *Introduction* has to be reshaped several times to match developments in the text. This might seem a wasteful way to proceed, but it tends to follow an important pattern in how the human mind works. This pattern is known as the 'hermeneutical circle'. It is this pattern and its implications that we want to explore in this chapter and, in the process, draw out its significance for teaching and learning.

---

1 Gadamer (1900–2002), along with Ricoeur (1913–2005), are the main thinkers associated with 'moderate' philosophic hermeneutics. (The current French president, Emmanuel Macron, worked as a research assistant for Ricoeur as a post-graduate student.) 'Moderate' indicates that it is possible to find meaning in a 'text', but not in a totally objective way. Gadamer's seminal book is entitled *Truth and Method*. The international Enhancing Catholic School Identity (ECSI) project, jointly sponsored by the Catholic Education Commission of Victoria and KU Leuven, is strongly influenced by Ricoeur's thought. Ricoeur taught at KU Leuven in the late 1960s and has influenced generations of noted scholars and their equally well-known doctoral students, including the ECSI's project leader in KU Leuven, Professor Didier Pollefeyt. Ricoeur, Gadamer, the Frankfurt school and Habermas have all significantly influenced the framing of the ECSI project.

2. THE HERMENEUTICAL CIRCLE

From a hermeneutical perspective all *learning is circular in character*. We can understand what this means with reference to how we engage with a poem.

2.1 Interpreting 'La Belle Dame Sans Merci'

John Keats wrote his famous poem 'La Belle Dame Sans Merci' in 1819. The immediate questions facing a reader is:

- *What is Keats trying to communicate in the poem?*

The question that philosophic hermeneutics poses is:

- *Can we infer from how we make sense of this text something about the nature of human understanding itself?*

La Belle Dame Sans Merci is set out in the box below. The first three stanzas are told by a narrator, the balance is told in the words of the main character.

O what can ail thee, knight-at-arms,
Alone and palely loitering?
The sedge has withered from the lake,
And no birds sing.

O what can ail thee, knight-at-arms,
So haggard and so woe-begone?
The squirrel's granary is full,
And the harvest's done.

I see a lily on thy brow,
With anguish moist and fever-dew,
And on thy cheeks a fading rose
Fast withereth too.

I met a lady in the meads,
Full beautiful, a faery's child;
Her hair was long, her foot was light,
And her eyes were wild.

I made a garland for her head,
And bracelets too, and fragrant zone;
She looked at me as she did love,
And made sweet moan.

I set her on my pacing steed,
And nothing else saw all day long,
For sidelong would she bend, and sing
A faery's song.

She found me roots of relish sweet,
And honey wild, and manna-dew,
And sure in language strange she said—
'I love thee true'.

She took me to her elfin grot,
And there she wept and sighed full sore,
And there I shut her wild wild eyes
With kisses four.

And there she lullèd me asleep,
And there I dreamed—Ah! woe betide!—
The latest dream I ever dreamt
On the cold hill side.

I saw pale kings and princes too,
Pale warriors, death-pale were they all;
They cried—'La Belle Dame sans Merci
Hath thee in thrall!'

I saw their starved lips in the gloam,
With horrid warning gapèd wide,
And I awoke and found me here,
On the cold hill's side.

And this is why I sojourn here,
Alone and palely loitering,
Though the sedge is withered from the lake,
And no birds sing.

The poem unfolds as a series of twelve word-pictures.[2] The twelve stanzas tell the story of a knight who, late one autumn, meets and falls in love with a mysterious girl whose attraction he experiences as wonderful, but ultimately deceptive. The experience of love does not end well for the knight who finishes where he began, 'alone and palely loitering' and amidst desolation.

Since the poem was written, literary critics have argued as to the poem's meaning and what it is that Keats is trying to communicate. The poem illustrates the role the hermeneutical circle plays in human understanding. To make sense of the poem, it is first necessary to read it through *as a whole*. It is then possible to see the significance of the individual word pictures represented by each stanza in building up this whole. *However, the meaning of the whole is more than just the sum of its parts.* This exercise reinforces the notion of *'holism'* being important in understanding all forms of human endeavour.

Human endeavour is the work of *subjects*. As subjects, we have reasons and motives for what we do. Human action is purposeful, and thus can be interpreted. This is not the case with objects. Objects are bound by universal laws and are not subject to interpretation. There is therefore a fundamental difference between the way in which information is collected and processed in the physical sciences and the way it is collected and processed in humanities and the human sciences.[3] Knowledge in the humanities and human sciences has to take note of holism. It is problematic to think that it is possible to break down a whole – such as a group's culture – into its constituent parts and think that this tells you all that there is to know about the culture. To make this mistake is comparable to thinking that a cake can be reduced to the sum of its ingredients. The latter are necessary to make the cake, but do not account fully for the final product!

The hermeneutical circle addresses the issue of holism and is represented schematically in the diagram below. The arrows indicate a continuing interchange between the whole and its parts as understanding develops.

---

2 Keats uses meter to isolate these word pictures. The first three lines in each stanza follow the same meter while the fourth line is truncated e.g. 'and no birds sing'.
3 A common problem in early anthropology was to think that, using the methodology of the physical sciences, it was possible to arrive at an *objective understanding* of another people's way of life. While anthropologists could make accurate observations of how another people lived, not knowing the local languages, and so being unable to access the input of insiders, they lacked an understanding of why things were the way they were, and so interpreted their results with reference to *meanings current in their own culture*, not to those current in the culture they were reporting on.

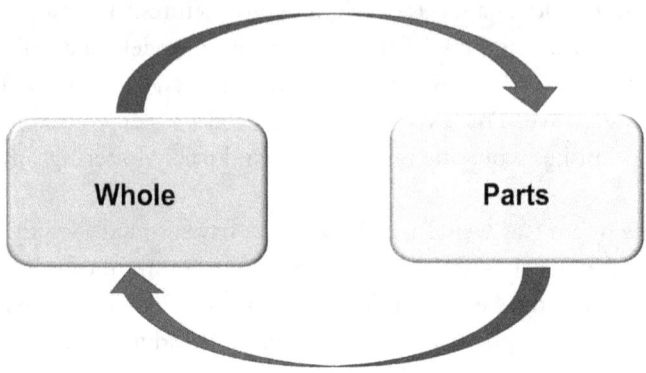

FIGURE 19.1: THE DYNAMIC RELATIONSHIP BETWEEN WHOLE AND PARTS

In 'La Belle Dame sans Merci', individual stanzas throw light on the meaning of the whole poem and, in turn, knowledge of the whole highlights the contribution of individual stanzas. This ongoing interaction between the whole and the part in creating meaning is what philosophers call 'the hermeneutical circle'.

We understand the whole in terms of the parts and vice-versa. However, in understanding any human endeavour *the whole is more than just the sum of the parts*. This is true of art, poetry, cuisine, architecture, and so on.

2.2 Levels of understanding

A *literal reading* of the poem takes it as a ballad telling the story of a knight, a beautiful lady, and the dangers of making poor choices. However, is this what Keats had in mind in writing the poem? To move beyond naive reading, it is necessary to know something about the context in which the poem was written.

Keats wrote it shortly after his brother, whom he had nursed through tuberculosis, had died. He was aware that he also had contracted the (in those days) incurable disease and had but a short time to live.[4] In 1819, he was in love with his neighbour, Fanny Brawne, and had to face the futility of love and its allure in his unhappy circumstances.

A *contextual reading of* 'La Belle Dame sans Merci' suggests that it can also be *interpreted symbolically*. In this understanding Keats, like the knight, is 'alone and palely loitering' and railing against both the fate that he now knows is his, and the futility of love.

---

[4] Keats was only 25 when he died.

When we add the context of the writer to our knowledge of 'the whole and the parts', it takes on a new meaning and we understand the poem in a new light. The hermeneutical circle does not close in on itself, but becomes more like a *spiral* as understanding grows.

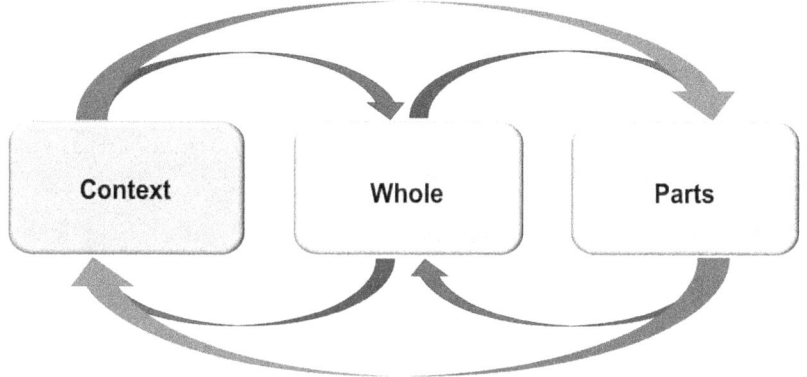

FIGURE 19.2: HERMENEUTICAL CIRCLE EXPANDS

2.3 Naive and post-critical understandings

Paul Ricoeur describes growth in understanding as a movement from a 'naive' understanding through a process of critique to a *'post-critical'* understanding.[5]

In the classroom students trust the pedagogical presentation of material by their teachers. Why would they do anything else? They are at school to learn and teachers are there to teach! Over time, teachers endeavour to develop the critical abilities of their students. In the case above, critique involves understanding the role that context plays in making sense of a poem. They do this by teaching them *to put questions to the material being presented to them.*

As this begins to happen, there is a gradual movement from what Ricoeur calls a 'hermeneutics of trust' to a 'hermeneutics of suspicion'. Across their education students must learn *to hold trust and suspicion in balance*. Without trust, there is no basis for learning, as all knowledge would have to be created from scratch, but without suspicion young people can easily become trapped in naive or fundamentalist understandings.

The pattern being outlined here has been generalised in the diagram below that represents the hermeneutical spiral. We usually start with a naive understanding of the unfamiliar to which we put questions (Critique 1).

---

5   The phrase is believed to have been first used by philosopher Michael Polanyi *In Personal Knowledge: Towards a Post-Critical Philosophy,* first published by the University of Chicago Press in 1958.

This leads to a 'new understanding' of 'the whole' which in turn leads us to put new questions to the parts (Critique 2) and so on. The movement from a literal understanding to a symbolic understanding of 'La Belle Dame Sans Merci' is an example of this process at work.

Understanding always remains open to new questions put either to the whole or to the parts. The aim of questioning is to arrive at *the best understanding* of the unfamiliar, rather than to a 'god-like', objective understanding of it. Since questions can arise from a culture different from that of the author, the meaning of the poem (or other work of art) can take on a life of its own.

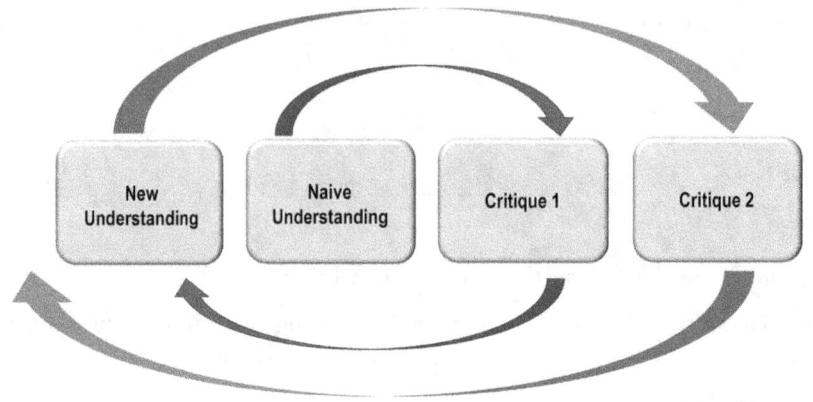

FIGURE 19.3: HERMENEUTICAL SPIRAL

Knowing something about the context of the author in interpreting 'La Belle Dame sans Merci' enables us to move beyond a literal understanding of the poem. We can ask questions such as: Does the poem reflect, or is it meant to indicate, how Keats felt at the time he wrote it? Is the knight 'alone and palely loitering' in the wintery countryside a symbol of Keats? Answering such questions leads to a new insight – the poem is better understood symbolically. The word pictures presented in each stanza contribute, each in its own way, to conveying *what the author feels*.

Keats seeks to convey how he feels through the medium of images and hopes that these *evoke a resonance in the experiences of the reader*. A connection can thus be made across time between the author and the reader, based on a shared appreciation of what is means to be human.

The 'whole' is no longer confined to the meaning the poem has for the author, but now includes the reader's own experiences as well. Great art and literature work evocatively in this way.

3. WAYS OF KNOWING

It is an axiom of pedagogy that teachers work 'from the known to the unknown'. But what about the case where the ideas being presented to the students are totally new to them and where there is apparently no 'known' to appeal to? *In the hermeneutical perspective, this situation never arises!*

When it comes to understanding something unfamiliar, a student *always begins from 'somewhere'*, whether he or she recognises this to be the case or not. This 'somewhere' is known technically as the *fore-structure of knowing*.[6] This 'fore-structure' still operates even when 'prior knowledge' is lacking. To explain how this works, it is helpful to briefly examine the work of US anthropologist, Edward T. Hall, who identifies three major ways in which people acquire their culture: through technical learning, formal learning, and informal learning.[7]

3.1 Technical learning

Education's stock-in-trade is *technical learning*. Here a topic is broken down into its constituent parts, the relationships between the parts are analysed, and then both are presented to students in a coherent manner. Learning then occurs as *the result of conscious effort*.[8]

For instance, a technical approach to teaching a new language breaks it down into its three major components: vocabulary, grammar, and syntax. In working with students, a language teacher does not begin from *tabula rasa* (no prior knowledge) because the students already have referents and can draw on what they have learned in their English classes. This enables them to move from learning 'vocab' in the new language – *cat, mat, slowly, on, sat, big,* and *blue* – to constructing simple sentences. *The cat sat on the mat. The big cat sat on the mat. The big cat sat on the blue mat slowly.* In the course of this progression, students are calling (implicitly) on their knowledge of English to create simple sentences in the new language.

This works as long as the word order in the new language is the same as that found in English. The students' initial assumption is that it will be. After all, why would they think otherwise! However, when this is not the case,

---

[6] See Gallagher's discussion of the contribution of Heidegger in shifting the 'centrepoint of the hermeneutical circle from the objective concerns about whole and parts to the transcendental conditions of interpretation', 61.
[7] Edward T. Hall, *The Silent Language*. New York: Anchor Books, 1973. Hall's classic work has proved seminal in its influence.
[8] Technical learning is commonplace in subjects like mathematics and science. It is becoming increasingly commonplace in sports as sports scientists break down performance into its constituent parts and isolate their biometric characteristics, and power determinants. They are then able to design nutritional regimes and training routines to ensure that an athlete can perform at peak power when required.

the teacher will correct the wrong assumption and indicate the new way of ordering words.⁹ In doing so, she or he is employing a second mode of learning. Hall names this *formal learning*.

3.2 Formal learning

Formal learning is *culturally determined*. In formal learning, there is a 'right' (or 'correct') way of doing things and a 'wrong' way. The matter is not generally open for discussion because there is no in-between position. The pattern in formal learning is: *Try, make a mistake, be corrected by someone who knows, and learn from your mistake*.

Culture provides the criteria for judging what is 'right/correct'. Much of early childhood learning involves formal learning. A particular group exercises a preference for doing things one way rather than another. While 'once upon a time' there may have been a reason for making a particular choice, this has generally been long forgotten. Consider, for instance, why it is that we choose to sit on chairs and not on the floor, as people do in many cultures. Again, why do we put flowers on a grave? These are choices that have been made at some point in time and we do not think to question them. They are taken as 'givens' in our culture.

If children ask 'Why?' when they are corrected for offending against the unstated formal norms of their culture, it is generally a mistake to provide a reasoned answer. While saying: 'Because it's the culture, dear', or possibly 'because that is the way we do things' may not seem at all adequate, it could well be correct!

Formal learning is a common mode of learning when people join a new organisation. Newcomers soon learn that there is 'a right way' and 'a wrong way' to do things based on the reactions of their new colleagues. They are often forced to use trial and error to work out the unstated assumptions and rules that guide group life. These are taken for granted by insiders who are often unaware of what they are, until they see them being transgressed.

Social media relies on formal learning to promote ideas about what is currently 'politically correct'. Rational discussion about 'political correctness' usually leads nowhere since the protagonists on both sides of a debate usually operate from different conceptions of what their culture holds as 'correct'. This happens most obviously when a culture is undergoing major change.

Formal learning, unlike technical learning, goes on *largely out of our awareness* and is usually highly specific. It is a form of learning that happens

---

9   In English we generally follow the word order subject-verb-object (SVO) in constructing sentences. This pattern is by no means universal. In Korean, Turkish and Tamil the order is SOV while in Arabic it is VSO. Italian and Spanish employ the SVO structure but, unlike English, adjectives do not always go before the noun they qualify.

cumulatively, incident-by-incident, case-by-case, since it deals with the right way and wrong way of doing *specific things*.

3.3 Informal learning

Informal learning happens when someone is invited to imitate a model, or *'to look around you and see how things work here'*. The content of informal learning is more general than is the case with formal learning. Not only does the learner learn how to act but, as well, they learn something *about the person* being imitated and the social context in which things happen. Both these factors qualify what is learnt in important ways.

When newcomers learn by observation, it is initially hard to know what to attend to. There is a broad range of things *that could be attended to* and previous experience helps them discern what are the most important things to focus on.[10]

While technical learning operates at a conscious level, what we learn formally and informally *generally happens out-of-awareness* and 'on the run' in the process of daily living. Formal and informal learning, as defined by Hall, are forms of *cultural learning* that, with some training, we can bring to awareness and utilise as resources in making sense of things. Both forms of learning depend on the existence of *cultural traditions*. Since they both happen outside of awareness, we are unaware of what we do not know. From time to time a teacher has to stop and ask: 'Why am I doing what I am doing?' to become more aware of what they have learned both formally and informally in teaching students.

When teachers speak about moving from 'the known' to the 'unknown', they are generally referring to technical learning. Technical learning often proceeds in a manner that is oblivious of what students learn formally and informally. However, despite the fact that these forms of learning happen largely outside of a student's awareness, they play a role when it comes to understanding the unfamiliar.

For instance, if students have learned informally from their peers that poetry is 'a waste of time', then they will approach 'La Belle Dame sans Merci' with a (negative) prejudice that inhibits learning because it stops them putting questions to the poem, or to the teacher about their presentation of the poem. On the other hand, if the student has informally come to 'love' poetry (i.e. he or she brings a positive prejudice) then the student can appreciate the skill Keats shows in changing the meter to isolate the stanzas

---

10 Many organisations use a 'buddy' system to help new people master the intricacies of formal and informal learning. A good mentor helps the newcomer focus their attention wisely, acquire *technical information* about how the local system *is supposed to work*, learn the 'right' way of doing things. It provides them with a role model to imitate, and is available to answer their questions.

from one another in creating a succession of word pictures that contribute to the overall impact of the poem.

The prejudices students bring to reading a poem can be positive or negative; they can open up questioning or close it down. They can allow students to grow in understanding or the opposite.

In this chapter we have explored some important aspects of the hermeneutical tradition which shape approaches to pedagogy. The idea of a 'hermeneutical circle', which becomes a 'hermeneutical spiral', is a construct which has proven helpful to many in seeking understanding. It is widely used in Church circles by those committed to social justice, and features in such methods of theological reflection as the enhanced *See Judge Act* model.[11]

---

11 For an example, see Jim & Therese D'Orsa, *Mission in Practice*. Mulgrave: Garratt Publishing, 2019, 51–55.

20

TRADITIONS AND CULTURE FROM A HERMENEUTICAL PERSPECTIVE

A great deal of what we know is held outside of conscious awareness. When we try to make sense of a poem, a new language, a paradigm in science, or a perspective on religion, we come to the task not only with a wealth of things we have already learned, but also with a range of biases or presuppositions that are held outside of our direct perception. As we have seen, context, history, culture, and community each play an important role in determining what, in hermeneutics, is called the *fore-structure of knowing* — that is the beliefs, values and sensibility we hold out of awareness (worldview in our previous discussion), but bring into play when confronted with the need to make sense of the unfamiliar. Fore-structure of knowing, or worldview, is important as we explore the subject of this chapter — the role traditions (with their deep connections to community, context, and culture) play in the meaning-making process.

1. TRADITIONS, UNDERSTANDING AND IDENTITY

1.1 Traditions – patterns of group life

When a group comes into existence and its members work together to do something significant, group life soon becomes patterned. Members are able to distinguish 'us' from 'not us'. They develop a sense of belonging that enables them to identify with one another. Patterns of thinking, feeling, valuing, learning and behaving develop that characterise members and come to distinguish them from non-members. For some groups, such boundaries are tightly drawn, while for others they are loosely drawn.

Over time, the reasons for adopting some patterns at the expense of others fade from collective memory and these cultural patterns, originally chosen consciously, morph into *traditions*, that is, into *the accepted way of thinking, valuing, feeling, and behaving*.[1]

---

1   A common understanding of culture is 'how things are done around here'. This definition provides a one-dimensional understanding of a much more complex reality. The notion of culture as a group's more or less comprehensive, more or less successful, design for living peacefully together in their

1.2 Narrative – carrier of traditions

Traditions are then *built into the narrative of the group* and so grow in significance. They are passed from one generation to the next in narrative form so that young people, or new members, soon learn that there is an accepted way of thinking, feeling, valuing and behaving if you want to belong to this group. The process by which this happens relies heavily on formal and informal learning, as traditions become a taken-for-granted aspect of the group's culture.

From time to time individuals and sub-groups within a culture question certain traditions. Generally, members do not welcome such questioning since it threatens the sense of belonging that goes with membership of the group. However, in some circumstances questioning leads people to explore why traditions take the form that they do.

Bringing traditions to consciousness in this way can lead to change, since traditions are human constructs that represent a preference chosen from among available options. As historical circumstances change, new options open up, and so new choices can be made. This means that, rather than being fixed in time, traditions can take on a life of their own and evolve over time, despite any internal opposition to change.[2] Thus, people talk about being part of a 'living tradition'.

An individual acquires his or her understanding of a group's traditions through formal and informal learning, but also through the technical learning that characterises schooling. Schools play a key role in helping students to both critique and appreciate the biases contained in what they learn formally, informally, and technically. Bias can be constructive or destructive, and discerning which is which is central to an effective pedagogy.

1.3 Culture as defining a 'hermeneutical space'

Our attempts to make sense of the unfamiliar are constrained by the 'imaginal horizon' that our culture imposes on us. People raised in a particular culture understand that life offers them a certain range of meaningful options. Options that lie outside this range cannot be imagined, even if they exist. Gadamer refers to this phenomenon as thinking within an 'horizon of

---

particular environment' (Luzbetak) is a more useful understanding of 'culture', as we have discussed in Chapter 7.

2 The Catholic Church distinguishes between *The Tradition* handed down by the apostles and early disciples and recorded in Scripture, and *traditions* that have emerged over time as preferred ways of thinking, valuing, feeling and doing things. The former is seen as unchangeable, and the latter capable of development. A major difficulty arises in knowing where the boundary lies between the two forms. Many traditions exist in regard to the way The Tradition is understood, explained, and celebrated. Because of the role traditions play in shaping how people understand their identity, such boundary issues are hotly contested and can limit the Church's capacity to change as historical circumstances change and new mission priorities arise.

meaning'. When an author writes, he does so within a particular horizon; when the reader reads what has been written, then she does so within her own horizon. Interpreting the text, involves a *fusion of horizons* in that the horizon of the reader is expanded by contact with the horizon present in the text.[3]

Belgian religious educator, Didier Pollefeyt, develops a similar idea. For him human understanding occurs within a 'hermeneutical space' bounded by culture. This 'space' defines the imaginal limit within which meaning can be made – a limit beyond which we cannot see possibilities. Culture imposes this horizon on our understanding, and it operates largely out of our awareness.[4]

When we try to make sense of the unfamiliar, we rarely encounter it as something entirely new. As people brought up in a culture, we have a sense of the whole that is our culture through the experience of living in it, even though we might have difficulty in articulating what the 'whole' is. This is so because our culture has become part of who we are; it provides important markers for how we understand 'who I am' and 'what is right for me'. For better or worse, we are trapped within a cultural horizon determined by the language we use and the traditions that define our identity. Language and traditions help define the imaginal horizon within which we construe what is possible. Traditions are embedded in our use of language.

Because we think within a cultural horizon, or 'cultural hermeneutical space', we always have some expectation of what the unfamiliar might mean. We therefore have something to which we can put questions. These expectations form part of what we have previously called our 'fore-structure of knowing' – the implicit framework we bring to making sense of the unfamiliar.

The 'fore-structure of knowing' is not a theoretical construct. It is real, as the following 'real-life' example illustrates:

> *As we (the authors) were driving to a seminar some decades back, we listened to a radio interview with a mother, recently arrived from South Africa. The interviewer was exploring her reasons for migrating to Australia. She recounted how she and her husband, both of whom had good jobs in South Africa, had debated for quite some time about whether or not to migrate. The catalyst for their decision was an incident involving their three-year-old daughter whom we will call Alice.*

---

3 Gadamer, 374–75.
4 Didier Pollefeyt, *The Lustre of Life: Hermeneutic-communicative concept of religious education* https://www.bne.catholic.edu.au

Alice had damaged her doll and when she was asked what happened she retorted unthinkingly, 'a Kaffir did it!' The wife explained to the interviewer that the family lived in a gated community within a white enclave and that her daughter rarely encountered black Africans. Despite this, at three years old, Alice had already absorbed a cultural bias just by being part of a particular cultural world. Her sense of 'the whole' included blaming black Africans when things went wrong!

The parents were so horrified by her remark that they decided it was time to leave. Blaming black people when things go wrong had become part of their daughter's 'fore-structure of knowing'. This happened because of her immersion in the culture, and not as something she had consciously learned or ever been taught at home.

Our purpose here is to point out culture's role in shaping the *fore-structure of knowing* that we bring to understanding the unfamiliar.

2. TRADITION AND TRADITION(S) IN THE LIFE OF THE CHURCH

The above discussion is a sociological/cultural anthropological approach to tradition providing insight into traditions of meaning as they evolve within any society or community. There are also other important understandings with regard to tradition that Catholic educators require when their educational role directly involves what is known as the tradition of the Church. This is obviously the case in Religious Education, but we would argue that, because of the nature of the worldview of the faith we espouse, one which embraces the sacramentality of all of creation, it also applies to all areas of learning.

In his encyclopaedic work, *Catholicism*, McBrien takes the reader through important points of distinction vis-à-vis tradition in post-Vatican II Catholicism. He refers to the 'wider' theological meaning of tradition as the whole *process* of 'handing on' to each generation the faith of the Church by a variety of means (shared life, liturgy, preaching, teaching, etc.). He also refers to a 'narrower' meaning viz the *content* of the post-Apostolic teaching that is handed on, which was the dominant understanding pre-Vatican II.

In its *Dogmatic Constitution on Divine Revelation*, the Second Vatican Council embraced the *wider meaning*, one which includes both content and process, and this is now normative for Catholics. 'The Church, in her teaching, life and worship, perpetuates and hands on to all generations all that she herself is, all that she believes'.[5] McBrien goes on to distinguish

---
5   *Dogmatic Constitution on Divine Revelation (Dei Verbum)*, 8.

between 'Tradition' (upper case) as the living and lived faith of the Church, and 'traditions' (lower case), as customary ways of doing or expressing matters of faith. As he explains it, if a tradition cannot be lost or changed without essential distortion of the Gospel, it is part of Tradition. If it is not essential (and he gives various illustrations of this such as compulsory clerical celibacy), it can be changed or even eliminated.[6]

More than two decades later, Lieven Boeve provided the following theological definition of what McBrien is referring to as Tradition (upper case):

The term tradition refers to the subject, the process, and the content of the transmission of faith through which the identity, the continuity, and the productive unfolding of the message of revelation in the community of faith is made possible.

He goes on to clarify that:

... not only is tradition the precondition which makes the identity, continuity, and unfolding of the message of revelation in the faith community possible, but that it also constitutes the precondition for making the faith community itself possible in as far as it makes faith possible. There is no Christian faith or Christian community outside the framework of the Christian tradition.[7]

In a new work, Gerald O'Collins discusses *Jesus as the Tradition Who is handed down within the community*. This is a powerful emphasis and takes the Christian educator deep into the heart of mission. It evokes the challenge to growth in vision, understanding and sensibility.[8] Given our goal as Catholic educators of enabling students to grow in capacity to carry on the mission of Jesus in all its richness in today's context, there are clearly few foundational understandings more important than that of tradition.

---

6   Richard McBrien, *Catholicism*. San Francisco: Harper and Row, 1981.
7   Lieven Boeve, *Interrupting Tradition: An Essay on Christian Faith in a Postmodern Context*. Louvain: Peeters Press, 2003, 20. Emphasis added. Boeve's motif of 'interruption' is taken from Johann Baptist Metz's political theology, which draws it from German philosopher and critic, Walter Benjamin's, 'Theses on History' and the emphasis on 'apocalyptic' memory of suffering.
    Elsewhere Boeve has discussed the dialogical and dynamic relationship between revelation, scripture and tradition as the reception of *Dei Verbum*, as normative in the life of the Church, proceeds. Lieven Boeve, 'Revelation, Scripture and Tradition: Lessons from Vatican II's Constitution *Dei Verbum* for Contemporary Theology'. *International Journal of Systematic Theology*. Vol 13, No 4, October 2011, 416–433.
8   Gerald O'Collins, *Tradition: Understanding Christian Tradition*. Oxford University Press, 2018. This treatment gives a clear, thorough, and reliable approach for those looking for a sound and readable introduction to this vital topic.

3. MECHANICS OF UNDERSTANDING

The biases and pre-conceptions (good and bad) that we pick up from our context, culture, and community, are shaped by traditions that exist within the culture. We acquire these in the form they take in the communities in which we live, beginning with our families. Teachers often see family traditions at work in the biased attitude some students bring to subjects like Religious Education, History and English. Our relationship to traditions plays a pivotal role not only in what we understand, but also in *whether or not we choose to understand*.

In Western cultures, traditions of learning are held mainly as *academic traditions* and the priority accorded them is often determined by their apparent utility. In schools this particular bias appears in the frequently asked question: 'How will learning this help me get a job?' The presumption here is that the purpose of school learning is 'to get a job'. Such an answer may make some sense in many settings, but it makes little sense, for example, to Aboriginal children living in remote communities where there is simply no work to be found nor, one assumes, for those students who come from families who have experienced long-term inter-generational unemployment, for whatever reason.[9]

In some communities, however, the preferences that sit behind traditions are decided, not by their apparent utility, but by their potential in promoting the community's ideal of 'human flourishing'. 'Human flourishing' and 'utility' seem to define the poles between which the choices underpinning most educational traditions sit.

3.1 Personal worldview

Our grasp of language and traditions provides us with a culturally determined *frame of reference* when it comes to understanding the unfamiliar. As we have seen earlier (Chapter 6), this is known in anthropology as our *personal worldview*.

Our worldview acts as a filter in processing new information by determining what we actually attend to. In the main this worldview is shaped by traditions that we have unconsciously absorbed and that tell us how we should think, feel, and value. They also tell us how we should react

---

[9] This matter 'hit home' to Jim D'Orsa when he was asked to review the operation of a Catholic boarding school for Aboriginal students drawn from remote communities. This was the first time he had faced the 'What for?' question about schooling in a context where there was no immediate or obvious answer. If the students had no prospect of getting a job when they left school, what was the purpose of the school in educating them? How was this purpose articulated? And how did it shape the curriculum and pedagogy of the school? To his surprise the school's leaders, who were relatively new to Aboriginal education, had not thought these questions through. They were running the school as if it were located in a major town where jobs were plentiful.

to the unfamiliar. The traditions central to our personal worldview reflect preferences that our group has chosen in the past.

3.2 A simplified model of understanding

The figure below outlines a simplified model of how understanding functions: as a person grows up, their worldview is shaped by traditions and language in a process that goes on largely outside of awareness.

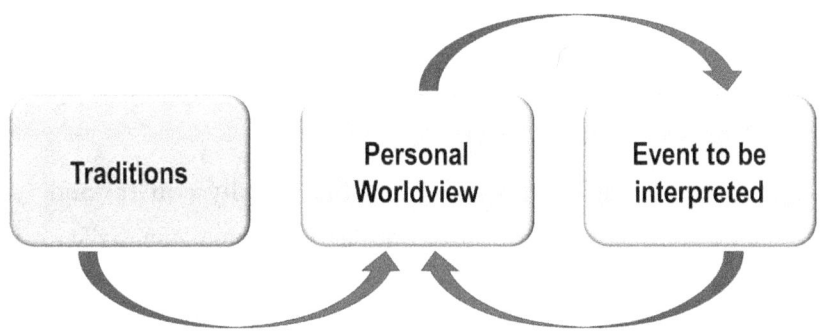

FIGURE 20.1: A SIMPLIFIED MODEL OF UNDERSTANDING

Our personal worldview provides us with important elements that we each bring to the task of understanding the unfamiliar ('event' in the diagram). Our personal worldview has two major components: *prior knowledge* held consciously in memory, and our *fore-structure of knowing* made up largely of things we have learned formally and informally about how to respond to the demands of living in a particular context, community and culture.

We stress that our fore-structure of knowing operates out-of-awareness and is not coincidental with *prior knowledge* of which we are aware. The fore-structure of knowing operates even when we have no prior knowledge of the unfamiliar. That is, a person's worldview embraces things held consciously (prior knowledge) and things held outside of awareness.

To engage with the unfamiliar ('event' in the diagram) we put questions to it based on *what we know* and the traditions that shape what we know. Thus, a hermeneutical circle is created between our personal worldview (which acts as 'a whole') and the new event (which acts as a 'part'). The new event puts questions to the whole, and the whole puts questions to the new event, and in this process there is a *fusion of horizons*[10] and understanding

---

10 E.g. Gadamer, *Truth and Method*, 306–307.

expands. Our expanded understanding *may be correct or incorrect* depending on the way in which the biases implicit in traditions shape the questions we put to the unfamiliar.

In most pedagogical decision-making, emphasis is placed on assessing prior knowledge, but not on what students bring subconsciously to the task, variously called fore-structure of knowing, pre-understandings, biases or prejudices. However, a short reflection on what happens in the classroom reveals that prior knowledge, on its own, rarely explains students' reactions to new material. Most teachers have prepared lessons with careful attention to prior knowledge only to encounter an insipid response from students. Other factors are clearly at work. The hermeneutical model outlined above suggests what these might be.

3.3 All meaning is linguistically and historically constrained

Meaning is carried by language. Traditions have meaning only to the extent that they can be put into words. They are limited by language, and the limitations that language imposes on meaning impacts on how we interpret the unfamiliar in two important ways.

First, the *background* people bring to reading a text determines its meaning for them. An illustration drawn from Biblical interpretation, courtesy of discussion provided by Rabbi Jonathan Sacks, may make this clearer. As Sacks explains, when God appears to Moses in the burning bush, Moses asks God what God's name is and the reply as it has found its way (via Latin and Greek) into most Catholic Bibles is 'I am who am'. This rendition of the text fits nicely with Aristotelian metaphysics (and with Catholic theologies envisaging God as a timeless, immutable, incorporeal, unchangeable Being). In common Catholic interpretation of the passage, the God of the Bible has become the God of metaphysics. But, as Rabbi Sacks points out, the text can equally and should be translated from the original Hebrew as 'I will be what, where, or how I will be'. God reveals Godself to Moses as the one who brought the people out of Egypt, as the one who is engaged in their history.[11] He notes the inclusion of the future tense which is entirely absent from all the early Christian translations. In the Jewish worldview, God is not only 'the Lord of history' but also the God who interrupts history.[12] God is most decidedly not 'the God of philosophy'. The Jewish and Catholic traditions have developed along different tracks due in no small part to *the constraints imposed by language in understanding sacred texts.*

---

11 Jonathan Sacks, *The Great Partnership: Science, Religion and the Search for Meaning*. London: Hodder and Stoughton, 2011, 64–65.
12 A phrase associated with the work of Lieven Boeve in *God Interrupts History*. London: Bloomsbury, 2007.

Second, the meaning of words is not constant, and many changes occur over time indicating that all understanding and meaning is historically constrained. Later constructions get imported back into the earlier interpretations, sometimes compromising the original meaning, sometimes expanding it, and sometimes changing it altogether. One has only to surf the net to find lists of words whose meanings have changed, sometimes substantially over time. Words such as 'gay' and 'queer', as used in contemporary parlance, are used in a very different way now from that of even the recent past.

Understanding is best thought of as a linguistic event in which the new is incorporated into a previously existing whole. This event is hedged around by traditions most of which are taken for granted. The event is dynamic in that the familiar and unfamiliar are brought into dialogue through the process of questioning. The art of the good teacher lies in helping students formulate their own questions.

3.4 As traditions change so does our relationship to them

The hermeneutical circle is not a vicious circle from which there is no escape. For most of us the familiar is unproblematic. However, when our attempts to use it in understanding the unfamiliar fail because we are unable to answer the questions we put to it, then we are forced to examine *the framework we are employing in making sense of the unfamiliar.*

Teachers can often help students here by challenging the common biases and presuppositions that they bring to class. They can challenge the 'common sense' way in which cultural traditions are often understood. In recognising that there are limits in what we bring to the task of understanding the unfamiliar, we become open to change, to new possibilities, to learning, and to expansion of the 'horizon' within which we normally think.

As we come to understand our faith tradition, for instance, we move from an uncritical acceptance of it, through a critical exploration, to a post-critical understanding. In a word, we *'befriend'* it, despite the limits obvious in those who share it, and an awareness of its own limits as well. To 'befriend' someone means to accept them *as themselves*, despite their limitations. 'Befriending' precludes the idea that friends need to be perfect![13]

The model we have been building up can be extended and is summarised schematically below:

---

13 James and Evelyn Whitehead, *Method in Ministry: Theological Reflection and Christian Ministry*, Revised Edition. Kansas City: Sheed & Ward, 1995, 9.

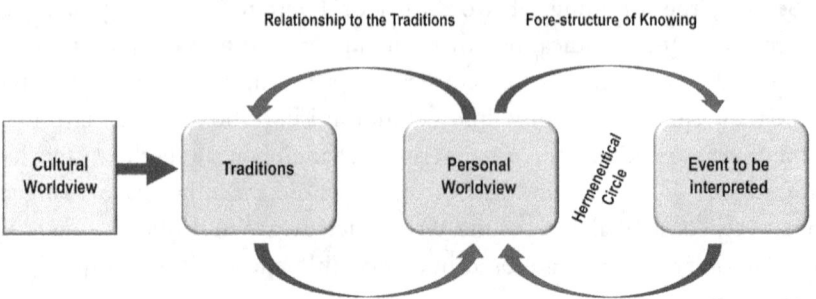

FIGURE 20.2: A MORE COMPLETE MODEL OF UNDERSTANDING

The fuller model can be explained as follows:

1. *The worldview of our culture enters the process of understanding through the operation of traditions alive in the culture. These are incorporated into a person's worldview through the processes of enculturation and education and reside there partly in-awareness (prior knowledge) and partly out-of-awareness (fore-structure of knowing).*
2. *When faced with the unfamiliar (the event to be interpreted) we experience an inner tension because the unfamiliar is different from what we understand to be the case, and so we question it.*

   Understanding grows as we find answers to these questions. In the example quoted above the question was: 'What is Keats trying to communicate in "La Belle Dame sans Merci"?'
3. *The answers to these internal questions do not generally come in a single flash of insight but are the result of successive interactions between the known and the unknown. As we move around the hermeneutical circle our understanding expands and the unfamiliar gradually takes on a new face. There is a 'fusion of horizons' between our understanding and that of the author.*

   However, when this does not happen, when we do not understand, we are forced to interrogate the traditions on which we depended and that now seem to be inadequate in helping us formulate questions. Instead of putting questions to the unfamiliar, we put them to the traditions that we rely on in making sense of the unfamiliar. Many Catholics have been forced to do this in trying to make sense of the sexual abuse crisis in the Catholic Church.
4. *The questioning of traditions changes our relationship to them by opening up a second hermeneutical circle, one that brings our personal worldview and the traditions on which we depend into dialogue.*

As a result, we may learn one of several lessons:

- *that our understanding of the tradition is mistaken or is too limited*
- *how our biases and preconceptions limit the questions we are prepared to ask*
- *that cultural changes have affected the traditions themselves and we need to reassess their value.*

In all three instances, we will find it necessary *to modify our personal worldview*. This then opens up new possibilities in understanding the unfamiliar by enabling us to put new questions to it.

In this chapter and the previous one we have explored the notion of 'understanding' from the perspective of moderate hermeneutics. The model outlined above seeks to explain how understanding works and suggests why some teaching strategies work better than others in promoting student (and teacher) understanding. For many teachers the model will put words around what they intuitively sensed was the case.

The treatment in this chapter differs from that of Lonergan in that it *contextualises* the process of understanding. This is of vital importance since events happen in a context, a culture and a community, and these are always shaped by traditions. This must be remembered if they are to be understood.

21

HERMENEUTICS AND THE EDUCATOR: LOCATING CRITICAL PEDAGOGY

In previous chapters we have explored the nature of human understanding from the perspective of 'moderate hermeneutics'. 'Moderate' generally indicates 'somewhere in the middle' which raises the questions: what is on either side? Are there other ways of 'understanding understanding' and, if so, what significance do they have for pedagogy?

Answering such questions necessarily engages us in key debates about the ethical purpose of teaching and the relationship between purpose and pedagogy. Put in simpler terms:

- *How do I construe my ethical purpose as a teacher and how does this impact on the choices I make in teaching and promoting student learning?*

This question was first raised in Chapter 11.

1. TEACHING AND ETHICAL PURPOSE

As we have noted in discussing the pedagogical relationship, every teacher has some implicit or explicit sense of 'doing the right thing' in working with students. In forming this sense, a teacher may draw on a number of sources: personal experiences of schooling; training as a teacher; traditions associated with the profession; empathy for young people and their culture; a desire to share what the teacher has come to know and love, and so on. For many teachers 'doing the right thing by students' equates to 'making a positive difference in their lives'.

The 'difference' that defines a teacher's ethical purpose is hardwired into his or her personal worldview. Since worldviews evolve over time, so too does a teacher's conception of the 'difference' he or she hopes to make. Ethical purpose is rarely a fixed quantity and so is capable of reformulation and even transformation. Because pedagogical choices reflect ethical purpose, *a teacher's approach to pedagogy can also evolve over time.* Whether or not an approach can be considered 'Catholic' will generally depend on the trajectory of this development and the values that guide it.

The *moderate hermeneutics* discussed in the previous chapter sits on a spectrum between *conservative hermeneutics* and *critical hermeneutics*.[1] All of these schools of thought shape the ethical purpose of education according to different values. Moderate hermeneutics shapes it in terms of *meaning-making*. Conservative hermeneutics interprets meaning-making in the restricted sense of *cultural reproduction*. Critical hermeneutics interprets meaning-making in terms of *the use and abuse of power*.

2. CONSERVATIVE HERMENEUTICS

A conservative approach to hermeneutics emphasises education's essential *reproductive purpose* of passing on the shared meanings that bind people in a society together. This is essential if a culture is to survive and thrive. From this perspective education is understood as having an important *cultural and civic role to play in a democracy*. Conservative hermeneutics assumes language is objective, ideology-free, and value-neutral. The creation of 'shared meanings' is equated to the acquisition of *cultural literacy* and *the discovery of 'truth'* (understood in an objective sense).[2]

Much schooling does involve passing on a cultural heritage and many teachers construe their ethical purpose in these terms. However, good pedagogy encourages students to think critically. A problem with conservative hermeneutics is its assumption that it is possible to arrive at an objective 'God-like' understanding of reality and that this can be expressed unambiguously in language. The problem with this is that all language is culture-dependent and therefore limited. This limitation crosses over into our understanding of truth.

Applied to a text, conservative hermeneutics holds that we can arrive at a full understanding of what the author had in mind when writing it and not be blindsided by his/her, or the reader's, use of language. Applied to lived experience, conservative hermeneutics holds that we can arrive at an objective understanding of the world around us, one free of the biases and constraints that culture and history impose on our use of language.

A conservative approach to human understanding is popular in politics, but also underpins many forms of fundamentalism, including religious fundamentalism. For almost two millennia, the thinking of Christian churches has been strongly influenced by a conservative understanding

---

1 Shaun Gallagher, *Hermeneutics and Education*, Albany: State University of New York Press, 205–275.
2 How truth is construed is a major issue in contemporary philosophy. Those who support an 'objective understanding' of truth hold that it is possible to understand things in a way that is *free of all human biases*.

of hermeneutics.[3] Sacred texts were often read from the perspective of 'naive literalism' – the meaning of the text being understood as if it were a contemporary work.

Conservative hermeneutics is also the *default position* behind the pedagogical thinking of teachers and curriculum designers who take the ethical purpose of teaching for granted. It is the hermeneutics that stands behind those Religious Education (RE) programs in Catholic schools where the Catholic tradition is treated uncritically.

Since the 1980s there has been a tension between the hermeneutics that stands behind most RE curricula (conservative) in Catholic schools and the hermeneutics that stands behind the pedagogy used by RE teachers in the classroom (moderate or critical).

3. CRITICAL HERMENEUTICS

At the other end of the hermeneutical spectrum we find *critical hermeneutics*. This has had a significant impact on pedagogy in Western democratic countries and on the way the Church has formulated its mission in many developing nations.

The critical approach to hermeneutics shares much in common with moderate hermeneutics in holding that language, as the carrier of meaning, is biased by traditions. It challenges the way in which power is used to form the traditions that shape the formal and informal learning that goes on in society, and that control what is deemed to be knowledge worth promoting in schools.

3.1 Three sources in critical pedagogy

Critical hermeneutics finds its place in Catholic education largely through the 'critical pedagogy' movement. This movement developed in the 1970s and has three interdependent sources:

- *critical theory*
- *the work of Brazilian educator, Paulo Freire*
- *liberation theology developed by the Catholic Church in Latin America as a response to the poverty and oppression of the poor*

These three movements have influenced one another in determining the scope and form of critical pedagogy. The diagram below indicates some of

---

[3] From early Christian times, however, the literal reading of scriptural texts has been balanced by allegoric and other readings. This practice dates back at least to Origen (c.184 – c.253 AD).

the key figures associated with the emergence of critical hermeneutics and critical pedagogy.

The ethical purpose of critical pedagogy is to liberate students from biases and traditions that are oppressive and which constrain their capacity to 'flourish' as human beings.[4]

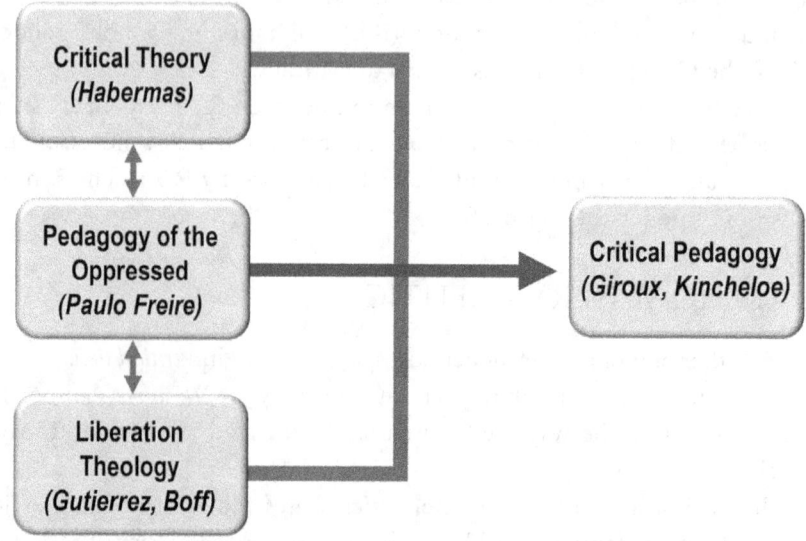

FIGURE 21.1: CRITICAL PEDAGOGY – MAJOR INFLUENCES

Critical educators do not reject traditions but suggest that *there is a major problem when people take traditions for granted*. Put another way, they suggest that much of what we learn formally and informally needs to be brought to consciousness and scrutinised critically. This is because of the tendency of traditions *to serve the interests of dominant groups in society, while at the same time marginalising others*. Traditions appropriated uncritically can easily work against building up a healthy church or society.

The aim of education from a critical perspective is to uncover the ways in which biases, and the traditions that support them, constrain and inhibit students' thinking, and therefore their capacity to understand the world in which they live. From the critical perspective education seeks to help students raise questions that lead to social changes. Critical educators have an 'emancipatory interest' in schooling that leads them to identify and critique traditions that oppress and marginalise others. They see this as a

---

4 The role of traditions in the construction of meaning is ambiguous. Traditions represent wisdom that develops out of past experiences. However, not all past experiences retain their value as contexts change. So the value of traditions has to be continuously discerned. If this does not happen then past criteria are used to judge present experiences with problematic consequences.

hopeful step towards effecting needed personal and social changes, creating new traditions and modifying older traditions.[5]

One example of this is that if, from a very early age, students find that God is always referred to as 'he', then they come to think of God as male. They do not do this consciously, but simply because this is the way language is used in their community. If the church to which they belong takes this linguistic usage for granted, then the language of their religious tradition introduces a bias that privileges males over females and this legitimises various forms of patriarchy. This bias also influences the way in which sacred texts, such as liturgical texts, are understood, so a bias against women becomes part of the religious tradition.[6] Female theologians, such as Sandra Schneiders, Elizabeth Johnson, Elaine Wainwright, and Susan Smith, who highlight the ways in which this bias plays out in Church life, are often labelled 'feminists'.[7]

A second example concerns many religious terms being dropped from common speech as our society becomes more aggressively secular. With this happening, after a time people lose, or no longer acquire, the language needed to articulate experiences that are religious or spiritual in nature, including prayer. This development may not be planned; it may just happen as a culture changes in a particular way. However it takes a good deal of critical reflection to identify what is happening and the values at stake, and to develop strategies to address the matter.

People of faith find the secularisation of language oppressive because the terms of public discourse are controlled in a way that seeks to exclude them from participation. The secularisation of common speech creates new and oppressive traditions![8]

---

[5] In an early book, *Knowledge and Human Interests* (1968), Habermas distinguishes three 'interests' that people have in constructing knowledge: an *instrumental interest* associated with controlling and manipulating one's environment; a *practical interest* which constructs knowledge through inter-subjective dialogue; and an *emancipatory interest* which is constructed through reflecting on experiences, the way in which these are interpreted, and how they shape a person's sense of self and his/her social obligations.

[6] Within the Catholic Church the unwillingness of Church leaders to use inclusive language in liturgical texts it not a linguistic issue; it is an ideological issue that proceeds from the bias noted above.

[7] See for instance, Elisabeth Schussler Fiorenza, *In Memory of Her: A Feminist Theological Reconstruction of Christian Origins*. London: SCM Press, 1983. See also Elizabeth Johnson, *She Who Is: The Mystery of God in Feminist Theological Discourse*. New York: Crossroads, 1994.
And Sandra Schneiders, 'Scripture: Tool of Patriarchy or Resource for Transformation' in *Beyond Patching: Faith and Feminism in the Catholic Church*. Revised edition. New York: Paulist Press, 2004.
And finally, Susan Smith, *Women in Ministry*. Maryknoll NY: Orbis, (2008). The fact that women theologians who point out this bias are labeled as 'feminist', which the labelers consider a disparaging term, is a further example of the bias.

[8] Catholic schools provide a valuable civic service in promoting a general religious literacy that is resistive to this trend.

Critical hermeneutics seeks to uncover the oppressive biases that operate in the cultural traditions that guide and form a society. Since these biases are usually held in place by dominant social groups pursuing an ideology, *critical hermeneutics has a political orientation*. Attempts to critique and reform traditions are seen as politically subversive.

4. CRITICAL THEORY AS A SOURCE OF CRITICAL PEDAGOGY

'Critical Theory' is a branch of modern European political theory whose most notable contemporary voice is Jurgen Habermas (1929-). The initial concern of critical theorists was the oppressive nature of 'European culture' and the need for a practical means to 'emancipate' oppressed social groups, such as low paid workers and immigrants, from its more pernicious traditions. This was seen as a major issue particularly in the post-colonial era (1970s and 1980s).

4.1 Narrow and broad conceptions of critical theory

The critical theory movement has subsequently broadened in scope to include the 'emancipation' of women and minority groups and, more recently, indigenous peoples. Taken up in the US, it has been concerned with the emancipation of Blacks and Hispanics from the worst impacts of a 'dominant power' that uses both education and its control of knowledge to maintain a position of white dominance.[9]

Critical educators are concerned to preserve democratic institutions in the face of all attempts by a 'dominant power' to subvert them. From the perspective of critical theory, broadly understood, education is caught up in the political struggle for emancipation from all that dehumanises people and so restricts the notion of 'human flourishing' to one where 'dominant power' approves.[10]

4.2 The 'socially critical school'

In Australia, writing in the context of secondary schooling, Stephen Kemmis, Peter Cole and Dahle Suggett translated the major themes of critical theory

---

9 As we have seen, in the modern period knowledge came to be defined as that which was determined by the methods of science. Knowledge and truth were associated with 'facts'; everything else was determined to be 'opinion'. In this understanding of knowledge, values and religion were excluded from being 'knowledge' and seen as only 'matters of opinion' about which everyone was entitled to form his or her own view. This form of scientism then invaded the school curriculum. The Romantic movement and the postmodern critics, particularly Lyotard and Foucault, challenged this way of colonising 'knowledge'.

10 Critical theory presents one face of the 'postmodernism' that began in the 1970s and continues unabated to the present.

into pedagogical terms in their influential book *Orientations to Curriculum and Transition: Towards a Socially-Critical School*.[11] They argued that 'the more we assert the necessity of schooling as a *preparation for life*, the more we assert that school life is not real life at all, but something which precedes real life and which must be different from it' (emphasis in the original). The result is that school life comes to be experienced by students as artificial.

The idea that schooling is 'a preparation for life' denies the concept that students' home, school and community experiences can be a starting point and the subject matter for education. It denies the concept that the articulation, interpretation and differentiation of these experiences should be the goal of schooling. The authors conclude that schools are part of society, not separate from it, that schooling is *a social process* and so it is important to consider the purpose of this process. Our argument supports the position of Starratt that ethical schooling involves an academic, social and civic curriculum.

The authors contrast three orientations that curriculum and pedagogy can take: *vocational/neo-classical, liberal/progressive* and the *socially-critical*. The table below provides profiles of these three approaches. Kemmis et al. suggest that 'current practice', and the forms of central office support offered to schools (at the time of their work), favour the vocational/neo-classical model. They also promote the concept that significant changes in the consciousness of teachers and their pedagogical choices are needed for pedagogy to move towards a liberal/progressive or a socially critical orientation.

In the table below, Kemmis et al. highlight the different ways in which teachers can legitimately construe their ethical purpose in teaching and how this is likely to be reflected in the pedagogical choices they make.

	Vocational/Neo Classical	Liberal/ Progressive	Socially Critical
School Concern	Preparation of Students for work	Preparation of students for life	Engagement of students in critical thinking and action
Dominant Curriculum Concern	Course or subject content/ structuring learning	Issues or processes/ facilitating student learning	Critical theory/group processes/ action orientation
Focus for Expression of Concern	Faculty and subject organisation	Total school/team teaching	Teaching team, students and community

---

11   Stephen Kemmis, Peter Cole, & Dahle Suggett, *Orientations to Curriculum and Transition: Towards the Socially Critical School*. Melbourne: Victorian Institute of Secondary Education, 1983.

Themes of Concern	Student discipline, teaching resources, curriculum packages, testing procedures Developing diligent obedient students	Student participation, group process, small group management, program review Developing caring co-operative environment	Student action, group processes and community linkages negotiated tasks Developing working knowledge and critical perspective on society

TABLE 21.1: CURRICULUM AND PEDAGOGY – THREE ORIENTATIONS[12]

5. PEDAGOGY OF THE OPPRESSED AS SOURCE IN CRITICAL PEDAGOGY

The thrust of a critical pedagogy is to *liberate young people from traditions and biases that are oppressive.*[13] Because so much of what young people appropriate from their culture happens through what Hall terms formal and informal learning (see Chapter 19), we often fail to recognise the oppressive nature of many of the 'givens' in our culture.

5.1 Paulo Freire

The 'father' of critical pedagogy is Brazilian educator, Paulo Freire, whose book, *Pedagogy of the Oppressed,* has been through multiple editions and translated into many languages.[14]

Freire quit his career as a lawyer in Brazil to work as an educator with peasant workers in remote villages. Many of his students were illiterate fishermen. He taught them how to read and write in order to help them gain some control over their lives. Freire's primary interest in working with marginalised people was 'emancipatory'. After listening to their descriptions of the hopeless conditions in which they and their families lived, he posed the question of 'Why?' He did this conscious of the fact that he was an 'outsider' putting questions to a reality that his students experienced and understood as 'insiders'. His aim was to help them understand their present reality in a new way, and within the wider construction of the world opened

---

12 Adapted from table in Kemmis, Cole, and Suggett, 20–21.
13 It needs to be noted that not all traditions are oppressive.
14 *Pedagogy of the Oppressed* was written in 1968 and was published in English in 1970 while Freire was living in exile. Copies had to be smuggled into Brazil where the book had been banned. Freire recounts how religious sisters smuggled copies into Brazil wrapped in the dust jackets of religious books they had acquired while studying elsewhere in Latin America. In 1992 Freire wrote *Pedagogy of Hope.* In this book he sets out his reflections on the experience of working with critical pedagogy in the twenty years since writing *Pedagogy of the Oppressed.* The book was not published in English until the year of his death in 1997.

up to them by being able to read, write and thus communicate in other than an oral manner.

For Freire, learning about the world in a literacy program had to coincide with his 'students' learning about the world that they experienced on a day-to-day basis. This learning also required putting their own questions (not his) to that world. This was not an exercise that they did as individuals, but in dialogue with other people living in and experiencing that same world. For him, literacy provided an avenue to greater freedom and to social transformation.

By asking: 'Why are things the way they are for you?', it became possible also to ask: 'Are there other ways of organising the world in which you live?' and, if so, 'How can we make such changes?' For Freire, learning involved a 'pedagogy of possibility' leading to social action. He saw that it was necessary to effect social change in order to 'humanise' the workers he dealt with (and their families).[15] He discovered that social changes that humanised workers eventually also humanised the people who oppressed them. The struggle for change operated at both levels.

Raising the awareness of the labouring classes and involving them in organised social change in the 1960s was not a task for the faint-hearted. In Brazil it also had political consequences. Freire was forced to flee the country and lived in exile with his family in Chile for a number of years. It was while in exile that he wrote *Pedagogy of the Oppressed*, a reflective account of his experiences as a critical educator.

Freire's approach to 'awareness-raising'[16] shared much in common with the approach taken by the early Catholic liberation theologians working with 'base Christian communities'. Freire readily acknowledges this.[17] And these two movements drew courage from each other.

One of the hard lessons Freire learned was that *he had to take the language spoken by his 'students' seriously*. He learned that rural workers spoke a 'common sense' form of language that was not the language of educators. If he wanted to engage in a meaningful dialogue with them about the

---

15 One research project Freire conducted explored the way in which parents punished their children. He found that rural workers used excessive corporal punishment, compared with fisherfolk, in order to keep their sons and daughters in line. Eventually he led his rural constituency to see that they were simply replicating in their own families the sort of oppression that they were experiencing at the hands of their 'bosses'!

16 Freire called his form of awareness-raising 'conscientisation'. It had a strong ethical as well as political orientation and gave moral purpose to his work that he always interpreted as a 'calling'.

17 Two Catholic priests, whose ministry was to Black and Puerto Rican communities living in New York, sponsored Freire's first visit to the United States. He was surprised at the similarities between the ways in which members of these communities saw the world and those of rural workers in Brazil and Chile. Both were overcome by the helplessness of their situation but in denial that this was the case.

conditions in which they and their families lived, then he had to understand their way of talking and talk *with* them rather than talk *at or to* them.

His approach to critical pedagogy changed over time. *Pedagogy of the Oppressed* records a praxis methodology as set out in the diagram below which has three steps: reflection, awareness-raising, and practice. The model is hermeneutical in that the 'student' begins with a certain construction of 'my reality' and, in dialogue with others, arrives at a new awareness of that reality, one that provides the impetus for social action. Social action then changes how 'my reality' is understood, and so a journey around the hermeneutical spiral continues.

Freire's starting point with rural workers was always their concrete reality and the generation of 'working knowledge' about that reality. This placed a value on what they understood to be the case – whether or not this was correct. Discussing this form of knowledge with peers was self-correcting and led his students to think beyond their immediate context. They then joined with others to effect change, first of all at the local level and later at regional, state, and national levels. These were the levels their 'bosses' invoked to justify keeping oppressive conditions in place.

Freire's initial model for critical reflection is set out in the diagram below.

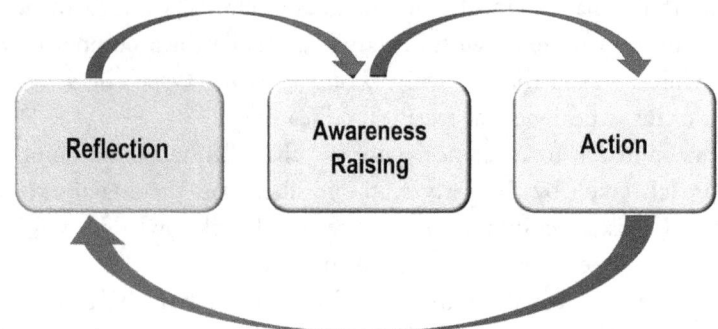

FIGURE 21.2: ONGOING PROCESS OF ACTION AND REFLECTION (FREIRE)

5.2 'Pedagogy of possibility'

In reflecting on his experiences of working with oppressed peoples in numerous contexts, Freire discovered that *awareness-raising alone does not lead to action*. Action can be displaced by a condition that he names *'hopefulness'*. This is often termed 'messianic hope' – the belief that 'somehow we will wake up tomorrow and all our problems will be solved'.[18]

---

18 See Paulo Freire, *Pedagogy of Hope: Reliving Pedagogy of the Oppressed*. New York: Continuum, 1997. In this book written towards the end of his life, Freire reflects on what he learned from working with marginalised people. He also writes on the development of his approach to education and social justice as portrayed in *Pedagogy of the Oppressed*.

He wrote that to be effective, awareness-raising has to co-opt the individual or collective imagination to arrive at what he called 'utopia' – a conception of what the world could look like. Co-opting the collective imagination in this way gives people something practical to place their hope in and work towards. In Freire's praxis model, change comes through a series of small, but decisive, steps that enable people living in a concrete situation to identify and name 'the difference' they wish to make to their present reality. They then have a moral purpose in acting to effect change and bring about social transformation because they can name the 'difference' they want to make. Arriving at 'utopia' involves a number of steps:

- *naming the present reality*
- *critically analysing that reality*
- *imaginatively reframing the situation*
- *defining moral purpose and generating hope*
- *taking action to realise these hopes*

As the diagram below shows, this process also involves a hermeneutical circle.

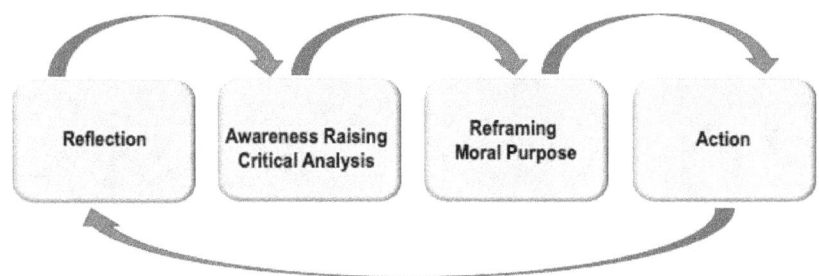

FIGURE 21.3: ACTION AND REFLECTION AS HERMENEUTICAL CIRCLE

Freire names this process the 'pedagogy of possibility'. It is a change model that educational and other leaders could profitably employ.

5.3 Dialogue in critical pedagogy

A critical pedagogy aims for two things: developing awareness and learning how to learn. *It is the empowerment that comes through the latter that makes the former meaningful.* Failing this, teachers become agents of what Freire calls a 'banking' or 'jug to mug' approach to pedagogy in which they pass on yesterday's understandings to young people who will blossom in tomorrow's world.[19] He also emphasises that the process by which students learn is *dialogical*.

Working with rural workers, and later in working with students, Freire discovered that *awareness-raising involves an exchange of interpretations* where people in a group respect the different ways in which others 'read the world' in which they both live.[20]

As we have already seen, we each read the world within a 'horizon' that we have absorbed formally and informally as the result of growing up in a particular context, culture and community. This helps us make sense of the world in that it enables us to navigate a known number of situations, but it can be a hindrance when we strike a totally new situation, since it limits our capacity to imagine something 'outside the box'.

In dialogue, it becomes possible to engage with people who have a different horizon and arrive at *a fusion of horizons*[21] that takes each partner in the dialogue beyond his or her previous position. In this way it becomes possible to re-imagine what is possible and so expand our understanding of the world and its possibilities. The fusion of horizons provides a new basis for hope, for reformulating our ethical purpose, and for engaging in social action to transform the world in some positive way.

---

19 No matter how advanced the technology students bring to the classroom today (hardware and software), within a few short years it will be superseded and will become obsolete. Learning *how to learn* in such a context is much more important that mastering particular hardware and software.
20 This notion is a central understanding in moderate hermeneutics.
21 A phrase and a process associated with the work of Gadamer in *Truth and Method*.

22

CONTEXTUALISING CRITICAL PEDAGOGY

In this chapter we take our discussion of critical pedagogy further, contextualising both its origins and also its contemporary contribution to pedagogies aligned with the vision of human flourishing which Jesus called the Kingdom of God.

1. LIBERATION THEOLOGY AS A SOURCE IN CRITICAL PEDAGOGY

Freire's work in developing critical pedagogy was closely linked to the development of liberation theology in Latin America. Methodologically, they share much in common. The main difference lies in the way they construe the values that drive ethical purpose.

Freire did not make his case on religious grounds, although he was aware of this possibility. He saw the churches, via the liberation theologians, exercising a prophetic role in Latin America. As he noted in *The Politics of Education* (1985):

> *This prophetic attitude, which emerges in the praxis of numerous Christians in the challenging situation of Latin America is accompanied by a rich and very necessary theological reflection. The theology of so-called development gives way to the theology of liberation – a prophetic utopian theology, full of hope. Little does it matter that this theology is not yet well systematized. Its content arises from the hopeless situation of dependent, exploited, invaded societies. It is stimulated by the need to rise above the contradictions that explain and produce that dependence. Since it is prophetic, this theology of liberation cannot attempt to reconcile the irreconcilable.*[1]

1.1 The birth of liberation theology

The birth of liberation theology is generally traced to a conference of the bishops of Latin America (CELAM) held in Medellin, Columbia, in 1968.

---

1 Paolo Freire, *The Politics of Education: Culture, Power and Liberation*. Westport CT: Greenwood Publishing, 1985, 139.

This conference was followed up by other major meetings in Puebla, Mexico, (1979), Santo Domingo, Dominican Republic (1992), and Aparecida, Brazil (2007). Each meeting issued a final, book length document, setting out in some detail the deliberations of the conference, and these provide a picture of the ebb and flow of liberation theology in Latin America and in the wider Catholic world.

Gustavo Gutierrez is the theologian regarded as 'the father' of liberation theology. His book, *A Theology of Liberation: History, Politics, Salvation*[2], introduced the rest of the Church to developments in Latin America. It has also had a significant impact on the development of Catholic social teaching and on theology more generally.

1.2 Liberation theology: process and structure

Liberation theology has a process, a structure and content. As a way of doing theology it is inductive, starting with the situation of people's lives. It follows the see-judge-act methodology first developed by the Young Christian Worker (YCW) movement in Belgium after World War I (and later adopted by the Catholic Action movement in Australia and elsewhere).

'Seeing' in this model means looking at the existential realities in which people live their lives, and the joys and sorrows these produce. Gutierrez argued that the 'pastoral' issues facing poor people, and those who minister to them, cannot be separated from the social issues confronting them, causing their poverty.

'Judging' means comparing this reality to what the situation would look like if the Kingdom of God, central to Jesus' mission and message, were present in this same existential reality. This is a hermeneutical endeavour.

'Acting' means taking action to effect a change in the reality of people's lives.

The parallels with Freire's 'pedagogy of possibility' methodology is clear.

In the practice of liberation theology, the see-judge-act methodology was employed by base Christian communities. These were informal groups of up to thirty people, who lived in the same neighbourhood, and who came together to reflect on the Bible, and its significance for their lives.

Liberation theology sought to address two major issues: the Church's need to stand *in solidarity with the poor and marginalised* just as Jesus did in his own ministry, and the *structural nature of human sinfulness*. If the Catholic

---

2 The notion of 'structural sin' (sometimes termed 'social sin') does not deny the reality of personal sinfulness as is sometimes claimed. It refers rather to the way in which evil can become structured into social arrangements. Such 'structural sin' facilitates individual wrong-doing, and renders resistance to its effects more difficult. Pope John Paul II included a discussion of structural sin and its relationship to personal sin in his 1987 encyclical *Sollicitudo Rei Socialis* (On Social Concerns), 36.

Church were to stand in solidarity with the poor and marginalised, then it needed to exercise a *'preferential option for the poor'* in major decision-making.

The critical orientation of liberation theology and the social activism of base Christian communities using the see-judge-act model soon ran into problems within the Catholic Church. These were the same problems that Freire's literacy groups encountered in civil society. Some Church leaders saw base communities as 'too political'. Critics also complained that exercising a preferential option for the poor was 'exclusive'. Sin, they argued, was always something personal. The see-judge-act model, in their view, presented a 'horizontal' view of religion.

Popes born in Europe (Paul VI and John Paul II), conscious of the menace of communism there and elsewhere in the 1960s and 1970s, were not impressed by the CELAM bishops' putative endorsement of liberation theology. The reason was that they saw parallels between its method of societal analysis and that of the European communists who were seriously oppressing vast populations and had been doing so for decades. Coming from communist-governed Poland, and having experienced, at first-hand, communism in practice, Pope John Paul II was understandably wary.

Early in his pontificate Pope John Paul II attended the CELAM meeting at Puebla (1979) where his opening address disappointed bishops supporting the approach of liberation theology. He did, however, subsequently adopt some of CELAM's recommendations, particularly that the Church exercise a preferential option for those who are poor and excluded. His predilection for the term 'solidarity' has subsequently raised an echo in many Christian hearts. This 'preferential option' or 'solidarity' with the poor became an important principle in Catholic social teaching.

It is important to recognise that liberation theology is a many-faceted and complex theological genre which has developed over the decades since Gutierrez produced his seminal work in 1971. It has attracted some outstanding scholars in many societies and cultures, and also across Christian denominations, because its subject matter lies at the heart of the Gospel. By the 1990s 'liberation' had become a major theme in Catholic missiology.

Cardinal Jorge Bergoglio, now Pope Francis, was the main writer of the bishops' document at the CELAM conference at Aparecida in 2007. His concern for the existential situation of the poor and marginalised, particularly the poor of Latin America, migrants flowing into Europe, and the victims of modern forms of slavery, is very well known. Under his leadership, liberation theology has now become more officially mainstream in the Catholic Church.

The three sources named in the preceding chapter – critical theory, the work of Paulo Freire, and liberation theology – have all made important contributions to the development of critical hermeneutics and critical pedagogy.

2. CONTEXT AND CRITICAL PEDAGOGY

Freire's concept of critical pedagogy draws attention to the role context plays in how pedagogical decisions are made, in particular *the ways in which teachers must read the context in the process of pedagogical decision-making*. Such reading of the context in which teachers teach and in which students learn can occur at three distinct levels.

2.1 Local school context

The immediate and obvious level at which teachers read the context is that of the school. Here traditions (often unstated) help define what constitutes 'good teaching'. Some of these traditions have their source in the internal life of the school, are often acquired as a result of formal and informal learning, and reflect preferences made over time by staff. They include things such as: having quiet classrooms, not going overtime when teaching, creating an interesting environment in the classroom, collaborating with colleagues in planning teaching, expanding the range of one's teaching strategies, and being involved (or not) in extra-curricular activities.

These traditions are *internal* and grow out of the culture of the school, reflect its history and its tolerance for risk-taking or ambiguity, and so on. The local context can be influenced by traditions that have *external* sources such as the attitudes parents hold about what constitutes 'good teaching'. In some cases, these attitudes are informed by social pressures, access to various forms of media, or by the parents' own experience of being at school. In a highly competitive educational market, external influences can also influence pedagogy indirectly via their impact on school leaders.

2.2 System context

The teaching context can also be read at a second level, that of the school system. Catholic schools now form part of a system. This system has an interest in promoting change in response to social movements sourced, for example, in public policy, union initiatives, policies of sponsoring bodies (such as local dioceses or Catholic Education Offices), and the media. At this level, resources are often made available to promote specific types of pedagogical developments. Testing regimes, such as NAPLAN and PISA, also become influential in shaping what happens in classrooms.

All testing regimes tend to invite teachers to 'teach to the test'. While some educational authorities decry this, teachers have to live with the reality that, in a competitive educational market where schools are ranked on results, 'teaching to the test' is a long-established tradition and integral to the formal and informal culture of most schools. Critical educators such as McLaren, Giroux, and Kincheloe, along with many teachers, decry this practice because of the limited conception of 'human flourishing' involved, and the marginalising effect it has on students, particularly those from low socio-economic and minority ethnic backgrounds.

While systems have drawbacks, they also offer possibilities when it comes to promoting better teaching and learning. Good teachers are generally not slow to make the most of these.

2.3 Cultural context

Context can also be read from a cultural perspective. This becomes important when there is a change of era in which cultural understandings, particularly competing conceptions of what constitutes 'human flourishing' and 'good teaching', are re-negotiated. Teachers are on the frontline as the resultant 'culture wars' or 'identity wars' are fought and won or fought and lost.

Thomas Oldenski, writing in the late 1990s, sets the situation out succinctly for our era by contrasting the tensions that now exist between two competing cultural worldviews – those of modernity and postmodernity.

> *Briefly stated, modernism offers the ideals of a democratic society – freedom equity and justice, as well as the notions of individuals' social responsibilities as agents of critique and change. Modernism values the individual as a critical being able to shape his or her own destiny and meaning. Likewise, modernism upholds high culture over popular culture. Knowledge is perceived as totalizing narratives identified with the development of reason, science and technology. Reason, science and technology become sources of power and dominance in establishing the privileged over those who lack them. The only source of this knowledge and power is however the metanarratives of the Eurocentric cultures and histories. Thus, schooling becomes a site of transmission of the canon of knowledge and culture, as defined by rationality, science and technology.*[3]

---

3 Thomas Oldenski, *Liberation Theology and Critical Pedagogy in Today's Catholic Schools*. New York: Taylor and Francis, 1997.

As we saw earlier, the privileging of Western culture, including its religious expressions and constructions of knowledge, over that of other cultures, is known as *classicism*.[4]

Classicism is a particular issue in the Catholic Church where theologies developed in Europe are, or have been, taken for granted as *the* expression of Christian faith. Theologians from Asia,[5] South America, Africa and Oceania challenge this position. Their protest is part of a wider post-colonial cultural movement that views the Eurocentric ways of constructing knowledge with suspicion.

Speaking of this trend Oldenski continues:

> *Post-modernism, by contrast, expands the concepts of freedom, equity, justice and a democratic society to include an understanding of these phenomena from the perspective of those histories and voices that have been silenced, erased or excluded from the Eurocentric meta-narratives of progress and human development. Postmodernism identifies these histories as "dangerous memories" ... since they force one to evaluate history as it has been developed and presented from the perspective of the dominant culture and the oppressor.*[6]

We see the difficulties these 'dangerous memories' pose in the defensive way mainstream Australia has dealt with the treatment of Aboriginal peoples in the period since white settlement.

Oldenski also notes:

> *Post-modernism values popular taste and the everyday in the lives of people as vital to shaping and understanding culture. It celebrates diversity and plurality. In regard to knowledge, postmodernism begins to raise questions about how knowledge is constructed, whose interests knowledge serves, and what values and assumptions underlie this knowledge.*[7]

This popular culture recognises that there are people in the community who are LGBTQI and that such people have rights, including the right to live in committed relationships protected by the law. This is one manifestation of a cultural shift, termed the 'postmodern turn', that acknowledges diversity in the community.

Contemporary culture now has a third phase and that is the 'postsecular turn' in which religion is accepted as part of the existential human

---

4   Classicism is not confined to Europe. It includes, for example, Chinese, Islamic and other counterparts, and it works at many levels.
5   See for example Peter Phan, *Christianity with an Asian Face: Asian American Theology in the Making*. Maryknoll N.Y: Orbis, 2003. See also *In Our Own Tongues: Perspectives from Asia on Mission and Inculturation*. Maryknoll N.Y: Orbis Books, 2003.
6   Oldenski, 9.
7   Ibid.

condition. The difficulty for teachers is that they are dealing with students and parents who are influenced by all three trends – modern, postmodern, and postsecular – and, given the contradictions implicit in them, they lack a coherent worldview. In the present complex cultural milieu, teachers may find themselves in the same position.

A cultural reading of the context in which teachers live, learn and teach can uncover similarities to the complexities of Jesus' own society and culture when he advised his followers to 'read the signs of the times' (Matt 16:3) and see God at work in what was happening around them. This brings us back to Ignatius' insight that it is necessary to 'find God in all things'.

2.4 Postmodernity and critical pedagogy

The advocates of critical pedagogy tend to hold views that align more closely with a postmodern sensibility than with either a modern sensibility or a postsecular sensibility. However, the situation is not clear-cut.

Teachers need to reflect on how they read the context in which they teach and how this shapes their pedagogical decisions. Those who adopt a critical stance to pedagogy tend to read the context in which they work in cultural terms and this reading helps them define their ethical purpose.

As Kincheloe notes of critical pedagogy:

> ... *critical pedagogy works to help teacher educators and teachers reconstruct their work so that it facilitates the empowerment of all students. In this context critical educators understand that such an effort takes place in an increasingly power-inscribed world where dominant modes of exclusion are continuously 'naturalized' by power-wielders' control of information. What does this have to do with teacher education, critics may ask? We live in a democracy, they assert. Why do we have to spend all this time with such political issues? Isn't our focus teaching and learning? But democracy is fragile, critical educators maintain, and embedded in education are the very issues that make or break it. Are teachers merely managers of the predetermined knowledge of dominant cultural power? Is teacher education merely the process of developing the most efficient ways for educators to perform this task? Do teachers operate as functionaries who simply do what they are told? Contrary to the views of many, these questions are not separate from the most fundamental features of teaching and learning.*[8]

The case made above is amplified when applied to a multi-cultural, multi-faith society and the need to build social cohesion across faiths and cultures. In this cultural context it becomes necessary to understand the

---
8   Joe L Kincheloe, *Knowledge and Critical Pedagogy: An Introduction*. Springer, 2010.

one who is 'other', and this cannot be done without understanding their religion or other life options. This cannot happen without engaging the one who is 'other' in dialogue. The *Enhancing Catholic School Identity* project has brought this realisation home to many Catholic teachers in this country.

However, it is one thing to know what is required, and something else to have the procedural knowledge necessary to make it happen. As Catholic schools become more multi-faith, they present a unique context in which interfaith dialogue can be pursued. At present *teachers in Catholic schools are pedagogically ill-equipped to deal with this development*. Addressing the issue is an important challenge now facing principals and system leaders operating from a postsecular perspective.

The three levels at which context can be read results in teachers framing their ethical purpose (the difference they choose to make) in quite different ways and, as a result, coming to quite different conclusions about what constitutes good pedagogy and human flourishing. It requires *dialogue within a staff* on this matter to develop a consensus about ethical purpose if the school is to pursue a coherent mission.

3. WHAT IS CRITICAL PEDAGOGY?

Critical pedagogy refers to the range of decisions that teachers make about what is appropriate in teaching and learning, and so what is 'good' for this child or this group of children. Critical pedagogy involves interpreting the cultural context with a particular bias that gives emphasis to what Ricoeur calls a 'hermeneutics of suspicion'.

Oldenski offers the following descriptive definition of critical pedagogy:

> *Critical pedagogy, as formulated by Freire, McLaren and Giroux, subverts the canon of knowledge and the neutrality this knowledge claims. It pushes the purpose of schooling beyond the transmission of the knowledge and the culture of Eurocentric metanarratives. It questions how knowledge is constructed, whose interest knowledge serves, whom knowledge excludes or silences, and what values and assumptions inform (the construction of) knowledge. Critical pedagogy draws upon post-modernism in rejecting the totalizing narratives of reason, science and technology that emerged from the Enlightenment. Critical pedagogy values popular culture as part of understanding the milieu and rejects the positioning of high culture over and opposed to popular culture. Thus, critical pedagogy includes the memories and voices of those who have been rejected and marginalised by mono-cultural Eurocentrism ... The voices of those who have been silenced and excluded through the exercise of power must be included in reconstructing*

knowledge and in the process of schooling. This inclusion requires valuing the experiences of students, (particularly those who are) marginalised and oppressed. Critical pedagogy begins with their experiences as a source of knowledge, including their everyday culture expressed in a variety of contemporary and familiar forms. Thus, schooling becomes less a 'banking' process and more a process of 'conscientization' as developed in the works of Freire, and expanded by McLaren and Giroux.[9]

Critical pedagogy then involves a 'critical reading' of the context that shapes the consciousness of teachers and the decisions they make about what is at stake in teaching and learning. It then seeks to translate this understanding into classroom practices. Critical pedagogy is attuned to and influenced by cultural currents swirling in society and addresses a number of fundamental questions such as:

- *What is knowledge?*
- *Whose interests does it serve?*
- *What impact (positive or negative) will this understanding have on my students' capacity to flourish?*
- *How to I assist students to understand and deal with the issue?*

The belief underpinning critical pedagogy, and critical hermeneutics in general, is that the voices that are excluded or silenced in society are those of people who, from firsthand experience, know how the 'great schemes' that are designed by power elites to help them, actually fail them. This is not something those in power, or their supporters, generally want to know!

Critical pedagogy proceeds from the understanding that young people have their own language and culture, their own 'more or less successful design for living together peacefully' in the postsecular environment, to quote Luzbetak whom we met in Chapter 7.[10] However, this design often lacks any input from history and is contextualised in a unique but limited way. Those engaged in critical pedagogy do not try to 'fill in the gaps' for students based on their own experience, but endeavour to enter into dialogue with them in a way that helps them develop the *contextually critical form of consciousness* needed to make sense of and thrive in the postsecular environment. Theirs is a *facilitating and accompanying role* quite different from that of power-wielders who prefer to live in the world of abstractions far removed from the concrete experience of the young people whose voices they silence. Critical educators seek to raise students' critical awareness of

---

9   Oldenski, 86. Material in brackets is not in the original.
10 Luzbetak, 156–7.

the context in which they live and lead them to put questions to their own experience and that of their community in the hope of transforming it.

4. NEXUS: CRITICAL PEDAGOGY – A CATHOLIC PEDAGOGY

The nexus between the development of liberation theology and the development of critical pedagogy is evident with Paulo Freire and Pope Francis providing important links between these two movements.

A *Catholic pedagogy must include a critical dimension* and this needs to apply across the curriculum, including the Religious Education curriculum. The questions central to critical pedagogy are unlikely to go away:

- *Who defines what is knowledge and how?*
- *Whose interests are served by creating knowledge in this way?*
- *What notion of human flourishing is embedded in the way we create knowledge?*
- *How does this way of creating knowledge allow students to make sense of the existential situation in which they live?*
- *Is this way of creating knowledge in the best interests of my students?*
- *How should I respond as a teacher in helping them to learn?*

A critical pedagogy seeks to achieve a degree of emancipation from the all-embracing relativism in the culture in which students now live. This can be viewed as a social task (improving the quality of their lives in a democratic society), or a religious task (creating Kingdom spaces in student's lives) or, importantly, both.

Either way, the questions above raise significant issues about a teacher's ethical purpose, how he or she formulates the pedagogical relationship with students, the 'difference' he or she seeks to make, and how pursuing this difference shapes pedagogical choices.

We conclude with the 'emancipatory' questions that Freire poses in his 'pedagogy of possibility':

- *How do you, as a teacher, imagine the 'utopia' that your teaching seeks to provide for yourself and the students you teach?*
- *What hopes does this open up for you and for them?*

23

HUMAN DEVELOPMENT, COGNITION, AND PEDAGOGY

As we explore aspects of student development and cognition, it may be helpful to review our recent journey.[1]

1. QUICK REVIEW

In Part D we explored the process of knowing as developed by Lonergan and qualified by hermeneutics. We saw that, according to Lonergan, the dynamism of human cognition operates at three interrelated levels: attending to the data of experience, developing insight (understanding), and validating what is understood (knowing). We have discussed the confusion caused by the use of 'understanding' to indicate both content and process, and also the confusion that follows when understanding is equated with knowing.

We have also explored the contextual nature of all understanding. This implies that all knowing, and therefore the meaning-making that depends on knowing, is contextual as well. What we know and hold to be true depends in large part on the culture in which we grow up and the historical circumstances in which this happens. This is obviously true for people growing up in other cultures and histories as well. Clearly the human capacity to misunderstand or misinterpret other peoples is significant. In a pluralised world this problem is amplified, particularly when we tend to take our culture and history as normative for others.

While exploring epistemological and hermeneutical assumptions may seem somewhat exotic, these assumptions have important social and educational consequences when it comes to how teachers (and students) understand the world and their membership of it.

The 'cognitive dynamism' outlined in Lonergan's epistemology is consistent with the understanding of how the brain functions, as currently

---

[1] In developing this chapter, we are indebted to the doctoral research of Margaret Kelleher, *From Biblical Story to Biblical Interpretation: A Critical Transition*. PhD Thesis: Melbourne College of Divinity, 2011.

understood by science[2] and research into 'what works' in the classroom. The 'surface learning' and 'deep learning' proposed in the models of learning discussed in earlier chapters correspond to 'understanding' and 'knowing' as defined by Lonergan.

Learning has been discussed so far in philosophical, and therefore abstract terms. This removes the discussion from the classroom situation where teachers are dealing with students *at various stages of personal development* where the learning situation is *concrete and specific*. The present chapter seeks to move discussion about pedagogy, and the relationship that sits at its heart, from the abstract to the concrete in addressing the question:

- *How does the dynamism of human cognition unfold in students, and what are the pedagogical implications of this unfolding?*

To answer this question, we seek to bring the insights of epistemology and philosophical hermeneutics into conversation with the findings of developmental psychology. We confine the discussion to those aspects of human growth and development that are relevant to schooling.

2. TWO TRADITIONS IN HUMAN DEVELOPMENT

There are two broad traditions at work in studies of the psychology of human development. The first derives from *cognitive psychology* and the pioneering work of Jean Piaget. The second is based on Erikson's theory of *psychosocial development*. We treat both in turn and explore their implications for learning.

Before embarking on this task, we reiterate the point that *all teachers have at least an implicit theory of how development issues impact on student learning*, just as they have an implicit theory about how students think and how they learn. In this chapter we seek to bring to consciousness teachers' assumptions about the impact of human development on student learning, so that their adequacy can be evaluated.

2.1. Cognitive psychology: Piaget and his successors

Piaget made a seminal contribution to education. He explored how children learn, and identified the stages by which this process unfolds. In doing so, he set the scene for later research into human development that resulted in the stages theories of Lawrence Kohlberg (moral development) and James Fowler (faith development).[3]

---

[2] See Daniel Helminiak, *Brain Consciousness and God: A Lonerganian Integration*. Albany: State University of New York Press, 2015.
[3] An assumption often imputed to stage models is that all human beings develop through a number of invariant stages irrespective of variables such as gender, culture and context.

Stage models of human development are presumed to identify *universal patterns*, a claim open to challenge given the limited nature of the sample groups studied in formulating the theory.[4] Despite their acknowledged limitations, stage theories offer valuable educational insights, and it is on these that we focus in seeking to develop a working model of student learning.

2.2 Piaget's stages of cognitive development

Working with subjects drawn from his clinical practice in Geneva, Piaget set out to explore the cognitive capacities of young people as they grow from childhood to adolescence. He conducted a number of ingenious experiments and concluded that the cognitive development of children passes through four recognisable stages. These are set out in the table below. It is important to point out that Piaget did not study the cognitive development of adults, and this left the question open as to whether there are stages beyond 'formal operations'.

Stage	Age
Sensorimotor	0–2
Pre-operational	2–7
Concrete Operational	7–11
Formal Operational	11+

TABLE 23.1: PIAGET AND COGNITIVE DEVELOPMENT

Piaget concluded that while the sequence of stages outlined above is fixed, there are notable differences in the rates at which children move through them, so that ages in the table are *indicative only*.

Piaget theorised that children have internal cognitive structures that change (adapt) in the process of maturation. New experiences cause a change in an already established equilibrium within the child's cognitive structure that has to be negotiated, and this leads to a progressive reorganisation and transformation of the child's cognitive structure. The move from stage to stage is gradual rather than abrupt, and consolidation in a particular stage usually precedes change to another stage. Both the cognitive structure and changes occurring as children move from stage to stage have to be inferred from the behaviour of the children.

The developmental transitions associated with schooling are those *from pre-operational to concrete operational thinking that occurs in the primary schooling years*, and from *concrete operational to formal operational thinking* that usually

---

4 The originators of stage models – Piaget, Kohlberg and Fowler – have usually been more cautious in their claims.

occurs during secondary schooling. If there is a stage beyond formal operations, then this too could also occur during the later years of secondary schooling.

2.3 Concrete operational thinking

In the concrete operational stages, the child (7–11 years old) can think logically and solve *concrete problems*. They understand definitions and are able to use these as the basis of classification and categorisation. They understand cause and effect and have a sense of time as past and present. However they struggle to understand abstract concepts and complex verbal constructions such as hypotheses. Their thinking is usually context specific. At this stage children understand symbolism as long as the examples are concrete and particular.

2.4 Formal operational thinking

In the formal operational stage, students (11+ years) can follow the form of an argument and can reason in a competent manner. They can master abstract concepts and understand relationships between such concepts. They can think beyond the present and project into the future and so commit to new possibilities. In this stage they begin to develop a capacity for reflexive thinking and so can reflect on, and be critical of, their own thinking. This means that metacognition now becomes a possibility. Formal operational thinkers are capable of complex symbolic thinking and of working with complex symbols.

Piaget hypothesised that learning new things is a *spontaneous process*. He concluded that as young people developed through the various stages, *their cognitive structure is transformed*. What prompts the transition from stage to stage, however, remains something of a mystery.

2.5 Some qualifications on Piaget's theory

Kelleher notes two repeated findings in empirical studies that have sought to replicate Piaget's work:

- *A majority of 15-year-olds have not reached the stage of formal operational thinking*
- *When the learning domain involved has a heavy reliance on verbal material, which is what tends to occur in Religious Education (and other areas), the students reach formal operational thinking even later that 15.*[5]

---

5 Kelleher 2011, 157.

As noted earlier, Piaget was concerned with the learning of children. Other researchers sought to explore whether there were further stages in cognitive development associated with young adults. They sought to explore *'post-formal operational thinking as a characteristic of adult thinking'*.[6] Of particular interest here is the work of William Perry (1970) who explored 'post-formal thinking' in males[7] and Mary Belenky and associates (1986) who explored the same phenomenon in women.[8] We include these explorations in this discussion insofar as they impinge on how students think and learn in the final years of schooling.

3. 'POST-FORMAL THINKING'

Attempts to explore 'post-formal thinking' in adults run into an immediate problem: young people who have reached the stage of formal operations *are capable of reflexive thinking and so of metacognition*. They have the capacity to exert conscious choices with respect to their thinking and 'how they think about thinking'. This capacity shapes not only what they choose to think about, but also how they do it. Of course, for many young adults including young teachers, this does not happen consciously, but happens because they grow up in a certain culture and take on board the epistemological and hermeneutical understandings with currency in that culture.

The situation is very problematic in Western societies where modern, postmodern and postsecular worldviews exist concurrently with each operating on a different set of epistemological or hermeneutical assumptions.

In adults the 'dynamism of human cognition' outlined by Lonergan is fully operational. So young adults *attend to their experiences*, including their social and psychological experiences, *gain insight into the framework they use* to make sense of their world, including the social and civic relationships within that world, and become aware of the role culture and faith play in shaping this framework. We note that the term 'framework' as used here is synonymous with the term 'worldview' as we have outlined it previously (Chapter 7).

The analysis of cognition in young adults therefore needs to occur *within a much wider framework* than the one adopted by Piaget for the purpose of studying growth and development in children. Studies, such as those by

---

6 The stage theories of Kohlberg and Fowler that depend on Piaget's theory of cognitive development are not limited in their impact by the fact that Piaget's theory is based on experiments with children and adolescents.
7 William Perry, *Forms of Intellectual and Ethical Development in the College Years*. New York: Holt Rinehart and Winston, 1970.
8 Mary Belenky, Jill Tarule, Blythe Clinchy, and Nancy Goldberger. *Women's Ways of Knowing: The development of Self, Voice and Mind*. New York: Basic Books, 1986. This book had at least 10 editions.

Perry and Belenky, confirm this observation. The schema Perry developed to analyse the thinking in college students in the US illustrates this need.

3.1 William Perry: thinking in adult students

In endeavouring to trace how thinking develops in young adults, Perry identified nine stages that they seem to pass through. To explain the data, he included variables such as the student's worldview, their attitude towards authority, and how they understood and validated knowledge.

A simplified version of his model is set out in the table below.[9]

Position	Title	Understanding of Knowledge	Worldview	Understanding of Authority
1.	Basic Duality	Right/wrong. Truth absolute.	Dualistic	Authority absolute – source of truth.
2.	Multiplicity Level 1	Diversity perceived, but seen as 'alien' or 'unwarranted confusion'. Truth Absolute.	Complex Dualism	Authority absolute, but now seen as incompetent.
3.	Multiplicity Level 2	Diversity and uncertainty accepted but seen as a temporary state. Truth Absolute.	Qualified Dualism	In some areas Authority has not found the answers yet.
4	Multiplicity Level 3	Diversity accepted as legitimate and widespread.	Dualism in transition to relativism	Authority and right/wrong Doubted.
5.	Relativism	All knowledge and values seen as contextual.	Relativism	Authority holds only in some areas, has some answers.
6	Need for commitment foreseen	All knowledge and values are relative.	Relativism	Need to orient oneself to a relativistic world through some form of personal commitment.
7	Initial Commitment	Commitment made and responsibility accepted.	Relativism	Authority accepted, but within a relativistic world.
8	Implications of commitment understood	Commitment made and responsibility accepted.	Relativism	Authority accepted, but within a relativistic world.
9.	Developing commitments	Commitment made and responsibility accepted.	Relativism	Authority accepted, but within a relativistic world.

TABLE 23.2: NINE STAGES OF COGNITIVE DEVELOPMENT (WILLIAM PERRY)

---

9   Table adapted from Kelleher, 160.

The table demonstrates how a much wider frame of reference is needed to research the thinking patterns of adults. The framework has to take into account how adults understand knowledge, and how they understand the process of knowing, including the role that authority plays in determining what is true. As adults mature, there is a progressive acceptance of diversity as a fact of life, a higher tolerance of ambiguity, and the realisation that, in a responsible person, *knowing is linked to doing*.

Perry discovered that young people make a series of *epistemological shifts* as they mature. They move away from an initial *dualism*, where issues are discussed in black and white terms, through *multiplicity* as diversity of viewpoints comes to be accepted and shades of grey acknowledged, towards *relativism* where knowledge and truth is seen to be contextual and provisional. As a result of these shifts, an adult comes to recognise that his or her commitments always rest on a fragile basis.[10]

The transitions that Perry identified are characterised by different epistemological and hermeneutical assumptions, that is different ways of understanding what knowledge is and how it is validated, and also what is personally meaningful and how this is justified. Within these shifts there was also growing acceptance of the need *to match what one knows to how one acts and to develop commitments that reflect one's values*. Growth towards maturity involves a gradual acceptance of the need for authority while, at the same time, being aware that all authority has inherent limits. Thus, sooner or later 'authority' has to be 'befriended'!

Belenky and colleagues studied post-formal thinking in a group of women and discovered that while there was a similar general pattern to that discovered by Perry, there were also important differences. These differences centred on how women understood and valued difference. The 'difference' that concerned women was in *how men and women interpreted personal experience*, particularly in the area of relationships. For women, commitment is expressed in relationships, for men it is often expressed in projects, values and causes. For women these three factors merely provide the context in which relationships can be formed.

Both research projects link cognitive development in young adults to their epistemological assumptions, a result confirmed by other research.[11] Kitchener and Kitchener, for instance, note that 'an individual's epistemological assumptions about the nature of evidence, knowledge, and

---

10 Perry uses 'relativism' in a special way here to indicate the provisional nature of truth. The term is more commonly used to mean 'every point of view contains its own truth'.
11 K.S. Kitchener & R.F. Kitchener, 'The Development of Natural Rationality: Can formal operations account for it?' in Jack Mezirow and Associates, *Fostering Critical Reflection in Adulthood: A Guide to Transformative and Emancipatory Learning*. San Francisco: Jossey-Bass, 1990. Also, Deanna Kuhn, 'Formal Operations in a 21st Century perspective'. *Human Development* 51(1), 2008, 48–55.

justification play a critical role in reasoning'. Even in scientific reasoning the assumptions that a person brings to problem-solving influence their perception of the problem, their evaluation of the evidence, and the criteria they use for evaluating theories.[12] This is as true for teachers as it is for students, and is a finding consistent with Lonergan's 'dynamism of human cognition' and his 'transcendental precepts':

- be attentive
- be intelligent
- be reasonable
- be responsible.

4. ERIKSON'S PSYCHOSOCIAL MODEL OF HUMAN DEVELOPMENT

Erik Erikson's understanding of human development grew out of his practice as an art therapist working with children, and later as a psychoanalyst.[13] In the latter capacity he identified a number of 'stages' that people pass through in the process of maturing. Erikson refocused psychoanalysis moving it from concern about the impact of early childhood events on later development (Freud) to the impact of social influences on human development.

Erikson's interest was in the role social interactions and relationships play in the development and growth of human beings as they move through the stages of development. In his theory, human development is cumulative with each stage building on the previous one, but the transition from stage to stage can be messy, leaving some tensions in the previous transitions unresolved. This can be problematic for later development.

The movement from stage to stage is marked by some form of *crisis* in which the developing person struggles to make sense of his or her life agenda within an existing frame of reference. *Crisis provides the context for growth, or neurosis.* As people negotiate these developmental crises, they emerge with psychological strengths that become an asset for the rest of their lives. That is, as people negotiate the crises associated with moving from stage to stage, they develop *essential life competencies*. The development of these competencies contributes to their sense of self-worth.

The table below summarises Erikson's model.

---

12 K.S. Kitchener & R.F. Kitchener, 'The development of natural rationality: Can formal operations account for it?' in J.A. Meacham & N.R. Santilli (eds), *Social development in youth: structure and content*. Basel: Kaeger, 1981, 173.
13 Erikson trained in this field under Anna Freud (the youngest daughter of Sigmund Freud), who was a pioneer in using psychoanalysis to treat children. Anna fled Vienna prior to the German occupation and spent the rest of her life in Britain. Erikson fled to the United States.

Stage	Age	Crisis	Competence	Dangers
1	0–1	Trust vs Mistrust	Learning to depend on adults.	Fear and belief that life is unpredictable.
2	2–3	Autonomy vs Shame and Doubt	Personal control over a range of choices.	Feelings of personal inadequacy and self-doubt.
3	3–5	Initiative vs Guilt	Ability to work with others and lead in play.	Guilt and lack of initiative.
4	6–11	Industry vs Inferiority	Confidence that 'I can do this'. Pride in accomplishments.	Self-doubt and poor self-image.
5.	12–18	Identity vs Confusion	Conscious sense of self leading to independence. Awareness of beliefs, values and ideals.	Confusion about personal identity values and beliefs.
6.	19–40	Intimacy vs Isolation	Developing close committed relationships with others.	Unable to sustain relationship, loneliness.
7.	40–65	Generativity vs Stagnation	Contributing to community. Has a sense of purpose in life. Care for others.	Feeling isolated, uninvolved, purposeless.
8.	65+	Integrity vs Despair	Sense of contributing to something worthwhile.	Sense that one has achieved little. Being a failure.

TABLE 23.3: STAGES OF HUMAN DEVELOPMENT – ERIKSON

The strength of Erikson's model is that it is holistic in looking at human development *across a life cycle and in a social context.*

4.1 Erikson and the pedagogical relationship

Of particular interest to educators are the transitions that occur in the school years (Stages 4 and 5) and the lingering effects of transitions that precede the school years (Stage 2 and 3).

Educators need to realise that they too are caught up in the process of human development, and that the school often constitutes the social context in which they make the transitions associated with movement through Stages 6, 7 and 8. As each of these transitions occurs, it is likely that the teacher will *come to understand the pedagogical relationship he or she has with students in a new light,* and so 'doing the right thing by students' can take on new meanings. The result is that, within a teaching staff, there are likely to be several legitimate understandings of the pedagogical relationship based on the fact that *staff members are at different stages of human development.* School leaders need to be aware of this situation in promoting particular approaches to pedagogy.

4.2 Erikson in the classroom

Starratt explores the ethical demands of schooling from within Erikson's model of human development.[14] He sets out a programmatic approach to 'doing the right thing by students' involving five major elements:

1. Developing the self-esteem of students
Starratt takes self-esteem as the starting point for healthy human growth. This emerges from the young child's developing sense of competence in dealing with the tasks of life, which leads to an appreciation of their talents.

2. Helping students discover and share their inner wealth
As self-esteem develops, students realise that their true wealth is what is inside them, in what they are, rather than what they possess or look like on the outside. This realisation provides the foundation for building healthy relationships, as well as for learning how to heal breaches in relationships, how to forgive another person, and how to ask for forgiveness from another person.

3. Learning to turn one's talents towards the community
Students need to learn that their talents are given to them primarily to enrich the community. Students can do this only if the school provides them with sufficient opportunities to be of service to others.

4. Exploring the nature of heroism
Starratt notes that deep in the heart of every person is the desire to do something special. He suggests that this capacity for personal transcendence be seen as heroism, and that it can take a variety of forms. One of central significance to the Christian is discipleship which makes demands in terms of relationships and service. In this context he suggests that Catholic schools need to provide a way of channelling the student's quest for the heroic.

5. Developing a capacity for self-governance (and personal commitment)
Self-governance operates at two levels. The first level is how students govern their personal, individual lives. The second is the capacity of students to govern their communal life together in the school setting.

Starratt contends that leaders in Catholic schools know how to construct learning environments and learning activities to promote these five basic pre-dispositions for human and religious growth, 'but what we lack are the

---

14 Robert Starratt, 'The Religious Development of the Catholic School Teacher'. Paper presented at the Annual Meeting of Catholic School Superintendents of Catholic Schools, New Orleans, 1984. Made available by Starratt. He returns to these themes in *Cultivating an Ethical School* (2014) linking them more explicitly to Erikson's model of human development.

staff development programs to develop those skills and attitudes in teachers to enable them to work with youngsters on these learnings'.[15]

Of particular educational interest is the transition associated with Erikson's Stage 5, the formation of a personal identity, which happens during the secondary school years and so forms the important background against which formal operational thinking begins.

5. STAGE 5: THE FORMATION OF PERSONAL IDENTITY

Erikson's Stage 5 has become of increasing interest to Catholic educators with the introduction of the Enhancing Catholic Schools Identity project. Stage 5 is concerned with the formation of personal identity, the conditions under which this happens, and the place of religion within this process.

5.1 Nature of personal identity

Erikson formulated the notion of 'identity crisis' to denote issues surrounding transition from Stage 4 (Industry vs Inferiority) to Stage 5 (Identity vs Confusion). In discussing identity, he identifies three components:

- *An inner dimension. Identity is part of the psyche of the individual*
- *The cultural and historical setting. These two factors determine the social milieu in which identity must be formed.*
- *Unresolved developmental tasks of earlier stages.*[16] *These exist as an unwelcome legacy that remains to be addressed.*

For Erikson, identity is *socially defined* and has three components:

- *how the individual perceives himself*
- *the congruence of this perspective with how the individual is perceived by the community*
- *how the individual perceives the responses of others.*

As socially defined, identity is shaped by *the roles that a person plays within a group*. These may be formal or informal and can change as the context changes. Students can exercise choice as to which role they choose to play, and the classroom often becomes the 'theatre' in which new roles are played out. Teachers need to recognise what is happening and interpret it accordingly.

---
15 Ibid.
16 Erik Erikson, *Identity: Youth and Crisis.* London: Faber and Faber, 1969, 82.

In negotiating the crisis of identity, the adolescent has to contend not only with conflicting forces within his or her psyche, but also with conflicting forces emanating from a rapidly changing contemporary society and culture. The competing demands generated by change have to be integrated into the psyche if one is to emerge from the crisis with an increased sense of inner unity. Without this, young people remain confused as to who they are and what life is about. The construction that students place on change in their society and culture is therefore important in identity formation.[17] Commenting on the dilemma this can create, Kelleher observes:

> *In the context of religious education, students will be challenged to integrate within their personality the conflicting patterns of belief and values from the school, which fosters a Christian community and advocates a particular perspective on life, with the powerful influence of a society whose values expressed in popular culture and the peer group, are frequently antithetical to the school's perspective and in which an anti-religion and atheistic agenda is currently being canvassed.*[18]

It is sometimes easy for teachers to forget the existential condition in which adolescents attempt to negotiate the crisis of identity, and to underestimate the cognitive demands that come with this challenge. In the face of these demands, many students simply 'bail out' and adopt a relativist position. That is, they refuse to engage with the challenge. This applies not only to religious issues, the 'refusal to engage' often applies to making career choices and even to study itself.[19]

6. THEORY OF IDENTITY FORMATION: JAMES MARCIA

Canadian developmental psychologist, James Marcia, has developed a working model of identity formation based on two variables, *exploration and commitment*. *Exploration* recognises a crisis, and that important issues need to be explored and options identified. *Commitment* marks the degree to which an individual is committed to a particular option. Marcia represents these as two independent 'axes', as in the following table:

---

17 Ibid, 92.
18 Kelleher, 189.
19 For a helpful outline of Marcia's theory, view 'James Marcia's Adolescent Identity Development' on Youtube at https://youtu.be/-JrZwmHU9xE

		Crisis	
		Yes	No
Commitment	Yes	Achievement	Foreclosure
	No	Moratorium	Diffusion

FIGURE 23.4: IDENTITY FORMATION (MARCIA)

Marcia uses 'crisis' in the same sense as Erikson, and the individual may ('Yes'), or may not ('No'), be exploring how to resolve it. Given that this is the case, then he may ('Yes') or may not ('No') be committed to resolving it. This situation creates the four *identity statuses* outlined in the diagram above.

1. **Identity Diffusion** corresponds to 'doing nothing'. Applied to a career it means not exploring options and so not being committed to any. In the case of ideology, it means not being interested and not being committed politically.

2. **Identity Foreclosure.** Here there is strong commitment to a particular option, but there has been no exploration of alternatives. In career choice it means 'I will become a lawyer because my father is a lawyer'. In religion it equates to 'I am Catholic because my parents are Catholic'.

3. **Identity Moratorium** corresponds to actively exploring, without being committed to any particular option. It is a state of intelligently 'keeping my options open'. In career terms it means exploring options without making a choice. In ideological terms it means being interested in politics but not committed to any party. In religious terms it equates to relativism – seeing one religion as good as another, without being committed to any.

4. **Identity achievement** means that there has been exploration and there is commitment to a cause, a career or a set of religious beliefs.

Marcia's identity model can be applied to the formation of human relationships. The model is helpful in explaining the ways in which students come to make choices as well as their attitudes to relationships. It is particularly helpful in explaining their attitudes to religion where helping secondary students move beyond 'moratorium' has become a major challenge.[20]

---

20 One of the major findings of the Generation Y Study into the attitudes and beliefs of young people, was that the majority of senior students who had attended Catholic schools could discuss religious topics intelligently, without being committed to what they knew. Mason et al judged this to mean the Catholic schools were failing. From a developmental perspective, this finding does not come as a surprise. See the report by Michael Mason, Andrew Singleton & Ruth Webber in *The Spirit of Generation Y*. Mulgrave: Garratt Publishing, 2007.

7. COLLECTIVE IDENTITY AND INDIVIDUAL IDENTITY

The process of individual identity formation always happens in a social context and depends on roles already existent in that context. This is because any role that an individual seeks to play in order to 'test' personal identity, has already been culturally defined by the group. This enables members to recognise what is going on and respond. Peer response is of particular importance in the formation of individual identity. Social interaction with others in the group influences the student's perception of their place in the group. In this context school life, seen as a milieu for social interaction, has an important influence on the development of an individual's worldview and the interpersonal and intrapersonal competencies associated with 'deep' learning. It is a milieu for learning independent of the classroom. This social influence is often at its strongest in extra-curricular activities.

Kelleher identifies a key tension associated with adolescence and the search for a personal identity open to faith.

> In adolescence, gaining acceptance within a group, and establishing one's identity as a member of a group, contributes to the broadening of the young person's horizon and social skills beyond the family. Group attitudes and values are internalized. At times the young person will need to negotiate situations where there is a clash between personal and group values, a painful experience, but one which may result in a stronger sense of personal identity. Membership of a group provides emotional support, a sense of belonging and establishes commitments to others beyond the family. The relationships between members of the group provide a context in which leadership roles may be adopted, but also where negative feelings ... are experienced.[21]

The models presented in this chapter raise important questions for educators when it comes to conceptualising the pedagogical relationship and its implications in the classroom.

Piaget highlights learning as a process *occurring within an isolated individual*. His is a highly individualistic model in which the goal is developing thinking skills. Many teachers understand the pedagogical relationship and doing the right thing by students within this framework.[22]

Erikson views learning as *occurring is a social context* in which roles play an important part. The way in which the teacher construes his or her

---

[21] Kelleher, 2014, 190–1.
[22] This way of conceptualising the pedagogical relationship is well spelt out in the work of development psychologist Deanna Kuhn. See Deanna Kuhn, *Education for Thinking*. Harvard University Press, 2008.

role becomes an important issue in how they understand the pedagogical relationship, and whether or not the classroom functions as *a social context for learning*. Not all teachers will construe 'doing what is right by the students' in these terms for a variety of reasons, including the level of their own personal development. However, this now seems an essential aspect of any sound approach to pedagogy, including any pedagogy that is 'Catholic'.

24

DIALOGUE AND PEDAGOGY: THE MISSION CONNECTION

The concept of dialogue has gained increasing prominence in philosophical, educational and theological discourse in the past half century. This has been driven by the need to understand and adapt to the increasing religious and cultural pluralism now found in all Western societies, and the consequent need to build social cohesion in those societies, as well as to offset the dangers posed by various forms of fundamentalist extremism.

In theological discourse there is now greater recognition of the fact that building the Kingdom of God is not something the Church can do on its own. Nor should it be. The 'missionary church' that Pope Francis envisages needs 'dialogue partners' to achieve its goals on behalf of the Kingdom of God. His position could not be clearer in its call to educators:

If there is one word that we should never tire of repeating, it is this: dialogue. We are called to promote a culture of dialogue by every possible means and thus to rebuild the fabric of society. The culture of dialogue entails a true apprenticeship and a discipline that enables us to view others as valid dialogue partners, to respect the foreigner, the immigrant and people from different cultures as worthy of being listened to. Today we urgently need to engage all the members of society in building "a culture which privileges dialogue as a form of encounter" and in creating "a means for building consensus and agreement while seeking the goal of a just, responsive and inclusive society" (Evangelii Gaudium, 239). Peace will be lasting in the measure that we arm our children with the weapons of dialogue, that we teach them to fight the good fight of encounter and negotiation. In this way, we will bequeath to them a culture capable of devising strategies of life, not death, and of inclusion, not exclusion.

This culture of dialogue should be an integral part of the education imparted in our schools, cutting across disciplinary lines and helping to give young people the tools needed to settle conflicts differently than we are accustomed to do. Today we urgently need to build "coalitions" that are not only military and economic, but cultural, educational, philosophical and religious. Coalitions that can make clear that, behind many conflicts, there is often in play the power of economic groups. Coalitions capable of defending people from being exploited for improper ends. Let us arm our people with the culture of dialogue and encounter.[1]

1. MISSION INVOLVES 'GOING OUT'

In his Easter message for 2020 Australian Catholic bishop, Vincent Long, draws on an image that Pope Francis also drew on from the book of Revelation – that of Jesus knocking on the door and seeking entrance. The problem is, as Pope Francis interprets the situation vis-à-vis the Church, that Jesus is already on the inside of the Church wanting the door opened so that he can get out![2] Bishop Long makes the point that today we meet the risen Christ beyond the boundaries of our individual and collective imaginal horizons when we engage in common cause with others in the service of those who are marginalised. This means going out to meet people where they are, not where we might want them to be.

Finding common cause requires dialogue in which we come to understand the person or group who is 'other' from within the limits imposed by their worldview and also our own. This task has both a cultural and a faith dimension.[3] Introducing students to the practice of dialogue is, therefore, an important cultural and also religious goal, since dialogue is an essential mode of engagement in pursuing the Church's mission and in building a cohesive society. In practising dialogue, it has become obvious to people of good will that they are entering an area that challenges and enriches their understanding and living out of their faith. And they are also entering an area where they will be improving the quality of civic and cultural life.

In this chapter we examine two important initiatives that seek to develop this understanding in the context of schooling, and explore their implications for pedagogy in Catholic schools. The first is an educational initiative mounted by the Tony Blair Institute for Global Change. This initiative was set up to promote intercultural dialogue as a pedagogical imperative in all schools.[4] The second is an educational initiative jointly

---

1 Pope Francis' speech on receiving the Charlemagne prize, 6 May 2016. http://www.vatican.va/content/francesco/en/speeches/2016/may/documents/papa-francesco_20160506_premio-carlo-magno.html
2 Vincent Long, Easter Message 2020, available at https://youtu.be/kK2nMi98fzs
3 Even today, some societies do not have such a clear separation of faith and culture as we have in the West.
4 The Congregation for Catholic Education envisages Catholic schools as centres for intercultural living and learning in its 2013 document, *Educating to Intercultural Dialogue in Catholic Schools*, http://www.vatican.va/roman_curia/congregations/ccatheduc/documents/rc_con_ccatheduc_doc_20131028_dialogo-interculturale_en.htmlLiving in Harmony for a Civilization of Love.

mounted by Katholieke Universiteit Leuven (KUL) and the Catholic Education Commission of Victoria (CECV) to promote dialogue as an essential goal in Religious Education and in the reformulation of the mission of contemporary Catholic schools in Australia. Dialogue links these two important endeavours.

2. DIALOGUE IN ACADEMIC DISCOURSE

Dialogue has become an important topic in many areas of study. Here we briefly consider three areas: education, philosophy and Catholic theology.

2.1 Dialogue in educational discourse

Schools provide an important context in which important civic and religious goals can be achieved. 'Dialogue', understood as a pedagogical approach, provides the 'how' in achieving these goals.

The *Tony Blair Institute for Global Change* (TBIGC) sums up the matter well in introducing its resource for promoting dialogue in schools, *Essentials of Dialogue*:[5]

> *All around the globe, education systems are struggling to prepare young people for the complex realities of a profoundly interconnected world. While many education systems are concentrating even harder on centralised curricula and standardised testing, there is a strong consensus that education should also give young people the soft skills that they need to make sense of, and play an active part in, a globalised society that is more closely integrated and interdependent than ever before.*
>
> *More than any other generation in human history, the students that we educate today will live alongside, work with, and relate to, peers with the widest possible range of cultural backgrounds, beliefs, values and perspectives. It is imperative that we give them the tools to build societies that welcome diversity rather than fearing it, that encourage an open-minded approach to the other, rather than the cultivation of prejudice, ones that include rather than exclude. The alternatives are too terrible to contemplate. Every day we see news reports that indicate what happens as a direct result of people rejecting diversity, celebrating intolerance, and wishing to impose their monolithic vision of reality upon others. We all know that we want to help students approach the diversity of the world in an open-minded way, but we want straightforward and simple classroom activities that can help us*

---

5 Tony Blair Institute for Global Change, *Essentials of Dialogue*, 2017. This 92-page resource can be downloaded from the https://exchange.youthrex.com/report/essentials-dialogue-guidance-and-activities-teaching-and-practising-dialogue-young-people

to achieve this – without disrupting our need to deliver the kinds of results that our curriculum, and our students' parents, demand.

The rapid growth in communications technology is one of the key drivers of this change, and it is important to reflect upon the fact that our students are almost certainly already participating in global discussions, through their access to social media. At best, young people are being subjected to poor examples of how to interact online, and at worst, we know that a great deal of radicalisation into violent extremism takes place online.[6]

Dialogue also features in the growing literature on *social-emotional learning* in the US and Canada[7] and in the *social pedagogy*[8] movements in Europe.

The quote above could, with little change, be applied to the Catholic Church in Australia that is becoming more multi-cultural in both its lay and clerical membership, which makes *dialogue within the Church* a necessary process in determining its future.[9]

2.2 Dialogue in philosophic discourse

In philosophic discourse, dialogue is seen as an indispensable element in promoting the *inter-subjective* learning that now characterises many of the 'human sciences'. The axiom here is that *you cannot validly treat human beings, who are subjects, as if they were objects*. The so-called 'hard sciences' study objects. An object is not free to respond to the same stimulus in a different way, whereas a 'subject' can. Subjects can exercise agency!

This axiom first became obvious in the field of anthropology. As we have already noted, early anthropologists studied the culture of those they saw as 'primitive' peoples. They made detailed observations (assumed to be 'scientific') of the surface dimensions of the cultures they were studying such as observable customs, patterns of relationship and social interaction, rituals associated with life-transitions, modes of communication, health care and governance. Very few mastered the language of people they studied. They then returned home and wrote up reports. What soon became clear is that, while their reports may have covered the 'what' of a culture

---

6 Ibid, 7.
7 See, for instance, the *SEL Field Guide* (2014) that can be downloaded from the URL: https://www.selpractices.org/about. While *Essentials of Dialogue* is mainly targeted at senior primary and junior secondary students, the SEL field Guide is targeted at teachers working with adolescents. The Guide explores how out-of-class activities can be used to generate social and emotional learning. Its *standards* and *teacher practices* can also be applied in the classroom.
8 For an introduction to social pedagogy see M.K Smith, *Social pedagogy: the development of theory and practice,* available at http://infed.org/mobi/social-pedagogy-the-development-of-theory-and-practice/
9 The *Plenary 2020* process is an attempt by Church leaders in Australia to engage in a form of dialogue with the membership of the Catholic Church community. At the time of writing the process has been temporarily derailed by the COVID-19 pandemic.

accurately, this had to be *interpreted* to get to the 'why'. Here, anthropologists encountered a hermeneutical roadblock. The researchers made the mistake of interpreting another culture from within the worldview of their own culture, and not that of the people they studied. It is *only in dialogue between 'insiders' and 'outsiders'* that the deeper elements of a culture (or any other human phenomena) are revealed.

The outsider needs to ask questions about what he or she has observed. Very often, because insiders take their culture for granted, they have difficulty explaining why things are the way they are, or even in knowing how to frame the right questions. However, since culture is 'the possession of a people' (Luzbetak)[10], insiders have access to collective resources that enable them to come up with answers. It is only when the insider and outsider enter into *serious dialogue* that the deeper dimensions of a culture are revealed. These include the values and cultural myths that give *meaning* to what is happening on the surface.

The path to learning through *serious dialogue* is *inter-subjective,* rather than *objective*.[11] This form of learning now applies in many areas of human endeavour, including the study of religions. *Dialogue provides an essential pathway to meaning* in intercultural and interreligious learning.

2.3 Dialogue in theological discourse

In the theological tradition 'dialogue' has a recent history. It entered official Catholic teaching only in 1964 when, during the Second Vatican Council, Pope Paul VI called for a 'dialogue with the modern world', a world in which he included not only the societies and cultures of, or connected with Europe, but also the new emerging nations with their various cultures and religions.[12] He established the Secretariat for Non-Christians[13] that same year to work through what dialogue with other religions might involve. For the next two decades, the Catholic Church's understanding of dialogue was

---

10 Luzbetak, 156–9.
11 In many instances early anthropologists did not speak the language of the 'primitive' people they visited. And the language typically did not have a written form and could not be studied in the usual way. One of the services missionaries performed for many indigenous peoples was to record their languages and give them a written form. A spectacular example of this was Alexandre de Rhodes SJ who worked in Vietnam in the 17th century (Peter Phan, *Mission and Catechesis: Alexandre de Rhodes & Inculturation in Seventeenth-Century Vietnam*. Maryknoll N.Y: Orbis, 2005). De Rhodes gave the local language an alphabetical form quite distinct from the character form used in China. To this day it retains that form. An example closer to home is the work of the Australian Sisters of St Joseph recording Tetum, the indigenous language of East Timor that had been banned during the Indonesian occupation (Margaret Press & Susan Connelly, *Mary MacKillop East Timor 1994–2006*. St Mary's: MMI, 2007). Without a written language a people lacks a literature, and has only an oral memory which tends to become distorted over time. Language is essential to all forms of meaning-making and is a principal marker of collective identity.
12 Pope Paul VI, *Ecclesiam Suam*, 2–15.
13 Renamed the Pontifical Council for Inter-Religious Dialogue by Pope John Paul II in June 1988.

formed principally in the context of inter-religious and interfaith dialogue (although in Europe and Latin America, the possibility of Christian-Marxist dialogue was also explored.)

The Protestant approach was somewhat different. A key figure here was missiologist Lesslie Newbigin[14] whose theological orientation was shaped by his cross-cultural missionary experience. He found that the UK he returned to from India in the 1970s was essentially a 'pagan' country in which many Christians had succumbed to the false interpretation of Christianity that characterised Enlightenment thinking. In his writings Newbigin sought to explain what was happening and what could be done to resist the developments that had occurred.

Newbigin saw a major problem in the way in which knowledge had come to be constructed in Western societies with 'facts' pitted against 'values'. The prevailing 'orthodoxy' was that facts were a *matter of science* and could be included in public knowledge. Values on the other hand were a *matter of opinion* and so belonged to the private sphere, and thus were to be excluded from the public square, a position Christians could not accept. A consequence of this construction of public knowledge was that religion was assigned to the private sphere. Returning home after long exposure to a totally different culture, Newbigin, through his many books, reset important parameters for dialogue between faith and culture in the West. In doing so he contributed to the emergence of a postsecular worldview.[15]

3. PERSPECTIVES ON DIALOGUE

Dialogue can be understood from a number of perspectives. It can be understood as a communal endeavour, for example, or as a personal endeavour. For many people 'dialogue' equates with 'scripted conversation' as happens in a play or TV series. Actors have a 'dialogue coach' to ensure they get their lines right. In this perspective dialogue *is a matter of words*.

As Catholic Church leaders have reflected on the significance of dialogue, particularly in the inter-religious context, they have come to realise that dialogue can take *a number of forms* and is an essential element in the Church's mission. Normative Catholic teaching, particularly as developed by Pope John Paul II, recognises four forms of dialogue:

---

14 Newbigin was a Scottish Presbyterian minister who, with his new wife, went as a missionary to India in 1934. He did much to bring Christian groups together, leading to his appointment as bishop of South India. His ecumenical work took him to Geneva to take up a senior position with the World Council of Churches. Following this appointment, he returned to India, and subsequently retired to the UK in 1975.

15 His most important books include: *The Gospel in a Pluralist Society*, SPCK/Eerdmans/WCC, 1989; *Foolishness to the Greeks: Gospel and Western Culture*, Eerdmans/SPCK, 1986; and *Truth to Tell: The Gospel as Public Truth*, SPCK, 1991.

- **Dialogue of life** *happens when people from different faith traditions live together as neighbours and in peace.*
- **Dialogue of action** *happens when people from different backgrounds work together to achieve some common purpose, for example to achieve some social good such as action for justice or the education of a child.*
- **Dialogue of theological exchange** *occurs when people seek to understand the religious meaning other traditions have for their participants and appreciate the richness embedded in these traditions.*
- **Dialogue of religious experience** *happens when people rooted in their own tradition share the spiritual riches of that tradition with others in their common search for God, and in prayer.*[16]

In this perspective dialogue is not just a matter of words; it is a means of *encountering another person or group at a deep human level*. The first two forms of dialogue noted above set conditions that make it possible for the latter forms to occur successfully. Being able to live together and work together meaningfully is a condition for exploring deeper life issues. This observation has important pedagogical implications for a Catholic school drawing students from a range of religious backgrounds.

In the classroom only some forms of interpersonal communication constitute dialogue. For example, discussion is not dialogue. Here the aim is to clarify an understanding. Debate is not dialogue. A debate pits one person against another in a win-lose situation. Nor is deliberation dialogue – here the aim is to build consensus.

4. ESSENTIALS OF DIALOGUE (2014)

The Tony Blair Institute for Global Change (TBIGC), mentioned above, provides an important and accessible resource for understanding dialogue and its pedagogical implications. The Institute was established by the former Prime Minister of the UK with a view to promoting greater understanding and social progress in our globalised world. In *Essentials of Dialogue*, TBIGC refers to dialogue in terms of encounter and the process of understanding:

> [In an] *encounter with those who might have different opinions, values and beliefs to my own, dialogue is the process by which I come to understand the*

---

16 Pope John Paul II, *Redemptoris Missio*, 1990, 57;
   http://www.vatican.va/content/john-paul-ii/en/encyclicals/documents/hf_jp-ii_enc_07121990_redemptoris-missio.html
   and the Pontifical Council for Interreligious Dialogue, *Dialogue and Proclamation*, 1991, 42. http://www.vatican.va/roman_curia/pontifical_councils/interelg/documents/rc_pc_interelg_doc_19051991_dialogue-and-proclamatio_en.html.

other's lives, values and beliefs better, and others come to understand my life, values and beliefs.[17]

Expanding on this understanding the TBIGC observes:

Through this mutual interchange students not only grow in their direct understanding of their own community, and the other individual, but they also develop an open mindset; learning to embrace diversity as a positive facet of contemporary global society. Participation in dialogue drives students to acquire and practise higher level thinking skills and to honestly and respectfully engage with a range of viewpoints. Through direct encounters with those who are different to themselves, students are empowered to overcome prejudice, and are armoured against those (such as religious extremists) whose narrative seeks to divide the world into a simple dichotomy of 'Us/Good and Them/Bad'. In addition, students acquire a range of skills, while simultaneously developing greater confidence and self-esteem as their opinions are engaged with respectfully by their interlocutors.[18]

Dialogue involves understanding the person or group who is 'other' *from within their frame of reference* rather than imposing our frame of reference on them. Doing this avoids making the same mistake as the early anthropologists.

Authentic dialogue must meet two basic conditions:

- *We acknowledge that we see the world from a particular perspective, and this leads us to take a particular stance towards it. At the same time, we recognise that 'the other' is similarly placed, and we are willing to establish what his or her view or stance is, and to face up to the questions this raises for us.*
- *We are willing to make the imaginative leap necessary to understand the world from within the other's worldview and stance.*

This requires the development of a number of skills, particularly the ability to listen to the other and to understand the world from within his or her perspective. In the classroom an important aspect of the teacher's role is *to facilitate real dialogue.*

With this approach, the teacher often acts in the role of facilitator, prompting and clarifying questions, and much agency is given to pupils, who are regarded as collaborators in teaching and learning. The approach was found to raise children's self-esteem, to provide opportunities for developing

---

17 Tony Blair Institute for Global Change Essentials of Dialogue, 2014, 7.
    https://www.tes.com/teaching-resource/the-essentials-of-dialogue-11604195
18 Ibid.

critical skills, to enable under-achievers to express themselves, and to create a climate of moral seriousness. Children were also helped to engage with ideas and concepts from different religious traditions, to be reflective about their contributions and to justify their own opinions. They also discussed how they arrived at their conclusions and were encouraged to recognize the possibility of alternative viewpoints and to be open to the arguments of others.[19]

Teachers have a responsibility *to establish the conditions in which dialogue can take place safely.* This means laying out the basic ground rules and expectations for dialogue to occur. *Students need to have worked together on common projects to create the conditions of trust needed for dialogue to become possible.*

The TBIGC sets out its guidelines for dialogue in question form:

- *How welcoming is the classroom to all students?*
- *Do wall displays reflect the diversity of your group?*
- *What is the seating arrangement?*
- *Does it encourage dialogue or are students in rows where they cannot see one another easily?*
- *Where does the teacher stand, sit or move?*
- *How do students show they want to speak?*
- *How do the students relate to one another?*
- *What activities are built into lessons that encourage collaboration rather than competition?*
- *How does the teacher deal with instances of disrespect and intolerance?*
- *Do these instances involve the participation of the other students exploring how the group feels when these instances of disrespect happen?*
- *How can the teacher draw in students who are reluctant to take part in dialogue?*
- *How do students know they are valued?*
- *Are different perspectives encouraged?*
- *Are all voices heard?*
- *Do students speak from the 'I' perspective sharing their own thoughts and experiences, instead of generalising?*[20]

The Institute goes on to note that:

It is unrealistic to expect any classroom to be an entirely 'safe' space for all students all of the time. Providing opportunities for student dialogue inevitably holds some elements of risk; these can be minimised through

---

19   Ibid,10. There may be differences in the way the word is used in everyday discussion and in an academic sense. In the above passage, Professor Robert Jackson is explaining the impact of dialogue in the classroom.
20   Ibid,10

suitable preparation and training ... Like all skills and competencies these will improve through practice.[21]

There are a number of important **process values** at stake in dialogue. The first is *trust*. Students will enter into the dialogue only when they trust the teacher as facilitator. The second is being able to *listen to others non-judgmentally* and become *active listeners*. A final precondition is *readiness*.

The TBIGC's *Dialogue Checklist* includes the following *Readiness Checklist*:

LISTENING
- *My students show respectful and attentive body language when in dialogue with others.*
- *My students can process what they hear to ask questions that clarify, challenge and seek a deeper understanding*
- *They can focus on the 'other' in the dialogue without being distracted by the teacher, their peers or others.*
- *My students listen carefully, process and reflect before speaking again, in order to avoid spontaneous responses that might be ill-thought through.*

RESPONDING
- *My students can ask questions that are open-ended and that seek meaning and significance.*
- *My students can ask questions formed by what they hear from others to further their understanding.*
- *They are able to ask questions that explore meaning and significance.*
- *They can articulate how they feel on hearing something from someone else.*
- *They can show that they value the ideas, experiences and beliefs of others even when they do not agree with them.*
- *They are able to respond empathetically to others.*
- *They can challenge others in the dialogue in a way that is respectful and open.*

REFLECTING
- *My students are able to identify the major influences on their lives, behaviour, beliefs and thinking.*
- *My students are able to place themselves in the local, national and global communities and understand how they contribute to these groups.*
- *They can find differences as well as similarities between their own lives, values and beliefs and those of others.*
- *They can articulate clearly what they have learned about the 'other'*

---

21 Ibid.

through their dialogue with them, focusing on specific points.
- *They are able to reflect on their own skills of dialogue (and those of others) and consider how these could be improved in the future.*
- *They can explain how their learning through dialogue may impact their behaviour or choices in the future.*[22]

The above serves not only as a readiness checklist, but also as an assessment tool for measuring progress.

In setting up the dialogue process in the classroom, the TBIGC's recommendation is that the teacher *starts with non-contentious subjects* and moves into more sensitive areas. This occurs as confidence in the process and trust among the group builds. In dialogue the teacher is not above the fray, but learns with the students. *Dialogue is a journey best made together.*

The teacher's skills as facilitator play an important role in whether or not this journey happens successfully. The TBIGC sets out these skills in question form as follows:

- *Are you able to be impartial on the topic? Be aware of your own pre-formed assumptions on the issue?*
- *How will you ensure students suspend judgment/start with an open mind?*
- *What are your techniques for ensuring that all feel they have a voice in the dialogue and that it is not hijacked by a few?*
- *How are you ensuring students feel safe enough to take risks?*
- *How can you model listening deeply and engaging in the dialogue?*
- *Are you encouraging responses to what is said as opposed to allowing the dialogue to become a Q&A session?*
- *How do you encourage students to show empathy towards one another?*
- *Are you ensuring that students are speaking about themselves and not on behalf of others?*
- *How do you encourage students to bring their own experiences to the dialogue?*
- *How will you measure the effectiveness of the activity?*
- *Do you have strategies to help students to recognise assumptions in their comments and/or questions and help them to rephrase in a less prejudicial way?*
- *Do you ensure that reference to people or groups not represented in the dialogue is fair?*[23]

---

22 Ibid, 26.
23 Ibid, 11.

Essentials of Dialogue provides teachers with the resources needed to be effective as facilitators of dialogue.

Many teachers of Religious Education are already well equipped for this role. The strength of this publication is its eminent practicality for both student and teacher. As the above outline makes clear, dialogue involves the development of important 'deep learning skills' that are vitally important in enabling 'difference' to be understood and valued. This is a significant step not only in building social cohesion within schools, but also in helping students acquire a sense of membership in the world as it is.

In a globalising world, the Church's capacity to enter into respectful dialogue with people who see the world differently from itself, is an important skill – a skill to be used in the promotion and understanding of its mission.

5. DIALOGUE AND INTERPERSONAL COMPETENCIES

In Part B, we explored the contribution anthropology makes to the understanding of pedagogical choices in Catholic schools. From anthropology we draw the concepts of worldview and culture and the need to bring different worldviews into conversation. We highlighted the inter-subjective nature of some forms of human learning and offered dialogue as a pedagogical strategy for learning from and with others.

To engage in dialogue is to develop a range of 'interpersonal skills' that are essential in our society and church in enabling groups, drawn from different backgrounds, to understand each other and to work together constructively for the common good. This is a matter of great concern to all educators, particularly in a society that puts significant emphasis on the 'hard skills' associated with mastering content and passing exams, sometimes to the detriment of other essential goals. These goals should not be a matter of either/or, but rather both/and. However, in our culture hard skills draw most resources, whereas the skills that enable people to live together with a degree of contentment tend to be relatively neglected, with predictable results.

The matters raised above have significance for how the mission of a school is construed, how success is measured, and the important place a dialogical pedagogy has within the school's mission.

6. DIALOGUE IN RELIGIOUS EDUCATION

6.1 Hermeneutical-Communicative model of Religious Education

The *Enhancing Catholic School Identity* (ESCI) project places emphasis on the Hermeneutical-Communicative (HC) model in teaching Religious Education.[24] This model of Religious Education developed by Didier Pollefeyt and Herman Lombaerts from KUL has been trialled in Catholic schools in Flanders where in some schools up to 90% of students are of Muslim faith.[25] Context has played a major role in the development of the model.

The HC model is an important component, together with the theology of Lieven Bove and other KUL scholars, in the development of the *Enhancing Catholic School Identity* (ECSI) project, jointly sponsored by KUL's Faculty of Theology and Religious Studies and the Catholic Education Commission of Victoria (CECV).[26] ECSI is now used in many dioceses in Australia, and in several other countries, as a means for reimagining and reframing the task of Catholic schooling in a postsecular cultural context. The ECSI project was designed as part of the *pastoral response* by the Catholic Church in Flanders to the demands of a changed cultural context that has impacted negatively on all faith communities in Europe over recent decades. The project is one outcome of extensive research carried out, often as empirical studies, by academics from universities across Western Europe. The HC model of Religious Education and ECSI are enduring results of this wider pastoral effort.[27]

The HC model is predicated on the notion that inter-religious dialogue is important in the formation of a religious identity, and that the task of Religious Education is to help young people to form an identity that respects *the particularity of the religious tradition into which they are born*. (It is not designed to 'convert' them from one tradition to another). The model acknowledges

---

24 Herman Lombaerts and Didier Pollefeyt, 'The Emergence of Hermeneutics in Religious Education Theories: An Overview', in H. Lombaerts and D. Pollefeyt (eds), *Hermeneutics and Religious Education*. Leuven University Press, 2004, 1–56.
25 Belgium Catholic schools are, in the main, what in Australia we call state schools. Teachers are paid by the state. All Catholic schools are open to students living in the local area, irrespective of their religion. The Catholic Education Office is a significant player in curriculum development since about 80% of schools in Flanders are 'Catholic'. However, it has a very limited role in the governance of Catholic schools.
26 It is beyond the scope of this book to go into detail about the technical side of the ECSI project which uses empirical data to assess the situation of individual schools. The ECSI project cumulates this data across school systems to create a form of statistical normativity that enables schools to see their situation in the context of the system to which they belong. Technical details can be readily tracked down on the internet via resources created by KUL for this purpose.
27 Much of this research is reported in academic journals in the field of Practical Theology published by KUL.

the fact that some students come from backgrounds in which there is no religious tradition at all. However, even here there will be a worldview playing in the background.

The teacher plays three roles in the HC model of Religious Education:

- **expert** in the Catholic tradition
- **witness** to the Catholic tradition
- **moderator of dialogue** between religious traditions.[28]

Pollefeyt set out the aim of the HC model as follows:

> ... to make students aware of the plurality of views of life, philosophies, ideologies and religions that characterise today's reality – both for the individual and the community – and to try to influence our interpretation of reality.[29]

In other words, to help students develop and articulate a coherent worldview.

The approach implicitly acknowledges a reality identified by Dillon working in the US context – that today Catholics exercise *personal interpretive authority* in matters of religion. She also makes the case that since the Second Vatican Council, substantive validation for doing this can be found in Catholic teaching.[30] It is through dialogue, including with the normative teaching of the Church, that a necessary corrective is applied that resists subjectivism (my way is 'the way') on the one hand, and relativism (all ways are equally valid) on the other.

The HC model is not without its critics. Questions are sometimes raised about the capacity of Religious Education teachers to moderate dialogue as envisaged by the model. Whether they qualify as 'experts' in the Catholic tradition has been challenged. The concern expressed is that the approach of the HC model will promote relativism. Others argue that the context for Religious Education in Australia is quite different from that in Flanders and so the case for adopting the HC model here is weakened. It has also been argued that asking students who do not have a sufficient grasp of their own religious tradition to enter into an intelligent dialogue with those belonging to a different tradition is foolhardy.

---

28 See Herman Lombaerts & Didier Pollefeyt, *Hermeneutics and Religious Education*. Leuven: Leuven University Press, 2004.
29 Didier Pollefeyt, 'Lustre of Life: The Hermeneutical-Communicative model of Religious Education' in *CEO Brisbane International Speaker Series*: 2013, available at URL https://ceo.brisbane.edu.au/formationleadership/identity/Documents/CI%20Readings/ISS_Pollefeyt_articles_book.pdf.
30 See Michelle Dillon, *Post secular Catholicism: relevance and renewal*. New York: Oxford University Press, 2018, 6.

At present the research base supporting the HC approach has not been sufficiently developed in this country to refute some of these objections. While it is obvious that the context here clearly differs from that of Flanders, the reality of a globalised world presents every society and educational authority with the challenge to improve intercultural and interreligious forms of learning, and this obviously includes Australia. In the case of Christian educators, there is the added imperative of constructing a sustainable and sustaining future for all of God's children, as each Catholic school community seeks to actualise aspects of Jesus' unifying vision of the Kingdom of God.

6.2 'Recontextualisation' within ECSI

The ECSI approach to Catholic schooling advocates the need for the Catholic faith to be 'recontextualised' to remain meaningful for students growing up in a postsecular world.

Recontextualisation is a concept promoted by KUL theologian Lieven Boeve, whose thinking is influenced by that of influential Belgian theologian Edward Schillebeeckx, as well as the postmodern philosopher and critic Jean-Francois Lyotard.[31] Boeve's contention is that, whenever faith crosses major cultural boundaries, it needs to be reformulated to be meaningful for people who think in a different frame of reference. In a particular culture, as history evolves, cultures also change. Forms of cultural and religious expression that were once meaningful lose their interpretive power. New forms of expression need to be developed that have interpretive power in the new context. The message of faith that was once contextualised in a different era, now needs to be 'recontextualised' if it is to be meaningful in a new context.[32]

Boeve also takes up Lyotard's critique of modern 'master narratives' as 'closed' and raises the question of whether, in recontextualising faith for a postsecular era, this needs to be done as an 'open' or a 'closed' story. Lyotard's critique of the master-narratives of modernity (communism, fascism and capitalism) is that they are all closed stories that have no place for people who do not support the dominant ideology – for those who are 'different'. Lyotard interprets Christianity as a closed story as well. Boeve argues that while this fits much of the historical evidence, it is not necessary that it be

---

31 Lieven Boeve, *Systematic Theology Truth and History: Recontextualisation* paper at NOSTER Colloquium 2008. Schillebeeckx himself was influenced in this matter by Hans-Georg Gadamer. https://www.kuleuven.be/thomas/uploads/file/lieven-boeve/Lieven-Boeve_Systematic-Theology-Truth-and-History-Recontextualisation.pdf

32 An enduring problem for all Christian denominations, including Roman Catholic, has been to assume that the formulation of Christian faith worked out over centuries in Europe is its definitive historical expression.

so. Jesus' message of the reign of God suggests that *God's mission is incomplete in human history*. As human needs and conceptions of human flourishing change, so too does the mission of the Church in response. In this sense the Christian story is better understood as an open story, and it is only in dialogue with others that a fuller understanding of this story will emerge. The story is *necessarily* 'open' because the Kingdom of God is incomplete in human history.

The history of Western Christianity illustrates that the process of recontextualisation began when Paul took the message of Jesus, contextualised as it was in Jewish culture, and recontextualised it for his Greek-speaking audiences. The process has happened several times across the history of Christianity. A major challenge for Church members in understanding the Catholic faith is the tendency to *take a particular contextualisation of faith as its definitive expression*. This confusion often sits behind the conservative-liberal divide within the Catholic community over matters such as 'truth' and 'law'.

Major recontextualisations of faith in Church history have been associated with:

- *important cultural shifts in the West*
- *important theological shifts in the way the Church has come to understand its mission.*

Both have created the need for faith to be reinterpreted if it is to remain meaningful as people begin to think within the new frame of reference.

Examples of recontextualisation occurred in the patristic period, in the late medieval period, following the Reformation, and, more recently, when the bishops assembled at Vatican II endeavoured to take the faith tradition as formulated during the Counter-Reformation and re-contextualise it to be more meaningful for people living in the postsecular world. Boeve interprets the present time as another example of a major cultural shift.

For Pollefeyt and Bouwens, Boeve's former colleagues at KUL, re-contextualisation is a major educational challenge now facing Catholic educators. They see recontextualisation happening in the context of dialogue:

> However, it is the theological (epistemological) conviction of this type of Dialogue School that the truth of Catholicism is not fixed and cannot a priori be known with certainty. The truth must rather be discovered and made true in lives actually lived through a continual process of interpretation. Believers are challenged to search for new insights into what it means to be Catholic in the midst of the present context, and to do so creatively, innovatively, and

with an open mind. Recontextualising Dialogue Schools are constantly in search of new ways to express and live the gospel. They are always looking for new ways to make it true today. When we do this, we stand with one foot in the Catholic tradition and the other in an unwritten future. The outcome of this search is uncertain, and it is possible that some valuable things from the past will disappear into the background. Nevertheless, we satisfy ourselves with new discoveries, and hope that the Holy Spirit accompanies us on the journey.

As the world evolves and changes, so do the idea of what it means to be Christian in this world and the way the original evangelical inspiration is given a concrete form. Catholic faith must change her profile and 're-contextualise' herself as she enters each new era. The process of re-contextualisation began already in the earliest days of Christianity, and it is now up to us to carry on this tradition in the 21st century. The Catholic tradition has always been developing and renewing itself in a great variety of ways, and it must keep doing this today. Whenever God walks beside us on this path, new revelations come forth, and the faith tradition further unfolds itself.[33]

6.3 ECSI – unresolved issues

Recontextualisation: how do we do it?

While the need for recontextualisation seems clear, the unresolved question facing Catholic educators is: 'How do we do it?' given that the cultural and religious landscapes are so confused. Furthermore, many Catholics, including teachers in Catholic schools, now belong in one or more of the modern, postmodern, and postsecular camps, some individuals drawing on all three! Lacking a coherent worldview, they fail to engage in meaningful dialogue about faith issues. Many parents who send their children to Catholic schools also lack a coherent worldview because of the epistemological confusion that now exists. Leaders face a difficult task not only in understanding the situation but also in knowing where to start in addressing it!

The ECSI project has introduced a new frame of reference for analysing the context in which Catholic schooling now functions. It also provides teachers with a form of discourse to discuss the situation and the challenges it poses. However, as noted above, the project also contains a number of

---

[33] Didier Pollefeyt & Jan Bouwens, 'Dialogue as the Future', Catholic Education Office, Brisbane: *International Speaker Series,* 2013 available at
https://www.bne.catholic.edu.au/formationandleadership/identity/Documents/CI%20 Readings/Pollefeyt%20and%20Bouwens%20-%20Dialogue%20as%20the%20Future%20 (May%202013).pdf

unresolved questions that will have to be addressed in future years if it is to deliver on its significant potential. It is likely that empirical research currently underway will provide answers to some, if not all, of these questions.

ECSI offers a way forward that casts the pedagogical relationship in Catholic schools in a new light, and with this, the role of the Catholic educator.

Mission and Identity

ECSI uses 'identity' as a major category in discussing the future of Catholic schooling. The term is interpreted in both a personal sense – the religious identity formation of students – and a corporate sense – the identity of Catholic organisations as particularly 'Catholic'. The project's promoters seem to eschew the use of the word 'mission' because of the negative connotations it carries in Belgium. In this country, 'mission' is associated with the grim failures of evangelisation in Rwanda for which the Catholic Church is Belgium carries some culpability. This is to confuse 'missions' with 'mission'. In the view of this book's author's, ECSI is a serious missional endeavour in its conception and pastoral intent.

As we have noted previously, dialogue is a *mode of mission* that can take many forms in response to human needs, both temporal and spiritual. No matter what form mission takes, those engaged in it have to seek *dialogue partners* in our multi-cultural, multi-faith and globalising world. They must be able to work with others to achieve common goals. This means they have to be able to understand how potential partners see the world and how this may differ from their own way of seeing it. And they need to be able to negotiate the difference. This is both an educational task and an expression of mission in a globalised world. As we have argued elsewhere 'Catholic' is what 'Catholic' does.[34] The issue of identity cannot be separated meaningfully from the issue of mission. This is a lacuna that Australian educators need to address in further developing the ECSI model, the meaning of re-contextualising faith in the Australian context, and the HC approach to Religious Education.

In this chapter we have explored the importance of dialogue in both an educational and a theological context. In exploring its relevance to the work of Catholic educators, to their pedagogical practice in schools, and to the mission of the Church, we underline the fact that all three are intimately related.

---

34 Jim and Therese D'Orsa, *Educator's Guide to Mission in Practice*. Mulgrave: Vaughan Publishing, 2019.

Part E
PEDAGOGIES FOR THE KINGDOM

In this concluding chapter, we seek to bring the themes explored previously into a provisional synthesis, and link this back to the understanding of a Catholic pedagogy, as outlined in Chapter 1.

25

TRANSFORMING POSSIBILITIES: PEDAGOGIES FOR THE KINGDOM

> *... and He said to them, 'Therefore every scribe who has been trained for the Kingdom of heaven is like the master of the household who brings out of his treasure what is new and what is old' (Matt 13:52).*

The purpose of this concluding chapter is not to summarise what has already been written previously. Rather, by bringing the main themes of the book into a coherent account, we are attempting to highlight what, from long experience, we see to be essential perspectives in developing the pedagogical orientation of a *Catholic* school community operating in the postsecular context.

In seeking to contribute to a conversation about pedagogy in terms of Catholic schooling, we have explored the topic from a number of perspectives. Our purpose in doing this was to question some of the taken-for-granted assumptions on which current pedagogical ideologies depend, and to acknowledge the contributions of important scholars, so as to open up fruitful conversation about pedagogy broadly conceived. Our ultimate focus is the young person, made in the image and likeness of God, capable of life-enhancing hope, and carrying great potential.

1. ETHICS: STARTING POINT FOR A CONVERSATION ABOUT PEDAGOGY

The English-speaking world interprets pedagogy largely in *instrumental and strategic terms* – what teachers do to promote learning among students in the classroom. This understanding contrasts with that developed in Europe where, as Van Manen suggests, pedagogy is often thought of in a different way, in terms of 'the good' pursued in the special relationship that exists between an adult and a child in the context of learning. This relationship is bounded by ethical considerations that flow from the power imbalance existing between adult and child, and from the child's vulnerability as a learner.

Understood in this wider sense, pedagogy is associated not only with teaching, but also with parenting, counselling, welfare and any context where adults work with young people to promote their growth and development. In this tradition of pedagogy 'what works in the classroom' is subject-specific and known as *didactics*. That has not been our consideration in this work.

We take it as axiomatic that an ethical understanding of pedagogy as described above is a more helpful starting place than the pragmatic understanding commonly accepted in the English-speaking world. In the ethical understanding of pedagogy, the onus is on the teacher to do what is 'good' or life-enhancing by 'this child or this group of children' and to avoid what is not good or which is destructive. How teachers construe what is right and good for students is partly a matter of personal choice and partly determined by the culture in which such choices are made. The Catholic Church community has a particular understanding of 'the good' that is strongly anchored in the living faith tradition that has sponsored schools for generations.

Pedagogical decisions are often made in the hurly-burly of the classroom and are generally made pre-reflectively and 'on the run', so the background the teacher brings to the classroom will, in a significant way, shape any pedagogical decisions made 'on the spur of the moment'. Much of this background consists of the pre-suppositions that teachers hold about teaching, learning and how students develop. These pre-suppositions develop as a consequence of living in contemporary Western culture with all its ambiguities.

The world of teaching does not provide much time for reflecting on the often-unstated beliefs that underpin teaching practice. Being asked to view this practice though an ethical prism may seem quite challenging to some.

1.1 Doing 'good' by students: the silent language of witness

Many of the presuppositions teachers hold have been acquired unreflectively in growing up in a particular culture and going to school in that culture. Any critical exploration of pedagogy has to take into account that the teacher represents *a way of being in the world for students still in the process of trying to work out for themselves how to be in that world.*

The pedagogical relationship provides a unique context for witnessing how to be in the world. This is important to Catholic education, as to all education. All teachers are witnesses to a way of 'being in the world as an adult'. Long after students have forgotten what they were taught in English, Science, Maths, Religious Education and so on, they remember the example of teachers and the lessons conveyed though *the silent language of witness*. The 'good' that pedagogy seeks to achieve, and the 'not good' that it seeks to avoid, are proclaimed in this language.

1.2 Doing 'good' by students – the worldview of the teacher

'Worldview' is an important concept drawn from anthropology. As we noted in Chapter 6, it involves three interrelated elements:

- *what a person knows and believes*
- *what a person has come to value*
- *the sensibility a person brings to thinking through and acting on issues.*

Sensibility includes 'gut reactions' to people and events that result in a person taking a *characteristic stance* to what life presents.

A person's worldview is held partly within awareness and partly outside of awareness. In regard to the latter, worldview contains what in hermeneutics is called 'the fore-structure of knowing' – the assumptions on which teachers depend. This dependence occurs while navigating the intricacies posed by the 'pedagogical moments' teachers encounter 'on the run' in normal classroom practice.

In discussing pedagogy, it is important for teachers to bring to conscious awareness the assumptions that they employ in addressing these often fleeting 'moments', and to test their validity. Put another way, it is important for teachers to understand the contours of their personal worldview and how this plays out in pedagogical decision-making.

A person's worldview is constructed in the process of growing up in a particular culture and community. It is one by-product of being educated in a culture and contains the biases (good and bad) that come with the experience of growing up in that setting. However, the shaping of one's worldview continues throughout life, so that both teachers and students have lifelong opportunities to bring their worldview into closer alignment with that of Jesus. For Christians, Jesus remains the model of human living and of pedagogy.

Worldviews are sourced in both faith and culture. As we have noted previously, in contemporary Western society a person's worldview can be sourced in any one of three cultural traditions. Many students, for instance, view knowledge from a modern perspective where science provides the only measure of 'certain' knowledge.[1] Other students are more oriented to the postmodern 'hermeneutic of suspicion', encouraged by the media,

---

1 See Philip Hughes, *Putting Life Together: Findings from Australian Youth Spirituality Research*. Fairfield Christian Research Association, 2007, 124–5.

and also through the educational process. They regard all knowledge as suspect and do not see any source of knowledge – science, history, religion, economics etc. – as privileged. For them, truth is a relative concept. A third group find their home in a postsecular cultural understanding. Here faith is taken as a fact of life that needs to be dealt with. While institutional approaches to religion may be out of favour, holders of this perspective still have to address their spiritual needs, so their stance is often what Marcia names 'moratorium' – 'searching, but not committed'.[2]

In the context of living between eras, the cultural situation for young people in the West is both complex and confusing. Some commentators speak of a 'fragmentation of culture' by which they mean that societies in the West are losing social cohesion. This is happening as any consensus about 'the plan for living together peacefully' (culture) progressively breaks down and, with this, confusion reigns over what constitutes 'the common good'.

The worldview of culture provides people living in a particular society with their default frame of reference in making sense of life, that is, in determining what is personally meaningful. Once this becomes fragmented, meaning becomes problematic.

There seem to be two major ways in which this is happening at present. Some commentators interpret the situation in terms of the disintegration of the once coherent worldview of modernity as the assumptions on which it rests have become discredited by postmodern critics; others interpret the situation in terms of *'bricolage'* – of people constructing their worldview by selectively combining fragments of the modern, postmodern and postsecular worldviews, but in a way that lacks the coherence that each of these offers.[3]

What is true of students would also seem to be true of teachers. Many lack a coherent worldview, and this has a bearing on the assumptions they bring to teaching young people, as well as to the witness they offer about what it means to be in the world as an adult.

As already indicated, an important task of this book has been to bring some of these assumptions to awareness so that they are open to critique and, where necessary, to change.

1.3 'Doing 'good' by students in matters of faith

Since, as we have argued above, all teachers are witnesses to their students, they are seen as standing for 'something', whether or not they acknowledge

---

2 See discussion in Chapter 23.
3 The work of Ann Casson of Canterbury Christ Church University UK explores the situation of bricolage in regard to students in faith-based schools in pluralist societies, e.g. Ann Casson. *Fragmented Catholicity and Social Cohesion: Faith schools in a plural society.* Oxford: Peter Lang, 2012.

this to be the case. In the context of a Catholic school, the nature of this 'something' is of vital importance.

We have postulated that an indispensable goal for a Catholic school is to help students develop a personal worldview open to faith, that is, that the experience of Catholic schooling might help create in them the realisation that faith is important in making sense of their lives. This realisation comes through what they learn, but also through what they experience in being part of a community. For many students the school provides the only context in which this realisation is likely to occur.

Childhood is the age of promise par excellence for young people. Possibility lies at the heart of all pedagogy and is inherent in the pedagogical relationship, the ethical purpose of this being to nurture potential and enable growth. The inclusion of faith in how a person makes sense of their world expands enormously the range of possibilities for children attending Catholic schools. It is incumbent therefore on teachers to explore the assumptions that they hold about faith and its place in their own lives, whether they are Catholic or not. School and system leadership play a vital role here.

Our experience has been that many teachers have a personal worldview in which their understanding of faith seems frozen in time. In most cases this 'time' corresponds to their secondary education; in some it is their primary education. They understand 'faith' as a thing, rather than as a relationship and a process in which persons and communities are involved. They have little, if any, sense that faith continues to evolve as human experience, and with it human culture and history evolve.

Other teachers seem to take a 'foreclosure' stance to their religious identity. They simply accept what they have been taught about faith even though, when examined, they think it is nonsense. It is 'Catholic nonsense' that they are expected to teach, and so they get on with this because it is their job. They feel no impetus to put further questions to their interpretation of the faith tradition even though it has generated their employment.

Less common is a 'diffusion' stance to religious issues. Teachers adopting this stance see faith as irrelevant to their lives. They formulate what is 'good' for the young people they teach in purely secular terms, guided by the largely indiscriminate way religion is treated in the government-provided curriculum.

In our experience a significant number of teachers in Catholic schools adopt a 'moratorium' stance to religious identity and are seeking answers to what they see as complex issues, but provide little evidence of any obvious commitment to what they learn. We encounter a number of these in our postgraduate work with teachers.

1.4 Dealing with a secular sensibility

While having a designated leadership role in a Catholic school is an incentive to developing a stronger religious identity, such a role generally requires more than what people know and believe, and have come to value, prior to taking it on. The impediment seems to be that, growing up in a secular culture, many teachers have developed a *secular sensibility*. That is, their initial response to situations is to accept *cultural* norms unreflectively. It is only on further conscious reflection that faith understandings are brought into play. This problem seems endemic in Catholic organisations of all types at the present time. Dealing with this matter is a central issue in the formation of teachers and leaders.

Some overcome the impediment at a personal level by developing their prayer life. Others may seek spiritual accompaniment or mentoring. At the group level some leaders employ a theological reflection method such as *See-Judge-Act*[3] to discern together with colleagues how to act as persons of faith in complex situations.

The secular sensibility also impacts on how teachers respond to pedagogical moments in the classroom, a situation where reflection is a luxury. If teachers are not aware of the way in which their personal worldview plays out in pedagogical decision-making, then they compromise the quality of their witness to students, even though they may be devoutly Catholic. Developing self-awareness is therefore important. It is part of the challenge to personal growth that is inherent in working with the young.

1.5 Doing 'good' by students: developmental awareness

Teachers, like students, are in the process of personal development. This process is ongoing and has its predictable crises, as Erikson suggests. In dealing with developmental crises, teachers are as prone as adolescents to 'opting out' or endlessly exploring options without committing to any. However, teachers' crises relate to matters other than identity. They may, for instance, relate to intimacy (who do I want to be with, who wants to be with me), to making a worthwhile contribution (generativity), or to seeing one's life as purposeful and meaningful (integrity).

---

3   This is a method associated historically with the work of Cardinal Cardijn and the Young Christian Worker movement. It has been further developed as the current context requires. For example, Jim and Therese D'Orsa, 'Doing Theology: a Process of Meaning-making', in *Leading for Mission: Integrating Life, Culture and Faith in Catholic Education,* Mulgrave: Garratt Publishing, 2013, 232–243.

As teachers mature and resolve these crises, their understanding of the 'good' that a pedagogical relationship with students can achieve changes. This was brought home to Jim D'Orsa recently in attending the reunion of a class he taught in the late 1970s, many members of whom are now grandparents. The participants' memories of their teachers (and their relationship with them) were frozen in time. However, the teachers had clearly moved on in their understanding of what is important in pedagogy and the 'good' that it can achieve.

Teachers interpret the pedagogical relationship from where they themselves are in the cycle of human development. Young teachers will perceive it differently from people in their 40s and 50s, who often see life in terms of contributions to be made. Later in life teachers look back with satisfaction on a contribution well made, or with regret at lost opportunities. The life-circumstances of teachers make it unlikely that there will be tight agreement on what constitutes the 'good' that pedagogy seeks to achieve, simply because the 'goal posts' for this shift as life moves forward. *Pedagogy is an area in which legitimate differences can be challenging.*

2. 'BEFRIENDING' THE WORLDVIEW OF FAITH

All teachers in Catholic schools sooner or later have to address their relationship to the worldview of faith. This includes dealing with the question of whether or not it has a place in their personal worldview, and if so, how. The reason for this is that they agree to support the ethos of the Catholic school, and so are bound by the ethical demands that go with being a witness for their students to the possibilities that accompany being an adult in the world.

To deal with this worldview requires a certain level of knowledge. This is a cognitive challenge that *can be met*. Most teachers appreciate the value dimension of the worldview of faith as they experience it in everyday school life. They seem to sense when this is absent. As noted earlier, the problematic area is that of *sensibility*, the stance one takes to matters of faith. Jim and Evelyn Whitehead suggest that the preferred stance to take is that of 'befriending' faith.[4] This, we suggest, is also an important stance to take to one's culture and to the necessary dialogue between faith and culture. To 'befriend' someone is to enter into a relationship, aware of both that person's strengths and limitations, and to not be put off by the latter. Like ourselves, our friends have both!

---

[4] James and Evelyn Whitehead, *Method in Ministry*, 9.

The Catholic faith tradition is lived in so many communities and in many traditions, To 'befriend' this tradition is to be aware of strengths as well as weaknesses in those communities and traditions. It is to be 'critical' and to teach students to be critical as a way of being in the world. The opposite of critical, as Paul Ricoeur points out, is to be 'naive'. To be 'critical' is to balance the 'hermeneutic of trust' essential in all learning (if you do not trust your teachers you are unlikely to learn), with the 'hermeneutic of suspicion' that challenges all forms of naivete by putting questions to the assumptions on which truth claims rest. This balancing act, integral to any form of critical pedagogy, acknowledges strengths, something that many teachers seem to overlook. In consequence, they have difficulty in 'befriending' a faith tradition that is in the process of transition. It is through the process of critique properly understood, that teachers and students arrive at *a post-critical faith,* which for most educated people today seems to be the condition of authentic faith.

3. TWO PERSPECTIVES ON THE WORLDVIEW OF CATHOLIC FAITH

3.1 Master narratives of modernity

In his critique of knowledge, influential postmodern critic Jean Francois Lyotard, advised that people should be suspicious of 'master narratives'. He had in mind modernity's master narratives of *knowledge* and *emancipation,* both of which arose in the 18th and 19th centuries as rivals in making sense of life to the hegemony previously enjoyed by the master narrative of Christian faith.

The 'master narrative of knowledge' endeavoured to displace the interpretive power of Christian faith with that of science and its promise of unlimited progress. The 'master narrative of emancipation' sought to replace the interpretive power of Christian faith with that of economics, and with it came the promise of a classless society and prosperity.[5]

The tragic events of the 20th century led Lyotard and other thinkers to question the plausibility and credibility of modernity's master narratives and to suggest that people should *be suspicious of all narratives that make hegemonic claims.* Lyotard's principal critique of metanarratives was that those who champion them *do not make space for people who are different,* who hold another view, or who reject the prevailing orthodoxy. Their humanity is regarded as less than that of the champion group and so they can be treated

---

5   Lieven Boeve, *Interrupting Tradition: An essay on Christian faith in the post-modern context.* Louvain: Peeters Press, 2003, 40–43.

differently. Instances of this dynamic at work both in Nazi Germany's treatment of Jews and minorities such as homosexuals and gypsies, and in Stalin's use of gulags, play in the background of this critique. However, the dynamic plays out in another key whenever one group views itself as 'superior' to another and their perceived superiority justifies the oppression of people seen as 'other'.[6]

A worthy aspiration of postmodern thinkers was to give a voice to those Lyotard names as the *'differend'* – the ones who are 'different'. His claim, and that of other postmodern critics, is that such people are victims, and they know from first-hand experience how the 'systems' put in place by those 'in charge' fail, or are deficient, in realising the false hopes they offer. The *differends'* critique of the system that has failed them is worth hearing because it is an important step on the road to change. This was the case for Freire's fisherfolk in Brazil in the 1960s, the workers in Polish shipyards in the 1980s, and it will be the case today for Uighur Muslims in China. Sadly, it continues to be the case for indigenous peoples around the world.

3.2 Open and closed master narratives

Lyotard regarded Christian faith as a hegemonic master-narrative. Lieven Boeve takes a more sanguine and, we believe, a more balanced view.[7] He notes that 'master narratives' provide an essential *interpretive device* that humans employ to deal with the ambiguities and uncertainties associated with living in complex societies. We all identify with a story in making sense of our lives. The more pertinent question, however, is: 'Which narrative does my story correspond to?'

Boeve distinguishes between two types of master narratives – *closed narratives and open narratives*.

Closed narratives are self-contained. Like the master narratives of modernity, they presume to be universally true, that is, true for all peoples and all times. Closed narratives, being self-contained, are generally not open to there being a transcendent dimension to human life. Life has to be interpreted within an immanent framework.

Open narratives on the other hand are contextual, and so are qualified in their truth claims. They claim: 'This is how it is for us, but this may not

---

[6] In a famous essay entitled 'Exorcising Plato's Ghost', in his book *The Dignity of Difference* (London: Continuum, 2002) highly regarded Jewish Rabbi, Jonathan Sacks, calls this belief the most pernicious known to humankind because of the suffering that it has caused throughout human history. It is a belief now entrenched in certain Catholic theologies of priesthood where ordination is understood as rendering clergy 'ontologically different' from other members of the community of faith. Some see this belief providing clericalism with a theological justification.
[7] Lieven Boeve, 'Can God escape the clutches of the Christian master narrative', in *Lyotard and Theology*. London: Bloomsbury, 2014, 59–74.

be how it is for you'. They confirm *a particular identity* without denying the right of others to affirm a different identity. Being indeterminate, they are open to the transcendent because they are open to the future being different from the present.

The question Boeve asks is this:

- *Does Christian faith represent an open or a closed master narrative?*

His argument is that, while historically Christian faith has been interpreted both ways, in the present context of radical pluralisation it is best re-contextualised as an open narrative. He argues that the contemporary experience of radical pluralism is *unprecedented in human history* and this creates the need to re-contextualise the faith tradition if it is to remain plausible and credible to people living in this situation. He argues his case largely on anthropological grounds – the human need to interpret life in terms of the *particular* 'narrative' people associate with, or see themselves as part of.[8]

3.3 Catholic faith as a closed master narrative

Older Catholics are familiar with Catholicism presented as a closed master story that excludes others. Many have family stories of marriages conducted in the sacristy, not in the church; of funerals people were forbidden to attend; of dealing with the fallout from divorce, and so on. A common thread running through all these types of experiences is the Church's denial of the right of the person 'who is other' to be different, and its exclusion of the one who is legitimately different.[9] While Vatican II changed the situation, *at the level of sensibility* the problem lives on in a number of areas, including towards those who are gay, lesbian or transgender.

There is a considerable lobby within the Catholic Church whose members still interpret Christian faith as a closed master narrative. These are the defenders of the 'Catholic tradition' understood as either built on 'absolute truth' or containing 'unchangeable law'. This way of *interpreting* the Christian story is proving particularly problematic in our pluralised cultural context, as people living in that context no longer see it as either plausible or credible. The issue is made more complex by the fact that the increased pluralism in society *invites Christians to explore the pluralism that exists within their own religious tradition*, as well as the pluralism in belief

---

8 Boeve, 2003, 90–91.
9 It was only at the Second Vatican Council (1962–5) that Catholic teaching moved away from the teaching that 'error has no rights' which had been used in 'Catholic countries' to oppress Protestant groups and provide the rationale for such exclusions.

that arises from the Church's presence in the many cultural regions of the world.

4. THE CHRISTIAN STORY AS OPEN NARRATIVE

The Christian story, and within that the Catholic story, is often presented as *the story of the Church* in an institutional sense. After all, this has been the body that has existed throughout nearly two thousand years. Church leaders in particular have often looked at the Christian story from this perspective. As a result, in the course of history, in many people's minds the message of Jesus as presented in the Gospels faded into the background and was superseded, or almost superseded, by 'Church teaching'. The Church began to proclaim itself, rather than the Gospel.

Things started to change in the 20th century with the Catholic revival in scripture studies. The 'ressourcement' movement focused the attention of the bishops at Vatican II on 'going back to the sources' and the major 'source' that needed to be consulted was the biblical text itself. New Testament studies made it possible to ask: 'What, essentially, did Jesus teach?'

4.1 The Kingdom of God as starting point

Scripture scholars agree that the central motif of Jesus' teaching is 'the Kingdom of God'. Respected scholar, John Fuellenbach SVD,[10] affirming the observation of John Bright, points out that Jesus never defined what he meant by 'the Kingdom of God', nor is it recorded that anyone ever asked him what the phrase meant.[11] This led some, including his immediate disciples, to place a specific political construction on what he was saying. Jesus clearly wished to avoid this, going to great lengths to clarify that the 'Kingdom of God' he spoke about had very little in common with the rule of the kind of messiah-king the Jewish people of the time were eagerly anticipating. Across time, Jesus' teaching, as both word and witness, would indeed present a real challenge to human arrangements, including political arrangements. However, the kingdom he spoke about has certainly not been embodied in any of them neither in his own time, nor since.

Jesus' hearers, including his critics, held a particular interpretation of Israel's master narrative. 'Law' had become the narrative's interpretive key, and observing the law had become the path to God's blessing. Jewish people of Jesus' time had arrived at *a particular interpretation of human possibility*,

---

[10] John Fuellenbach is a Divine Word priest-scholar who has devoted a considerable portion of his academic career to the study of this central motif in the synoptic gospels. As a member of a missionary congregation, he responded to the imperative to clarify this key to Jesus' understanding of his mission.

[11] John Fuellenbach, *The Kingdom of God: The Message of Jesus Today*, Maryknoll N.Y: Orbis, 1995, 25.

both for themselves individually and for the people collectively. The public worldview and the public imagination were trapped within a *particular horizon of meaning*.

Jesus offered an alternative construction of human possibility. He sought to change the imaginal horizon within which people could respond to the challenge presented by his parables. 'The kingdom of God is like ...' heralded an *unexpected* comparison. Jesus showed much creativity and clearly went to considerable effort to introduce *a very different kind of kingdom – God's Kingdom*.

Jesus' teaching, while novel, was not entirely new. It drew on religious understandings having currency at the time, particularly the prophetic, apocalyptic, and ethical expectations of what the longed-for rule of the Messiah-king would be like, as Fuellenbach explains.[12]

Jesus' teaching owed much to the great prophets of the Old Testament, particularly Isaiah with whom he identified when he publicly proclaimed the essence of his mission in the synagogue at Nazareth (Lk 4:16–20). Isaiah had envisaged God creating 'a new heaven and a new earth' (Isaiah 65:17). This apocalyptic vision of *radical transformation* is central to Jesus' own understanding of the Kingdom of God as presented in the synoptic Gospels. Transformation was not, however, something that would happen only in the future but, as Jesus made clear, it needed to happen in the present *so that people had hope in and for the future*. Nor was it something that applied only to individuals, for it had *an important social* dimension applicable within and beyond one's own society, as Jesus made clear in his healings and parables such as within the Good Samaritan account (Lk 10:25–27).

Jesus saw his mission as offering people hope that God really was breaking into human history to effect much needed change. His healings and his social choices offered this hope in a concrete way. What his disciples did not immediately understand was that discipleship involved becoming active agents in the process of making the Kingdom of God present.

4.2 Ethical demands of the Kingdom

A strong ethical current ran through the Jewish religious tradition. The touchstone of ethical behaviour was the way in which the most vulnerable were treated. 'Code' for the most vulnerable was 'the widows, orphans and aliens', aliens being people from other places, not one's own society or culture. These were groups who in a traditional village society were least likely to have anyone to protect them. Justice, in the biblical tradition, requires *living in right relationship* with God and one's fellow humans,

---

12 Fuellenbach, chapters 1–3, 27–50.

the touchstone of authenticity in matters of justice being that the most marginalised groups are given prime consideration.

Jesus challenged the limited understanding of human possibility embedded in the worldview and public imagination of his society. The parable of the Good Samaritan (Lk 10:25–37), the encounter with the woman at the well (Jn 4:4–42), the praise given to the Roman centurion (Matt 8:5–13), are examples of an altogether different understanding of what could be. Jesus also discounted the idea that God's blessing could be earned, since God cannot be controlled in this way. God acts out of love, and so the capacity for having faith in God always comes as God's gift. The parable of the Prodigal Son (Lk 15:11–32) affirms love as pure gift.

Jewish leaders were not open to Jesus' ideas about human possibility, nor did his views about God appear to be orthodox, so they rejected his call to conversion and transformation, just as they had rejected John the Baptist before him. They were locked into 'their' story and not open to changing course.

4.3 Creating kingdom spaces in students' lives

Jesus' notion of the Kingdom is open-ended. No matter how bad the situation is, it can always be made better through the creation of 'kingdom spaces' in people's lives. Jesus did this for those whom he healed, for the crowds he fed, for the people he taught, and for the disciples he befriended. Freire helped his fisher folk create 'kingdom spaces' for themselves; teachers do this regularly for students and for groups of students when they do 'good' by them. The 'kingdom spaces' created in school life are often *social spaces* that are necessary to open up new possibilities for students among their peers and in society, particularly for those who are marginalised.

No matter how good things may seem occasionally to be, they can always be better, because human possibility is limited only by imagination. The insights that faith brings to human imagining, particularly where the marginalised are concerned, are often critical in creating 'kingdom spaces' in those students' lives. A school's broader program, sometimes termed 'extra-curricular activities', often provides 'spaces' where students discover their talents and come to realise that they have something to offer the community. Having the opportunity to be of service to others helps build their sense of self-worth, the bedrock on which personal, including religious identity, is constructed

The human possibilities embodied in Jesus' teaching about the Kingdom of God also include the notions of forgiveness and compassion. These are constituent elements of a life lived in right relationship with God, other people, and the whole of creation.

In talking about the Kingdom of God, Jesus was not speaking of a 'spiritual kingdom' as those who wish to maintain the status quo sometimes claim. God's Kingdom, or a situation where God's vision for the world makes the running, includes all the aspects of life and living – material, spiritual, psychological, ideological, environmental and so on. As Fuellenbach notes:

> No Jew could ever envisage a purely spiritual Kingdom without expecting as well a complementary historical and political realization on behalf of Israel. Jesus went beyond these physical and material aspects of God's Kingdom, but he definitely did not abandon them.[13]

Jesus' teaching that the Kingdom was present, but not yet fully realised, should have headed off attempts to turn his teaching into a closed master narrative such as 'The Church is the Kingdom of God', but it did not. Such a closed narrative could not, and does not, give an adequate account of God's mission in human history.

4.4 The open nature of God's mission within human history

As theologian Peter Phan and others have pointed out, prior to Vatican II, Catholic missionary activity around the world was organised on the basis that 'God's Church has a mission'.[14]

In this context, 'mission' was understood as preaching the Gospel and setting up faith communities. Because mission was clearly envisaged as what the Church was doing, *it was also envisaged as under its control*. At Vatican II it was realised that, rather than the Church having a mission in any foundational sense, *mission comes from God; God is at work in the universe and in human history; God sent Jesus as that mission incarnate to demonstrate the essentials of that mission and to invite others to join in the grand project. The Church is the community of disciples intentionally so committed*.

This change in perspective requires at least two important elements:

- *a more inclusive understanding of mission*
- *an appreciation that people other than Christians need to be involved in God's mission if the Kingdom of God is to be realised in human history.*

Thus, the conceptual basis on which mission is organised and engaged has changed. Now, rather than claiming that the sentence 'the Church has a

---

13 Fuellenbach, 33.
14 Peter Phan, 'Proclamation of the Reign of God as Mission of the Church', *In Our Own Tongues: Perspectives from Asia on Mission and Inculturation*, Maryknoll N.Y.: Orbis, 2003, 32–44.

mission' expresses the foundational understanding of mission, we say *'God's mission has a Church'*.

God is the driver of mission. The Church is by its nature God's agent in history, *but not necessarily God's only agent*. This realisation makes it very difficult to interpret the narrative of Christian faith is closed terms. God's Spirit is at work in the whole world. *Prayerfully discerning where God is at work in the world, is now a necessary part of Christian adulthood.* This brings us back to the foundational spiritual insight of Ignatius of Loyola – *God can be found in all things* – one might add: 'If you know how to look'.[15]

God's mission, as exercised through the community of communities we call Church, currently takes many forms, including ecumenical and inter-religious dialogue. We simply do not know what forms it might take in the future, when new 'kingdom spaces' will certainly need to be created. Nor do we know who might be needed as dialogue partners in continuing Jesus' mission in a particular context. For all of these reasons, we would argue that Catholic faith is therefore best interpreted as an open story. As we, at Jesus' own invitation, make our own his prayer to the Father: 'Your kingdom come on earth as in heaven …' (Matt 6:10) we express aspirations meaningful only in terms of an open story.

5. PEDAGOGY AND HUMAN POSSIBILITY

Pedagogy, as we have discussed, seeks to realise the possibility that lies in each child or group of young people. The teacher's conception of human possibility for this child, and for these children, will be shaped by the role that faith plays in the way that the teacher imagines the future. Cultural constructions of human possibility in a secular society are necessarily limited. It is therefore important that teachers have the opportunity to 'befriend' the Catholic faith tradition, seeing it as an open narrative, one with which they can identify, and which they and their students can bring into dialogue with contemporary culture.

Pedagogy has both an individual and a social dimension. How teachers construe what is 'good' needs to take both into account. Doing good for students requires more than knowledge of 'what works in the classroom' since such knowledge is often formulated without reference to 'this student or this group of students'. While researchers, such as Hattie, can identify the 'effect size' of individual 'interventions', even a short time in the classroom

---

[15] In New Testament teaching, God's Spirit guides the Church. This has sometimes been interpreted as Church leaders having the 'inside running' with God when it comes to making decisions. The lesson of scripture would seem to be that God has a sense of humour. God lets leaders learn from their own mistakes, particularly from their own hubris. Pope Francis' move towards a more synodal Church seeks to address the problem of faulty discernment by leaders.

indicates that these must work in concert, and that the 'whole' is often much more significant than the 'parts'. With that proviso, however, knowing what the parts are remains important.

The current pedagogical emphasis on 'deep learning' represents one construction of 'doing the right thing by students' but as we have argued, while it is valuable it nevertheless lacks a coherent theory of learning. Here we proposed that Lonergan's outline of the dynamism of human cognition as qualified by the insights of hermeneutics, meets this need, and we addressed some of the anomalies in learning such as confusing understanding with knowing. Lonergan's 'imperatives': *be attentive, be intelligent, be reasonable and be responsible*, offer an important insight into what learning seeks to achieve. Once understanding has been validated, the issue for a disciple of Jesus remains: How can I put my knowledge, and my talents, at the service of the common good, bearing in mind that in our time the common good urgently includes care for the earth, our common home?

5.1 Pedagogy: an ethical framework – care, critique, and justice

Throughout this book we have viewed pedagogy in ethical terms. An *ethic of care* expressed in and flowing from genuine Christian relationship is clearly essential. This is a foundational insight of John Baptist De La Salle. We have also argued that, in dealing with both the cultural tradition and the religious tradition, teachers in a Catholic school need to be guided by an *ethic of critique* that recognises both strengths and limitations in what is being proposed so that naivete is avoided in learning. The equation seems simple:

No critique = No care.

Jesus' teaching implies a notion of 'human possibility' that has both an individual and a social dimension. In a Catholic pedagogy, an ethic of care and an ethic of critique need to be balanced by an ethic of justice understood in Biblical terms, that is as right relationships with God, one's fellow humans and the natural world.[16] Despite the development of a substantial corpus of magisterial teaching on justice, and notwithstanding some excellent programs involving action for justice, ecological engagement, and other social learning projects, the tendency in Catholic circles has been to focus predominantly on the individual dimension of human potential. Despite

---

16 In *Cultivating an Ethical School* (2014) which has stimulated and guided aspects of our discussion, Starratt draws his conclusion on philosophical grounds. See Chapter 3, 'A Multidimensional Ethical Framework', in *Cultivating an Ethical School*, 45–58.

rhetoric to the contrary, pedagogy in Catholic schools is, in practice, often construed in *highly individualistic terms* by teachers, students and parents.

Teachers are witnesses to young people of what 'being in the world as adults can mean. This witness needs to be offered not only by a particular teacher, but also by other members of the school community. The effectiveness of the witness is compromised when there are serious contradictions between various teachers' approaches to the relationship between faith and culture. Teachers have the opportunity to open up to students what 'being part of the school community' means at a time when students are forming their own ideas about what 'human possibility' entails, and seeking to bring these to realisation. Working with young people as they negotiate this challenge is important especially in the secondary school years when students endeavour to resolve the crisis of identity.

A shared approach to 'Catholic pedagogy' makes it possible to maximise the 'good' that teachers seek to accomplish in helping students realise the possibilities open to them. Such 'good' accompanies and enables the young person to develop a worldview that is other-centred rather than self-centred. In the process, it also enhances and transforms the relationships that constitute the young person as human – those with self, God, others, and the natural world. In time, the young person's worldview thus becomes the Biblical 'heart' that affects positively all that it responds to, initiates, and seeks to transform.

SELECT BIBLIOGRAPHY

Books and Journals

Anderson, Gerald (ed). *Biographical Dictionary of Christian Missions*. Grand Rapids: Eerdmans, 1998.

Beer, Peter. *An introduction to Bernard Lonergan: exploring Lonergan's approach to the great philosophic questions*. Victoria: Sid Harta Publishing, 2010.

Blenky, Mary; Tarule, Jill; Clinchy, Blythe & Goldberger, Nancy. *Women's Ways of Knowing: The Development of Self, Voice and Mind*. New York: Basic Books, 1986.

Bergmam, Roger. *Catholic Social Learning: Educating the Faith That Does Justice*. New York: Fordham University, 2011.

Bevans, Stephen. *Wisdom from the margins: Systematic theology and the Missional Imagination*. Catholic Theological Society of America (CTSA Proceedings), 2001: 56.

Bevans, Stephen. 'Doing Mission Today: Where we do it: How we do it, What we do'.
http://mohmv.com.au/Resources/Stephen%20Bevans%20Keynote%202.pdf

Bevans, Stephen. *Constants in Context: A Theology of Mission for Today*. Maryknoll N.Y: Orbis, 2004.

Bevans, Stephen & Schroeder, Roger. *Prophetic Dialogue: Reflections on Christian Mission Today*. Maryknoll. N.Y: 2011.

Biggs, John & Collis, Kevin. *Evaluating the Quality of Learning: the SOLO Taxonomy*. New York: Academic Press, 1982.

Boeve, Lieven. *God Interrupts History: Theology in a Time of Upheaval*. London: Continuum, 2007.

Boeve, Lieven. *Interrupting Tradition: An essay on Christian faith in a postmodern context*. Louvain: Peeters Press, 2003.

Boeve, Lieven. *Lyotard and Theology*. London: Bloomsbury, 2014.

Brown, Raymond. *An Introduction to the New Testament*. New Haven: Yale University Press, 1997.

Brown, Raymond. *The Churches the Apostles Left Behind*. New York: Paulist Press, 1984.

Brueggemann, Walter and Erikson, Amy. *The Creative Word: Canon as Model of Biblical Education*. Second Edition. Philadelphia: Fortress Press, 2015.

Daw, Joan. *Young People, Faith, and Social Justice*. Box Hill: Yarra Institute Press, 2013.

De La Salle, John Baptist. *Meditations in Time of Retreat*.
https://www.lasallian.info/wp-content/uploads/2012/12/Meditations-2007.pdf

De La Salle, John Baptist. *The Conduct of Christian Schools. Lasallian Sources: the Complete Works of John Baptist De La Salle Vol 6.* Landover MD: Christian Brothers' Conference, 1996. https://www.lasallian.info/wp-content/uploads/2012/12/Conduct-2007-reprint.pdf

Del Colle, Ralph. *Christ and the Spirit: Spirit Christology in Trinitarian Perspective.* New York: Oxford University Press, 1994.

Delio, Ilia. *Making All Things New: Catholicity, Cosmology, Consciousness.* Maryknoll N.Y: Orbis, 2015.

Dillon, Michelle. *Catholics in Transition.* Maryland: Rowan and Littlefield, 2013.

Dillon, Michele. *Postsecular Catholicism: Relevance and Renewal.* New York: Oxford University Press, 2018.

D'Orsa, Jim & Therese. *Catholic Curriculum.* Mulgrave: Garratt Publishing, 2012.

D'Orsa, Jim & Therese. *Leading for Mission: Integrating Life, Culture and Faith in Catholic Education.* Mulgrave: Garratt Publishing, 2013.

Erikson, Erik. *Identity: Youth and Crisis.* London: Faber and Faber, 1969.

Faggioli, Massimo. *Vatican II: The Battle for Meaning.* Mahwah N.Y: Paulist Press, 2012.

Freire, Paulo. *The Politics of Education: Culture, Power and Liberation.* Westport CT: Greenwood Publishing, 1985.

Freire, Paulo. *Pedagogy of Hope: Reliving Pedagogy of the Oppressed.* New York: Continuum, 1997.

Fuellenbach, John. *The Kingdom of God: The Message of Jesus Today.* Maryknoll N.Y: Orbis, 1995.

Fullan, Michael. *The Meaning of Educational Change.* Columbia: Teachers College Press: 1984.

Fullan, Michael. *The New Meaning of Educational Change.* New York: Routledge, 2015.

Fullan, Michael & Quinn, Joanne. *Coherence: The Right Drivers in Action for Schools, Districts, and Systems.* London: SAGE, 2016.

Fullan, Michael; Quinn, Joanne; McEachen, Joanne. *Deep Learning: Engage the World, Change the World.* London: SAGE, 2018.

Gadamer, Hans-Georg. *Truth and Method.* 2nd Revised edition. London: Sheed & Ward, 1989.

Gallagher, Shaun. *Hermeneutics and Education.* New York: The University of New York Press, 1992.

Gallagher, Shaun. *Phenomenology.* Basingstoke: Palgrave Macmillan, 2012.

Gowdie, Jill. *Stirring the Soul of Catholic Education: Formation for Mission.* Mulgrave: Garratt, 2017.

Greeley, Andrew. *The Catholic Imagination.* Berkeley: University of California Press, 2000.

Green, Michael & McGregor, Darren. 'Looking for New Wineskins: The Marist Experience' in Jim & Therese D'Orsa, (eds and authors). *New Ways of Living the Gospel*. Mulgrave: Garratt, 2015.

Green, Michael. *Now with Enthusiasm: Charism, God's Mission and Catholic Schools Today*. Mulgrave: Garratt Publishing, 2018.

Groome, Thomas. *What Makes Us Catholic: Eight Gifts for Life*. New York: HarperCollins, 2003.

Gutierrez, Gustavo. *A Theology of Liberation*. Maryknoll N.Y: Orbis Books, 1973.

Hall, Edward. *The Silent Language*. New York: Anchor Books, 1973.

Hattie, John. *Visible Learning: A synthesis of over 800 meta-analyses relating to achievement*. London: Routledge, 2009.

Hattie, John & Donoghue, Gregory. 'Learning Strategies: A synthesis and conceptual model' *npj Science of Learning*, 23 May 2016.

Hattie, John & Zierer, Klaus. *10 Mindframes for Visible Learning: teaching for success*. London Routledge, 2017.

Helminiak, Daniel. *Brain Consciousness and God: A Lonerganian Integration*. Albany: State University of New York Press, 2015.

Henman, Robert. 'Can brain scanning and imaging techniques contribute to a theory of thinking?' in *Dialogues in Philosophy Mental and Neuro Sciences*, 2013: 6(2), 2013.

Hiebert, Paul. *The Gospel in Human Contexts: Anthropological Explorations of Contemporary Missions*. Grand Rapids: Baker Academic, 2009.

Hiebert, Paul. *Transforming Worldviews: An Anthropological Understanding of How People Change*. Grand Rapids: Baker Academic, 2008.

Hughes, Phillip. *Putting Life Together*. Melbourne: Fairfield Press, 2007.

Hyland, Sabine. *The Jesuits in Latin America, 1549–2000: 450 Years of Inculturation, Defense of Human Rights, and Prophetic Witness*. Saint Louis: The Institute of Jesuit Sources, 2009.

Irvin Dale & Phan, Peter (eds). *Christian Mission, Contextual Theology, Prophetic Dialogue*. Maryknoll N.Y: Orbis, 2018.

Johnson, Elizabeth. *She Who Is: The Mystery of God in Feminist Theological Discourse*. New York: Crossroads, 1994.

Kemmis, Stephen; Cole, Peter & Suggett, Dahle. *Orientations to Curriculum and Transition: Towards the Socially Critical School*. Melbourne: Victorian Institute of Secondary Education, 1983.

Kirk, J. Andrew. *The Mission of Theology and Theology as Mission*. Valley Forge PA: Trinity Press International, 1997.

Kirk, J. Andrew. *What is Mission? Theological Explorations*. Minneapolis: Fortress Press, 2000.

Kincheloe, Joe. *Knowledge and Critical Pedagogy: An Introduction*. Springer, 2010.

Kitchener, Karen & Kitchener, Richard. 'The development of natural rationality: Can formal operations account for it?' in J.A. Meacham & N.R. Santilli (eds). *Social development in youth: structure and content*. Basel: Kaeger, 1981.

Kitchener, Karen & Kitchener, Richard. 'The Development of Natural Rationality: Can formal operations account for it?' in Jack Mezirow and Associates. *Fostering Critical Reflection in Adulthood: A Guide to Transformative and Emancipatory Learning*. San Francisco: Jossey-Bass, 1990.

Kuhn, Deanna. 'Formal Operations in a 21st Century perspective.' *Human Development* 51(1), 2008.

Kuhn, Deanna. *Education for Thinking*. Harvard University Press, 2008.

Kirsi, Tirri & Toom, Auli. 'The Moral Role of Pedagogy as the Science and Art of Teaching.' IntechOpen, 2019. This chapter will be included in the forthcoming Springer volume Kursi, Tirri (ed). *Pedagogy in Basic and Higher Education – Current Developments and Challenges*.

Lombaerts, Herman. 'The Lay State' – an Indicator of the Transformations in the Church: The contribution of Brother Michel Sauvage', *AXIS Journal of Lasallian Higher Education* 5, no. 3, 2014.

Lonergan, Bernard. *Insight* (Vol 3, of the Collected Works of Bernard Lonergan). Edited by F.E. Crowe and R.M. Doran. Toronto: University of Toronto Press, 2013.

Lovat, T., Dally, K., Clement, N. & Toomey, R. 'Values pedagogy and student achievement: Contemporary research evidence'. Dordrecht, NL: Springer, 2011.

Lovat, Terence. *The art and heart of good teaching: Values as the pedagogy*. Singapore: Springer, 2019.

Lovat, Terence. 'Values education as good practice pedagogy: Evidence from Australian empirical research'. *Journal of Moral Education*, 46, 2017.

Lowney, Chris. *Heroic Leadership: Best Practices from a 450-year-old company that changed the world*. Chicago: Loyola Press, 2003.

Luzbetak, Louis. *The Church and Cultures*. Revised edition. Maryknoll NY: Orbis Books, 1988.

Lyotard, Jean Francois. *The Postmodern Condition: A Report on Knowledge*. Manchester University Press, 1984.

Marcia, James. *Adolescent Identity* https://www.academia.edu/12364473/ADOLESCENT_IDENTITY_JAMES_MARCIA eadedn21

Martin, James. *The Jesuit Guide to (Almost) Everything*. New York: HarperOne, 2010.

Martos, Joseph. *Doors to the Sacred: Historical Introduction to Sacraments in the Catholic Church*. Missouri: Ligouri Press, 2014.

Mason, Michael; Singleton, Andrew & Webber, Ruth. *The Spirit of Generation Y*. Mulgrave: Garratt Publishing, 2007.

Mazzonis, Querciolo. *Spirituality, Gender, and the Self in Renaissance Italy: Angela Merici and the Company of St. Ursula (1474–1540)*. Washington: The Catholic University of America Press, 2007.

Naugle, David. *Worldview: The History of a Concept*. Grand Rapids: Eerdmans Publishing, 2002.

O'Malley, John. 'Does Church teaching change?' in *When Bishops Meet*. Cambridge MA: Harvard University Press, 2019.

O'Malley, John. *What Happened at Vatican II*. Cambridge MA: the Belknap Press, 2008.

O'Malley, John. 'How the first Jesuits Became Involved in Education' in George W. Traub, *A Jesuit Education Reader*. Chicago: Loyola Press, 2008.

O'Malley, John. *Vatican 1: The Making of the Ultramontane Church*. Cambridge MA: the Belknap Press of Cambridge University Press, 2018.

Oldenski, Thomas. *Liberation Theology and Critical Pedagogy in Today's Catholic Schools*. New York: Garland Publishing, 1997.

Perry, William. *Forms of Intellectual and Ethical Development in the College Years*. New York: Holt Rinehart and Winston, 1970.

McEvoy, James. *Leaving Christendom for Good: Church-world Dialogue in a Secular Age*. New York: Lexington Books, 2014.

Pagola, Jose. *Jesus: An Historical Approximation*. Miami: Convivium Press, 2014.

Phan, Peter. *Christianity with an Asian Face: Asian American Theology in the Making*. Maryknoll N.Y: Orbis, 2003.

Phan, Peter. 'Proclamation of the Reign of God as Mission of the Church' in *In Our Own Tongues: Perspectives from Asia on Mission and Inculturation*. Maryknoll N.Y: Orbis, 2003.

Phan, Peter. *Mission and Catechesis: Alexandre de Rhodes & Inculturation in Seventeenth-Century Vietnam*. Maryknoll N.Y: Orbis, 2005.

Poutet, Yves. *Origins and characteristics of Lasallian pedagogy*. Translated by Julian Watson FSC, Finian Allman FSC, Celsus Clark FSC, and John Walch. Manila: De La Salle University Press, 1997.

Press, Margaret & Connelly, Susan. *Mary MacKillop East Timor 1994–2006*. St. Mary's: MI, 2007.

Rahner, Karl. *Trinity*. London: Burns & Oates, 1970.

Rayez, Andre SJ. *Lasallian Studies 1952*. Anonymous unpublished translation.

Schroeder, Roger. *What is the Mission of the Church? A Guide for Catholics*. Maryknoll NY: 2008.

Roxburgh, Alan. *Joining God, Remaking Church and Changing the World: the new shape of the world in our time*. New York: Morehouse Publishing, 2015.

Rummery, Gerard, fsc. 'The Coming of the Teaching Brothers' in Jim & Therese D'Orsa (eds). *New Ways of Living the Gospel*. Mulgrave: Garratt Publishing, 2015.

Sacks, Jonathan. *The Dignity of Difference: How to avoid a clash of civilizations*. London: Continuum, 2003.

Sacks, Jonathan. *The Great Partnership: Science, Religion and the Search for Meaning*. London: Hodder and Stoughton, 2011.

Schein, Edgar. *Organisational Culture and Leadership*. 5th edition. Hoboken N.J: Wiley, 2017.

Schneiders, Sandra. *Beyond Patching: Faith and Feminism in the Catholic Church*. Revised edition. New York: Paulist Press, 2004.

Schneiders, Sandra. *The Revelatory Text: Interpreting the New Testament as Sacred Scripture,* second edition. Wilmington: Michael Glazier, 1999.

Schussler Fiorenza, Elisabeth. *In Memory of Her: A Feminist Theological Reconstruction of Christian Origins.* London: SCM Press, 1983.

Sedmak, Clemens. *A Church of the Poor: Pope Francis and the Transformation of Orthodoxy.* Maryknoll N.Y: Orbis, 2016.

Senge, Peter. *The Fifth Discipline: The Art and Practice of the Learning Organization.* Revised edition. London: Random House, 2006.

Sinek, Simon. *Start with Why: How Great Leaders Inspire Everyone to Take Action.* New York: Penguin, 2009.

Sire, James. *Naming the Elephant: Worldview as a Concept.* Downers Grove IL: Intervarsity Press, 2004.

Smith, Susan. *Women in Mission: from New Testament to Today.* Maryknoll N.Y: Orbis Books, 2007.

Starratt, Robert. *Cultivating an Ethical School.* New York: Routledge, 2012.

Starratt, Robert. *Ethical Leadership.* New York: John Wiley & Sons, 2004.

Tan, Jonathan. 'Missio Inter Gentes: Towards a New Paradigm in the Mission Theology of the Federation of Asian Bishops' Conferences (FABC)', *Mission Studies,* Vol 21, No 1, 2004.

Tarnas, Richard. *The Passion of the Western Mind: Understanding the Ideas that have Shaped our World View.* New York: Random House, 2005.

Taylor, Charles. *A Secular Age.* Cambridge MA: Belknap Press of Cambridge University Press, 2007.

Tekippe, Terry. *What is Lonergan up to in Insight?* Collegeville: The Liturgical Press, 1996.

Tekippe, Terry. *Bernard Lonergan: An Introductory Guide to Insight.* Mahwah N.J: Paulist Press, 2003.

Timperley, H; Wilson, A; Barrar, H; and Fung, I. *Teacher Professional Learning and Development: Best Evidence Iteration.* Auckland: New Zealand Ministry of Education, 2007.

Van Manen, Max. *Pedagogical Tact: Knowing what to do when you do not know what to do.* London: Routledge, 2016.

Whitehead, James & Evelyn. *Community of Faith: Models and Strategies for Building Christian Communities.* New York: Seabury Press, 1982.

Whitehead, James & Evelyn. *Method in Ministry* revised edition. Kansas City: Rowman and Littlefield, 1995.

Theses

Braniff, John. *The Marist Brothers' Teaching Tradition in Australia: 1872–2000.* PhD. University of Sydney, 2005.

Hayes, Christopher. *Paradoxes, parallels and pedagogy: A case study of Ignatian pedagogy and of teachers' perceptions of its implementation in Australian Jesuit schools.* PhD. Australian Catholic University, 2006.

Kelleher, Margaret. *From Biblical Story to Biblical Interpretation: A Critical Transition.* PhD. Melbourne College of Divinity, 2011.

Sharkey, Paul. *The Ignatian renewal: a case study of a long-term, multi-phase process of educational change.* PhD. RMIT University, 1999.

Van Grieken, George. *To Touch Hearts: the Pedagogical Spirituality of St. John Baptist De La Salle.* Doctoral Dissertation, Boston College, 1995.

Vatican Documents
Documents of Vatican II
Lumen Gentium (Dogmatic Constitution on the Church)
Gaudium et Spes (Pastoral Constitution on the Church in the Modern World)
Dei Verbum (Dogmatic Constitution on Divine Revelation)
Gravissimus Educationis (Declaration on Christian Education)

Selected Post Vatican II Documents on Catholic Education
Sacred Congregation for Catholic Education:
The Catholic school (1977).
Lay Catholics in schools: witnesses to faith (1982).
The religious dimension of education in a Catholic school (1988).
The Catholic school on the threshold of the third millennium (1997).
Educating together in Catholic schools: A shared mission between consecrated persons and the lay faithful (2007),
Educating to Intercultural Dialogue in Catholic Schools: Living in Harmony for a Civilization of Love 2013.

Papal Documents
Pope Paul VI, *Ecclesiam Suam* (On the Church), 1964.
Pope Paul VI, *Evangelii Nuntiandi* (Evangelization in the modern world), 1975.
Pope John Paul II, *Sollicitudo Rei Socialis* (On social concerns), 1987.
Pope John Paul II, *Redemptoris Missio* (On the permanent validity of the Church's missionary mandate), 1990.
Pope Benedict XVI, *Verbum Domini* (On the interpretation of Sacred Scripture in the life of the Church), 2010.
Pope Francis, *Evangelii Gaudium* (The joy of the Gospel), 2013.
Pope Francis, *Laudato si'* (On care for our common home), 2015.
Pope Francis, *Gaudete et Exsultate* (On the call to holiness in today's world), 2018.

Other Vatican Documents
Congregation for the Clergy. *General Directory for Catechesis*, 1997.
Special Commission of Bishops and Cardinals. *The Catechism of the Catholic Church. Second* Edition. Huntingdon: Our Sunday Visitor, 2000. Original Latin version promulgated by Pope John Paul II in 1997.

Pontifical Biblical Commission. *The Interpretation of the Bible in the Church*, 1993.

Other Episcopal Documents
Catholic Bishops of NSW and the ACT *Catholic Schools at a Crossroads*, 2007. https://www.csnsw.catholic.edu.au/wp-content/uploads/2018/03/catholic-schools-at-a-crossroads.pdf

Other Documents
Charting the Progress of the Hewlett Foundation's Deeper Learning Strategy 2010–2015. https://hewlett.org/wp-content/uploads/2017/04/Deeper-Learning_2017_RTI-.pdf
Characteristics of a Jesuit Education 1986. jesuitinstitute.org/Pages/CharacteristicsJesuitEducation.htm
Ignatian Pedagogy: A Practical Approach. 1993, 2nd edition 2013. www.sjweb.info/documents/education/pedagogy en.pdf
Kolvenbach, Peter-Hans S.J. 'Ignatian Pedagogy: A Practical Approach', 1993. https://www.educatemagis.org/documents/ignatian-pedagogy-letter-from-father-general-kolvenbach-sj/
National Research Council *Education for Life and Work*. 2012. https://www.nap.edu/resource/13398/dbasse_084153.pdf
Pollefeyt, Didier. 'The Lustre of Life: Hermeneutic-communicative concept of religious education.' https://www.bne.catholic.edu.au
Pollyfeyt, Didier & Bouwens, Jan. 'Dialogue as the Future: A Catholic Answer to the 'Colourisation of the Educational Landscape'.' Catholic Education Office Brisbane: International Speaker Series, 2013. https://www.bne.catholic.edu.au
SEL Field Guide (2014). https://www.selpractices.org/about
Smith, M.K. *Social pedagogy: the development of theory and practice* available at URL: http://infed.org/mobi/social-pedagogy-the-development-of-theory-and-practice/
Starratt, Robert. 'The Religious Development of the Catholic School Teacher'. Paper presented at the Annual Meeting of Catholic School Superintendents of Catholic Schools, New Orleans 1984. Made available by the author.
Tony Blair Institute for Global Change (TBIGC). *Essentials of Dialogue* 2017. https://exchange.youthrex.com/report/essentials-dialogue-guidance-and-activities-teaching-and-practising-dialogue-young-people
Queensland Brain Institute. *The Brain: Learning and Memory: From Research to Practice* 2017. https://qbi.uq.edu.au/learning.

Values Education Project
Curriculum Corporation (for the Australian Government Department of Education, Science and Training), *Values Education Study Final Report* 2003.
Australian Government Department of Education, Science and Training, *National Framework for Values Education in Australian Schools* 2005.

Select Bibliography

Curriculum Corporation, *Implementing the National Framework for Values Education in Australian Schools:* Report of the Values Education Good Practice Schools Project Stage 1. 2006.

Curriculum Corporation, *At the Heart of what We Do: Values Education at the Centre of Schooling.* Stage 2. 2008.

Education Services Australia. (Hamston, Julie; Weston, Jane; Wajsenberg, Jenny; & Brown, David.) *Giving Voice to the Impacts of Values Education – The Final Report of the Values in Action Schools* project, 2010.

Lovat, Terence; Toomey, Ron; Dally, Kerry; Clement, Neville. *Project to Test and Measure the Impact of Values Education on Student Effects and School Ambience.* Final Report for the Australian Government Department of Education, Employment and Workplace Relations. The University of Newcastle, 2009.

INDEX

A

Ad Gentes 32, 33, 34, 359
A Framework for Formation for Mission in Catholic Education 158
Anders, Wilhelm 359-361
anthropology 3, 15, 31, 77, 90, 91, 94, 97, 98, 124, 150, 214, 231, 240, 247, 253, 266, 314, 322, 333
    cultural 3, 90, 91, 98, 124, 240, 247
    mission 3, 91
Aquinas, Thomas 58, 214
A Sense of the Sacred 160, 163-5, 166, 167, 170, 174
atomistic paradigm 143
Australian Values Education Project (AVEP) 170

B

Barat, Madeleine Sophie 49
Barry, Mother Gonzaga 49
Belenky, Mary 299-301
Bergman, Roger 62
Bevans, Stephen 27, 28, 107, 349
Boas, Frank 90, 359
Boeve, Lieven 20, 129, 130, 133, 134, 265, 268, 325, 326, 338-40, 349
Bosco, Don 50
brain science 2, 211, 213, 240
Braniff, John 51, 354
bricolage 334
Brown, Raymond 11, 244, 249
Brueggemann, Walter 105, 106, 107, 108, 109, 110, 349

C

Cardijn, Joseph (Cardinal)
    Young Christian Workers 336
Carey, Sr Loreto 163
Catholic Curriculum: a Mission to the Heart of Young People 1, 82-4, 128
Catholic Education Commission of Victoria (CECV) 251, 313, 323
Catholic imagination 25-7, 350

Catholic pedagogy 2, 8, 23, 24, 45, 51, 113, 129, 141, 294, 329, 346, 347
Catholic Schools at a Crossroads 96
CELAM 285, 287
Champagnat, Marcellin 49
charism 1, 18, 45, 49, 51, 100
Chavoin, Jeanne-Marie 49
Chevalier, Jules 49
Cleary, Br John 160
cognitive development 297, 299, 301
Colin, Jean Claude 49
Comenius, John Amos 45, 55
common good 59, 60, 143, 169, 322, 334, 346
condition of belief 86, 94
Congregation for Catholic Education 19, 20, 22, 40, 59, 63, 65, 96, 132, 133, 150, 157, 162, 312, 355
Council of Trent 78, 114-16, 120
Cramoisi, Mother Raphaela 49
critical pedagogy 273, 276, 278, 280, 285, 288, 289, 291, 292, 294, 351, 353
cultural myths 98, 99, 101, 315
culture 1-5, 8, 10, 13, 14, 17, 18, 20, 21, 24, 27-30, 34, 40, 41, 43, 51, 54, 58, 59, 61, 62, 64, 65, 70, 73, 77, 79, 81, 83-104, 107-110, 113-21, 123, 124-8, 130, 131, 133, 136, 137, 149, 151, 157, 158, 165, 167, 174, 180, 202, 220, 221, 227, 232, 240, 242-45, 247, 249, 250, 253, 256-58, 261-4, 266, 267, 270, 271, 273, 274, 277, 278, 280, 284, 288-96, 299, 306, 311, 312, 314-16, 322, 325, 326, 332-7, 342, 345, 347

D

deconstructionists 129
Deeper Learning 191, 192, 203, 356
Deep Learning 191, 198, 201, 204, 207, 350
Dei Verbum 33, 145, 264, 265, 355
Delany, Bishop Daniel 49
De La Salle, John Baptist 45, 47-9, 51, 53, 57, 65-75, 89, 178, 179, 210, 346, 349, 350, 353, 355

Meditations in Time of Retreat 72, 74, 349
pedagogical vision 23, 45, 51, 54, 60, 63, 68, 72, 74
The Conduct of Christian Schools 70, 71, 74, 178, 350
d'Houet, Marie-Madeleine 49
dialogue
    between faith and culture 88, 109, 110, 316, 337
    culture of dialogue 311, 312
    dialogue and pedagogy 311
    dialogue partners 212, 311, 328, 345
    Dialogue and Proclamation 37, 317
    dialogue with the world 35, 124
    forms of dialogue 38, 316, 317
    inter-faith dialogue 231
didactics 144, 332
Dignitatis Humanae 33
Dillon, Michele 152, 324, 350
Dilthey, Wilhelm 241, 242
discernment 55, 58, 61, 72, 106, 109, 131, 345
divine pedagogy 145
Duff, Alexander 30

E

Enhancing Catholic School Identity (ECSI) 4, 20, 88, 96, 97, 133, 134, 160, 174, 212, 251, 292, 323, 325, 327, 328
    Hermeneutical-Communicative Approach 212, 323, 324
Educating to Intercultural Dialogue in Catholic Schools: Living in Harmony for a Civilization of Love 96, 132, 133, 355
empirical research tradition 177
Erikson, Erik 302, 305
Essentials of Dialogue 313, 314, 317, 318, 322, 356
ethical approach 140, 184, 186, 210
Evangelii Nuntiandi 9, 35, 36, 37, 62, 125, 355
evangelisation of cultures 124

F

faith and culture 4, 5, 8, 24, 34, 40, 58, 86, 88, 90, 96, 103, 108–10, 113, 114, 119, 120, 123–27, 136, 174, 180, 312, 316, 333, 337, 347

fore-structure of knowing 247, 257, 261, 263, 264, 267, 268, 270, 333
formation 1, 16, 40, 49, 51, 56, 60, 67, 69, 70, 72, 127, 131, 133, 151, 157, 158, 161, 165, 305, 306–8, 323, 328, 336
Fowler, James 296, 297, 299
fragmentation of culture 334
Francis, Pope 21, 23, 33, 36, 38, 39, 63, 88, 104, 109, 118, 127, 131, 135, 149, 152, 287, 289, 294, 311, 312, 345, 354, 355
    Laudato si 39, 63, 149, 355
Freire, Paulo 19, 152, 275, 280–8, 292–4, 339, 343, 350
    conscientisation 281
    pedagogy of possibility 281, 283, 286, 294
Fuellenbach, John 10, 11, 341, 342, 344, 350
Fullan, Michael 4, 101, 139, 140, 147, 190, 201, 202, 204–8, 235, 350
fundamentalism 274

G

Gadamer, Hans Georg 212, 239, 241, 251, 262, 263, 267, 284, 325, 350
    fusion of horizons 239, 263, 267, 270, 284
Gaudium et Spes 33, 34, 62, 124, 355
Giroux, Henry 19, 289, 292, 293
goals 11, 18, 19, 26, 36, 63, 96, 131, 144, 157, 159, 179, 180, 187, 188, 203, 311, 313, 322, 328
Gonzales, Justo 107
Goodyear, Charles 225, 226
Gowdie, Jill 158, 350
Green, Br Michael 49, 51, 99, 158, 351
Gutierrez, Gustavo 286, 287, 351
    A Theology of Liberation 286, 351

H

Hall, Edward T 90, 257–9, 280, 351
    formal learning 257, 258, 259
    informal learning 157, 257, 259, 262, 275, 280, 288
    technical learning 257, 258, 259, 262
Hartenstein, Karl 31
Hattie, John & Donaghue, Gregory 189, 190, 198
Hattie, John 13, 139, 140, 147, 177, 178, 181, 185, 189, 190, 201

Hattie, John & Zierer, Klaus 185
Hayes, Christopher 51, 63, 354
Hebblethwaite, Margaret 55, 56
Herbart, Johann Friedrich 45
hermeneutical circle 251, 253–5, 257,
    260, 267, 269, 270, 283
hermeneutical space 262, 263
hermeneutical spiral 255, 260, 282
hermeneutical theory 14
    conservative hermeneutics 274
    critical hermeneutics 274,–6,
        278, 288, 293
    hermeneutics of suspicion 255,
        292
    hermeneutics of trust 255
    moderate hermeneutics 212, 271,
        273, 274, 275, 284
    textual hermeneutics 241, 249
Hiebert, Paul 81, 82, 85, 91, 93, 351
historical critical consciousness 78
historical critical method 247
historic effect 78–80, 244
Hughes, Philip 333, 351

I

Identity formation 133
Ignatian Pedagogy: A Practical Approach
    55, 62, 356
Ignatius of Loyola 44–7, 51, 53, 54, 64,
    65, 71, 131, 210, 345, 360
    finding God in all things 54, 57,
        58, 61
    Spiritual Exercises 56, 64
imaginal horizon 26, 28, 30, 167, 220,
    262, 263, 342
Irenaeus 108
    Type C theology 107–9

J

John Paul II (Pope) 10, 25, 37–9, 67, 100,
    108, 135, 286, 287, 315–17, 355
    Redemptoris Missio 10, 25, 37,
        38, 100, 317, 355

K

Katholieke Universiteit Leuven (KUL)
    20, 133, 134, 160, 161, 313, 323,
    325, 326
Keats, John 252–4, 256, 259, 270
Kelleher, Margaret 295, 298, 300, 306,
    308, 355
Kemmis, Stephen & colleagues 278–80,
    351

Kincheloe, Joe 19, 289, 291, 351
Kingdom of God 5, 9–11, 22, 23, 26, 31,
    32, 34–8, 81, 87, 100, 127, 129,
    131, 212, 248, 285, 286, 311, 325,
    326, 341–4, 350
kingdom spaces 294
Kirk, Andrew J 32, 351
Kitchener, K S & R F 301, 302, 351, 352
Kohlberg, Lawrence 296, 297, 299
Kolvenbach, Peter Hans 54, 61, 62, 356
Kuhn, Deanna 301, 308, 352

L

La Belle Dame Sans Merci 252, 256
Leading for Mission 83, 336, 350
liminality 85, 94
Lombaerts, Herman 48, 323, 324, 352
Long, Bishop Vincent 312
Lovat, Terence 159, 174, 175, 352, 357
Lowney, Chris 58, 352
Ludolph of Saxony 55
Lumen Gentium 33, 34, 53, 127, 355
Luzbetak, Louis 91, 92, 93, 117, 262, 293,
    315, 352
Lyotard, Jean Francois 126, 128, 278, 325,
    338, 339, 349, 352

M

MacKillop, Mary 50, 315, 353
Marcia, James 151, 152, 306, 307, 334,
    352
Martin, James 55, 145, 352
Mazzonis, Querciolo 47, 352
McBrien, Richard 264, 265
McEvoy, James 120, 130, 353
McGregor, Darren 49, 51, 351
Merici, Angela 47, 48, 352
metanarratives 128
    closed story 325
    open story 129, 130, 326, 345
missiology 3, 27, 30, 31, 36, 91, 287
mission 1, 25, 28, 29, 31–7, 39, 41, 47, 65,
    82, 83, 91, 99, 128, 158, 163, 260,
    290, 311, 312, 315, 328, 336, 344,
    349, 350, 351, 353, 354
    forms of mission 25, 29, 35, 39,
        40, 45, 328, 345
Mission and Justice program 163

N

Nagle, Nano 49
naive literalism 247

National Catholic Education Association
(NCEA) 160
  vision and values 100
National Catholic Education Commission
(NCEC) 158
National Framework for Values
  Education in Australian Schools
  167, 168, 356, 357
National Research Council (NRC) 191,
  192, 201, 234, 356
Naugle, David 83, 352
Newbigin, Lesslie 316
new pedagogy 4, 43, 139, 140, 190, 207,
  208, 234
Nostra Aetate 33, 35, 36

O

Oldenski, Thomas 19, 289, 290, 292, 293,
  353
O'Malley, John 59, 60, 95, 114, 119, 120,
  121, 353
Origen 107, 275
  Type B theology 107, 108

P

Paul VI, Pope 9, 35–9, 124, 125, 127, 287,
  315, 355
pedagogical choices 1, 11, 18, 24, 25, 54,
  143, 251, 273, 279, 294, 322
Pedagogical Tact 22, 145, 354
pedagogy
  Catholic 23
  ethical approach 140
  pedagogy: phenomenological
    approach 4
  pragmatic approach 2
Perry, William 299–301, 353
Phan, Peter 36, 290, 315, 344, 351, 353
phenomenological approach 4, 140, 146,
  159, 202, 216
phenomenology 3, 55, 140
Piaget, Jean 212, 296–9, 308
  cognitive development 297
pietas 59, 60
pluralisation 130, 340
Polanyi, Michael 255
Polding, Bishop John Bede 50
Pollefeyt, Didier 251
Pontifical Council for Inter-religious
  Dialogue 37
post-critical faith 133, 338
postmodernity 14, 127, 128–32, 289
postsecular age 80, 131, 134

pragmatic approach 2, 4, 139, 180, 190,
  191, 201, 207, 210
Prophets of Deconstruction 128

R

Ratio Studiorum 55, 178
Rayez, Andre 70, 353
Reck, Sr Carleen 161, 162
recontextualisation 99, 326, 327
Redemptoris Missio 10, 25, 37, 38, 100,
  317, 355
reflective practice 71, 140, 148, 201, 202
reflexive modernity 151
Rice, Edmund 50, 172
Ricoeur, Paul 212, 241, 244, 251, 255,
  292, 338
Roxburgh, Alan 12, 353
Rummery, Br Gerard 68, 70, 353

S

Sacks, Jonathan 149, 268, 339, 353
Schein, Edgar 93, 101, 353
Schleiermacher, Friedrich 241, 242
Second Vatican Council (Vatican II) 19,
  22, 29–33, 35, 36, 53, 55, 58, 59,
  61, 62, 74, 91, 95, 100, 113, 117,
  119, 120, 123, 124, 126, 127, 130,
  152, 160, 179, 214, 264, 265, 315,
  324, 326, 340, 341, 344, 350, 353,
  355
secularisation 117, 119, 129, 130, 163,
  277
  of government 119
See Judge Act 260
Senge, Peter 16, 354
signs of the times 34, 117, 133, 241, 291
Sinek, Simon 174, 185, 354
Sire, James 81, 84, 354
Smith, Susan RNDM 47, 277, 314, 354,
  356
social pedagogy 314
Spiritual Exercises 56, 64
Starratt, Robert 4, 140, 143, 144, 149,
  151–3, 159, 206, 279, 304, 346,
  354, 356
structural sin 286

T

Tan, Jonathon 33, 354
Taylor, Charles 85, 86, 94, 114, 118, 128,
  149, 244, 289, 354
  condition of belief 86
  social imaginary 114

technology in schools 147
Tertullian – Type A theology 107, 108
The Catholic School 19, 40, 59, 63, 157, 162
The Characteristics of Jesuit Education (1986) 55
The Enlightenment 47, 48, 65, 86, 116, 117, 128, 143, 292
The long nineteenth century 119, 361
theology 2, 3, 28–34, 36, 40, 41, 58, 66, 77, 91, 95, 104, 107–10, 116, 124, 131, 214, 231, 232, 247, 265, 275, 285–8, 294, 313, 323, 349
Tony Blair Institute for Global Change (TBIGC) 212, 312, 313, 317, 318, 319, 320, 321, 356
Essentials of Dialogue 313
tradition/s 2– 4, 9, 11, 12, 14, 17, 18, 19, 20, 22, 24, 34, 40, 43, 45, 47, 50, 51, 54, 61, 62, 69, 71, 77, 79, 80, 85, 87, 88, 96, 102–7, 109, 110, 115, 118, 131, 133–5, 139, 140, 143, 144, 147, 158, 165, 172, 175, 177–80, 199, 201, 209–11, 220, 231, 232, 237, 240, 244, 247, 249, 250, 259–71, 273, 275, 276–8, 280, 288, 289, 296, 315, 317, 319, 323, 324, 326, 327, 332, 333, 335, 338, 340, 342, 345, 346
Traub, George W 59, 353

U

Universal call to holiness 53

V

Values Education Study 168, 169, 356
values infusion 160, 161, 166, 167, 170
values pedagogy 157, 159, 161
Van Grieken, George 69, 70, 72, 73, 355
Van Manen, Max 4, 22, 140, 143, 145–8, 152–4, 159, 202, 210, 331, 354
Vision and Values 100

W

Whitehead, James & Evelyn 104, 113, 269, 337, 354
Wilhelm, Anders 31
Woods, Julian Tenison 50
Worldview 78, 81, 82, 83, 87, 93, 103, 123, 132, 134, 300, 333, 337, 338, 352, 354
    definition 21
    personal worldview 3
    worldview of culture 85, 86, 89, 93, 98, 334
    worldview of faith 103, 123, 134, 337

Y

Young Christian Worker Movement 286, 336
See Judge Act 260

www.ingramcontent.com/pod-product-compliance
Lightning Source LLC
Chambersburg PA
CBHW051348290426
44108CB00015B/1930